ON THE JOHN UNIVERSITY™

The path to higher education OTJU *starts with a good sit down.*

WORLD HISTORY

ON THE JOHN UNIVERSITY™

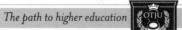

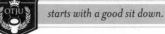

The path to higher education OTJU *starts with a good sit down.*

WORLD HISTORY

SWEETWATER
PRESS

SWEETWATER
PRESS

On the John University: World History

Produced by arrangement with Cliff Road Books

ISBN-13: 978-1-58173-742-4

Book design by Miles G. Parsons
Cover design by Ford Wiles
Contributors: Kelli Dugan, Eldon Dugan, Megan Roth

Printed in the U.S.

The Cradle of Civilization

It's no wonder civilization sprang from Mesopotamia.

It had everything: diverse geography, untapped raw materials, thousands of people.

Those elements, combined with the fertile soil of the land lying between the Tigris and Euphrates rivers, gave birth to agriculture, trade, and culture.

Of course, people drove the innovations. So warfare, bloodshed, and politics were the prices paid for advancement in the Fertile Crescent. As the body count rose, life expanded and eventually prospered, but it all began in this one spot recognized today as the Cradle of Civilization.

The word Mesopotamia, derived from the Greek meaning "between the rivers," actually refers to an entire region rather than a specific locale, and evidence of life in this area dates back to around 8000 BC. Historians believe the agricultural revolution, capable of sustaining large cities by ancient standards, took hold around 6000 BC.

The portion to the north of present-day Baghdad, Iraq, is known as Al-Jazirah, or The Island, to the Arabs. Babylonia is the region to the south. Broader definitions extend the region's boundaries from the Zagros Mountains in the northeast to the Arabian Plateau in the southwest, and from the Persian Gulf in the southwest to the Anti-Taurus Mountains in the northwest.

Sometime between 3500 and 3000 BC. nomadic tribes traded their hunting and gathering ways for agriculture and stability and settled the city-states of Sumer, a region that prospered—except for a brief sixty-year occupation by the Akkadians to the north—for about fifteen hundred years.

In 2000 BC, the Amorites conquered Sumer and made Babylon the new capital, establishing Babylonia as the apex of Mesopotamian life.

Except for brief invasions by the Hittites and Kassites, the Babylonian Empire endured for a thousand years until the warrior Assyrians from the north came knocking in the eighth century BC.

But let's not put the cart before the horse. It hasn't even been invented.

Mesopotamia's rich soil might have been fabulous for farmers, but it was void of natural resources imperative to trade such as stone, metals, and timber. This encouraged the eventual rise to trade routes with Syria and Asia Minor, where those items were plentiful. In fact, a model of a sailing boat was discovered in the excavation of a Sumerian tomb dating to 3500 BC.

In short order innovations including wheeled chariots—most probably drawn by donkeys—appeared to spur land trade. But writing was by far the most important development spawned by this region, and that advance will be addressed in good time.

It should be noted, however, that uniformity of language made education possible, and for that, all mankind owes a huge debt. And we're not just talking about readin', writin', and 'rithmatic.

Formal education in Mesopotamia was created to train scribes and priests, but fundamental teaching quickly gave way to higher learning in law, medicine, and even astrology.

And just as in Egypt, libraries became the center for all intellectual training and education.

The sheer diversity of Mesopotamian life makes quantifying its contributions to mankind difficult. For more than three thousand years, the region supported myriad peoples, languages, and cultures. Its divisive factions, spread over numerous periods and eras, meant geography held little unifying power. And because the capital city shifted in time with the ruling culture, Mesopotamia's historical record remains jagged, yet celebrated for its eccentricity.

Sumer Rising

Is an area void of thriving urban centers less civilized simply because it is removed from bustling activity? Can rural dwellers bound by a common code of economic, social, political, and religious beliefs not claim civility because they live in the sticks?

The answer to both questions is no, and Sumer exemplified both ways of life in relative harmony beginning around 3100 BC when Sumerians of all walks kept records, erected architectural marvels, and created expressive works of art that melded form and function.

They plowed fields, used bronze field tools, and used the river to trade between cities. They erected temples.

They held an array of jobs the land would support and arranged trade with other cities to obtain the things they could not produce for themselves.

Innovation, though, is the key indicator of a progressive civilization, and Sumer had no shortage of ingenuity. Sumerians created both the potter's wheel and the first known wheeled contraption.

Sumerian Roots

The first inhabitants of what would become known as Sumer were called Ubaidians, and beginning sometime around 5000 BC they set up house from Adab and Eridu to Nippur and Ur. Within a few hundred years, the settlements were holding their own and even welcomed newcomers from the Syrian and Arabian deserts.

But it was a northern tribe of joiners, called Sumerians, who talked a little funny and acted even stranger that set up shop around 3250 BC and pretty much took over. The region flourished because of their influence, and a legacy of art, architecture, crafts, religion, and even philosophy emerged.

Written language in the form of cuneiform, or writing on clay, took hold and remained the most common form of Middle Eastern communication for several thousand years.

What followed was a long line of leaders and dynasties, each remarkable in its own way and all collectively responsible for the shaping of mankind.

Crash Course

Sumerian Rulers

Etana was the first recorded king of Sumeria, and he really hit his stride around 2800 BC. He is remembered, without much detail, as a stabilizer of the lands.

Not long after Etana stepped down, an upstart by the name of Meskiaggasher launched a rival southern dynasty at Erech. He assumed control of everything between the Mediterranean Sea and the Zagros Mountains.

Around 2750 BC, Meskiaggasher's son, Enmerkar took the reins and routed Aratta in the northeast. Enmerkar's strongest general, Lugalbanda, succeeded him. The epic tales surrounding their exploits, passed down through oral storytelling, are the basis for most everything known about ancient Sumeria.

Lugalbanda was followed by Enmebaragesi, who prevailed over Elam and commissioned Nippur's Temple of Enlil.

The last ruler of the Etana Dynasty was Enmebaragesi's son Agga, who fell to Mesanepada, king of Ur, around 2670 BC.

Mesanepada established the First Dynasty of Ur and made Ur the capital of Sumer.

When Mesanepada died, power shifted to the city of Erech under the leadership of Gilgamesh until about 2650 BC.

Around 2500 BC, Mesilim took control, but his was the last great reign of Sumer.

Infighting began, military resources were depleted, and Eannatum took the throne.

Around 2365 BC, Uruinimgina instituted sweeping social reform, but a military power he was not.

Lugalzagesi, governor of nearby Umma, overthrew Uruinimgina in the mid-twenty-third century BC, and ruled unchallenged for the better part of two decades.

Invaders Arrive

Sargon the Great didn't wait for an invitation. He conquered the whole country in a little more than eighty-five years. The Semitic ruler made Agade, in the northernmost corner of Sumer, his capital, and it quickly became the most powerful city in the world. In short order, the northern Sumer natives adopted the customs of their invaders, becoming an assimilated people called the Akkadians. From this point forward, Sumer became interchangeable with Akkad.

But the party didn't last all that long.

The Gutians, hill people from the Zagros Mountains, decimated Agade—and eventually all of Sumer—during the reign of Sargon's grandson, Naram-Sin. The Sumerians ultimately prevailed against their mountain-folk invaders, but it took a couple of hundred years.

It wasn't until Utuhegal, king of Erech, triumphed over the Gutians—just before the turn of the twentieth century BC—that the Sumerians finally celebrated their Independence Day.

It was Ur-Nammu, one of Utuhegal's most trusted generals, who founded the Third Dynasty of Ur and established himself as a true renaissance man. Not only was Ur-Nammu a brilliant military leader, he also brought about massive social reform and enacted laws almost three hundred years before Babylon's celebrated Hammurabi.

Ur-Nammu's son, Shulgi, followed skillfully in his father's diplomatic footsteps, but he also championed education and commissioned academies across the kingdom to satiate his intellectual lust. But uncouth, barbaric Semitic neighbors pushed their way into Sumer and Akkad around the turn of the millennium and overtook cities such as Isin and Larsa. Taking advantage of the mayhem, the residents of Elam sacked Ur and imprisoned its last king, Ibbi-Sin.

For several hundred years, Sumer and Akkad remained embroiled in violent civil wars between Isin and Larsa and even Larsa and Babylon.

It wasn't until Babylon's great Hammurabi defeated Larsa's Rim-Sin in the mid-seventeenth century BC, that peace returned, and he reigned as the sole leader of Sumer and Akkad.

EVERYDAY HISTORY

THE SAIL

Almost 10,000 years before steam and oil began powering ships, Mesopotamian sailors harnessed the wind with a little help from their friends and a lot of help from a little-known plant called hemp.

Archaeologists date hemp's first use for this purpose to 8000 BC, and within five thousand years hemp was one of the world's largest textile exports.

From Mesopotamia, hemp seeds were carried by birds and wind to Asia, Europe, and Africa. And the strong fiber wasn't used just for the sails themselves but to engineer ropes and rigging to control the sails as well.

By the sixteenth century, though, expanded trade routes and world exploration demanded that ships withstand perilous treks for which hemp really wasn't the most effective material.

Hemp gave way to Holland's canefis, or canvas, which was popularized by Christopher Columbus's voyages to the New World, but even that method was short-lived.

By the nineteenth century nylon was helping sailors stretch their budgets and the lengths of their trips, but the Industrial Revolution took the wind out of the lightweight, malleable material fairly quickly.

Sumerian Politics

- All Sumerians worshipped three common gods: Anu, the sky god; Enlil, the lord of storms; and Ishtar, the morning and evening star.
- The Creation, an epic poem, theorizes that humans were created solely to eliminate work from the gods' busy schedules.
- After the common gods, each city had its own god that was believed to live inside the city's temple.
- The earliest Sumerian cities were called temple towns because each was built around a temple erected in honor of the local god. Markets and other public buildings sprang up outside these temples.
- The temple towns grew into city-states, the cornerstone of modern civilizations.
- City-states were ruled by leaders, called ensis, whose most important job was to oversee local irrigation.
- Kings—more often than not—were selected because of their military prowess and ranked just below the gods, but just above the priests assigned to interpreting the will of the gods.
- This structure established kings and priests as a collective upper class.
- Scribes, who tended to the scholarly duties of the temples, were upper middle class by modern-day standards and oversaw the burgeoning legal system and the economy.
- Nobles fell behind scribes on the Sumerian food chain and owned most of the land.
- Merchants, artisans, and peasants accounted for most of the population, and only slaves fell lower in the social order than this working class.

SUMERIAN SHOWOFFS

Sumer might have existed more than 5,000 years ago, but there's really very little about the civilization one can consider primitive. The Akkadians especially took full advantage of the innovations about them.

They recorded everything on sandstone tablets and used intricate cylindrical seals to roll their signatures into the wet clay of these "documents." Thousands of the clay tablets have been excavated from temple ruins, documenting the contracts, credit issues, loans with compounded interest, and business partnerships that drove the Akkadian economy. For picture drawing they developed a stylus which led directly to the cuneiform writing style of stylized symbols.

The most monumental advance came when someone figured out that the symbols could represent individual sounds instead of just a single item, and the written word was born. By 2800 BC, the use of syllabic writing had reduced the number of signs from nearly 2,000 to 600.

The Plow

Like many of our most enduring marvels, the plow surfaced in Mesopotamia around 4500 BC in its most rudimentary form, the ard. It consisted of nothing more than a pole with a spear-like point that farmers dragged across the earth to dig ruts for seed cultivation.

The ard gave way to more complex wooden plows, typically pulled by men, but as the practice spread to less arid parts of the world, domesticated animals such as oxen were incorporated into the equation.

Meanwhile, the Chinese had already created stone points for their plows by 3000 BC, allowing for the digging of deeper furrows with far less effort. It was the Chinese who developed the first iron plow tip around 500 BC, almost five centuries before it occurred to Western farmers. Chinese farmers also developed the first moldboard, or a curved metal plate designed to scoop tilled earth away from the plowed tracks to prevent the earth from sliding back into the ruts.

Sumerian Mythology

The Creation: Sumerians believed the world had once been covered with water and rife with chaos. The mother of Chaos, Tiamat, was a massive dragon who mounted an army of dragons to stave off the gods who assembled with the sole purpose of bringing order out of chaos.

Tiamat is said to have come straight for the gods with her mouth wide open, and Enlil, god of the winds, did his thing: He pumped Tiamat so full of air she was stopped in her reptilian tracks. Enlil swiftly cut Tiamat open and laid half the corpse down to form the earth and the other half arched above to form the heavens.

Then, the gods beheaded Tiamat's husband, mixed his blood with clay and, *voila*, mankind sprang into existence.

Epic of Gilgamesh: This tale recounts the title character's trip to the ocean floor in search of the plant of life. He stopped on his way home, though, for a quick bath in a lake, and a serpent yanked the plant. Watching the snake shed its skin as it slithered away, Gilgamesh understood that aging is simply the curse of mortality. Seems a bit anticlimactic, but it *has* endured longer than any other known work of literature.

The search for eternal life is actually a common theme in Sumerian literature. Consider the story of Adapa, a fisherman who talked shop just a little too long one day with Ea, the god of water. The other gods didn't appreciate Ea sharing divine secrets, so they invited Adapa up for a chat. Ea told him not to eat or drink anything while visiting for fear it would be a trick. Anu, the god of the sun, offered Adapa the water and bread of life, his reasoning being it couldn't hurt to make the fisherman immortal if he already knew so much inside information. But Adapa, heeding Ea's advice, turned down the offer and missed his one shot at eternal life.

The Sumerian version of the Great Flood story recounted in the Christian Bible is based on a character named Ziusudra. Careful. It gets a little tricky here. Ziusudra was the inspiration for the Babylonian character, Utnapishtim. The story of Utnapishtim and the flood was repeated in the *Epic of Gilgamesh*. Tradition holds that surviving the flood rendered Utnapishtim immortal, and he is the Yoda-like figure who tells Gilgamesh exactly where to find the plant of life.

POLITICAL SCIENCE 101

LEGAL MUMBO JUMBO

A defining characteristic of any civilization is the population's ability to police itself.

If the U.S. Constitution's Bill of Rights seems harsh, take a minute to consider what abiding by these little Mesopotamian gems must have been like. Be advised, the laws have been paraphrased, but zero liberties were taken in recounting them. At least there were only 12:

Family Matters: If a son disowned his father, dad was entitled to chop junior's hair off, enslave him and sell him for money. If a son disowned his mother, she too could chop off the ingrate's locks, drive him from the hous, or even the town, and strip his citizenship and inheritance, but he remained a free man. If a father disowned a son, junior was out on the street and lost everything. If mom did the same, junior had to leave and couldn't take any furniture. Adulterous wives were thrown into the river for their offenses, but men leaving their wives were required only to pay "one half mana of silver."

Work Ethic: If an overseer or fisherman was ordered to serve the king and, instead, he sent a stand-in, the guy who laid out is put to death, and the guy he sent in his place inherited his house.

Insurance: If bad weather or unruly farm animals damaged land rented to a farmer, the tenant was partially reimbursed for the loss of productivity.

Bookkeeping: When a business owner gave his clerk any form of merchandise (grain, wood, oil, etc) it was the clerk's responsibility to provide a "strict account" and money for any and all transactions. It was then the business owner's responsibility to provide the clerk with a receipt for the money paid.

Fenced In: If a man bought a slave who wasn't technically on the market, the broker of the deal was responsible for paying all damages.

Beware of Mauling Lions: If a lion killed anything trespassing on an owner's property, the owner was required to pay damages for the mauling, but he was allowed to keep any carcasses.

Basic Economics: Vendors could purchase only set amounts of merchandise as set forth in written agreements with owners. Any merchandise left over after the transaction remained the property of the owner to do with as he pleased.

Short-term Leasing: Shepherds of small cattle were allowed to drive their herds into the city gates and put them to pasture on fields owned by other men, but in doing so the shepherds assumed all pasture-tending responsibilities for the duration of the stay and were required to pay the owner of the field sixty *qa* per day.

Child Support: If a man sold a slave girl for profit and then discovered she was the rightful property of another man, the seller was required to refund the exact purchase amount to the buyer. If, however, she had borne children by the time the discrepancy was discovered, the seller was also required to pay one half shekel per child to the buyer.

Right of Renegotiation: If a man with a daughter of marrying age had promised—either in writing or verbally—a particular dowry for the right to marry her but he then falls upon hard times and loses a portion of the property, the man is allowed to adjust the amount of the dowry without the father-in-law or son-in-law seeking legal recourse.

Bereavement Fee: If a man gave his daughter a dowry, and she died in a reasonable way, the dowry reverted to the father.

Widow Wages: If a woman married, bore no children, and her husband died, her dowry was refunded to her out of her late husband's estate. If the woman had no dowry, a judge examined the late husband's affairs and gave her a "proper" share in line with the estate.

Sargon the Great

Somebody had to be first, and Sargon of Akkad figured why not him.

He assumed control of Mesopotamia in 2334 BC, and in just under six decades he built the world's first super power. Restless, to say the least, Sargon amassed his empire by conquering all of southern Mesopotamia and portions of Syria, Anatolia, and Elam. In doing this, he not only created the region's first Semitic dynasty but also the Mesopotamian military tradition.

The capital city he erected, Agade, was destroyed when his dynasty fell, and the site has never been located, so all of what is known about Sargon has been pieced together through legend and more than two thousand years of cuneiform literature that was written centuries after his death.

Like all great tales of legendary leaders, Sargon's roots are muddled, but folklore holds that he was found floating down the river in a basket by a gardener who took him in and raised him. His birth father is unknown, but his mother was believed to have been a priestess in a town on the middle Euphrates.

He made his bones on the battlefield and stepped into power after defeating Lugalzaggisi of Uruk, who had already united the city-states of Sumer and claimed domain over all lands reaching to the Mediterranean. Sargon was able to maintain his supremacy by triumphing in battle time and again as each of the city-states Lugalzaggisi had conquered attempted to win back independence rather than submit blindly to a new ruler.

After the homeland was secured, Sargon took his military prowess and natural charisma on the road, cutting a victorious swath from northern Syria and southern Anatolia to Susa, in what is now western Iran. His dominance allowed trade in Agade and throughout Mesopotamia to flourish as he opened routes with the Indus Valley, the Oman coast, settlements along the Persian Gulf, Badakhshan, Lebanon, the Taurus Mountains, Cappadocia, Crete, and arguably Greece.

Jericho

As early as 7000 BC, at least 10 acres of this oasis city near the banks of the Jordan River boasted mud and brick houses built on stone foundations. As the city grew, the need to fortify its perimeter became paramount to protect its multiplying wealth from opportunistic outsiders. There is evidence that a ditch and a twelve-foot stone wall eventually encircled the city. That might not sound impressive, but considering that they had only their hands with which to dig and that the stones for the wall were carried—or more probably dragged—from a riverbed almost a mile's walk away, it's a pretty staggering feat.

Records indicate the city was updated throughout the centuries and within several hundred years the wall increased to about fifteen feet and a stone tower rising twenty-five feet was added.

Round houses were replaced by rectangular ones built of more sturdy materials, and religious structures were eventually erected.

Wheat and barley were the primary cash crops, but hunting and trade with neighboring areas also contributed to Jericho's economy. Residents domesticated goats for milk and meat, while birds were hunted for their meat and trappings.

The abundance of salt, sulfur, and pitch made Jericho attractive in trade circles, and these natural resources allowed residents to obtain items such as obsidian, turquoise, and other stones.

Excavations at the Jericho site reveal sociological evidence that a dominant ruling class was most likely linked closely with religious practices. But artisans and merchants also left behind clues. Fertility figurines were quite popular, but Jericho's artists also carved life-sized human forms.

Catal Huyuk

Catal Huyuk in southern Turkey also emerged as a social and cultural hub for Mesopotamian life sometime around 7000 BC, but it was larger and somewhat more advanced than Jericho. At its peak, Catal Huyuk housed around six thousand people spread about thirty-two acres.

The rectangular houses were architecturally unremarkable, but they were built in a formation that literally closed ranks to protect the city center. Roofs and terraces served as the primary means of getting around, and each house was actually its own little fortress within a fortress.

The uniformity of housing indicates a strong ruling class at Catal Huyuk, and the volume of shrines suggests an imposing religious hierarchy. The shrines were full of fertility worship and death imagery.

From jewelry, mirrors, and weapons found buried among the dead to the intricately carved statues adorning the shrines, archaeological evidence indicates Catal Huyuk operated at a much more advanced level both culturally and artistically than Jericho.

Archaeologists began digging around Catal Huyuk shortly after the discovery of a Neolithic site in the 1950s. Excavator James Mellaart and his team gained international fame after finding unique and extravagant works of art.

Shuruppak and Larsa

Shuruppak, located just south of Nippur on the banks of the Euphrates River, is the site of present-day Tall Fa'rah in south-central Iraq. Tradition holds that Shuruppak was ground zero for the great flood, believed to have destroyed all of mankind except for the obedient Ziusudra. Having been commanded by a god to build an ark to ride out a devastating flood—sound familiar?—Ziusudra then recreated life on earth. His reward? Eternal life.

Guess Noah missed the boat on that one.

Back in the "it's real and we can touch it" world, excavations in the 1900s revealed that the city of Shuruppak resurrected itself at least twice between the late prehistoric period and the twentieth century BC.

The digs unearthed—among other things—well-built dwellings and cuneiform tablets documenting administrative records and even language development.

Although it was most likely founded in prehistoric times, the city of Larsa came to prominence as an ancient capital of Babylonia sometime around 2025 BC. Larsa apparently coexisted with nearby Isin for more than a century while both cities got their respective houses in order. By 1932 BC, though, Larsa had overshadowed Shuruppak, its longtime rival.

During its height, Larsa was ruled by an independent dynasty led by Naplanum, whose thirteen successors effectively replaced Sumerian with Akkadians as the predominant culture. Agriculture and domestication of livestock flourished. Irrigation and trade with distant lands improved Larsa's position. The arts, especially under the rule of Warad-Sin's son Rim-Sin, were embraced. Rim-Sin resurrected the old Sumerian schools.

But Babylon's Hammurabi lay in wait.

In 1763 BC, Rim-Sin fell to Hammurabi, and Babylonia assumed control over southern Mesopotamia.

EBLA

During its heyday, Ebla was the word in northern Syria, Lebanon, and other parts of northern Mesopotamia. Situated on what is now Tel Mardikh in northwestern Syria, Ebla dominated the region from about 2600 until 2240 BC, opening trade routes as far away as Egypt, Iran, and Sumer.

The organizational skills unearthed at Ebla in 1975 by a University of Rome team of archaeologists boggled the mind. Not only do the seventeen thousand cuneiform tablets date to the third century BC, they were discovered practically in the order in which they had been filed.

Agriculture flourished in Ebla, which was rich in barley, wheat, olives, figs, grapes, pomegranates, and flax and accommodating to herds of sheep, goats and pigs. It didn't hurt that seventeen smaller city-states in what is now Lebanon and southwestern Turkey fell under Ebla's control.

With access to silver and timber in these outlying regions, Ebla became a manufacturing and distribution hub, and linen and wool became its chief exports.

And because the city was a peaceful one, Ebla was allowed to prosper longer than most neighboring cities. Ebla was ruled by nonhereditary kings who appointed fourteen governors as department heads. Decision making was shared, however, by the king and a council of elders. Research also reveals the city flourished as a major educational center.

And all was well until Sargon the Great—or possibly his grandson, Naram-Sin—destroyed the city during a conquest, but the people of Ebla reportedly held on—impoverished and downtrodden—for almost 250 years.

The Amorites ultimately sacked Ebla and took the city for their own, but at least the invaders took the time to rebuild the palace and at least one temple. Ebla succumbed finally to regional upheaval and chaos sometime between 1650 and 1600 BC.

Ur

The rulers of Ur realized what dominant military powers have preached for millennia: Control the port, and you can control the world or, at the very least, your little corner of it.

The city's geographical location—roughly halfway between present-day Baghdad and the head of the Persian Gulf—destined Ur for economic and political dominance.

In the Christian Bible, the city is referred to as Ur of the Chaldees, referring to the Chaldeans. The locale is important to Christian scholars who study its mention in the book of Genesis as the starting point for Abraham's family's migration toward Palestine in 1900 BC.

Despite its cross-religion appeal, Ur actually evolved into the primary worship center for the Sumerian moon god Nanna as well as his Babylonian counterpart Sin. The temple in their honor towers seventy feet above the Iraqi desert.

Among the first village settlements of Sumer around 4000 BC, Ur emerged as a dominant power about 2,200 years later. Conqueror and builder of temples, Mesanepada, founded Ur's First Dynasty around 2650 BC. He was succeeded by his son, Aanepadda, who built the temple to the goddess Ninhursag.

Few records regarding the Second Dynasty have ever been located, but historians have pegged Ur-Nammu as the first king of the Ur's Third Dynasty. Ur-Nammu—in case you weren't paying attention earlier—resurrected the empire of Sumer and Akkad, won control of the port and transformed Ur into Mesopotamia's hotshot city.

Art and education flourished.

But just before 2000 BC, the Elamites captured Ur's king Ibbi-Sin and sacked the city.

Over the next few centuries, a rebuilt Ur became part of the kingdoms of Isin, Larsa and eventually Babylonia.

It was King Nebuchadnezzar II of Babylonia during the Chaldean Dynasty who really took an interest in Ur, commissioning a large-scale building plan.

But when Persia conquered Babylonia, Ur began to decline.

Crash Course

Sumer Trivia

- The latter years of Sargon the Great's fifty-six-year reign were littered with uprisings. Literature blames Sargon's sacrilege for the unrest, but historians are generally more comfortable accepting that excuse as a worthy scapegoat for one man's inability to truly hold influence over an empire of that size.
- The Sumerians developed the first calendar, adjusted to the phases of the moon. The lunar calendar debuted later with the Semites, Egyptians, and Greeks.
- Cuneiform writing paved the way for epic literature, and three key tales have survived for thousands of years. These works address the creation, the mythical Great Flood, which is recounted in almost every ancient civilization, and the Epic of Gilgamesh.
- The majority of Sumerian priests were also mathematicians long before the concept ever existed. They actually developed a notation system for tracking the nation's massive public-works program. Not only did the system involve a decimal point, but it was based on cycles of sixty, laying the foundation for time and degree measurement.

HAMMURABI

As Sumer declined, Mesopotamian power shifted northward to the city of Babylon under the reign of Hammurabi. It marks a time of conquest and unparalleled order shrouded in brutality.

Politically, the rise of the Babylonian empire coincides with the union of the Akkadians and the Sumerians, but Hammurabi's forty-three-year reign, beginning in 1792 BC, established more than a geographical relocation. It effectively laid the foundation from which all future legal systems would borrow, in spirit if not deed.

Indeed, the notorious Code of Hammurabi includes 282 random laws establishing the first known due process, but its procedures and subsequent punishments ranged from highly enlightened to unthinkably barbaric. It was truly comprehensive and sent crystal clear messages that hoodlums of any sort would not be tolerated.

"An eye for an eye," anyone?

The code's sheer length and complexity place it, for most historians, far above anything similar found in the Assyrian culture some thousand years later. The actual document was recovered during a 1901 excavation of Susa. The timeless words were inscribed on a cylinder that had been transported from Babylon to Elam sometime around 1100 BC.

A portion of the historic document reads: "When the lofty Anu, King of the Anunnaki and Bel, Lord of Heaven and Earth, he who determines the destiny of the land, committed the rule of all mankind to Marduk;...when they pronounced the lofty name of Babylon; when they made it famous among the quarters of the world and in its midst established an everlasting kingdom whose foundations were firm as heaven and earth—at that time, Anu and Bel called me, Hamurrappi, the exalted prince, the worshipper of the gods, to cause justice to prevail in the land, to destroy the wicked and the evil, to prevent the strong from oppressing the weak,...to enlighten the land and to further the welfare of the people."

Of course, no one ever accused Hammurabi of being a one-dimensional ruler. He also:

- Commissioned the construction of a massive canal between the city of Kish and the Persian Gulf. The canal not only irrigated a huge portion of the arid land but also protected cities to the south from flooding when the mighty Tigris overflowed.

- Ordered temples and forts constructed, the largest of which was a sanctuary for Babylonia's national deities, Marduk and his wife.
- Levied fair taxes that not only paid for his unbending form of law and order, but left enough in the cookie jar for a few beautification projects, including palaces and temples.
- Erected a bridge across the Euphrates, allowing Babylon to expand along the river's banks. Trade flourished.

People prospered. Life was good—until Hammurabi died in 1750 BC.

The Kassites, hungry for the wealth and opulence they had watched Hammurabi's subjects amass, swooped down from the mountains to the north eight years after his death, and raided the city several times before deciding to stay awhile—600 years give or take.

Unlike their Semitic predecessors, the Kassites were most likely Indo-European, and they are most frequently remembered for penning the Amama letters. The historic letters chronicle the give and take between Babylonian and Syrian rulers seeking aid from their Egyptian counterparts against insurgents and invaders.

The Kassites were finally cast out, but Babylon sputtered along for another four centuries or so, until Assyria's power descended from the north, sucking Babylonia under control of the Nineveh kings. Babylonia rebelled.

Sennacherib practically decimated the city, but the blight was short-lived. Esarhaddon restored the region to prosperity.

In the seventh century BC, Nabopolassar liberated Babylonia with the help of the Medes, establishing an independent dynasty.

What became the second Babylonian kingdom got its start with Nabopolassar's death in 605 BC when his son, Nebuchadnezzar II, assumed the throne and unleashed all holy hell.

NEBUCHADNEZZAR

Like Hammurabi, Nebuchadnezzar was a true renaissance man.

He was a statesman, warrior, and visionary responsible for not only restoring Babylonia's former glory but elevating the empire to the most powerful nation in the Near East.

But Nebuchadnezzar's bloodthirsty mean streak captured most of the glory.

Egypt made the mistake of conspiring with the Assyrians to subjugate Babylonia again, and the young Nebuchadnezzar met them head-on at Carchemish. He left his Egyptian aggressors gasping for air.

Not one to waste a lot of time, Nebuchadnezzar quickly convinced Palestine and Syria they were better off under his watch, consolidating all the trade from the Persian Gulf to the Mediterranean under Babylon's control. Having sewn his wild oats, Nebuchadnezzar turned his sights toward preservation and beautification of his capital. He strove to make Babylonia the crown jewel of the Near East, and by all accounts he succeeded.

The city was reportedly enclosed by a wall fifty-six miles long and wide enough for chariots to patrol its plateau. Inside the wall lay a metropolis about two hundred square miles in size, larger than most by ancient standards. And because the Euphrates River flowed right through the center of town, trade thrived day and night.

A sacred paved road, the Processional Way, connected the temple of Marduk with the seven-tiered ziggurat that Nebuchadnezzar had commissioned. On the nearby mound of Kasr, he built his palace with the famous Hanging Gardens in his line of sight.

Palaces and temples and roads and gardens aside, things did not end well for Nebuchadnezzar. He succumbed to some form of dementia and reportedly crawled around like a common animal eating grass. The once great king died in 562 BC.

Power Structure

Each city had a god who reigned supreme.

While powerful, the king was merely the agent of that god, meaning all taxation was in the name of the deity and went directly to the temple. The priests actually held more power than the king because only they could ordain him to rule. While that might sound a little undermining for a king, it actually strengthened his position.

Rebellion didn't sound so appealing if it meant risking one's eternal soul for crossing the agent of the city's god. Church and state were inextricably linked.

Kings, seeking perpetual divine forgiveness, not only built extravagant temples but furnished them lavishly and provided food and slaves. The structures were actually deeded tracts of land, and a portion of the city's annual budget was allocated for their upkeep.

All subjects, poor and wealthy gave until it hurt.

Only the priests, who were not allowed to amass wealth or worldly belongings, were exempt from paying financial homage. Ironically, however, the priests were charged with maintaining the temples themselves, so they were allowed to conduct business—up to and including the use of slave labor—which meant the overseeing and de facto ownership of vast tracts of land and the people who worked them.

It was from Babylon that the Greeks brought to their city-states and then to Rome—and ultimately to us—the foundations of mathematics, astronomy, medicine, grammar, lexicography, archaeology, history, and philosophy. The Greek names for the metals and constellations, for weights and measures, for musical instruments, and many drugs, are translations—often simply transliterations—of Babylonian terms.

There's no question the Greeks and Romans get a lot of credit for laying the groundwork for modern society, but one should remember that a significant portion of the processes and terms attributed to the Greeks are actually derived from the Babylonian civilization. From constellations and musical instruments, to weights and measures and even pharmaceutical concoctions, it turns out the Greeks weren't as pioneering as the world once thought.

Babylonian Mythology

Now keep in mind that every single city had its own god, but the Babylonians took their religious worship to far greater lengths than that. Most professions—and even most mundane tasks—were assigned their very own gods as well.

At one point an official census pegged the number of official and unofficial Babylonian deities at somewhere around sixty-five thousand. Tradition holds that most Babylonian gods—unlike the transcendent Sumerian gods on which they were based—lived on earth, in the temples erected for them. They ate and drank to excess and were known to impregnate pious women in the dark of night.

- The oldest and most divine of the Babylonian gods came directly from the skies and included:
- Anu, the immovable firmament.
- Shamash, the sun.
- Nannar, the moon.
- Baal, the earth.

But that was only the beginning. Each family prayed to its own set of household gods for everything from bedtime prayers to their morning coffee. Not to mention, each and every person had a very own personal god who offered protection from harm and provided general happiness.

The tradition eventually gave way to the Persian practice of Zoroastrianism that held a strong belief in guardian angels and became the basis for the similar Christian belief. Sixty-five thousand deities seemed a little excessive after a while, though, and a periodic paring down began integrating minor gods into major ones as attributes of those deities. That's actually the process by which Marduk, a sun god, became the Grand Poobah of all Babylonian gods.

Culture Shock

Greek Historian Herodotus wrote in *The Histories* the following disturbing account of one Babylonian practice that would make ladies of every age cringe, or at the very least, blush. This version was translated by Aubrey de Selincourt in 1954:

> There is one custom amongst these people which is wholly shameful: every woman who is a native of the country must once in her life go and sit in the temple of Aphrodite [that is, Ishtar] and there give herself to a strange man. Many of the rich women, who are too proud to mix with the rest, drive to the temple in covered carriages with a whole host of servants following behind, and there wait; most however, sit in the precinct of the temple with a band of plait string round their heads—a great crowd they are, what with some sitting there, others arriving, others going away—and through them all gangways are marked off running in every direction for the men to pass along and make their choice. Once a woman has taken her seat she is not allowed to go home until a man has thrown a silver coin into her lap and taken her outside to lie with her. As he throws the coin, the man has to say, 'In the name of the goddess Myllita'—that being the Assyrian name for Aphrodite. The value of the coin is of no consequence; once thrown it becomes sacred, and the law forbids that it should ever be refused. The woman has no privilege of choice—she must go with the first man who throws her the money. When she has lain with him, her duty to the goddess is discharged and she may go home, after which it will be impossible to seduce her by any offer, however large. Tall, handsome women soon manage to get home again, but the ugly ones stay a long time before they can fulfill the condition which the law demands, some of them, indeed, as much as three or four years. There is a custom similar to this in parts of Cyprus.

End of an Empire

Comparing Mesopotamian cities to present-day metropolises such as London or New York City is really an apples-to-oranges sort of deal, but there's no doubt that locales such as Jericho and Catal Huyuk were the urban centers of their day.

- Thousands of people lived in one close-knit area.
- Trade flourished.
- Religious and political alliances formed.
- Occupational specialties beyond farming emerged.
- Artistic capabilities were embraced and encouraged.

These combined contributions made it possible for inventions such as writing, the wheel, the plow, and even the manipulation of bronze to emerge beginning around 4000 BC. Yet within thirty years of Nebuchadnezzar's bizarre passing, the once mighty Babylonian Empire crumbled. The civilization's demise is due in large part to the inept rulers who followed.

One such winner included Nabonidus, who literally watched while the city fell down around his ears. This might not have happened if the amateur archaeologist had spent half as much time ruling his own nation as he did excavating Sumer's antiquities. Nabonidus's primary fault was complacency.

The Babylonians—so comfortable in their wealth and trade—forgot that opportunistic invaders are always waiting for the slightest misstep.

The art—and more importantly, practicality—of war were forgotten.

By the time the Persian Empire's Cyrus came knocking, the Babylonian priests had gorged themselves on the riches of Babylon's masses, and the masses saw a simple solution: Let him in.

And, why not? Babylon's pinhead ruler by this point was Nabonidus's son, Belshazzar, who was so oblivious to the world around him that he threw a lavish party while his own people conspired his toppling.

The Persians promptly stormed his party and killed Belshazzar in 539 BC, ruling Babylon for the next two centuries until Alexander the Great crippled the Persian Empire and ruled an even more expansive kingdom until his death in 323 BC.

Abu Musa Jabir ibn Hayyan (Geber)

Born in Iran in 721, Abu Musa Jabir ibn Hayyan grew up in Yemen. As an adult, the future Father of Chemistry lived in Iran and followed in his father's footsteps practicing alchemy. He is also known as Geber, the Latin version of his name.

Many of the chemical elements, processes, and laboratory equipment used today were discovered or invented by Geber.

He developed chemicals such as hydrochloric acid and aqua regia, one of the few substances that can dissolve gold.

He is also credited with the discovery of citric acid, acetic acid, and tartaric acid.

Geber applied his chemical knowledge to improving the way steel and other metals were made, preventing rust, and engraving gold. He also developed the use of manganese dioxide in glassmaking—a process that remains in practice today—to counteract the green tint produced by iron.

Because his literary works rarely made sense, the term gibberish is believed to have originally referred to his writings.

In his *Book of Stones*, he claimed to have intentionally written to "baffle and lead into error everyone except those whom God loves and provides for."

In 803, he was placed under house arrest where he remained for several years before his death.

A crater on the moon is named for Geber. The lunar impact crater is located in the rugged south-central highlands of the moon.

Assyria Arises

The history of Assyria, the third and northernmost dominant region of Mesopotamia, is a bit more complicated—primarily because it carries forward to the present time. The earliest proof of Assyrian life dates to around 5000 BC in Nineveh, which was excavated by British archaeologist Sir Max Mallowan in 1932. Though not as old, Ashur and Arbel have been identified as the two other great Assyrian cities, and all three are believed to have been bustling urban centers by 2500 BC.

Between 2371 and 612 BC, Assyria flourished during what is commonly called its First Golden Age. It began with the reign of Sargon of Akkad and lasted until Nineveh's fall.

Sargon, the first king with the gumption to subjugate peoples outside his own city walls, set the precedent for all future imperial conquest. How else can one explain his control of everything north of Akkad to Ashur and west to the Mediterranean?

But it was Shamshi-Adad I who, in 1813 BC, united Ashur, Nineveh and Arbel; overtook Arrapkha; and rounded out what would become the core of Assyria with Nimrod. He also revived Cappadocia as an Assyrian merchant stronghold.

Now try to keep up. There might be a pop quiz:

- In 1472 BC, Assyria was annexed for about seventy years by a Mittanian king.
- Ashuruballit vanquished the last vestiges of Mittanian control by 1365 BC, laying the foundation for the first Assyrian Empire.
- That empire was successfully established in 1307 BC by Adad-narari and lasted for almost sixty years.
- The Middle Assyrian Empire and a period of tremendous expansion began in 1307 BC under Tiglath-Pileser. It is also during this period that Arameans began immigrating to Assyria, setting the stage for future conflict.
- By the time Tiglath-Pileser's son, Ashur-bel-kala, took the throne, the Arameans had infiltrated deep into Assyrian territory and disrupted life for the better part of a century.
- Assyria began to re-emerge as a power in 934 BC.

- Ashur-dan II rebuilt Assyria strategically by commissioning the construction of government offices in all provinces and stimulating the economy with a plow-distribution program that boosted grain production substantially. His four successors followed his lead and helped Assyria regain its former prominence.
- Ashur-dan II was succeeded by his son, Adad-nerari II, and then Tukulti-Ninurta II, Ashur-nasir-pal II and Shalmaneser III.
- Adad-nerari II defeated the Aramean chief at Nisibin, and the rest of the infiltrators followed suit.
- Ashur-nasir-pal II placed all lands south of Lebanon to the Zagros Mountains under Assyrian control.
- Another series of sharp-witted rulers—including Tiglath-Pileser III, Sargon II, Sennacherib, Esarhaddon, and Ashurbnaipal—helped Assyria assert its dominance from Egypt to Cyprus and Anatolia all the way to the Caspian Sea.
- The Assyrian Empire collapsed around 612 BC, and its people survived in relative obscurity for another 600 years give or take. The Persians, who were known to use Assyrians as troops, put the kibosh on an attempt to resurrect the empire in 350 BC by castrating 400 Assyrian leaders.

CRASH COURSE

ASSYRIAN INGENUITY

The next time you lock your bathroom door and settle in for a little quality reading time, take a moment to thank the Assyrians. Locks and keys originated in Assyria, as did dozens of other modern-day conveniences often taken for granted.

They're the reason time is broken into sixty-unit cycles.

They also pioneered the postal system, magnifying glasses, libraries, iron smelting, flush toilets, batteries, arches, aqueducts, and even guitars.

But Assyrian innovation was not limited to physical items.

The Assyrian government is also credited with introducing the idea of imperial administration, or the division of land into smaller, more manageable territories overseen by local governors who then report to a centralized authority figure—in Assyria's case, a king. This system is the very basis of the American federal-state system, and it has been replicated time and again for millennia.

Assyria also provides the mythological basis for the Old and New testaments of the Bible. It was the breeding ground for the first epic ever written, the *Epic of Gilgamesh.* It is the very birthplace for the ideas that spawned Hellenism, Judaism, Christianity, and Islam.

Pop Quiz #1

1) What is considered the first widely recognized civilization in what would be known as Mesopotamia?
   a) Assyria
   b) Babylon
   c) Aragon
   d) Sumer

2) Which Babylonian ruler's "Code" is considered the basis of modern-day law and order and gave us little gems like "an eye for an eye?"
   a) Nebuchadnezzar
   b) Hammurabi
   c) Nabopolassar
   d) Nebuchadnezzar II

3) Which of the following were Babylonian gods?
   a) Anu, the immovable firmament
   b) Shamash, the sun
   c) Baal, the earth
   d) All of the above

4) What was the name of the road connecting the temple of Marduk with the seven-tiered ziggurat commissioned by Nebuchadnezzar?
   a) Kasr Path
   b) Yellow Brick Road
   c) Processional Way
   d) Highway to Hell

5) What is the term for Sumerian writing that paved the way for modern literature and preserved works including the *Epic of Gilgamesh*?
   a) Hieroglyphics
   b) Sanskrit
   c) Cuneiform
   d) None of the above

6) Which Sumerian leader assumed control of Mesopotamia in 2334 BC, and in just under six decades built the world's first super power?
   a) Sargon the Great
   b) Philip of Macedon
   c) Alexander the Great
   d) Ivan the Terrible

ANSWERS:

1) d
2) b
3) d
4) c
5) c
6) a

Egypt's Beginning

Rivaled only by China for longest running historical record, ancient Egypt prevailed as the world's first true super power for more than 3,000 years. And it had everything: cunning leadership, architectural marvels, military domination, economic prosperity, pageantry, and deceit.

Ancient Egypt is divided into three primary segments: the Old Kingdom, Middle Kingdom and New Kingdom, spanning thirty-one dynasties—or ruling families—and 3,000 years.

But the true pomp and circumstance of this pioneering civilization lay buried for almost two millennia until a little tyrant by the name of Napoleon invaded the area in 1798, unearthing archaeological proof of the innovation and imperialism that had been Egypt and its glory.

The Old Kingdom, 3100–2125 BC

Spanning the first through the eighth dynasties, the Old Kingdom emerged when Menes unified what had been two separate regions, damned the Nile to create the capital city of Memphis and set about ruling that corner of the world.

When Menes's line ended about 200 years later, a prosperous but politically divided dynasty took the reins. Infighting aside, the ensuing periods spawned opulent tombs and mankind's first architectural marvel: the pyramid.

Egyptian life cruised along without any significant strife—but a long line of nifty inventions—for a few centuries, and then the Old Kingdom imploded politically during the seventh and eighth dynasties.

Little is known about the period between Pepi II's death and the start of the Middle Kingdom, except that—according to Greek historian Herodotus—his sister, a vengeful woman named Nitokris killed hundreds of subjects to avenge her brother's death.

Instability reigned again during the seventh and eighth dynasties with the country actually resplintering. The north was ruled from Herakleopolis and the south from Thebes.

Everyday History

Paper

While the applications of paper are numerous, perhaps the most important is that it gave man the ability to communicate in a relatively quick and cost-effective way. It was the Internet of the ancient world, bridging both cultural and geographical gaps.

Papyrus, used by the Egyptian beginning around 4000 BC, was the first paperlike material, but the pounding of reeds was certainly not man's first attempt to capture ideas for posterity. Clay tablets, waxed boards, and even silk had all been tried, but it wasn't until AD 105 that the Chinese developed something akin to modern-day paper.

Granted, hemp paper had been in use since about 49 BC in Asia, but paper's inventor, Cai Lun, produced a thinner, lighter-weight alternative to the popular silk or bamboo sheets of his day. He used a pressed blend of bamboo, fish net, and bark.

Of course, the Chinese also used paper as its own art form and even as clothing, but it was Buddhist monks who exported papermaking to Japan in the early seventh century. It is believed that sometime around AD 750, Chinese prisoners of war bartered the art of papermaking for their freedom from the Arabs. About 250 years later, the Arabs constructed the first-known paper mill in Xativa, Spain.

Around 1350, French monks started using paper to copy religious texts, mass production of paper from the Germans (assisted by the Italians) and then Johann Gutenberg's moveable-type printing press changed everything in 1453.

Prior to the printing press, books had been produced by hand and were typically reserved for the eyes of royalty and clergy because of time and expense required to produce them. The introduction of the printing press created the ability to mass produce the written word, signaling the inevitable spread of printed material among all social classes. The more people who could read, the more books were needed, and the demand for paper rose accordingly.

Within the next 200 years, paper production and trade went global: the first paper plant opened in Mexico around 1680; the first modern paper mill, the brainchild of William Rittenhouse, followed in

Philadelphia; Frenchman Rene-Antoine Ferchault de Reaumur ushered in the use of wood for this marvel, replacing the recycling of rags and other fabrics.

It wasn't until 1852, though, that Englishman Hugh Burgess engineered a more efficient wood pulp that was improved over the next fifteen years, paving the way for American C.B. Tilghman to add sulfites to the process. By 1907, Swede C.F. Dahl's sulfate method debuted in America sparking the means for true mass production.

Pyramids Emerge

Papyrus, or paper made from reeds, and the first documented evidence of bureaucratic red tape.

During the Third Dynasty, the world's first architect, Imhotep, designed the Step Pyramid at Saqqara. He did so during his time off from being a doctor, sculptor, astronomer, and scribe.

Sneferu started the pointed craze with his pyramid at Medum, followed by two others at Dahshur. But while Sneferu might have been the first pharaoh to commission true pyramids, he was upstaged by Khufu's Giza Pyramids. It is believed 100,000 labored on the marvel for three straight months during the annual flooding of the Nile.

Yes, there are actually three pyramids at Giza, but the still-standing Great Pyramid was the tallest building in the world for more than four thousand years. An estimated 2.3 million limestone blocks were used in its construction, but sadly, the engineering masterpiece was pillaged to build Cairo. Despite the plundering, the pyramid's estimated weight remains about six million tons.

Pepi II is believed to have ruled for ninety of his one hundred years, following his older brother's sudden death.

His sister, Nitokris, is said to have invited the people she held responsible for his untimely death to a party. She then flooded the banquet hall with water piped in from the river and promptly killed herself.

THE MIDDLE KINGDOM, 2125–1550 BC

What Northern Egypt needed at this time was a hero, and Mentuhotep fit the bill. Not unlike Menes, he quelled the unrest—this time at Herakleopolis—and unified the fragmented nation.

When Amenenhet I ascended the throne and launched the Twelfth Dynasty, he shifted the capital back to Memphis and oversaw a renaissance of Old Kingdom artistic influence. He then ruled jointly with his son, Sesostris, for ten years but was murdered while Sesostris was handling some family business in Libya.

Two generations later, the kingdom was reorganized into four regions under Sesostris III and another golden period of Egyptian art and sculpture dawned. Literature—written in Middle Egyptian—flourished as did the official recording of Old Kingdom works. The most famous Middle Egyptian literary work was *Instruction for Merikare*, the official guide book for all future kings.

The first acknowledged female monarch, Queen Sobeknefru, marked the end of the line.

During the Thirteenth and Fourteenth dynasties, Egypt was plunged again into a confusing array of short-lived rulers who either accomplished very little or just didn't bother documenting their existence.

A wimpy, ineffective line of leaders followed, leaving Egypt vulnerable to attacks by the Asiatic Hyskos. These squatters swept in and hung around for about two centuries. In the first century AD, the Jewish historian Josephus described them as godless barbarians who ruled in name only during the Sixteenth and Seventeenth dynasties.

Known also as the Shepherd Kings or Desert Princes, the Hyksos leveled Memphis and built their own capital at Avaris. Despite their torrid reputations, they did introduce pottery and looms, new musical instruments, exotic breeds of animals and new crops. But the art of war is where the Hyksos truly shined. From composite bows and cutting-edge cutlery to the horse-drawn war chariot, the Hyksos introduced their own form of enlightenment.

The New Kingdom, 1550–1295 BC

A new line of Egyptian-born rulers emerged quietly in Thebes. The greatest of these leaders, Ahmose, founded the Eighteenth Dynasty that launched the New Kingom and forcibly showed the Hyksos the door.

Soon after, Thutmose I swept through the Near East and Africa like a man with a plan. His grandson, along with Queen Hatshepsut, transformed the nation into a true world power, while Amenhotep III launched an aggressive artistic revolt. Akhenaton and Nefertiti introduced the concept of one—and only one—god, and then came Tutankhamen.

When the Nineteenth Dynasty arose, and Seti I set about restoring monuments of days gone by, it might have appeared that a time of rest and reflection had finally engulfed the embattled region, but then came Ramses II and an array of wars and meaningless treaties between Egypt and the challenging Hittites to the East.

Order in Egypt was restored briefly under Setnakht, and then Ramses III, considered the last great king, let loose on the Sea Peoples—no joke, that's really what they were called.

What followed was a period of economic decline and fizzling of culture.

Euclid of Alexandria

Euclid was a reclusive Greek man who lived in Egypt three centuries before the birth of Jesus Christ. His life was important, his impact on the world everlasting.

Known as the "Father of Geometry," Euclid developed geometric proofs. Many of the axioms and proofs you tried to master in high school can be traced to this mathematician who studied at Plato's Academy. The work he did remains the basis for the math we know and love—twenty-three centuries later. Six of his works survive to this day: *Elements, Data, Catoptrics, Divisions of Figures, Optics,* and *Phaenomena.*

Everyday History

The Clock

- Ancient peoples noted that stationary objects threw shadows that corresponded with the sun's movement through the sky.
- By 1500 BC, the Egyptians had invented a shadow clock, a version of the sundial. It consisted of a foot-long horizontal bar with a T-shaped appendage affixed to one end. The T threw a shadow on the bar's calibrated markings. In the morning, the T faced east and in the after noon was turned toward the west.
- The sundial prevailed as the universal timepiece for centuries, even though it could not effectively measure minutes and seconds. By 1400 BC, crude water clocks were being used in Egypt to measure the passage of night. The rate of flow into or out of a vessel could be regulated by the size of the hole used.
- The Romans used sundials and water clocks and divided the day and night into twelve equal hours. Daylight was dividedinto twelve equal parts, as was the night. In turn, the hours grew or shrank according to the season. As an added bonus, no two clocks in Rome were synchronized.
- A monk at Chartres is credited with the invention of the hourglass in the eighth century AD, but they were not intended for keeping daylong time. They timed sermons and lectures, kept track of workers hours, and measured the speed of ships.
- Fire clocks arose during the same time as hourglasses. The expense of candles and oils assigned them to royal households. Of course, they proved every bit as inaccurate and impractical as their predecessors.
- Monks, who needed to know the hour of their appointed prayers, are responsible for the first mechanical clocks. These marvels were weight driven and sounded the hour by ringing bells.

- During the sixth century, the standard consisted of seven canonical hours, varying by season and church decree. Escapements regulated the fall of the weights in measured intervals. The interrupter applied the force of the falling weight to the clock's machinery at spaced intervals. The rhythm of start and stop measured minutes and eventually seconds.
- The first clocks to break the day into twenty-four standardized hours appeared around 1330. Lacking faces or hands, they chimed the hour. Soon villages had large clocks sounding the hours from belfries.
- By the sixteenth century, the hour was broken into quarters.
- Minute and second hands would not be added until the arrival of the pendulum.
- By 1670, clocks with faces and a full complement of hands had become commonplace.

Famous Egyptians

Queen Hatshepsut

Not exactly a huge fan of dynastic etiquette, Queen Hatshepsut declared herself pharaoh when her husband, Thutmose II, died. Claiming that the deity Amun-Ra spoke to her directly—which raises an entirely separate set of issues—Hatshepsut announced that she would rule in the place of the underage heir, her nephew, until he had "come of age."

Amun-Ra reportedly called her his "sweet daughter," anointed her king of Upper and Lower Egypt, and the rest is crazed, cross-dressing history. Seriously, Hatshepsut routinely wore men's clothing and even donned a false beard for emphasis.

But no one really complained when for twenty years the economy soared, temple construction flourished, and her nephew, Thutmose III, came of age and accepted his spot as pharaoh.

Thutmose III

Call it sour grapes, but Thutmose III's decree that Hatshepsut's name be removed from all temple walls seems reasonable in light of the two decades he sat stewing in resentment.

Considered by many historians as the greatest pharaoh on record, Thutmose reportedly never lost a battle and triumphed as a statesman and diplomat.

These traits were put to the test early when a brood of neighboring rulers attempted to shake him down before he really had time to settle into the throne. It really wasn't pretty, but Thutmose prevailed.

He mobilized his army, crossed the Sinai Desert and marched directly into pro-Egyptian Gaza and started strategizing.

Taking a time-warp tip from Robert Frost, Thutmose took a road less traveled to Megiddo over a narrow pass and prevailed in his bid to take the focal point of his conquest. He then had a moat dug around the city and denied passage to any visitor at the gate who did not pledge allegiance to his rule. The siege lasted seven months.

Having established his military prowess, Thutmose III then confronted Palestine, Syria, and Nubia before negotiating an unprecedented peace among Egypt and the neighboring nations.

Amenhotep III and Tiyi

Amenhotep III, who ruled during the peak of Egypt's ancient prosperity during the Eighteenth Dynasty, bucked the dynastic trend and married a commoner, Tiyi. And while it could be argued that he made his choice based on some obscure political alliance, love appears to be the true motivation.

As a symbol of his affection, he is said to have engineered for Tiyi a massive lake in her hometown of T'aru. But he wasn't finished.

Amenhotep the Romantic then held a festival on the water, while he and Tiyi sailed in their boat, the Disk of Beauties.

Akhenaten

Akhenaten, son of Amenhotep III and Tiyi, actually tried to single-handedly shift Egyptian religion to the worship of one god. He was ultimately unsuccessful in wooing the rest of the nation to his sun worship—earning the nickname Heretic King—but he did have an eye for art.

He commissioned untold statues and paintings in addition to the renowned busts of his bride, Nefertiti, and mother, Tiyi.

Merenptah

Merenptah, son of Ramses II, inherited a mess.

His father had ineptly allowed foreigners to overtake the west side of the Nile Delta, with the eastern side following suit. Ramses II's excessive building projects had almost bankrupted the empire, and invasion was imminent.

But as Meryawy, the Libyan ruler, prepared to overrun the Delta, Merenptah had a dream. "His Majesty saw in a dream as if a statue of the god Ptah stood before his Majesty. He said, while holding out a sword to him, 'Take it and banish fear from thee'"

Merenptah opted to take up arrows instead of the proverbial sword and ordered a nonstop deluge on the invaders for six straight hours. Then he let loose soldiers in chariots, and the Libyans folded.

Ramses III

The Sea People—who had already laid waste to most of the neighboring regions—were knocking on Egypt's door by land and by sea.

Ramses III didn't waste a second. He mobilized an army to the south and demanded that all ships not taking on water secure the mouth of the Nile.

The Sea Peoples gravely underestimated the power of the Egyptian navy, not to mention Ramses military cunning. He ordered the banks of the Nile lined with archers and issued grappling hooks to the navy. The Sea People were so shocked to be hauled onto the banks of the Nile, they succumbed in short order to Ramses's army in hand-to-hand combat.

Peace reigned, but Ramses was not so lucky in love.

Tiye, listed in the historical record as one of his "minor" wives, plotted to kill Ramses so her son, Pentaweret, could seize control. Tiye masterminded a faux rebellion that ultimately failed, but Ramses was mortally wounded in battle and died before the conspirators stood trial.

Saladin

Anyone born inside a grand castle is probably destined to do great things. Such was the case for Saladin. His castle was in Tikrit, where he was born sometime in 1137 to 1138. The Kurd's destiny was to become Sultan of Egypt and Syria, and a major Muslim political and military leader.

The Ayyubid dynasty, which Saladin founded, eventually would rule over Egypt, Syria, Iraq, Hejaz, and Yemen. But Saladin is most well known for joining and leading the Muslim armies during the Crusades and recapturing Jerusalem in 1187. During this time, Saladin established a solid reputation throughout Europe as a gallant knight.

Cleopatra: The Last Pharaoh

Modern-day soap-opera writers could take a page or twelve from history and create the perfect femme fatale based on the life and times of Cleopatra VII, Queen of the Nile. It's a tale of conspiracy, murder, extortion, politics, infidelity, suicide, and even a little incest. We're not aware of any evil twins, but you get the picture.

To be fair, it's also a yarn that's been spun so many times over the past two thousand years that the line between fact and fiction has been liberally blurred, so light another match, and we'll try to sort it out.

Family Business

Sigmund Freud would have had a field day with this power-hungry despot whose mother was most likely her aunt and who married not one but two of her own brothers. But let's start at the beginning.

Born in Alexandria in 69 BC, Cleopatra VII was the third eldest daughter of Ptolemy XII, who was overthrown and fled to Rome when she was only eleven. Oddly, their line was of Macedonian descent, tracing its roots to Ptolemy I, a protégé of Alexander the Great and military genius who ascended the throne upon the exalted leader's death in 323 BC.

In Daddy Ptolemy's absence, Cleopatra's oldest sister Berenice took control of Egypt but reigned for only three years. In 55 BC, Ptolemy enlisted the help of the Roman general Pompey and reclaimed his throne; he had Berenice beheaded and her husband killed in an unspecified manner.

When her father died in 51 BC, Cleopatra inherited the throne jointly with her brother, Ptolemy XIII, under the watchful eyes of Pompey. As was custom, she married her co-regent brother, who was only twelve, for appearances, and pretty much had the run of the country for three years.

Teen Queen

So by the age of seventeen—possibly eighteen—Cleopatra ruled one of the most powerful countries in the world, and it would prove to be a zany ride.

Despite Tinseltown's depiction, Cleopatra definitely favored her father more than Liz Taylor; yet despite her masculine features, she reportedly possessed an irresistible charm and seductiveness that served her well. More importantly, she was intelligent—fluent in nine languages—and a cunning politician.

By 48 BC, the young Ptolemy's advisers—most notably a fellow by the name of Pothinus—conspired against the queen, stripped her of her crown and forced her and her younger sister, Arsinoe, into exile in Syria. Unhappy with her new digs, Cleopatra promptly mounted an army on Egypt's border and bided her time.

Rendering unto Caesar

Meanwhile, Pompey was attempting to wrest control of the Roman Empire from Julius Caesar and failing miserably.

Following a humiliating defeat at Pharsalos, Pompey sailed to Alexandria seeking protection from Egypt's king, his former ward. Fearing retribution from Caesar, Ptolemy's advisers decided it wasn't in their best interests to back the disgraced general, so they stabbed him to death in front of the young king.

Caesar was less than enthused when Ptolemy's runners presented him with a gift outside Alexandria's gates—Pompey's freshly skewered head. Combatants or not, Caesar and his rogue general had been buds back in the day, so the offering was far from copacetic.

Appalled by the cruelty shown his former comrade, Caesar stormed the city, seized control and demanded that Ptolemy and Cleopatra disband their armies and convene for a little tete-a-tete.

Cleopatra knew she couldn't just stroll through town without Ptolemy's lackeys taking a clean shot, but neither did she want the matter swept under the carpet. Her solution? She had herself rolled up in an oriental rug and delivered directly to the emperor. To say he was impressed that she had the cajones her brother clearly lacked was an understatement. The world's first power couple was born.

Of course, the tantrum Ptolemy pitched the next day when he saw the couple cavorting publicly didn't help his cause. Caesar had the petulant pharaoh arrested, but the boy king's army stormed the palace.

Six months later, what became known as the Alexandrian War ended when Pothinus died a martyr on the battlefield, and Ptolemy XIII drowned in the Nile as a fleeing coward.

Caesar restored Cleopatra's crown, and she promptly married her youngest brother, Ptolemy XIV.

Roman Romp

Drunk with power, the victorious soul mates set sail for a two-month cruise down the Nile. The rendezvous might have lasted longer, but rumor has it that Caesar's troops refused to play chaperone, forcing him to return to his imperial duties.

Given that Cleopatra gave birth to a son a few months later, and her most recent legal husband was only twelve, most historians connect the dots when she named the tyke Ptolemy XV yet insisted on calling him Caesarion, or "Little Caesar."

The romance flourished. Caesar dispatched three legions to protect Cleopatra in Egypt, but after only a year he imported her to Rome along with Caesarion and Ptolemy XIV.

For almost two years, Cleopatra enjoyed Caesar's villa, his ceaseless gifts and his attention. He went so far as to commission a statue of his mistress in the temple of Venus Genetrix.

Yes, mistress.

Caesar was married to Calpurnia, and the mighty ruler's countrymen were appalled at how readily he seemed to forget that fact. When rumors began circulating that he planned to pass a law making it legal for him to marry Cleopatra and name Caesarion his heir, things got ugly.

An angry mob of Roman senators surrounded and stabbed their ambitious dictator on March 15, 44 BC.

Cleopatra didn't hang around long enough for her group hug.

She and her troupe hightailed it to Egypt, where her husband died under suspicious circumstances, and she named Caesarion co-regent. Within two years, she was right back in the quick of Roman affairs.

Cleopatra's Undoing

With Caesar dead, control of the Roman Empire was divided among Octavian, Marcus Lepidus, and Marc Antony. Octavian, who was Caesar's great nephew, later became Emperor Augustus.

Marc Antony was still a little uneasy about what had gone down, so in 42 BC he invited Cleopatra to meet him in Tarsus, so he could grill her about her alliances.

Imagine his surprise when she arrived on a barge dripping with bling and accompanied by maids in sea-nymph costumes. Cleopatra made certain to get Antony's attention and dressed as Venus.

The ruse worked, and what began as a night on the barge turned into months in Alexandria. When winter gave way to spring, Antony returned reluctantly to his imperial duties, and within the reasonable amount of time Cleopatra had twins, Cleopatra Selene and Alexander Helios.

Time passed, Antony married Octavian's half-sister, Octavia, and the couple welcomed two daughters, both named Antonia.

But Antony just couldn't quite get Cleopatra out of his system.

On his way to plunder Parthia in 37 BC, he made a detour to Alexandria. The next year he married his love, and the happy couple welcomed bundle of joy no. 3, Ptolemy Philadelphus.

Octavia looked the other way from her husband's indiscretions, but when he blew off her announced visit so he could to tend to his Egyptian drama queen, the Roman subjects took notice.

The final straw came in 34 BC, when Antony named Alexander Helios king of Armenia; Cleopatra Selene queen of Cyrenaica and Crete; and Ptolemy Philadelphus king of Syria. Octavian took particular exception, though, to Caesarion being named "King of Kings" and Cleopatra anointed "Queen of Kings." The Roman senate declared war on Egypt, and playing house hadn't done much to hone Antony's tactical skills.

The pair and their respective armies fought pathetically off the coast of Actium and fled in shame when Octavian prevailed.

Knowing their days were numbered, Cleopatra dabbled with poisons in search of a painless escape and commissioned a mausoleum for all of her worldly possessions.

In 30 BC, Marc Antony marched to meet Octavian's brood outside the gates of Alexandria only to watch all of his men desert him unapologetically. Octavian fingered Cleopatra and Marc Antony as traitors, and Cleopatra locked herself away in her mausoleum to avoid his wrath.

She feigned death.

Marc stabbed himself in the stomach, but then learned her death was a ruse.

Thrilled, but a little woozy, Antony was toted to the mausoleum where he died in Cleopatra's arms.

A negotiator to the end, Cleopatra refused to let Octavian enter the mausoleum until he promised to divide her kingdom among her children. The future emperor had her flanked and taken prisoner. Her children were left unharmed.

After burying Antony in a ceremony befitting a king, Cleopatra turned her energy to her own suicide. It is believed she allowed an asp—a highly venomous snake—to bite her, and Octavia found her dead. So much for her potions.

At thirty-nine, she was laid to rest next to Marc Antony, and Egypt became a Roman province.

To neutralize any future threat from Caesar's son, Octavian had Caesarion strangled by his teacher. The other children became Octavian's wards.

Everyday History

The Calendar

Calendars rule our lives. They tell us when to do what we do. Farming, football, holidays, what color shoes to wear, and when it's time to put anti-freeze in the radiator.

Without them there would be no play dates, no luncheon with the girls, and no reasonable way to duck out of church-related activities. Grab some two-ply and hold on tight as we delve into the when, where, and why of humanity's most wonderful invention: Linear Time.

Mankind has always been in love with the moon. Before there were houses and agriculture, the moon was a constant friend in the night sky. There are discernable patterns that can be used as references in time.

Ancient man quickly realized that the phases of the moon could be used to safely predict when ancient woman needed to be avoided, as there was no chocolate. The lunar phases proved to be downright useless, though, when it came to predicting the seasons.

Early farmers and hunters needed a way to predict the advent of snows, rainy seasons and when to plant those first crops. The seasons are dictated by the solar year. It takes the earth 365 days to orbit the sun. The seasons mark the return of the earth to same place in its solar orbit, literally, like clockwork.

The moon has a shorter orbit around the earth. A lunar year lasts only 354 days, and lunar months will never match the seasons. The first calendars were skewed and slightly wacky but a step in the right direction.

The Babylonians pioneered a lunar calendar and stubbornly stuck with it for untold years. Tackling the problem of predicting the seasons in multiple moon cycles proved to be tricky. An astronomer named Meton amended the lunar calendar in 432 BC The Metonic cycle consisted of a nineteen-year calendar made up of seven years with thirteen months and twelve years with twelve months.

Intercalation, as it was called, solved the wandering month issue. Seasons were predicted with only a small amount of confusion. The Greeks adopted the Metonic cycle. Historian Herodotus makes mention of intercalary months in his fifth-century BC writings.

The Egyptians skipped lunacy completely and developed a solar calendar that became the standard around the (Roman) world. They were the first civilization to discover the length of the solar year and create a practical calendar. The key to the Egyptian breakthrough was, of course, the Nile River. The flooding that marked the beginning of the agricultural season occurred at the same time every year. Their primitive calendar consisted of a high water mark.

The Egyptians noted quickly, though, that even after a few years the lunar cycle got out of sync with the rising of the river. Early Egyptians realized that twelve months of thirty days accurately predicted the seasons as long as they added five days to the end of the year.

Some genius noticed that Sirius, the brightest star in the sky, rose once a year in perfect alignment with the sun. The heliacal rising of Sirius became the Egyptian New Year and marked the beginning of a five-day religious festival. Thus was born the "civil" year adopted throughout the empire by 4241 BC.

Julius Caesar adopted this calendar as his Julian calendar and spread it across the world. It was still in use during the sixteenth century AD. That pesky quarter of a day caused a slow wandering of the months, though certainly not enough to matter for the first 1,500 years.

Pyramid

Prior to 2630 BC, the tombs of Egyptian kings, or pharaohs, were called mastabas and resembled mud fallout shelters. But Djoser, a Second Dynasty pharaoh, wanted something a little more befitting a man of his stature. What began as a standard mastaba wound up being about 200 feet tall with tomb after tomb staggered atop one another. The Step Pyramid at Saqqara laid the groundwork for all pyramids to come.

Credited with having the Giza Pyramids built, Khufu decreed that all temples be closed and sacrifices stop, effectively putting priests out of work. But before you crown him jerk extraordinaire, remember that he fed and clothed the pyramid builders.

The Seven Wonders

No. 1: Great Pyramid of Giza

"Soldiers! From the top of these pyramids, forty centuries are looking at us."

Napoleon Bonaparte is believed to have uttered these words when his troops invaded Egypt in 1798, and he witnessed the glory of the pyramids.

Decidedly the most wondrous of the wonders in question, the Great Pyramid of Giza reigns supreme for two simple reasons: It's the oldest on the list, and it's still standing.

Egyptian Pharaoh Khufu commissioned the monument during the Fourth Dynasty—sometime around 2560 BC—to serve as his own burial tomb. It stands in the city of Giza in what is today part of Greater Cairo.

Although there are technically three Great Pyramids, only Khufu's tomb is granted the high honor. They have also been called "The Granaries of Joseph" and "The Mountains of Pharaoh."

Considering the two million limestone blocks used in the construction had to be carried onto the site from an unidentified source, it's no wonder it took an estimated twenty years to construct. The real mystery is how the architectural feat was completed at all.

Some historians believe workers first built a ramp that was raised as the monument grew taller, allowing them to push or pull the blocks into place. Another theory suggests that long levers were used to manipulate the blocks.

Transformed in recent history into a tourist trap, the Great Pyramid sits alongside the other Giza pyramids and the Sphinx. The area, referred to today as the Giza Plateau, also houses a museum showcasing the Sun Boat which is believed to have carried Khufu's body to his final resting place.

And in this particular case, size really does matter because the Great Pyramid is large enough to house the cathedrals of Florence and Milan, St. Peter's in Rome, and Westminster and St. Paul's in London.

No. 2: Hanging Gardens of Babylon

Believed to have been located on the east bank of the Euphrates River, just south of present day Baghdad, the Hanging Gardens of Babylon live vividly in imaginations only, yet conjure visions of lush fruits and vegetables interspersed among waterfalls and frolicking exotic animals.

More than a thousand years after Hammurabi ruled the Babylonian kingdom, the Mesopotamian civilization reached its pinnacle under Nabopolassar. But it was his successor, Nebuchadnezzar II, whom historians credit with building the gardens sometime around 600 BC.

The oasis was reportedly commissioned as a gift for Nebuchadnezzar's homesick wife who missed the mountains of Media.

And yet, Babylonian records make no mention of these glorious structures.

Some accounts have surfaced in the writings of the Greek historians Berossus and Diodorus.

A prevailing theory is that Alexander the Great returned home with tales of amazing gardens and palm trees in Mesopotamia, but the rest has been the work of overactive imaginations and poetic license.

According to writers of the day:

"Streams of water emerging from elevated sources flow down sloping channels....These waters irrigate the whole garden saturating the roots of plants and keeping the whole area moist. Hence the grass is permanently green and the leaves of trees grow firmly attached to supple branches....This is a work of art of royal luxury and its most striking feature is that the labor of cultivation is suspended above the heads of the spectators."

Excavations have uncovered what some archaeologists believe to be the palace, the vaulted building and an irrigation well mentioned in some of the accounts.

Arguments rage, however, as to whether these finds are too far removed from the banks of the Euphrates, leaving some historians to theorize that the gardens actually lined the walkway from the river to the palace.

No. 3: Temple of Artemis at Ephesus

There's just something about a ripped woman carrying a bow.

At least that seems to explain how the Temple of Artemis at Ephesus came to be the only one of thousands of temples constructed during the ancient world to make the list.

Artemis, by the way, was the Greek goddess of hunting and nature, and Ephesus was located near present day Selcuk, just south of Izmir, Turkey.

While the marble temple itself was not constructed until around 550 BC, its foundation has been traced to the seventh century BC, and some of the most renowned names in ancient architecture and sculpture, as well as other artists, had a hand in the project.

Croesus, king of Lydia, commissioned the temple, and Greek architect Chersiphron designed it. Finishing touches were added by the likes of Pheidias, Polycleitus, Kresilas, and Phradmon.

In simplest terms, the structure was a working temple, meaning visitors from artisans and merchants, to tourists and kings, paid tribute to the goddess when visiting.

An odd coincidence occurred on July 21, 356 BC, when a man named Herostratus torched the temple on the very same night the man who would become Alexander the Great was born.

According to Roman historian Plutarch's writings, the goddess was "too busy taking care of the birth of Alexander to send help to her threatened temple."

It took almost twenty years, but when Alexander's troops conquered Asia Minor, he helped rebuild the storied temple. Of course, he wasn't the structure's only exciting visitor over the years.

St. Paul attempted to spread the gospel of Christianity in Ephesus in the first century AD, but an indignant brood of Artemis worshippers set him straight rather quickly and put him back on the road.

Even though the Ephesians rebuilt the temple after the Goths decimated it in 262, the structure held little religious significance by the fourth century because the majority of the former patrons had converted to Christianity.

And in 401, the final blow was leveled by St. John Chrysostom, who had the structure razed. Its existence wasn't discovered until the late nineteenth century.

No. 4: Statue of Zeus at Olympia

To put this one in perspective, keep in mind that Olympia was the site of the first Olympic games in 776 BC, and the statue on its peak honors the unquestionable god of gods at that time.

No matter what form they've taken after almost 2,800 years at the hands of mankind, the original games stopped wars in their tracks and pulled athletes from around the globe.

The temple wasn't constructed until around 450 BC, when the architect Libon designed it, but popular opinion at the time held that the simple Doric style was too understated. Athenian sculptor Pheidias was commissioned to overhaul the statue.

The structure remained untouched until the first century AD when Roman emperor Caligula attempted unsuccessfully to have the statue moved to Rome. The temple was ordered closed in 391 when Theodosius I banned the Olympic games as pagan rituals and sacrilege.

The marvel was successfully transplanted to a palace in Constantinople, but a fire ravaged it in 462. Only rubble remains today.

Pheidias caught more than his share of flak from contemporaries for designing the statue of Zeus so out of proportion it appeared he would rip the roof off if he stood from his seated position. Scholars and historians have argued for centuries, though, that the proportions were by absolute design not flaw.

It was the detail of the throne on which he sat, however, that attracted the most praise. Pausanias reportedly wrote:

"On his head is a sculpted wreath of olive sprays. In his right hand he holds a figure of Victory made from ivory and gold,...In his left hand, he holds a sceptre inlaid with every kind of metal, with an eagle perched on the sceptre. His sandals are made of gold, as is his robe. His garments are carved with animals and with lilies. The throne is decorated with gold, precious stones, ebony, and ivory."

No. 5: The Mausoleum at Halicarnassus

King Maussollos of Carina was entirely unexceptional as a ruler, but the tomb constructed on his behalf is a different story.

As the Persians gobbled up their massive empire—including Mesopotamia, northern India, Syria, Egypt, and Asia Minor—smaller cities such as Carina were so far removed from the action they were typically left to their own devices.

So there sat Maussollos, doing nothing special, except moving his capital to Halicarnassus on the Aegean Sea, in what is now southwest Turkey.

Maussollos ruled from 377 until 353 BC His wife and sister Artemisia commissioned his tomb, which historians believe might not have actually been completed until three years after his death.

On top of a rectangular foundation sat a staggered podium, which was reached by statue-lined stairs. The podium held the burial chamber and sarcophagus constructed of white alabaster and accentuated with gold. It was enclosed by Ionic columns.

Like a cherry on top of an ice cream sundae, a sculpture of a chariot pulled by four horses adorned the tomb's pyramid-shaped roof.

And it was the scores of statues—inside and out—that truly elevated this structure to wonder status. They depicted people, lions, horses, and other animals.

The project also required the assistance of four Greek sculptors: Bryaxis, Leochares, Scopas, and Timotheus, each of whom completed one side.

An earthquake damaged the roof and colonnade some 1,600 years after it was completed, but it wasn't until the late fifteenth century that mankind disrupted its beauty.

The Knights of Malta reportedly invaded the region and built a massive crusader castle. When they decided to fortify their headquarters in 1494, they raided the Mausoleum for stones. By 1522, the tomb was almost bare.

And just in case it hasn't clicked yet, this marvel is the reason all modern-day large tombs are referred to as mausoleums.

No. 6: The Colossus at Rhodes

The shortest-lived of the wonders, the Colossus at Rhodes stood only fifty-six years, yet its symbolic importance as a monument to unity has endured for more than 2,300 years.

Constructed at the entrance of the harbor of the Mediterranean island of Rhodes in Greece, the Colossus honored the Greek sun god, Helios, but signified something even greater than that.

Ancient Greece was composed primarily of impotent city-states, and Rhodes was no different.

Left to its own devices, Rhodes thrived and even found an ally in Ptolemy I Soter of Egypt. But in 305 BC, the Antigonids of Macedonia attempted, but failed, to sever this alliance as an affront to Ptolemy's reign.

More importantly, when they took their toys and went home in 304 BC, the Antigonids left behind a substantial arsenal.

The Rhodians saw no use for the weapons and military equipment in the absence of conflict and sold their spoils to fund the monument immortalizing their victorious unity.

Commissioned by sculptor Chares of Lindos, the Colossus took twelve years to complete, incorporating bronze and white marble primarily. It towered about 110 feet and was the inspiration for French sculptor Frederic Bartholdi, who gave the world the Statue of Liberty almost two thousand years later.

The Colossus fell prey to an earthquake around 226 BC that weakened the marvel's knee, reportedly its weakest point.

Ptolemy III Eurgetes of Egypt offered immediately to pay for all restoration expenses, but an oracle forbade the toppled monument's resurrection.

An invading band of Arabs pillaged the Colossus's remains in AD 654 and sold the remains to a Syrian Jew. Tradition holds that nine hundred camels were required to carry the load.

No. 7: The Lighthouse of Alexandria

Six of the seven wonders might have been beautiful and grandiose explorations of architecture and engineering, but the Lighthouse at Alexandria holds a different distinction.

The lighthouse actually served a purpose, ensuring the safe return of sailors into the great harbor on the ancient island of Pharos in Alexandria.

Of course, it doesn't hurt that it was briefly the tallest building on earth.

Ptolemy Soter, commander of Alexander the Great's armies, assumed Egypt's throne when the great conqueror died. He moved the capital to Alexandria, but a logistical issue kept nagging at him.

The island of Pharos lies just off the coast with a dike connecting it to the mainland.

Ptolemy Soter knew that dangerous sailing conditions warranted the construction of a lighthouse, so he began the project in 290 BC. It would not be completed until sometime during the reign of his son, Ptolemy Philadelphus.

Roman coins actually featured the structure which helped mark the harbor for sailors by reflecting sunlight during the day and fire at night. Of course, tradition also contends that the reflecting mirror was used to spot and incinerate enemy ships from a relatively safe distance.

According to Arab traveler Abou-Haggag Al-Andaloussi, who visited the Lighthouse in 1166, the monument was composed of three stages and the height of a modern-day forty-story building.

An internal core reportedly operated as a shaft to hoist fuel for the fire, while the mirror on top reflected light, and a statue of Poseidon kept watch from atop the structure.

But times change, and so do rulers, who eventually moved the capital to Cairo.

The earthquake-ravaged wonder stood longer than any of the five others that had long disappeared. In fact, when the Egyptian Mamelouk Sultan, Qaitbay, sought to strengthen Alexandria's defenses in 1480, he chose the Lighthouse's site for his fort.

Crash Course

Ancient Civilization

- Egyptian historian Manetho cranked out the first comprehensive chronology of Egypt in 270 BC.
- It is believed that Stonehenge was built sometime between 3100 and 1550 BC, but it is generally accepted that the work was completed in several different phases during that lengthy period.
- The Peloponnesian Wars refer to the historic twenty-five-year clash between Sparta and Athens.
- Sakkarah Step Pyramid, located just south of Cairo, is believed to be one of the oldest man-made structure still standing.
- The Romans introduced mankind to the first paved roads sometime around 300 BC.
- Herod Antipas ordered the execution of John the Baptist.
- Hammurabi's Code has become almost synonymous with the vengeful mantra, "an eye for an eye."
- Attempting to go out with a bang, Herostratus sought immortality by setting fire to the Temple of Artemis. We're quite certain the gods frowned upon arson, though, and mankind was even less forgiving of the jackass responsible for destroying one of the Seven Wonders of the Ancient World.
- Cheops commissioned the Great Pyramid of Giza.

Chinese Culture Rises

- Seven thousand years ago, the fertile plain between the Yellow and Yangtze rivers gave rise to agricultural settlements. Four areas were settled, and separate cultural identities developed, but little is known about them.
- Pottery and burial sites are all that remain.
- The Yellow River culture, called the Yangshao, is the oldest known site in China.
- The Dapenkeng culture arose on the southeast coast of China.
- The Qingliangang culture appeared in the Yangtze River Valley.
- Another culture, called the Lungshan, grew in the southern bend of the Yellow River and apparently overran the Yangshao.
- These first settlements were clusters of earthen huts surrounded by rice and millet fields. Chinese folklore opens a small window into this otherwise forgotten period. The tales begin with the first king, Fu Xi.

Genghis Khan

The long-bearded, fearsome Mongolian Genghis Khan earned his status by bringing together many of the nomadic tribes of northeast Asia and founding the Mongol Empire. He then invaded East and Central Asia, eventually occupying most of those lands.

Khan actually was born with the name Temüjin. At about age forty (the year 1206), after uniting several tribes under his own rule, he was acknowledged as "Khan," a title for Turkic and Mongolian rulers. He was not referred to as Genghis until after his death.

Royal Lineage

Fuxi, whose reign began in 2852 BC, is credited with the discovery of the essential order of everything. He invented a crude form of writing, the Eight Trigrams, to aid in record keeping and investigating the natural world. His most celebrated contribution was in binding the Chinese conscience with the natural world.

Shennong, the second great king, is said to have invented the plow. He taught the people how to find the best soil and which crops to plant. The Farmer King told the people which herbs were edible and how to best use them.

Huangdi, the Yellow Emperor, is revered as the greatest of the first three kings. He is thought to have ruled from 2697 to 2598 BC. Huangdi defeated his brother, the Flame King, and took over his kingdom.

A war chief, Chi You, led an army of evildoers and giants against Huangdi and lost the battle. He is credited, however, with inventing war and the first metal swords, and is said to have eaten rocks. The truth hurts. The empire was a collection of mud villages surrounded by rice. Why not add a little garnish?

The Three Great Kings were followed by the Three Sage Kings.

Yao, the first in the trio, realized that his son was not suited for leadership and made a peasant his heir.

Shun was revered for his great virtues and his dedication to his father. He passed over his son and made Yu the last Sage King.

Yu established the first dynasty in China, the Xia, which lasted from 2205 until 1766 BC.

In case you haven't noticed, Chinese tales showcase a culture where virtue was placed above bloodline, and it appears to have served them well.

Xia Dynasty

Yu earned his throne by building canals and ditches to control the devastating floods of the Yellow River. This project took thirteen years to complete and reorganized the entire country.

The village patriarchs retained a large degree of independence. They had their own armies and regulated their own trade. Protection from the annual floods cemented the dynasty's power.

Erlitou was the capital of the Xia Dynasty. The city is situated in a valley of the Lo River. The fairly recent discovery of the city and its palace are the only reason the dynasty is no longer considered to be myth.

Yu named an heir to his throne and met resistance from powerful village patriarchs. His son, Qi, was made king, and merit was ousted by birthright.

Qi assumed leadership and had the villages that had opposed him destroyed. When Qi died, his five sons fought over the throne. There were no clear rules governing succession.

The son who won the throne fell to carousing and womanizing. A village patriarch seized the throne and was murdered by a court official who took power.

Qi's great-great-nephew marshaled an army and took his rightful place on the throne.

Despite its rocky start, the Xia Dynasty managed to survive for centuries.

The moral of this story? Men appointed ruler by birth—as opposed to merit—grow lazy and corrupt. As generations pass this moral lassitude grows and leads to the fall of the dynasty. A good man takes office and the cycle renews itself.

The last king of the Xia Dynasty, Jie, was the tyrant's tyrant.

Jie blew all the empire's money building palaces, married a hated woman, and spent his days playing with her. His neglect of state duties was second only to his persecution of perceived enemies.

Shang Rise and Decline

Jie jailed the patriarch of the Shang clan, a man named Tang, but committed a critical oversight. He forgot to kill Tang and eventually set him free.

Tang began quietly winning the support of the other cities. He declared his divine right to leadership and took the capital by force.

In 1766 BC, Tang became the first Shang emperor. Tang was a just and wise leader who earned the title Tang the Completer.

The cycle had renewed itself.

Tang died after a thirty-year reign.

Yi Yin, the chief court official, presided over the court until Tang's sons came of age. Tang had three sons, and—curiously—they all died under Yi Yin's supervision.

Tang's grandson, Tai Jia eventually took the throne, and the Shang Dynasty lasted for seven hundred years. The capital city was relocated five times during this period.

One of these capital cities had an earthen wall around it that was thirty feet high and ninety feet wide. The wall's existence reflects a high degree of organization and power. It also shows weakness on the part of the builder.

In building the wall, the Shang Dynasty was cut off from the rest of the world, and the only possible threat would have come from neighboring villages.

Wu Ding, the twenty-second Shang king, came to power around 1200 BC. Very little is known about him or the culture as a whole.

Wu Ding is believed to have spent his early years among the poor. Legend states that he did not speak for the first three years of his reign.

It is said that he brought such wisdom and peace to the land that no one dared say a word against him. It is also reported that he conquered a vast area and ruled by military might. The only facts remaining are those implied by the few artifacts which have been unearthed. These finds indicate there was a flourishing bronze industry that created beautiful vessels, weapons, and ornaments.

Written language was widespread, and there were ornate burial pits lined with human sacrifices. One burial pit was lined with seventy-three skulls. These all indicate a powerful central authority.

The last Shang king, Zhou, was a tyrant of the worst sort. He was vice-ridden and lost the respect of the people quickly.

Zhou developed a love of torture and put many people to death. When not occupied in his torture chambers, he threw lavish parties and had bizarre orgies. The nobles were appalled by his cruel behavior while the dynasty crumbled.

To the west sat an independent tribe, the Zhou, who enjoyed open trade with the Shang and paid them tribute. Their chief, Wen, visited the Shang capital and was imprisoned.

He was ransomed for a large sum of gold and slave women. Wen could not leave without making an effort to protect Zhou's subjects from his brutality. He offered to give Zhou a large tract of fertile land on the Lo River if he would promise to stop torturing people.

Zhou agreed and sent Wen home.

Paint

The benefits of paint extend far beyond the product's decorative and expressive properties that have helped define and imprint cultural nuances for thousands of years.

It has literally helped seal, protect, and preserve some of mankind's most inspiring creations as far back as 2000 BC. It was the Egyptians and Chinese who crafted mixtures of oils, resins, and pigments to adorn temples and tombs.

Like most of the innovations discussed to this point, these coatings were tinted with everyday materials founding near at hand, including white lead, clay, and gypsum (white); charcoal, graphite, and coal (black); gold powders and lithage (yellow); red lead, cinnabar, and iron oxides (red); copper carbonate and indigo (blue); and malachite, terre verte, and verdigris (green).

Binding agents included beeswax, gelatin, sap, and even animal fat. The precursor of varnish appeared around 1500 BC when resins were "run" with linseed oil.

An amber-linseed oil concoction became the most popular varnish for protecting weaponry, but gums replaced this scarce commodity.

Zhou Chokes

Wen returned home and started gathering support to oppose the Shang king.

Many of the feudal lords joined him, sickened by King Zhou's behavior.

The sages of the court, who read the oracle bones and divined prophecies, packed up their trappings and headed west.

Wen, however, was one hundred years old by this point and did not live to lead his followers into the Shang capital.

Wen's son, Wu, carried on the fight. Eight hundred feudal lords joined him with their own armies.

A fifty-thousand-man army of the Zhou tribe marched on the Shang palace. The king's army numbering six hundred thousand met them twenty miles outside the capital.

The Battle of Muye should have been a rout for the Shang forces, but the Zhou had two things in their favor, and the tide quickly turned for them:

The feudal lords had supplied the tribe with three hundred war chariots, while the Shang men had none. The Zhous also had a just cause, the king's men—exhausted by tyranny—were willing to defect.

With the Zhou armies racing toward them, the Shang front line turned around and drove back remaining Shang force.

The king retreated to his palace and donned his ceremonial jade armor in preparation for his last stand.

The Zhou army burned the palace down around him.

Wu speared the king's charred head on a stake and displayed it at the city gates for all to see.

The Western Zhou Dynasty came to power in about 1100 BC.

Zhou Dynasty

Wu took power and scourged the capital of Shang loyalists. After this initial violence, he disbanded his army and declared peace. Wu had to rule using tact and influence or face the same fate as Zhou.

The feudal lords were strong willed and numerous. During this period there were 1,763 territories ruled by independent lords who paid homage to the king. Diplomacy was the key to staying in power.

Wu allowed Zhou's son, Lufu, to take control of the Shang's old capital, keeping two of his brothers present as watchdogs.

When Wu died, his son was too young to rule, and his brother, Tan, took power as regent. Lufu's two brothers decided to install him as king and a brief civil war broke out.

Lufu and one of the brothers died in the battle. Tan restored peace and ruled for seven years until Wu's son Cheng came of age.

Cheng took power and kept his uncle on as his chief adviser.

Tan organized the state into an efficient bureaucracy. The system oversaw distribution of land, taxes, and the appointment of officials.

Tan's most important task was writing a book of ritual that cemented the king's divine right to govern. This display of ritual power negated the need to control the feudal lords with force.

Having secured the center of his realm, Cheng looked toward the borders of his kingdom. He sent his brothers to the outskirts of his domain to build forts which gave rise to new cities. These new colonies formed a ring around the kingdom.

Cheng fought nonstop to keep these colonies safe from outside tribes not under his control. He was the first Chinese ruler to popularize the phrase "Mandate of Heaven" to justify his actions. The mandate gave him the right to go to war and his victories proved its validity.

When Cheng died his son, Kang, took his place. He expanded the kingdom's territory to the north, further validating the Mandate of Heaven.

Kang's son, Zhao, took power in 977 BC. He marched to the south with six armies and never returned.

It was forbidden to speak of Zhao's death, and his son, Mu, was put on the throne. The nobles made it clear that they did not want him going to war with outside tribes. The mandate had been undermined by his father's defeat.

The mandate gave the king power to wage war, but he dared not wage war unless the outcome was certain. The king had a duty to protect his divine power, but Zhao's defeat cast doubt on the mandate's validity.

While the central state celebrated Mu's power with ritual ceremony, the outskirts of his kingdom fell away.

EXTRA CREDIT: The Mandate of Heaven stated that the king rules by the authority of the Deity Above only to the extent that the king remains just, equitable, and worthy of his people. This concept effectively ended the hereditary succession system, and for centuries to come, all kings would claim that the supreme god supported their rule.

> The Eastern Zhou dynasty was divided into two timeframes. The first, the Spring and Autumn period, also known as the One Hundred Schools of Thought, lasted from around 771 to 481. Iron was discovered, bringing advances in agriculture technology and massive population growth but resulting in conflict among the city-states.

Sputtering Along

Over the next two hundred years, the Western Zhou Dynasty slowly lost its hold on the country.

The feudal lords consolidated their power and drew away from the king.

Each generation of kings became less respected and more despotic.

The last emperor, You, brought the dynasty to its knees.

You placed his concubine on the throne with their bastard as his heir and banished his wife and son.

An earthquake and consequent famine shut agriculture down for years. Landslides and floods ravaged the land. Invading barbarians, who had plagued the kingdom for years, swept out of the west and menaced the capital.

The Quan Rong were joined by relatives of You's first wife and laid siege to the city.

You died in battle in 771 BC. The palace was looted and his concubine stolen.

Some of the lords remained loyal to his son Ping and declared him king. The Zhou Dynasty would carry on.

The capital, Hao, was clearly too close to the barbaric frontier, and Ping moved to the east. His new capital would be Loyang. The old city and its lands were given to the Duke of Chin.

Ping fled east with his fair-weather lords to rule a diminished kingdom. His western frontier was in shambles and open to invasion.

The Duke of Chin bore sole responsibility for the defense of the west. Noblemen fought one another for territory and plotted to take the throne. Ping refused to fight his nobles, so they grew powerful.

During Ping's fifty-year reign, the nobles consolidated the Chinese states into twelve major powers.

Huan, Ping's grandson, came to power and started a feud with a noble. The Duke of Cheng seized control of the palace where the king worshipped. These ceremonies were some of the last powers the king still held.

Huan waited eight years to retaliate. He was wounded in battle, and the palace was never freed.

His grandson, Xi, was unable to repulse the invading forces of the

Yi and Ti tribes. These nomadic people easily overran the weak Zhou armies.

The central states, the Cheng, Wey, Jin, and Zhou were on the verge of collapse.

The Duke of Qi decided to organize an army and fight for his land.

Duke Huan declared himself hegemon in 679 BC. He used force to unite the four states against outside invasion.

Huan drove the barbarians out of the central states and retained his title. The Duke of Qi held power over the central states and was king in all but name.

Xi died after a five-year reign, and his son took power.

When Xi's grandson, Xiang, became king, he waged war on his half brother, Shu Tai, who had enlisted the Ti to help him take the throne.

Shu Tai's plot was discovered, and he went to Huan, the hegemon, for protection. Huan defused the situation and restored peace. The Duke of Qi died six years later and left no heir.

Xiang attempted to take military power back and failed. He tried to take the Cheng state and enlisted barbarians to aid in his war.

The campaign ended with the Ti invading Zhou and placing Shu Tai on the throne.

Xiang, who was exiled, met with the Duke of Jin and bought his allegiance.

The Duke of Jin would defeat Shu Tai and reinstate Xiang. He would become hegemon.

Duke Wen took control of the government and set his sights on the Chu state to the south.

PHILOSOPHY 101
THE I CHING

Brief History

The *I Ching* is one of the oldest works of human literature. For centuries, people have consulted it to predict the future. *I Ching* translates as "The Book of Changes." The book is over 3,000 years old, but the philosophy behind it is even older. Chinese mystics developed keen sensitivities about the world around them through contemplative activities and meditation, and they recorded what they figured out. From one generation to the next they passed down these "ancient Chinese secrets," and by 1200 BC they began to get recorded. Eventually Confucius got in on the act, helping to codify some of the material. By the seventeenth century, Jesuit missionaries got interested in the I Ching, and in 1876 the first complete English language translation appeared.

How to Consult the Oracle

The *I Ching* is some fun reading in and of itself, but most treat it like an oracle that provides answers (however enigmatic) to their questions. It reveals how the forces of the universe are working at any given time. While there are many ways to approach the I Ching, the best way is to use three coins or sticks and toss them six times. Afterward, instructions included in most editions show how to develop a six-line figure known as a hexagram. There are 64 possible hexagrams. Each one tells something different about a situation.

The Hexagrams

A hexagram is actually composed of two trigrams (3 lines + 3 lines = a 6-line hexagram). The trigrams are divided into eight natural elements: Heaven, Thunder, Water, Mountain, Earth, Wind, Fire, and Lake. So, in any given hexagram, you might have a combination of Fire + Water (you can imagine this produces conflict) or Mountain + Earth (two elements that go together more smoothly). The combination of the two trigrams gives you your answer.

ZHOU DECLINE

The Chu had built a wall to contain the barbarians and block the Jin soldiers from entering the southern lands.

To the east and west the Ch'in and Qi faced each other in a struggle for power. The Eastern Zhou king was an ineffectual centerpiece waiting for the first blow to fall.

The four states slowly expanded their territories. They beat back barbarian tribes and took smaller states by force.

The dukes who led their armies into battle ruled their states independently of King Xiang, the ceremonial figurehead.

Xiang died after a long reign, and his son ruled for six years. Xiang's grandson ruled for six years and was succeeded by his younger brother, Ding, in 606 BC.

The Duke of Chu pounced on his chance to invade the Zhou lands and assert his power. He did not take the capital but did assume the title of king. This self-styled king of the Chu continued to expand his territory until he held lands on two sides of the Zhou state.

King Ding was followed by three generations of heirs.

His great-grandson, Jing, took the throne in 544 BC, and after a twenty-four-year reign died before formally appointing an heir. His sons made separate claims on the throne, and civil war broke out.

The war destroyed what was left of the Zhou state and signaled the loss of the Mandate of Heaven.

King Ching II took the throne but had little power to support his rule. The country was war torn, and the surrounding states were quarreling over Zhou territory.

China lost cohesion and gradually fell under the control of warlords.

Out of this chaos rose a reformer called Kong Fuzi, whose following lasted for a thousand years.

Philosophy 101

The Art of War

During this time *The Art of War* was penned by Sun Tzu, a general who fought for the Duke of Wu. Having experienced firsthand war's ill effects on China, Sun Tzu encouraged quick, decisive action and warned against the sieges and prolonged engagements that sapped the strength of the army. He emphasized the importance of psychological victory over the enemy. In this celebrated work Sun Tzu wrote, "Supreme excellence consists in breaking the enemy's resistance without fighting." The book taught a system of unity and order that could be attained by the individual. Sun Tzu's teachings were as methodical and unifying as Confucius's methods. They gained popularity among the warlords who sought to gain the upper hand.

Another philosophical trend, Daoism, was started in the sixth century BC by a sage named Laozi. Daoists believed there should be no central form of government. They believed that the only thing that mattered was the Dao, or the Way. This force was believed to be the genesis of all power in the universe. The Daoists appealed for a return to primitive farming communities that would allow for spontaneous interaction with nature. This idea was at odds, however, with Chinese culture and the prevailing philosophies of Confucius and Sun Tzu.

The Legalists were another school of thought that influenced Chinese culture during the same period. They believed that people responded only to fear of pain or a desire for pleasure. If that were really the case, then a strong social system had to be in place to enforce strict laws which would keep society ordered. The ruler would issue laws, and the people would obey. The common people would live and work for the ruler. They had no rights. The economy existed to enrich the government and pay for the army. The Legalist system led to dehumanized government and a distrust of scholars. Socialism was the center of the system, and materialistic merchants were frowned upon.

Everyday History

Gunpowder

Guess what you get when you combine charcoal, sulfur, and potassium nitrate with fire?

Kaboom!

The Chinese were more than a little startled to discover this for themselves around the middle of the eleventh century. But after the initial ringing in their ears subsided, and the smoke cleared, the experiment continued with great success.

Turns out, if you concoct that same little cocktail in an open-ended container, the force of the explosion actually propels the object forward with significant force.

It took more than three hundred years, though, for the Europeans to put their own distinct—and bloody—spin on the phenomenon By the Middle Ages, bombs and cannons were coming into their own and shifting greatly the battlefield advantage in favor of the ones with gunpowder.

Of course, the relatively unstable material presented quite a few logistical problems.

Sometimes components separated during travel and had to be mixed right in the middle of the battlefield despite the level of incoming fire. Sometimes the whole barrel just blew up.

For the next one hundred fifty years or so, the name of the game was attempting to determine the proper ratios at which the gunpowder would propel items at the enemy without burning up en route. Like many successful ventures, somebody in the right position at the right time made an educated guess based on the evidence available at the time, and trial and error worked.

In this instance the guess was that longer grains burned longer, and they were absolutely right in this particular case. Using longer grains to ignite cannons meant there was more surface area to burn—yielding more gas—and causing a more substantial build up of pressure. The more pressure the cannon could mount, the further the projectile would fly.

World in Transition

In this demoralizing environment, the four states waged prolonged and bitter wars against one another and with barbaric tribes that encroached on their lands. China was being torn apart by civil war.

The dukes waged war in order to keep and increase their power. Civil war broke out in every state, as powerful men vied for control of each state. The Zhou monarchs ceased to have any control or significance in the eyes of the dukes.

The Zhou Dynasty died out around 400 BC, and a period of civil chaos followed, called the Warring States period. Warlords fought for control of fertile regions unchecked by a central authority.

In the fifth century BC, Mongol and Turkish tribes to the south spread the use of cavalry to the Chinese warlords. By 300 BC these same tribes formed the Xiongnu federation to seize Chinese lands.

Local lords started building walls to keep the raiders out. This practice eventually gave rise to the Great Wall.

Enter Confucius

Jesuit missionaries, two thousand years later, latinized Kong Fuzi's name. They called him Confucius, and his teachings spread throughout the world under that name. Confucius had a knack for precise record keeping and an eye for detail that made him a natural for the position.

He developed an interest in the rituals used to honor ancestors and divine beings. He studied the oral tradition that had passed these rituals down for centuries and gained a reputation as a walking encyclopedia of ritual performance.

He gained a following and was hired by a high-ranking official to tutor his children. Confucius offered order in a time of armed upheavals and social strife. Virtue was prized over violence and a philosophy was born.

He taught that a study of the past could lead to an orderly life. Performance of duty to the state and one's family could reshape the world. He brought a sense of order to chaotic times.

Unification Begins

The Qin state took control of China and started the classical period of unification in 221 BC.

Qin Shi Huangdi was the first ruler to take the title of emperor. He pulled the country together and defined the national identity. The name China is actually derived from Qin.

The state then stripped control from the local dukes and assumed total control of China. The landed gentry were replaced by administrators and 120,000 prominent families were forced to leave their land and move to the capital at Xian.

The emperor craftily placed them in palaces and gave them allowances to live on. The presence of the aristocracy drew merchants and craftsmen, and the city rapidly became a cultural center.

Huangdi had all of the city walls in China torn down and collected and destroyed all private weapons. He nurtured the central bureaucratic power and created an elite class of officials dependant on him for their power.

The new concept of group responsibility meant that entire families could be executed or enslaved for the wrongdoing of one person. The emperor dictated every detail of people's lives.

Commerce, manners, ideas, art, and literature were under strict governmental control.

Writing was standardized and a uniform legal code was introduced.

A system of weights and measurements was adopted and uniform metal currency was distributed.

Officials were chosen by merit as opposed to social position.

The laws were strict and the punishments severe. You could be boiled alive in a cauldron for treason or torn apart by chariots. Mutilation was a common punishment for lesser crimes.

A system of canals and an imperial highway network was constructed to improve communications and distribute food and goods.

Vehicles were built to a standard size so wheels would all fit the ruts caused by heavy traffic.

The iron swords modernized the army and allowed for great conquests. Huangdi's armies pushed as far as present-day Vietnam. He also expanded on the huge earthen wall for northern defense. The early version of the Great Wall was a logistical feat that employed 300,000 men.

Huangdi also burned copies of Confucius's works and burned 460 scholars at the stake. His attempt to control the thoughts of the people caused a deep seated resentment to grow among the literate classes.

When Huangdi died, he was buried with large numbers of his concubines and all of the construction workers. The workers were killed to keep the vaults' treasures a secret. Some 7,500 life-size statues of soldiers were placed in the vault to guard him, and they remain a popular tourist attraction.

Huangdi had pushed the empire to its limits, and a rebellion took place after his death. Forced labor, high taxes, and compulsory military service had angered the nobles who had been stripped of their power.

The second Qin emperor committed suicide after four years in office. After several decades of strife, Liu Pang declared himself emperor.

Han Dynasty

The Han Dynasty started in 206 BC, when Gau Zu took the throne.

His policy of expansion and absorption of more and more territory greatly increased the size of the empire. This expansion was made easy by the fact that China started as a collection of warring states and tribes. The natural trend was one of absorption.

The wealth and power of the empire attracted many tribes who wanted to share in the prosperous culture. The sheer mass of Chinese people made them impossible to overwhelm. Later invaders would adopt the culture that was too massive to subvert.

Wudi

Wudi is considered the most important emperor of the Han Dynasty. He ruled from 141 BC to 87 BC.

Known as the Martial Emperor, he spent vast sums of money expanding the empire in all directions.

He embraced Confucius's teachings and repealed the legalist policies of the Qin Dynasty.

He instituted a training program for civil service candidates. This selection process led to the famous civil-service examination, which served as a model for the Western World.

Later Han rulers, as well as high officials, would receive proper Confucian educations.

The emperor conducted rituals to bring good harvests and ensure the welfare of his people. All aspects of Chinese life were dominated by religious ritual and were highly structured.

The Han period was one of cultural growth, pushed by strong central control and a population explosion. Standardized rituals, art, literature, and writing cemented the Chinese identity.

The first dictionary was written.

Textbooks on medicine and mathematics were produced.

Systems of astronomy and magic were developed.

The Chinese invented the decimal system, paper, silk production, the horse collar, and the plowshare.

They were the dominant culture in eastern Asia and looked down on other cultures as inferior.

The biggest problem for Wudi and the Han Dynasty was the violent tribes to the north and west of the empire. Countless tribes were attracted by China's wealth and abundant food supplies. China's weak and ill-defined borders encouraged barbaric invasion.

The Mongol tribes proved to be the greatest threat to China. Their highly mobile horsemen armed with composite bows proved too much for the thinly scattered infantry stationed on China's borders.

The Xiongnu were the strongest tribe and won control of the area that bordered northern China. Their second ruler, Mao-tun, realized that in order to compete with China he would need a similar state organization.

The Xiongnu government offered the same ritual government led by a Son of Heaven and began to absorb the frontier settlements. By 140 BC, they posed a large threat to the Han, and Wudi was determined to push them back and sever links with other hostile tribes.

He also needed to protect the trade routes to the west. A lively trade had developed with the middle-east that had earned the empire large profits.

Wudi stopped sending gifts to appease the Xiongnu and began looking for allies to help in the fight.

Forging Alliances

Wudi heard of an exiled tribe driven to the west by the Xiongnu and sent an envoy to win an alliance.

Zhang Qian traveled across the harsh Taklamakan and made contact with countless tribes. He returned home after thirteen years and set the emperor's eyes on the west.

The routes to the north and south of the great desert became the Silk Road.

Meanwhile, a new breed of horse had been discovered in what is now Uzbekistan that could revolutionize Wudi's cavalry. It was called the Celestial Horse.

The warfare against the nomadic tribes continued and was punctuated by great losses on both sides.

General Li Guangli defeated the Ferghana king and forced the Ferghana to become a tributary state in 104 BC. He brought some of the legendary horses back to China.

The conflict with the Xiongnu continued after Wudi's death in 87 BC.

In 51 BC, the Xiongnu became protectors of China's borders and were well compensated for this service.

Growing Pains

- The constant strife in the West took its toll on the Han Dynasty.
- Once a path to the West had been discovered it had to be maintained. As the West demanded more and more silk, the Han Dynasty grew richer.
- Every small state and tribe along the route had to be subdued and controlled in order to keep the road open.
- Middle-eastern nations such as Parthia became middlemen for this expansive trade and became rich.
- China also expanded far into the south. They needed the fertile lands to support an ever-increasing population.
- Every defeated tribe or nation was forced to pay ritual observance to the emperor, and Chinese culture continued to envelope its subject nations.
- The spread to the south reached as far as Korea. Control of Korea gave them control of sea trade with Japan. Naval superiority was key in expansion to the east and west.
- The Chinese showed no interest in the Western cultures they made contact with. This egocentric ideology was the foundation of China's national character.
- The Chinese thought of the world as divided by five concentric rings.
- The imperial holdings made up the center which was surrounded by rings of barbaric tribes held under varying degrees of control.
- The inner barbarians paid tribute and protected the borders.
- Most were dependent states with a Chinese official calling the shots. These states were allowed to keep their cultural identities as long as they swore loyalty to the emperor.
- The outer rings were outside of the borders and were held at bay by armed outposts and superior numbers.
- China was the only civilization, and all other peoples were barbaric.
- As the Voice of Heaven, the Emperor was charged with helping to enlighten the savages and spread the word of God.

Crash Course

Too Much Too Fast

- Wudi's empire building pushed China to its limits.
- There were shortages of horses, and too many peasants were called away from the agricultural fields to die in battle.
- Foreign missionaries and political hostages had to be expensively maintained.
- Population growth meant that families were given less land to live from.
- Taxes were raised, but corrupt officials pocketed much of the money before it reached the capital.
- The central government grew weak, as powerful, landed families bought the emperor's favor and high ranking officials ceased to be appointed by merit.
- The Han Dynasty was in shambles by the middle of the second century AD. Five hundred years of discord tore the dynasty apart.
- Weak emperors, army rebellions, and scheming local lords reduced China to utter dissolution. The local lords raised private armies and took control of government posts. In AD 184, the Daoists led two rebellions, and the northern borders were overrun by warring nomadic tribes. Nineteen Xiongnu tribes had to be settled in the Shansi region to ward off invaders.
- The Han Dynasty lost control in AD 189, when the army revolted and destroyed the capital. The empire fell into confusion and struggled for thirty more years.
- Several powerful families revolted in the north, and the last Han emperor stepped down in AD 220. As the government weakened and lost control of the north, the royal household and many inhabitants fled south.
- The center of control was removed to the south where it would stay.
- The Tartars took control of northern China and opened the border for nomadic tribes.

- These invaders generally took on Chinese customs and set up Chinese forms of government. Many took Chinese wives and became absorbed into the culture.
- The Turbo Turks took the Han capital of Loyang and held the emperor hostage in 311. Fifty years later the Tibetans organized an army and invaded China. They quickly took over the rich farmlands of the north and marched into southern China in 380.

EXTRA CREDIT: Chinese folklore might hold that ancient Chinese warlords often sent messages hidden inside cakes, but fortune cookies are not Chinese. San Francisco and Los Angeles lay claim to the delicious treats.

Printed Type

No better method than the printed word has existed—uninterrupted—for the preservation of human thoughts, emotions and history. There is no closer thing to time travel to date.

From stop signs and pulp fiction to blueprints and great works of literature, the printed word has defined humanity and shaped the world. Where would we be without instructions?

Get comfy, and find the matches as we delve into the history of printing.

The Chinese can be credited with the first successful attempt at block printing.

During the third century AD, they reproduced holy images and texts, using carved wooden blocks and black ink made from the residue of burned oils and wood dissolved in liquid. Precise replication was needed to ensure that the mystical qualities of these religious materials remained pure.

Block printing began to take off during the Tang Dynasty (AD 618–907). The rulers of the period were open to all religions. The Daoist and Confucian scholars, the Christian missionaries, Zoroastrian priests, and Buddhist monks had a message to spread.

The emperor's library held close to forty thousand manuscripts by the early seventh century.

The Buddhists led the pack when it came to block innovations. Duplication was, after all, the basis of their faith. They used carved blocks lying face up. Ink was applied to the wood. Paper was then laid on top and rubbed with a brush. But in AD 845, foreign religions were outlawed. Everything was destroyed, and the first great innovations in printing vanished.

Meanwhile, Buddhism and printing had been imported to Japan. In 735, the Empress Kouken ordered one million copies of a dharani, or charm, to be dispersed in order to ward off a smallpox epidemic. These are the earliest examples of copper block printing. Ironically, the empress died of small pox the same year that her project was completed.

The oldest surviving printed book is the Diamond Sutra of 868. This was a collection of Buddhist scriptures printed on sheets that were 2?–feet long by 1–foot wide. The sheets, pasted together, made a single

16–foot long scroll. They contained lessons on the nonexistence of all things and encouraged the reader to mass produce the text. The Lord Buddha would be present wherever a copy was found.

Other printed texts gained popularity at the same time, including Daoist magic, essays on dream divination, and dictionaries. Hand-copied reproductions were still preferred for sacred texts.

Calligraphy had a rooted tradition among the rich. Printed texts belonged to the poor. Systematically, the government became the engine for large-scale printing.

In 953, the National Academy presented the emperor with one hundred thirty volumes of the Confucian Classics. It took twenty-one years to produce.

The first great dynastic history was completed at the end of the tenth century after seventy years of work.

The Tripitaka, completed in 983, consists of one hundred volumes encompassing 130,000 pages. This entire Buddhist canon was printed from individual blocks.

The Daoist canon followed in 1019. It only had forty-nine volumes.

Marco Polo reported that Kublai Khan was printing paper money in the eleventh century.

With 30,000 characters, the collective alphabet of the Orient made widespread adoption of moveable type too much of a hassle.

THE DARK AGES

The next three and a half centuries are known as China's Dark Ages.

This collapse coincided with the fall of Rome and the ensuing European turmoil.

The southern regions witnessed the rise and fall of six dynasties, and the northern lands were ruled by a succession of kingdoms. This was a time of bloodshed and social chaos. The populations of the great cities declined as the bulk of the people fled from barbaric invasions from the north.

In the midst of the turmoil, Buddhism slowly filtered into China along the Silk Road, and mysticism took hold of a desperate people.

Order was restored in AD 581 by a tough general, named Sui Wendi.

China's Dark Ages had come to a close.

Universal Sexuality

The Chinese have always seen the universe and man's place in it as cyclical. The interaction of yin and yang, the positive and negative cosmic forces, ordered the universe. Their balance was reflected in nature and in the union between man and woman. Women were believed to possess magical powers and secret sexual knowledge. They were sexually superior and in control of sexual behavior. Men were seen as blind pupils who fed off the woman's essence during sex. Sexual relations of the ruling class were ritualized, and concubines were chosen to supervise royal sexual activities. They ensured that ceremonies were followed and that the emperors' partners were healthy. Only wives could stay in the bedroom overnight. The concubines had to leave before dawn. Virginity prior to marriage was a must for any woman seeking to be the top wife.

SILK

A popular legend states that, in 2640 BC, Lady Hsi Ling-shi, wife of the mythical Yellow Emperor, was drinking a cup of tea when a cocoon fell into it. As she fished the cocoon out, it unraveled into a long strand. Silk had been discovered. Lady Hsi Ling-shi is also credited with inventing the loom. Did you know?

- An ivory cup with a silkworm pattern has been dated to 7000 BC.
- A silkworm cocoon has been found in northern China that dates to 3000 BC.
- Silk was originally worn only by the emperor and high ranking officials.
- The emperor wore robes of white silk within his palace and robes of yellow—the color of the earth—outside of the palace.
- Silk was used to make musical instruments, bow strings, rag paper, and clothing, making an early impact on trade and the economy.
- An Egyptian mummy, dated around 1000 BC, was discovered near Thebes with strands of silk woven into her hair.
- In the fifth century BC, six provinces were producing silk.
- The empress ceremonially opened the silk season.
- Women were in charge of raising the worms and producing the silk.
- After the cocoons were unraveled, the silk was dyed and woven into fabric. The process was considered a state secret.
- Smuggling out silkworm eggs, cocoons, or technical secrets was a crime punishable by death.
- Greeks and Romans made reference to the kingdom of silk in the fourth century BC.
- Ambassadors went as far as Mesopotamia and Persia with gifts of silk. Silk was used to pay taxes and officials during the Han Dynasty.
- By 200 BC, silk production had reached Korea through Chinese immigrants. The knowledge reached India soon after.
- A Han embassy reached Baghdad in AD 97.
- Silk was very popular in Rome and became available to commoners by AD 380.

- When the Goths besieged Rome, Alaric demanded 4,000 silk tunics as part of his ransom of the city.
- A Chinese princess married a Khotan prince and smuggled silkworm eggs to him in her hair in AD 440.
- In AD 540, two Nestorian monks arrived at Justinian's Byzantine court with silkworms hidden in bamboo.
- Silk rapidly spread around the world and is still revered as a luxury textile.

Horses

The Chinese began domesticating horses in northern China around five thousand years ago.

During the Shang Dynasty, between 1600 and 1050 BC, horses were buried with their owners to be used in the afterlife.

Military might, in the Zhou Dynasty, was measured by the number of an army's chariots.

The horse became a key element in controlling the land and its people. They were also relied on for communication and transport.

As northern tribes invaded with superior cavalry, the chariot was replaced by highly mobile mounted troops.

The invention of the horse collar, the breast strap, and stirrups gave the Chinese complete control of the animal. Stirrups allowed for the use of lances and made heavy cavalry possible.

The horse became a status symbol.

Mounted hunting and polo became fashionable.

The Chinese never had success breeding strong horses and constantly sought to import superior breeds.

CONCUBINES

Keeping concubines is an ancient tradition that spans much of Asia.

Men have always found having more than one woman in their lives to be desirable. The number of women a ruler kept reflected his power and status.

The Chinese also wanted to have large families. Sons were important because they took care of the family and made sure that the ancestors were properly revered.

The poor were discouraged from procreating by inheritance laws that said all sons got an equal share of property when a father died. Poor farmers with small holdings could not have many children for fear that the small portions of land could not sustain a family.

The ruling classes, by contrast, were encouraged to take concubines to ensure the family line's stability. Multiple wives guaranteed an heir and often gave the emperor options. Emperors often had hundreds of women and used techniques of seminal retention to allow them to service all of their women. This also put a ceiling on the amount of sperm given to any one wife or concubine.

One emperor of the Tang Dynasty boasted forty thousand women in his household.

Women gained security and social position by becoming concubines. They could persuade the emperor and have a voice in the government if they won his favor. The man was duty-bound to honor and sexually satisfy each of his wives and concubines, however.

Keeping a balanced household was as important as running the empire. A man was judged by his ability to run his house and please all of his women.

The concubines were assured of their rights and of their sons' equal shares of the estate as long as they remained in the household.

Concubinage has been banned in modern times but is still thought to exist.

To be the emperor's mother was also a great honor and meant living like royalty.

Art 101
Ceramics

Ceramics have long been an area of artistic achievement in China.

They met daily household needs and were used in the performance of religious rituals. Some of these rituals—sacred to the culture—made up the fabric of Chinese society. Ceramic vessels ensured that the dead had food, shelter, and servants in the afterlife. Ornate vessels were given to Buddhist and Confucian temples. They were also used as diplomatic gifts.

The ceramic arts became dominant during the Tang Dynasty but did not become refined until the Song Dynasty.

The Song Dynasty produced elegant white-ware pieces. These innovations carried into the Mongol Yuan Dynasty when the empire's porcelain center moved to the Jiangxi province.

The Ming Dynasty followed and further refined the art.

The Mongol rule forced states to come into contact with one another and different styles were consolidated.

Eventually glazes and painted decorations became prominent in Chinese porcelain.

Jiangxi produced the finest porcelain. It was closest to the source of raw material and had a large labor force to draw on. It also drew upon well-organized transportation.

Innovations in the manufacturing process—such as the introduction of red and blue glazes—were made at Jiangxi.

The Ming Dynasty founded an imperial porcelain factory that is revered as producing the finest porcelain ever made.

Over time the porcelain changed from plain white to red and blue. Light green porcelain was very popular and eventually multi-colored works developed. The most famous color scheme is the highly sought after blue-and-white pattern.

Ming porcelain became popular all over Europe. The pieces were prized as rarities of uncommon beauty.

By AD 1600, one-third of all the silver mined in Peru and Mexico was sent to the Far East to pay for silk, spices, and ceramics.

Crash Course

Tea

Legend holds that the Chinese discovered tea in 2737 BC.

The Emperor Shen Nung, a scholar and scientist, decided that water should be boiled before drinking to ensure good health. While touring his provinces his servants made camp and started boiling water for consumption when some dried leaves fell into the water and turned it brown. The emperor tasted the brown liquid and found it to be refreshing and invigorating. Tea spread throughout the land in short order after this accidental discovery.

Buddhist priests brought tea with them to Japan.

Arab traders brought tea to the Middle East, where Italians discovered it and brought it to Europe.

By AD 1600, there were regular shipments of tea brought to Holland, France, and the Baltic coast.

The English East India Company became a major importer of tea soon after.

Tea was first served in English coffee shops in 1660.

It was said to give energy and sexual potency and to promote good health and long life. Tea was very expensive, and a black market quickly sprang up in England.

The Kowtow

China was a land ruled by ritual and ceremony. The kowtow was a ritualized expression of the emperor's superiority over his subjects. The practice started in the second century BC before the advent of tables and chairs. People sat on bamboo mats to eat meals and have conversations. These mats reflected the owner's status and increased in richness and size with rank. Sitting down on the mat meant going down on both knees, and resting the weight of the body on the heels. This simple posturing was the precursor of the kowtow. When furniture made its way into Chinese life, the old forms of sitting and bowing gained ritual prominence in Chinese society. Different bows were used to distinguish social status. Servants bowed to lords; minor officials bowed to high ranking ones, and family members bowed to elders. Over time the kowtow evolved to three separate prostrations, with the forehead touching the ground each time. This was the bow reserved for the emperor. As God's appointed leader and the world's bridge to heaven, he demanded that this ritual be performed by all who came into his presence. The Western world refused to acknowledge this perceived arrogance, which crippled diplomatic relations for centuries.

Chinese New Year

The Chinese New Year begins with the second new moon after the winter solstice, so how did pyrotechnics become part of the show?

Tradition holds that a horrid monster once stalked Chinese villages around the time of the new year in search of food. But one year, the monster attacked while the villagers were building a bamboo bonfire. Once ignited, the bamboo made loud popping sounds and burst into flames.

Scared out of its wits, the monster scurried away, and a tradition was born.

Chinese custom prohibits sweeping the house on New Year's Day because you might get a little overzealous and sweep your fortune right out the door. And when you do resume cleaning, the tradition is to sweep toward the center of the house, not out. After the fifth day, it is acceptable to carry out the trash, but only through the back door.

Crash Course

China

- The pig was first domesticated in China almost ten thousand years ago. One of the most prolific breeds of pig in the world is the Meishan breed. They reach puberty at less than three months and generally have litters of fifteen to seventeen.
- Souchong is a high-quality grade of black Chinese tea, and Lapsang Souchong is a distinctively smoky flavored version of Souchong.
- China produces about 19 percent of the world's corn crop, or about 4.5 billion bushels.
- One species of yam is used to make a dye in southern China.
- During the Tang Dynasty—around AD 900—the Chinese were 'farming' fish exclusively for the emperor's consumption. Some sources date the beginnings of Chinese fish farming as far back as 3,500 years ago. Today China farms more freshwater fish than any other country.
- There are more than four hundred varieties of kiwi fruit in China, where they have been consumed for over seven centuries.
- Chopsticks originated in China almost four thousand years ago, and the replacing of knives with chopsticks for eating at the table supposedly indicates the increased respect for the scholar over the warrior in Chinese society.
- Macao and Woosung, founded by Chinese immigrant Norman Asing in 1849 is the first recorded Chinese restaurant in the United States.
- The chemical compound MSG is often used to enhance the flavor of Chinese food. Some people with sensitivity to MSG exhibit symptoms such as headaches, chest pains, facial pressure, burning sensations, and sweating. The U.S. Food and Drug Administration continues to list it as GRAS—meaning Generally Recognized As Safe—but all foods containing MSG must state so on the label.

A History of Measurement

- Historians believe that pyramid builders issued yardsticks and rulers to the craftsmen so that there would be a standard way of measuring.
- In AD 950, the Anglo-Saxon king, Edgar, established the length of a yard by a rod that he kept stored at Winchester. He said all measurements the length of a yard should be the same length of that one particular rod.
- In the 13th century, Edward I established the Iron Ulna, a master yardstick set in iron that all builders were to use as a standard. Medieval town halls had a yardstick attached to a wall that provided the local standard of measure.
- In 1324, Edward II declared an inch to be three barleycorns, round and dry.
- In ancient Babylon and Egypt, the cubit was the length from a man's elbow to the tip of his middle finger. A man's foot was a common unit of measure, as were the joints on his first finger. Since human feet—and fingers and arms—are not all the same length, without a standard, a builder could end up with several different sizes of stones and bricks and a crooked building.

Today, lengths can be measured by lasers:
Light produced from the electronically excited helium and neon atoms is
Amplified by the
Stimulated
Emission
Radiation produced by housing the laser gain tube between two highly reflective mirrors.

Pop Quiz #2

1) What year did Egypt begin using papyrus?
   a) 6000 BC
   b) 4000 BC
   c) 3000 BC
   d) 2000 BC

2) Who was Euclid of Alexandria?
   a) Father of Chemistry
   b) Father of Mathematics
   c) Father of Geometry
   d) Father of Physics

3) Who is credited with inventing the hourglass?
   a) A monk at Chartres
   b) Thutmose III
   c) Saladin
   d) Alexander the Great

4) Who inherited the throne when Thutmose II died?
   a) Thutmose III
   b) Ramses II
   c) Ramses III
   d) Hatshepsut

5) Who created the lunar calendar?
   a) Egyptians
   b) Babylonians
   c) Greeks
   d) Persians

6) Which of these is NOT one of the Seven Wonders of the World?
   a) Great Pyramid of Giza
   b) Temple of Artemis at Ephesus
   c) Lighthouse of Alexandria
   d) Acropolis

Answers:

1) b
2) c
3)a
4) d
5) b
6) d

England's Beginning

By 4500 BC, a people arrived in England with the knowledge to unlock the secrets of agriculture.

These inhabitants were short, dark, and wiry, possessing physical traits still found among the English today. These hearty folk made the first pottery in England and are responsible for the first buildings of significant size on the island. Life became slowly sedentary as people became tied to the land.

Roaming gave way to routine as man achieved greater levels of comfort and control over his environment. Much hard work led to the felling and burning of forests to make way for a new agricultural landscape dotted with farmsteads and villages.

As the population steadily grew, the concept of private property came into existence along with the trappings of class. Soon there were chieftains organizing commerce and building religious centers. An elite priesthood formed that was the base of education. These priests were taught mathematics and astronomy in order to observe seasonal rituals that tied in to agriculture.

This religion gave rise to the first stone circles.

Life went on in much the same way for fifteen hundred years until metallurgy became prevalent among the British people. From humble beginnings in copper and gold jewelry, men were soon smelting tin from Cornwall with copper from Ireland to make bronze tools and weapons.

The Celts had arrived in England bringing with them the roots of Gaelic language and culture. The Beaker people earned their name by the small drinking cups buried with their dead in round barrows that still dot the English countryside. Starting in 2500 BC, large stone monuments were built by rich chieftains and wealthy cattle barons. Dynastic rulers may have directed the building of Stonehenge and other similar temples.

The economy was also boosted by trade with Mediterranean and Baltic peoples. After a thousand years of uninterrupted prosperity and building, there came a change in climate that led to increased tension among the tribes. The building projects stopped as suddenly as they began, and the production of weapons and shields skyrocketed. It was during this time the first fortresses were built.

Life carried on for hundreds of years with little or no change. Iron was introduced around 750 BC, leading to the creation of bigger, badder weapons. The ruling aristocracy consisted of chieftains and high kings who were constantly fighting one another. The war chariot and the use of cavalry made killing one another more efficient. Weapons continued to improve with the advent of skilled craftsmen.

Chieftains employed goldsmiths, jewelers, armourers, and bards to improve the standard of living of their clans. The aristocracy produced fierce warriors, hard drinkers, and tellers of wild tales. They dressed in cloaks and trousers. They wore ornate golden armbands and necklaces. Prior to battle they put on blue body paint and spiked their hair up with lime. The dominant religion of the time was the druid priesthood.

This ancient bickering and slaughter carried on unchecked until the second century BC. A group of Celts from the north of France, known by the Romans as the Belgae, settled in southern England following a series of sea raids. These newcomers carved out kingdoms for themselves and eventually consolidated under one leader.

Caswallon, based in Hertfordshire, was acknowledged as the high king of the south of England. Julius Caesar reported as much after a minor expedition to the island in 54 BC. Cunobelinus, heir to Caswallon, ruled into the next century. Emperor Claudius ordered the full scale invasion of England in AD 43. The Roman invasion is commonly seen as the cutoff point of the prehistoric era in Britain.

Crash Course

But How Did They Get There?

- The first inhabitants of England arrived 700,000 years ago. Homo erectus arrived via land bridge compliments of the Ice Age. These ancestors to modern man were the first "human" inhabitants of England.
- Ice a mile thick was commonplace during this time.
- Woolly mammoths and woolly rhinos roamed the Thames River valley. Herds of reindeer and bison populated the southern plains.
- Interglacial periods of mild weather broke the severe climate periodically making for a more friendly environment for our struggling ancestors.
- The oldest human bones found in England are those of a young woman dating back 250,000 years. It is suspected that her people hunted mammoths and hippos.
- Small bands of hunters, armed with stone and wooden weapons traipsed over England for countless millennia.
- A spearhead made of yew wood found at Clacton–on-Sea is considered to be the oldest wooden tool in the world. It has been dated to the same period as the unfortunate girl's remains.
- By 70,000 BC, groups of Neanderthals were inhabiting caves in England.
- Neanderthals are commonly recognized by heavy protruding brows and thick jaws.
- They were expert hunters and wizards when it came to making fire. Considered to have a larger brain capacity than modern man, they made rough clothing from animal skins, buried their dead, and were blessed with spoken language. They most likely had a form of religion.

- Sadly these noble savages died out around thirty-five thousand years ago. It would seem that modern man ran them out or killed them off.
- Starting around at about 12,000 BC, the ice sheets began to melt and be replaced by forest. By 7500 BC, water had cut England off from the rest of Europe. At this time the population was roughly ten thousand people.
- These remaining people were broken into small tribes that held territories of approximately two hundred square miles.
- They roamed their lands in dugout canoes, killing wild ox, red deer, and wild boar, snaring birds, and spearing fishing. Constantly on the move, these fine fellows had time to invent the bow and arrow and produce the first works of art on the island. Dogs were also domesticated in order to help hunt deer and begin some of the first herds of domesticated livestock.

Architecture of Ancient England

Hill forts were built on high ground to offer a commanding view of surrounding areas. It was easy to spot the enemy and fend off attacks from on high.

The originals date from the last millennium BC and were small, consisting of no more than three acres. They were home base for raiding chieftains out to steal their neighbors' cattle.

Larger forts consisted of walled villages bustling with farmers, herders, and tradesmen, all dependent on the protection of their overlord. There were sleeping quarters and market places alongside animal pens and places of worship. Often surrounding land was used to sow crops and to pasture sheep and cattle. The largest villages were centers of trade and religious festivals drawing crowds from miles around.

A ditch was dug around the contours of the hill. A rampart was built of stone and timber on the inside of the ditch, often reaching heights of fifty feet from the wall top to the bottom of the ditch. There were two entrances front and back guarded by large wooden gates topped by sentry platforms commanded by men wielding spears, slings, and bows. These gateways were often decorated by the heads of slain enemies.

England is also home to hundreds of megalithic structures known as henges. These giant stone circles date from 3500 BC to roughly 1500 BC. They were built using a standard measurement called the megalithic yard, or about 2.72 feet. Giant calendars aligned with the yearly movements of the sun and moon proved useful in planning and regulating agricultural practices as well as timing mystic rituals to propagate the changing of the seasons. The great powers of the earth and sky were worshipped here to ensure the fertility of both the herds and the women. The priests who designed these circles had a sophisticated knowledge of astronomy and may have seen the circles as representing the order of the heavens and earth. Thus, the great magical powers afforded these places held the world together and assured the continuation of life as embodied by the culture. The exact nature of the rituals remains unknown. It has been theorized that ritual dances were held in costume coupled with human and animal sacrifice.

The most impressive thing about the stone circles is their mere existence. Fifty-ton stones do not move themselves. Organized manpower was led, fed and motivated by great leaders working in tandem with the high priests. These building projects took years of hard labor to produce. During the project men had to be housed, clothed, and provided with tools and materials. The facts point to a centralized authority with surplus capital, raised primarily by plunder, trade, and possibly taxation.

Rule of Thumb

Although the phrase itself is quite benign, the origins of the saying "rule of thumb" have sparked debate for hundreds of years. Many historians hold—and teach—that the phrase is derived from a snippet of English common law that forbids a man from striking his wife with anything wider than his thumb. The argument has been made that even though that is, in fact, the true root of the saying, it would be unthinkable to acknowledge its awful genesis because the world has become so politically correct,. Regardless. it makes for interesting conversation when thrown out at a dinner party between intellectuals and scholars, who typically agree that the phrase is actually no more than a unit of measurement used by medieval carpenters. Traditional wisdom holds that the length of the thumb's first joint is roughly an inch long, so—provided carpenters were careful in their calculations—it's more likely "rule of thumb" referred to skilled craftsmen eyeballing a measurement rather than taking the time to scale it out.

THE CELTS

Celt is a name given to a people who shared a common culture that grew along the Atlantic seaboard of Europe. They had similar religious beliefs, art, and architecture. The Celtic culture spread along the Atlantic seaboard and down the rivers of Western Europe.

Many of their wartime technologies were adopted by the Romans and have come over the years to be identified as Roman without acknowledging their Celtic influences. Polished stone axes made of native British stone dating to 4000 BC can be found as far afield as Portugal.

The people of this region shared a unique and rich culture that flourished until the powerhouse empires of Greece and Rome destroyed them. They wore golden neckbands and bracelets and dressed in an ornate manner. They were taller than their Greek and Roman counterparts. They were regarded as fierce drunkards with inferior technologies and cultures, yet widespread adoption of Celtic ideas and innovations indicates the exact opposite was actually true.

The Gallic chieftain Vercingetorix gave Caesar his first taste of defeat in 53 BC. His victory was due in part to superior military technology. The Celtic warriors had sturdier helmets and larger, stronger shields. The Romans copied these ideas, and we now recognize the helmet and shield designs they stole as classic Roman armament.

The Britons—Celts who lived in England—defeated Caesar with their superior war chariots. These barbarians built better wheels and faster chariots than Rome had ever seen. The Roman troops were forced to retreat in the face of superior technology. Language suggests that the Romans adopted Celtic transport designs which were far in advance of their own clumsier versions.

The Celts were proficient road builders and their wooden roads crossed England and stretched into Europe as far as northern Germany. These roads—built by laying oak planks on birch runners—were wide enough to allow two-way traffic of large carts. Many Roman roads were built neatly on top of these wooden tracks. The first Roman road, the Appian Way, dates to 312 BC, yet there is a wooden road in South Wales that predates this celebrated path by at least two hundred years. It's no surprise then that Roman history—much like its roads—obscures the accomplishments of these ancient races.

Shrouded in Mystery

Celts are seen as barbarians because the only written records we have of them are Latin texts. These histories are, for the most part, propaganda. The Romans needed to justify the wholesale slaughter of their reportedly superior people. The texts that have survived are copies made hundreds, if not thousands, of years after the original manuscripts had been written. The church also had a zero-tolerance policy against pagans and destroyed all traces of pre-Christian classical literature. The Irish Celtic church is the only reason that any pre-Christian classical texts exist today. In the fifth century AD, intellectuals fled from Gaul to Ireland to escape invading Goths and Huns. The Christians in Ireland were open to outside beliefs and came from a strong Celtic background. They embraced knowledge and the local traditions in an attempt to peacefully introduce Christianity to the local culture.

Druids

The druids are rumored to have practiced ritual human sacrifice. A scholar called Poseidonius, who traveled through Celtic Gaul and Iberia in the second century BC describes one such ritual.

"The druids have an especially odd and unbelievable method of divination for the most important matters. Having anointed a human victim, they stab him with a small knife in the area of the diaphragm. When the man has collapsed from the wound, they interpret the future by observing the nature of his fall, the convulsion of his limbs, and especially from the pattern of his spurting blood."

This from a man who championed the druids as noble savages. No one knows for certain if the druids practiced human sacrifice.

Of course, the Romans had no problem crucifying traitors by the thousand and throwing criminals into the arena to be torn apart by wild animals, so who's to judge.

Druid Dominance

The Celts had an elite class of intellectuals known as the druids, whose power extended over the entire culture and allowed them to move freely throughout the Celtic lands.

It is said that a druid could walk between two opposing armies and order the combatants to lay down their arms.

They were the guardians of literature and of historical, scientific, medical, and religious knowledge.

The information was so vast that it took twenty years of training to become a druid.

Druid leaders insisted that all knowledge be transmitted orally as it was believed that writing relaxed the power of memory and inhibited learning.

Literacy was common among the druids and was used for any number of mundane daily tasks.

They used Greek and Roman alphabets and had their own alphabet called Ogham.

The druids were also the final authority on Celtic law and administered justice with the aid of law codes written in verse.

They held a power that was both judicial and religious, transcending all political boundaries.

This omnipotence made them a target of destruction by the Romans. Because the druids were the backbone of Celtic society, the Romans made it a point to wipe them out.

According to Caesar the druids had started in Britain and spread to Gaul.

Their center in Gaul was at Chartres but was removed to the island of Anglesey off the coast of Wales after Caesar destroyed Gaul.

Metallic Mastery

The Celts had a high degree of technical sophistication. Their blacksmiths were thought to be magicians, producing superior blades that could cut through bronze and inferior iron blades

In addition, it has been proven that the Celts had iron plowshares as early as the fourth century BC. The Romans report that they had an iron harvester in the first century AD.

The Roman historian Pliny wrote: "On the vast estates in the provinces of Gaul very large frames fitted with teeth at the edge, and carried on two wheels, are driven through the corn by a team of oxen pushing from behind."

The large combs beat the ears of corn off the stalks and deposited them in a container. A replica that worked as recorded by Pliny was built in the 1980s, based on a bas-relief sculpture.

These harvesting machines, called the Gallic vallus by the Romans, disappeared by the third century AD. Harvesting reverted to back-breaking labor until the machine was reinvented in 1831.

Gallic Gold

In the first century BC Gallic chieftain Vercingetorix issued gold coins with his portrait and name on them. At this time Rome had no gold coins because they did not have enough gold. They would not have enough gold to mint coins until they conquered Gaul. The Celts imitated the Greeks' gold coins long before Rome had the wealth to do so. Gaul was incredibly wealthy, and this wealth arose from hundreds of mines. Some reached depths of one hundred feet and used Archimedes's screw pumps to keep them dry. One historian estimates that these mines produced seventy tons of gold. Mines such as these require a system of agriculture and trade to support them. A complex social organization was needed to sustain large mining operations. This large scale operation of gold production and trade went on for three hundred years.

Celtic Life

The Celts lived in large towns that were centers of trade. These towns were either razed by Roman legions or built over by Roman towns.

In the country, Celts lived in two-story farmhouses that were often divided into several rooms.

In Britain there was an ancient tradition of building round stone houses that could be quite sophisticated. They were often built around courtyards and had stone floors complete with in-floor plumbing.

Celtic builders were held in particularly high esteem and paid annual retainers.

One example of their ingenuity is the crannog. These were timber-framed circular homes built in the middle of lakes. Boulders were sunk until they broke the surface of the water and a foundation of stone and rock was laid on top. These houses could be as large as fifty feet in diameter.

As Celtic trade became prosperous the towns grew. Several have been discovered that were actually larger than Rome. These towns usually grew close to mines.

The Celts minted their own gold coins and had bustling market places.

Iron goods and tools were sold along with glassware, jewelry, and enameled decorative items. These towns had separate craft and religious districts and aristocratic neighborhoods boasting beautiful homes. The towns shared trade routes that reached China and Africa, but most of their trade was with Rome.

The Celts were not shy about showing off their wealth. They wore gold torques, bracelets, armbands, brooches, clasps, and rings. They wore tunics embroidered with gold.

This is the reason Rome became interested in the Celtic world.

Pillaging and Plundering

The broad term "barbarians" was used by the Romans to refer to anyone who lived outside the realm of Roman influence, especially the Scottish, whose Celtic tongues grated on the civilized sensibilities of the Empire. In fact, Emperor Hadrian built a wall in 122 separating Rome and present-day Scotland.

The Germanic tribes to the North included the Vandals, Lombards, Alemanni, Goths, Franks, and Burgundians. While these tribes were not nomadic like the Huns, they were illiterate.

In 376, the Visigoths were forced from their homeland near the Danube by the powerful Huns. Desperate, the Visigoths pleaded with Emperor Valens to allow them refuge inside the walls of the Roman Empire.

Valens agreed but taxed them heavily for the privilege. They protested. He showed them the gates. They rebelled and killed Valens less than two years after their arrival.

In time, a Visigoth named Alaric ascended the ranks of the Roman army, but he left the empire when his father died to assume the Visigoth throne. When the Romans refused to pay a bribe in 410, Alaric laid siege to Rome.

A man of some morals, Alaric prohibited his men from assaulting women or pillaging churches. With the ground rules firmly in place, the Visigoths ravaged Rome for three straight days, leaving the once "eternal city" easy prey for the other Germanic tribes. Meanwhile:

- The Ostrogoths, hailing from present-day Ukraine, conquered most of Italy, Greece, and the western Balkans.
- The Vandals overtook Rome's North African territory.
- The Franks conquered France.
- The Saxons overran southern England.

The Indus River Civilization

For lack of a better term, the ancestral lands of present-day India and its neighbors fizzled.

Although there is evidence that an industrious people urbanized the northern fringe of the Indus River only a few centuries after Mesopotamian civilizations began dotting the landscape, this mysterious metropolis disappeared almost as quickly as it emerged.

This false start of the Indus Valley Civilization has fascinated historians for thousands of years, but it wasn't until the 1920s that excavations began on one of the mounds in Harappa in Pakistan.

The dig revealed not just a city beneath the earth but at least eighty sister villages and towns. The civilization was promptly dubbed Harappan, but it is frequently interchanged with the Indus River civilization.

While historians disagree about the actual founding date for the civilization, they tend to concur that the ancient city of Herappa was founded circa 2600 BC.

Harappa—not unlike Mesopotamia, Egypt, and Greece—grew up on the banks of a volatile river, so flooding and frequent devastation were a way of life for its earliest inhabitants. Archaeological digs have uncovered evidence that Mohenjo-Daro in the south was rebuilt six times and Harappa, itself, resurrected at least five times.

Horticulture apparently drove the Harappan economy, though there is evidence of domesticated camels, cats, dogs, goats, sheep, and buffalo, so it was not an entirely one-dimensional existence.

It also appears that the world's first city planners were Harappan, and they might have been just the slightest bit obsessive-compulsive in their designs. Not only was each and every Indus Valley city laid out using a perpendicular, crisscross methodology, but city architects used the exact same floorplan, if you will, every single time they rebuilt a city following a calamity.

And despite their apparently cramped quarters, the Indus Valley Civilization was anything but primitive when it came to plumbing. Evidence of drains, sewers, and even latrines has been detected.

Historians have also ascertained that the Harappans traded frequently with Mesopotamia because their seals have turned up in

Sumerian digs as have depictions of animals—such as tigers—that could never have survived in Mesopotamia.

Very little information regarding any sort of formal organized religion exists among the Indus River ruins. Based on seals and other artifacts, natural forces appeared to hold prestige, and there might have been some form of goddess worship, but details are too sketchy to say for certain. These same artifacts reveal a pictographic script, but to date no linguist or historian has had any success breaking its code.

Several theories have attempted to explain the sudden disappearance of the once vibrant social structure, but what happened is really anyone's guess. Perhaps the repeated flooding took its toll, and they just migrated elsewhere for greener—or at least drier—pastures, assimilating completely to their adopted homes. Others believe the Indo-European Aryans wiped them out in their conquest of Persia and northern India. Regardless, they disappeared and took their answers with them.

The Indus Valley Civilization intrigues historians, but because no trace of Harappan life appears to carry forward from its brief appearance, it doesn't make for a very good starting point.

Sanskrit Literature

A few major pieces of Sanskrit literature:

- *The Vedas: Rig, Yajur, Sama,* and *Atharva*
- *The Mahabharata*
- *The Ramayana*
- *Mrichakatika*
- *Natya Shastra*
- *Vikramorvasiyam*
- *Malavikagnimitram*
- *Abhijñanasakuntalam*

The Aryans

Starting implies forward progress, and for that one must look to the Aryans, a warlike band that, by all accounts, shunned all things Harappan. This nomadic bunch hailing from the outer realm of Euro-Asia apparently had no need.

There is no evidence Aryans built cities, organized states, or even adhered to a written language. What is known is that this group, also known as the Vedic civilization, split into tribes, called the *jana.* Originally based on kinship, these tribes eventually shifted focus to geography. In turn, the jana evolved into the *janapada,* or nation, while the *jana-rajya,* or tribal kingdom, gave way to the *jana-rajyapada,* or national kingdom.

The name Aryan is actually derived from the Indo-European root word, *ar,* meaning noble, and given their warrior characteristics, no one seemed to argue with the title.

Archaeological evidence indicates these tribes began migrating south to conquer Persia and India sometime in the earliest centuries of the second millennium BC In turn, they adopted the "noble" moniker to distinguish themselves from their conquests, and it also served as the base name for the Persian territories they overran, known today as Iran.

The Aryans infiltrated India from the northwest, settling eventually in the Indus Valley, but unlike the Harappans, their populations shifted along the Ganges floodplain. The milder, more predictable river provided more habitable conditions.

The Aryan religion was dominated by a god of storms or god of the sky, depending on the interpretation. He was called Dyaus Pitor.

The Aryan culture centered on warfare, and Aryans were known to rush into battle on horseback and in chariots. The tribes were ruled by war chiefs, known as *raja.*

This culture and religion are inextricably linked, and because the Vedic religion is the foundation of Hinduism, its influence is still felt today. Even in the Rigveda, or the collection of praises to the gods, the god Indra, is a conquering god who decimates cities and any enemies in the path.

The Rigvedic Period

Beginning around 1700 BC, the earliest recorded history of the Aryans in India takes its name from that series of religious praise poems, the Rigveda, believed to be the oldest piece of literature in the region.

During this earliest Rigvedic period which, most scholars agree, lasted about seven hundred years, the Aryan population was contained primarily to Punjab near the northern tip of the Indus River and the Yamuna River, a major tributary of the Ganges. The war chief, or raja, ruled over each tribe with the assistance of a council. Each jana had its own chief priest, and religion was based on sacrifices to the gods.

By the close of this period, the Aryan social structure had settled into four distinct groups called the *catuvarnas*, meaning "four colors." Priests, or Brahmans, perched at the top of the order, followed by warriors and nobles called Kshatriyas, craftspeople and merchants called Vaishyas, and servants called Shudras. This hierarchy established what became the caste system, and by the end of the period there was no room for advancement outside one's birthright.

The Brahmanic Period

The next 500 years, known also as the Later Vedic Period, saw the Aryan migration across the Doab, the large plain separating the Yamuna River from the Ganges. This period saw a marked shift in religious focus from the Rigveda to the Brahmanas, or priestly book.

This Epic Age gave rise to the literary heroes of Indian culture, including the *Mahabharata* and the *Ramayana*. While these works were not composed until sometime between 500 and 200 BC, it is widely accepted that they were recited in the oral tradition centuries earlier.

Aryan life at this time seems to have been dominated by music, dance, and lyrical poetry more so than the visual arts so prominent in Greece or Egypt. Oddly, there is no evidence of writing in Aryan culture until around 300 BC when Brahmi script was developed.

By 200 BC, and the dawn of the Vedic period, the Aryan culture had shed its outward warrior bravado and assimilated into the native cultures. It is at this point that the culture recognized as Indian began to congeal.

Speaking Volumes

Although some fourteen major languages are spoken in India today, four primary groups of people—based on the languages they spoke—populated the region's vast landscape.

Indo-Europeans comprise the majority of the population, speaking myriad tongues related to such European languages as Greek, German, or even English. Evidence indicates these people first appeared sometime between 2000 and 1600 BC, and it appears they brought with them their own social system and religions practices.

Second in size but dating further back are a group who speak Dravidian languages, and it is believed this group most likely penned records from the Indus River civilization coinciding with Mesopotamia in time frame. An even smaller group nestled in the northern mountains speak languages more closely kin to Chinese, Tibetan, or Mongolian.

The smallest—and most probably oldest—Indian group speaks languages from the Australoid family, or tongues spoken by natives of southeast Asia and Australia. While the Australoid way of life appears to be dying out, as recently as forty years ago this group was still vital in the forests of the Deccan Plateau.

Because each region of India is dominated by its own unique language, the result is a vast—yet surprisingly fluid—network of tongues. They include:

- Hindi
- Urdu (very closely related to Hindi but uses Arabic script)
- Bengali
- Marathi
- Assamese
- Sindhi
- Oriya
- Punjabi
- Kashmiri
- Nepali
- Telugu (Dravidian)
- Tamil (Dravidian)
- Kannada (Dravidian)
- Malayalam (Dravidian)

Alexander's Impact

It's no secret that Alexander the Great's goal in life was to conquer the entire world. That said, Alexander's conquests did in fact carry him into what is now Pakistan and India after his romp through Mesopotamia, but there's no record of any significant military action during his visit. It appears he and his men just decided it was time to go home and left.

In truth, Alexander made it only as far as Gandhara, due west of the Indus River, and turned back, but his mere presence in the region did leave two lasting impressions: It marked the permanent co-mingling of Indian and Greek culture, and it inspired India's first great homegrown conqueror to start rallying the troops.

From the end of the Harrapan period sometime around 1750 BC until the Brahmanic period, trade between India and Mesopotamia ceased. For whatever reason these routes were resumed sometime around 700 BC, and by the time Alexander made his appearance in India, commerce between the two regions was quite robust. The great conqueror's presence inspired the spread of that trade to Greece, and the door for cultural exchange was opened permanently.

Chandragupta Maurya

India's Chandragupta Maurya reign began in 321 BC with the unification of all the kingdoms of northern India. Then he hit the road. With virtually no troops, Chandragupta Maurya managed to wrestle control of the Magadha region just south of the lower Ganges. From there he took the entire Ganges, and an empire was born.

Most strategically, Chandragupta Maurya took advantage of the instability in the west left behind by Alexander's departure. He marched westward, taking the entire Indus Valley, Gandhara, and Arachosia. It didn't hurt his street cred any that he trounced the Selecids, or the Greek rulers of Persia and Bactria, along the way.

And because behind every great king is a great opportunist, meet Kautilya, a shrewd and calculating priest who designed the government by which Chandragupta Maurya would rule. The duo became the architects of the first unified state in Indian history, complete with brutal laws and strictly regulated commerce.

Buddhism

Buddhism, which will be discussed in greater detail, was the most popular reaction to the priestly abuse of power. While no one will argue the faith's merits as a religion, the discipline is also considered equal parts therapy and philosophy.

Buddhism's founder, Siddhartha Gautama was descended from nobility yet driven to find an end to human suffering. After years of meditating on the subject, he "awakened" to the idea that all human suffering is caused by human desire but that human desire can be satiated when one truly understands the meaning of all things, including oneself. This revelation gave him the name Awakened One, or Buddha.

It's a simple faith, really, that shunned the magic and rituals of Brahmanism and contradicted directly the Rigvedic teachings of coercion and strife by stressing the importance of mediation and self-reflection.

By striving to achieve the Buddhist "middle way" between extremes, Asoka found peace as a ruler. He then swore off meat and warfare, shifting the nation's focus to nonviolence ruled by "right," or dharma.

Asoka became a live-by-example sort of ruler, and he demanded religious tolerance as king. While he personally preferred—and lived—Buddhism, all religions were welcome in his kingdom, and by the beginning of the Gupta Dynasty the majority of India's inhabitants had embraced vegetarianism, and the death penalty had vanished from the law books.

And while he never succeeded in transforming India into a purely Buddhist nation, Asoka is largely responsible for the religion's rapid expansion. He dispatched monks to Burma, Tibet, Nepal, Persia, Mesopotamia, Syria, and Israel. Although the western missions were not as well received, the eastern evangelical crusades successfully spread Buddhism from Nepal and Burma into Tibet and China. That is not to say the movement had zero impact on the west. In fact, Barlaam, a Catholic saint of the Middle Ages and Renaissance, is based on Siddhartha Gautama. And one of the most celebrated stories involving the Buddha-inspired saint recounts the conversion of a hateful king named Josaphat with whom many similarities can be drawn to Asoka.

Ironically, Asoka's desire to spread the Buddhist word outside the confines of India actually ensured the faith's survival. When the Muslims later defeated the Hindus and seized control of India, Buddhism disappeared as an organized religion in India.

In 184 BC, the last of Asoka's ineffectual successors was assassinated, and the Mauryan Empire came to an end. Unification faltered in the absence of a strong leader and fragmented groups again dominated the landscape. A universal empire would re-emerge eventually to the north, setting the stage for one of the most innovative periods in Indian history.

Asoka

The next great conquering king of the Maurya Empire, Asoka, reigned from 272 until 232 BC. Of course, part of the reason we know anything at all about him has less to do with his exploits and more to do with the re-emergence of a written Indian language for the first time since the vanishing act of the Harappans.

Regardless, Asoka maintained meticulous records throughout his forty-year reign, and his was a busy little palace. Almost upon coronation, he launched an aggressive campaign to conquer the rest of the subcontinent, or the Dravidian regions to the far south and the Kalinga to the north.

By all accounts, the brutality associated with the conquest of Kalinga plunged Asoka into a religious conversion, a quite common occurrence during the late Brahmanic period in response to the rampant abuse of power by the priests.

THE GUPTA DYNASTY

Chandragupta I ruled for only fifteen years beginning in AD 320, but he laid the foundation for the resurrection of a great Indian empire. Like Chandragupta Maurya, he conquered Magadha, established his capital at Patna where the Mauryan capital had been and proceeded to consolidate the fragmented eastern kingdoms of northern India. And while Chandragupta reinstituted several of Asoka's successful government procedures, his heirs re-shaped the empire.

Chandragupta's son, Samudragupta—whose forty-five-year reign began in 335—continued his father's expansion and diplomacy, but it was his son, Chandragupta II who extended the kingdom into an empire spanning the north and western Deccan. Chandragupta II, who was also called Vikramaditya, or the "sun of power," assumed the throne in 376 and reigned over India's most profound cultural age.

This golden age—like most—was characterized by unprecedented magnificence in architecture, sculpture, and painting.

The definitive work of the period is undoubtedly the wall paintings of Ajanta Cave in the central Deccan, representing the various lives of the Buddha.

Ajanta, which is filled with Buddhist sculptures, consists of twenty-nine caves in all, and the work is believed to have been completed sometime between 460 and 480.

In addition to their beauty, the cave paintings are also considered the most accurate depictions of daily life in the region at that time.

The rock temple at Elephanta houses an eighteen-foot statue of one of the principal Hindu gods, the three-headed Shiva.

Kalidasa was the most revered writer of this period. While he was a gifted lyrical poet, he is most recognized for his dramatic works.

Three of Kalidasa's plays have survived the ages, and all three resonate with comedy, epic heroism and more than a hint of eroticism.

The Hun Migration

Sometime around 480, however, the Guptas succumbed to an onslaught of migrating Huns, whose original territory to the north of China apparently just wasn't large enough.

In hindsight, the Guptas could take a little comfort knowing the Huns marched all the way to Rome, but some eighty years of fending off the invaders left them a little too jaded—and exhausted—for a "big picture" perspective.

In 480, the Huns successfully overran northern India, and it took only twenty years for that stronghold to extend to the western portion of the Guptan Empire. By 550, Guptan royalty had vanished.

The warring Huns were quick to invade and assume control, yet they appear to have had little interest in asserting their own beliefs and social structure in their adopted homes. On the contrary, Huns throughout India and Europe were slowly assimilated into the cultures of their conquests, and they eventually lost all identity.

By 606, Guptan descendent Harsha re-established an Indian empire in the northern portion of the nation, where he ruled for more than four decades. Harsha—a great military tactician, statesman and patron of the arts—made Kannauj his capital. The sprawling city encompassed almost five miles along the Ganges and was rife with ornate buildings. And his system of taxation was progressive, to say the least.

Harsha allocated only about one-quarter of all tax collections for government administration. The rest he earmarked for charity and rewards, with the lion's share dedicated to art, literature, music, and religion. This time frame became known as the period of "Greater India," when its culture and trade dominated the Bay of Bengal and began shaping the development of nearby Burma, Cambodia, and Sri Lanka. But conquerors would soon head south from Afghanistan, and by 1100, Muslim rule would become the order of the day.

The Muslim Invasion

In 1192, Muhammed of Ghor, a Muslim general, sacked Delhi and set in motion what would become known as the Delhi Sultanate. The Slave Dynasty, so called because its first leaders had been Mamluks, or slave soldiers, lasted a little less than one hundred years and tore itself apart in civil war by 1290. During this period, Islam became the primary religion as many Hindus and Buddhists in what would one day become Pakistan began adopting the beliefs of their conquerors.

This shift set the stage, however, for the most powerful reign of the Delhi Sultanate when the Khalji Dynasty wielded control over even the southernmost portions of India for brief periods during the next thirty years.

By 1320, though, the Delhi Sultans began to lose their grip on the region. During the twenty-five-year reign of the Tughluq Dynasty political upheaval became commonplace, punctuated by rebellions and civil wars. In 1351 southern India regained its independence as a Hindu state and while the Deccan remained an Islamic state, it also declared its independence.

The power of the Delhi Sultanate evaporated in 1398 when Mongol invader Tamerlane, or Timur, sacked Delhi.

Indian Warfare

Military acumen played a vital role in the development of Indian culture from the civilization's earliest days. In fact, a permanent militia emerged quickly to maintain order at home and deter invasion from abroad.

Moreover, the constant military presence gave rise to a warrior class known as the Ksatriya, and the concept of serving one's country and defending one's nation became a noble pursuit.

In turn, Hindu military science was dominated by two particular types of warfare.

Dharmayuddha is war waged on the principles of dharma. In simplest terms, these righteous and socially acceptable wars provided the means for defending the Ksatradharma, or the law of kings and warriors.

By contrast, *kuttayuddha* was unjustified war, and it was typically cloaked in secrecy and cunning. This particular brand of warfare was not only frowned upon but openly shunned because it discounted the Hindu traits of valor and ethical standards.

A large amount of Hindu ink is dedicated to extolling the virtues of one approach and demonizing the other in the *Ramayana* and *Mahabharata* epics as well as in the Arthasastra treatises of Kautalya, Kamandaka, and Sukra.

It is also clear from examining these works that Hindu warriors made use of the Caturangabala, a well-organized network of chariots, elephants, cavalry, and infantry. Anyone who questions the validity of this particular method might be interested to know that the enduring game of chess has also been called Caturanga in its honor.

It has also been argued—primarily by a troupe of German-born Indian scholars—that India was the birthplace of firearms because of the ancient presence of gunpowder in the region. Yet the region was also known for weaponless warfare and martial arts.

WEAPONS

- Depending on which guide one chooses to follow, Indian weapons can be classified into either four or three categories.
- Dhanur Veda—the formal name for Indian military science—classifies them as the *mukta*, the *amukta*, the *mukta-mukta*, and the *yantramukta*.
- The Nitiprakasika, by contrast, recognizes only three: the mukta, or those which are thrown; the amukta, or those which are not thrown; and the *mantramukta*, or those which are discharged by mantras.
- Bows and arrows—the primary weapon of the mukta group—were the principal weapons of that historical period.
- *Agnicurna*, more commonly known as gunpowder, was composed of between four and six parts saltpeter, one part sulfur, and one part charcoal from burned indigenous trees.
- Historical evidence indicates all four warrior classes were adept archers, but according to historian H. H. Wilson "the Hindus cultivated archery most assiduously and were very much like Parthians in their use of the bow on horseback."
- The *blindipala* was most likely a heavy club with a broad tail end used for cutting, hitting, striking, and breaking, and it was a defining advantage to the Asuras in their struggle with Kartavirya Arjuna.
- The *nalika* is straight and hollow handgun or musket. A smaller version was typically the weapon of choice among foot soldiers. The larger version was less than portable and required carts to transport it into battle.
- The *cakra*, by contrast, was a circular disc used for felling, whirling, serving, cutting, and breaking.
- The *tomara* actually existed in two forms: an iron club and a javelin.

- The *pasa* was a triangular-shaped noose tricked out with lead balls, and this lethal little number could be manipulated in any of eleven different ways against an aggressor.
- The *vajra*, or thunderbolt, was the first known amukta weapon, made from the offered backbone of Rishi Dadhichi by Indra.
- The *parasu* is a battle axe made of steel with a wooden handle.
- The *gada* is a heavy iron rod with some one hundred spikes on its crown. Not only was this little gem used to successfully fend off human foes and elephants, it also could be turned into an alarming little projectile with the help of a little gunpowder.
- The *mudgara* was a hammer-shaped mace used to break heavy stones.
- The *sira* was a bucket-like instrument curved on both sides and with a wide opening made of iron.
- The *pattisa* was a long razor-sharp staff.
- The *sataghni* is the first-known cannon, and its name translates to having the power to kill one hundred at a time.

LET THE SWASHBUCKLING BEGIN

Indian swords, or *asi*, were typically fifty inches long and their place of origin could be determined by the color of the iron used to forge them. For instance, black iron was used in the Anupa, white iron in the Sataharana, gold colored in the Kalinga, oily iron in the Kambhoja, blue-colored in Gujarat, gray-colored in the Maharashtra, and reddish white in Karnataka.

But swords were also named for the characteristics they carried:

- *Nistrimsa* meant cruel.
- *Visamana* meant fearful.
- *Khadga* meant powerful.
- *Tiksnadhara* meant fiery.
- *Durasada* meant unassailable.
- *Srigarbha* meant affording wealth.
- *Vijaya* meant giving victory.
- And *dharmamula* meant the source of maintaining dharma.

Tradition holds that the Hindus imparted their knowledge of sword forging to the Persians who, in turn, educated the Saracens, and the Damascus blade was born.

The blades, so called because of their watery designs, were eventually imported or copied by the Romans, Greeks, Arabs, Persians, Turks, and Chinese.

It is believed that the original Damascus steel, known as wootz, was the world's first high-carbon steel.

Panini

Panini might have been the world's first self-proclaimed Grammar Master. This ancient Sanskrit expert offered a scientific, and surprisingly comprehensive, theory of phonics, phonology, and morphology. Because of these exploits, he is considered the founder of Hindu language and literature, yet very little is known about Panini the man.

It is generally agreed that he was born in Shalatula near Attock on the Indus River in present day Pakistan. His date of birth has been listed in four different centuries—spanning the fourth to the seventh BC—making him quite tricky to pin down. Given the mystery surrounding its greatest scholar, it is no wonder that the word Sanskrit actually translates to "complete" or "perfect" and was considered the language of the gods. Panini's most celebrated work, *Astaadhyayi*, differentiates between the language of sacred texts and the common language of everyday communication. In this work, he was the first to set grammatical rules and regulations.

Did You Know?

Born in AD 476, Aryabhata was India's first documented astronomer, and he is credited with creating the concept of zero. It might not seem like much at first glance, but that simple little goose egg revolutionized everything from mathematics and economics to engineering and medicine. He also was the first to theorize that the earth spins on its axis.

Religious Roots

Very little is known about the oldest religious practices in India because so much of the Harappan civilization of the Indus River Valley remains shrouded in mystery. It is a commonly accepted theory that they worshipped numerous gods, and there is even some evidence of Hindu worship, but details are sketchy at best. That said, at least three major world religions—Hinduism, Buddhism, and Islam—trace their roots to India.

Modern Hinduism began around 1500 BC when the Indo-European Aryans arrived from west Asia, bringing with them their own gods and beliefs. This polytheistic belief system was well-documented in the *Rigveda* and other epic literary works, but its most widely recognized tenet remains reincarnation, or the thought that people can be reborn as other beings after death.

The problem for some folks, though, was that Hinduism could be a little rigid, what with its sacrificial rites and priestly decrees. Freer spirits began searching for more accommodation in their spiritual guidance and settled on Buddhism around 500 BC.

Gautama Buddha's new way held that people could free themselves from the cycle of reincarnation by following a few basic, and essentially people-friendly, rules:

- Be a good person.
- Place enlightenment above pleasures of the flesh.
- Meditate.

It's no surprise Buddhism spread rapidly across East Asia, yet Hindu gods were not abandoned completely—not even by some of the most disciplined Buddhists. By AD 600, the region had reverted to a primarily Hindu nation with the Buddha becoming just another—if highly revered—Hindu deity.

Muslim conquests. beginning around AD 1100 in India, shifted the tide, yet again, toward Islam, which demanded that Allah be the one and only god. The widespread conversion took stronger hold in northern India than southern India, where Hinduism remained strong.

Hinduism

When the Aryans invaded India around 1500 BC, they didn't come empty handed. The Aryans brought their sky gods, and as the cultures mixed, so did the deities. The *Rigveda*, the epic Sanskrit poem composed around 1200 BC, provides the first written evidence of Hindu practice. Of course, folks either sang or recited it for about two thousand years before it was finally written down between AD 400 and 600, during the Gupta period.

Although it is called a poem, the *Rigveda* is more accurately a compilation of hymns, magic spells, and instructions for ritual sacrifice. The majority of the gods mentioned in this work are male and most are sky or weather gods, including Indra, the god of weather, and Varuna, the god of the sky, rain, ocean, and underworld.

In addition to widespread animal sacrifice, early Hinduism was also characterized by the use of hallucinogenic drugs, such as soma, that were believed to induce direct conversations with the gods. By 600 BC, the Hindu concept of reincarnation was embraced widely, but the belief lost its luster after a few centuries. Apparently the idea of perpetual life became tiresome.

What's more, any devout Hindus began having difficulty reconciling animal sacrifice with karma and stopped the practice hoping it would free them from the reincarnation cycle.

Around 300 BC, a few new gods made their way into the mix.

Before long, Vishnu and Shiva began replacing Indra and Varuna as the primary gods.

Sometime over the next millennium—toward the end of the Gupta period—a new Mother Goddess who held cows in the highest esteem came onto the scene, and beef-eating gradually declined as a result. Probably not too hard to see why some believers were thrilled to discover the flexibility and all-around warm-fuzzy feeling Buddhism offered.

Hindu Gods to Know

Shiva was a fertility God who made the crops grow. He was believed to spend most of his time on top of Mount Kailas in the Himalayas meditating. Meditation, his worshipers believed, provided him the spiritual energy necessary to rule the universe. Tradition holds that the Ganges River actually sprang from Shiva's head, blessing its waters from day one.

Vishnu was believed to have been repeatedly reincarnated in numerous forms. Two of the most celebrated forms for his worship were Krishna and Rama. The epic poem, the *Ramayana*, tells the story of Rama.

Krishna appears in myriad stories in a host of different forms. Sometimes he is a child or a great and respected leader; other times he uses a flute to call people's souls or he frolics amorously with Hindu goddesses. His most famous appearance comes in the *Bhagavad Gita* in which he instructs the young Prince Arjuna how to act and helps him distinguish good and bad.

Language and Literature

The Harrapans gave the world one of the earliest writing systems around 2500 BC, but because no one has ever successfully cracked its code, its usefulness doesn't extend far past proving the Indus River civilization used it to track property.

Following the Aryan invasion in 1500 BC, these pictographs disappeared inexplicably and the region remained illiterate for the better part of a thousand years. It appears that the Persians inspired India's inhabitants to resume writing sometime around 500 BC, but they adopted Sanskrit rather than any known Persian script.

With the exception of the celebrated *Rigveda*, three primary literary works—penned sometime around 300 BC—set the tone for Indian culture and decorum: the *Ramayana*, the *Mahabharata* and the *Bhagavad Gita*.

Ramayana

The *Ramayana* chronicles the epic battle between the god Vishnu and a demon called Ravana. Looooonnnng story short, the gods had foolishly made a pact that prevented them from fighting Ravana, and he promptly started screwing with them just because he could.

But Vishnu was clever.

He opted to be reborn as a man, nullifying his divine promise and leaving him free to fight his nemesis. The story goes that Vishnu was reborn as Prince Rama, slated to ascend the throne when his father died. But daddy changed his mind on his deathbed and appointed Rama's brother king instead.

A dispirited Rama, his wife Sita, and his other brother Lakshmana took to the trees—literally—trading palace life for the simplicity of the forest. Unfortunately for Rama, Ravana's demon sister fell in love with the dissed prince. This next bit plays out a bit like an episode of Jerry Springer.

When Rama refused to leave Sita for his new admirer, she attacked, forcing Rama and Lakshmana to fight her off. Scorned, she ran home to Ravana and told him how terribly she'd been mistreated. Understandably, Ravana didn't take kindly to tree people beating up his sister, and it certainly didn't hurt that she told him what a hottie Sita was. He went to take a look for himself and fell hard for Sita, whisking her home with him where she pined away for Rama.

Recognizing the tough spot they were in, Rama and Lakshmana paid a visit to the king of the monkeys—no joke—to ask for assistance. The primate king Hanuman did not disappoint. It helped that he possessed the power to shrink and enlarge himself at will. The rest gets a little fuzzy. Hanuman found Sita and told her Rama was on his way to save her. Ravana caught Hanuman and set fire to his tail. Hanuman set the whole island ablaze. Sweet monkey justice.

Mahabharata

The Mahabharata is actually a collection of little stories revolving around one central story that goes a little something like this:

The five good Pandava brothers quarrel with their cousins, the Kaurava brothers, over control of the cities of the Upper Ganges and Jumna rivers. It might be helpful to know the Pandava brothers were outnumbered five to one, yet their alliances with many Hindu gods assures the ultimate triumph of the underdogs. Krishna played a crucial role in turning the tide.

Although uplifting, the morale boosting tale also chronicles the Aryan conquest of India between 1000 and 800 BC. It was believed to have been composed around 500 BC but not written down in Sanskrit for at least another 200 years. Of course, because the Pandava brothers were obviously Aryan, it's reasonable to believe the the Dravidians would probably have switched around the good and bad guys.

Bhagavad Gita

Bhagavad Gita is only one of the smaller, companion stories to the longer *Mahabharata*, but it is revered for laying out the Hindu faith and philosophy for all posterity. An imminent battle sets the stage. Prince Arjuna is upset because he will have to kill his own relatives, some of whom are fighting on the other side. But Krishna steps in, disguised as a charioteer.

The Hindu god tells the prince to stop fretting because lost life is a matter of perspective. Any family members he loses in battle will be reborn into new bodies, and besides, people shouldn't get so preoccupied with their own tiny little souls. The real power, Krishna says, is in becoming part of that great soul that is the entire universe. Solid logic, especially when the guy spouting it has the reins.

Digging Deeper

The truly beautiful thing about history is that it never sleeps.

In fact, while you've been otherwise occupied, crews of archaeologists somewhere discovered something about someplace you might not even know existed.

And in the best cases, the archaeologists themselves discover things even they didn't know might be there.

Since you're not going anywhere anytime soon, we thought we'd take a few minutes to bring you up to speed on some of the most recent excavations and their impact on accepted world views. These accounts aren't ripped from the headlines in the same sense as your favorite crime drama, but they are proof that all the news that's fit to print doesn't necessarily involve political shenanigans or the revolving door of celebrity rehab.

Greek History

Stone Age hunters begat early farmers who parlayed their manipulation of agriculture into the earliest recognized civilizations led by the Minoan and Mycenaean kings.

Spurred by a series of wars and invasions, the region was plunged into a period known as the Dark Ages.

In 1100 BC, a northern tribe called the Dorians invaded and swept down the west coast.

Between 500 and 336 BC, the area was divided into city-states.

Except for the writings of three recognized historians—Herodotus, Thucydides. and Xenophon—archaeologists have relied on temple ruins, pottery, sculpture, and other random artifacts to piece together the larger story.

The result is a six thousand-year chronicle of life, death, conquest, innovation, art, and architecture. The civilization yielded some of the greatest philosophical thinkers, the basis for modern politics, and a paradox of sophistication and simplicity unparalleled since the decline of its Golden Age.

A Guide to Greek Gods

- **Zeus (Roman: Jupiter)**
  Zeus was King of Olympus and god of the sky. He was known for hurling thunderbolts, ruling the universe, and committing adultery.
- **Hera (Roman: Juno)**
  Hera was the wife and sister of Zeus. She was Queen of Olympus and the goddess of both marriage and childbirth. She punished the women that became Zeus' mistresses.
- **Poseidon (Roman: Neptune)**
  Poseidon was the brother of Zeus and the god of the sea. He carried a large trident (fork) and waved it to created tumultuous seas and storms, sinking ships. Poseidon was also the god of horses. He often disguised himself as a stud.
- **Hades (Roman: Pluto)**
  A brother of Zeus, Hades was god of the underworld. He pined after Persephone and eventually kidnapped her. He was also god of the dead and of wealth.
- **Hestia (Roman: Vesta)**
  Hestia was the sister of Zeus and goddess of the hearth. She was a protector of family, the home, and stability. She showed no interest in male gods Apollo and Poseidon and remained a virgin-goddess.
- **Athena (Roman: Minerva)**
  Smart and good with crops. Daughter of Zeus alone. She didn't have a mother. In fact, she just sprang from Zeus' head. This made her his favorite child. Goddess of wisdom, the city, and protector of agriculture, she could be tough like her father. He let her carry his special shield, the aegis. Anyone who looked at it turned into stone.
- **Hephaestus (Roman: Vulcan)**
  Really ugly but good with tools. He was the child of Hera. She gave birth to him for revenge on Zeus for giving birth to Athena. Her vengeance was short-lived, however. Hephaestus was lame and considered so ugly that Hera threw him out of heaven. Despite his dysfunctional childhood, he grew up to be the god of the forge and fire and husband of Aphrodite.

- **Ares (Roman: Mars)**
  Ares was the god of war and the son of Zeus and Hera, both of whom hated him. He was famous among the Greeks for being a coward, as it was common for him to retreat in battle. The Romans, on the other hand, saw him as brave and heroic, and in Roman mythology, he was the lover of Aphrodite, goddess of love.
- **Apollo**
  Apollo was the son of Zeus and a Titan, Leto. He was god of light, arts, medicine, and music. When the mortal Cassandra wouldn't return his affections, he cursed her with the gift of foretelling the future. Though she was always honest, no one believed her prophecies, which was part of her lifelong curse.
- **Artemis (Roman: Diana)**
  Artemis was the twin sister of Apollo and the goddess of hunting. In her chastity, she protected young girls and was known for having a fiery temper. When a hunter, Actaeon, spied on her while she was bathing naked, she had him torn to pieces by his own dogs. In the temple at Ephesus, a statue depicts her with numerous breasts, symbolizing her as a goddess of childbirth.
- **Aphrodite (Roman: Venus)**
  Aphrodite was the daughter of Zeus and Dione, but in some stories she is said to have emerged from the foam of the sea. She was the goddess of love, and like her father, she found it difficult to remain faithful to her spouse. Renowned for her beauty, she cheated on Hephaestus with Ares, Hermes, Dionysus, and the handsome mortal Adonis.
- **Hermes (Roman: Mercury)**
  Hermes was the son of Zeus and the nymph Maia. He was messenger of all the gods and said to be the most cunning. He was famous for lying and stealing and became known as the god of commerce and the marketplace.

INSPIRED: GREEK MUSES

The ancient Greeks believed nine Muses inspired human creativity.

The Nine Muses

Calliope	Muse of epic poetry and eloquence
Euterpe	Muse of music or of lyric poetry
Erato	Muse of the poetry of love
Polyhymnia	Muse of oratory or sacred poetry
Clio	Muse of history
Melpomene	Muse of tragedy
Thalia	Muse of comedy
Terpsichore	Muse of choral song and dance
Urania	Muse of astronomy

Nine Facts

1. The early Greek poet, Hesiod, was the first to name the Muses in the Theogony.
2. Homer famously invoked the Muse in The Iliad and The Odyssey.
3. Like his epic predecessor, Virgil invoked the Muse at the beginning of the Aeneid.
4. In English poetry, one of the earliest invocations comes from Geoffrey Chaucer. In The Canterbury Tales, the Man of Law calls on the Muse of poetry to help him tell a moral story.
5. John Milton invokes the aid of a Muse at the beginning of Paradise Lost.
6. The earliest sites of the Muses' worship were Pieria, near Mount Olympus in Thessaly, and Mount Helicon in Boeotia.
7. In Roman, Renaissance, and Neoclassical art, artists often distinguished Muses by certain props so viewers could recognize them.
    - Calliope carries a writing tablet
    - Clio carries a scroll and books
    - Erato carries a lyre and a crown of roses
    - Euterpe carries a flute

- Melpomene wears or holds a tragic mask
- Thalia wears or holds a comic mask
- Polyhymnia usually has a thoughtful look on her face;
- Terpsichore carries a lyre
- Urania carries a staff which she points at a globe.

8. Plato complimented the poet, Sappho, by calling her "the tenth muse." Since then, other female poets to earn that compliment have included Anne Bradstreet and Sor Juana Inés de la Cruz.
9. Muse comes from Latin Musa, from Greek Mousa. The name of Mnemosyne, the goddess of memory and mother of the Muses, comes from the Greek word mnïmosunï "memory," which comes from the Greek and Indo-European root men which means "to think." Men is the root word of amnesia, mental, and mind.

Zeus Upstaged?

A *New York Times* story, dated February 5, 2008, shook the very foundation of the ancient world by announcing that a team of archeologists had unearthed evidence of a religious altar on the summit of Mount Lykaion that appears to predate the belief in Zeus, pulling the proverbial rug out from under all that is known and accepted about the region that gave the world politics, the Olympics, and volume upon volume of Greek mythology texts.

The find, located in the vicinity of Arcadia, was actually discovered in the summer of 2007 by a team from the University of Pennsylvania who uncovered ashes, bones, and even evidence of animal sacrifices. The kicker is not that this evidence exists but that it apparently was deposited sometime around 3000 BC, some nine hundred years before late Bronze Age Greeks like the ancient Myceneans and Minoans surfaced in the region.

The best part is that the discovery was purely accidental.

The excavation crew, digging in a known sanctuary to Zeus, found what Penn's David Gilman Romano described as material which "suggests that the tradition of devotion to some divinity on that spot is very ancient" and "very likely predates the introduction of Zeus in the Greek world."

In case you missed this earlier—or have lived your entire life in this particular room—Zeus was the preeminent god of Greece, having surfaced sometime around 1400 BC and most likely hailing from high atop Lykaion.

The Greek traveler Pausanias, writing in the second century AD, described the sanctuary of Zeus on the mountain, forty-five hundred feet above the rural countryside.

"On the highest point of the mountain is a mound of earth, forming an altar of Zeus Lykaios, and from it most of the Peloponnesus can be seen," Pausanias wrote. "Before the altar on the east stand two pillars, on which there were once gilded eagles. On this altar they sacrifice in secret to Lykaion Zeus. I was reluctant to pry into the details of the sacrifice; let them be as they are and were from the beginning."

Jack Davis, director of the American School of Classical Studies at Athens, who visited the site several times, told the *Times* in an e-mail,

"Evidence uncovered certainly points to activity at the altar in prehistoric times....The trick will be in defining the precise nature of the site itself before historical times."

But hold onto your drawers.

Ken Dowden, director of the Institute of Archaeology and Antiquity at the University of Birmingham, in England, is quoted in the article saying he isn't the least bit surprised to discover evidence that migrating Greeks adopted a sanctuary honoring gods of an earlier religion.

"Even Christians would on occasion reuse a pagan sanctuary in order to transfer allegiance from the preceding religion to Christianity," said Dowden, who played no role in the Mount Lykaion excavation.

"You have some god being worshiped on a mountaintop, and the arriving Greeks have translated the god as 'Zeus,' their god of the sky, lightning, weather and so on," Dr. Dowden told the *Times.*

And like the real estate mantra, "Location, location, location," it was reportedly Mount Lykaion's proximity to Olympia—only twenty-two miles away—that caught Romano's interest in the first place. Olympia is perhaps the best known sanctuary of Zeus and became the focal point of the Pan-Hellenic games from which the modern Olympics descended.

Romano's team began by excavating a hippodrome on a high meadow where horse and chariot races—among other games—had been staged. Meanwhile, the research team mapped the altar site and dug a test trench. They found bones—primarily those of sheep and goats—as well as a few bronze trinkets, a seal stone emblazoned with an image of a bull (perhaps suggesting Minoan Cretan influence) and burned altar stones indicating the use of sacrificial fires.

The potsherds found on the altar site are consistent with five thousand–year–old styles, methods and materials, but their mere presence doesn't necessarily mean they were created in the same place.or time, in which they were incorporated into worship.

One theory suggests they were simply antiquities belonging to those peoples who offered them to the gods as offerings. Of course, they could actually be remains from an earlier Bronze Age settlement, but the location at that particular time in history would not have been especially inhabitable.

ARCHAEOLOGY 101

ANCIENT CIVILIZATIONS

Of course, Zeus's altar is only one in a long line of present-day archaeological discoveries re-shaping accepted facts about the ancient world.

In January 2008, a team of U.S. archaeologists announced it had discovered the ruins of a city dating back to the period of the first farmers seven thousand years ago in Egypt's Faiyum oasis. According to officials with the Supreme Council of Antiquities, an electromagnetic survey revealed "the existence in the Karanis region of a network of walls and roads similar to those constructed during the Greco-Roman period."

The artifacts unearthed consist of the remains of walls and houses in terracotta or dressed limestone. Also found were large quantities of pottery and the foundations of ovens and grain stores. The site lies only four miles from Fayyum Lake, and preliminary evidence indicates it most likely was settled along the water's edge.

The remains are believed to date to the Neolithic period, specifically sometime between 5200 and 4500 BC. The city itself remains buried, but future excavations are planned.

Archaeologists believe the palace city discovered in 2004 at the Erlitou site in Yanshi City in central China's Henan Province, might possibly be the earliest palace city ever discovered in China. Before the discovery of the Erlitou site, the Yanshi Shang Town, built some thirty-six hundred years ago, was believed to be the earliest Chinese settlement.

Officials with the Chinese Academy of Social Sciences' Institute of Archaeology believe the design of the city—measuring slightly more than three hundred square yards—became the model in capital city design for later dynasties. Indeed, crisscrossing roads, the rectangular palace city, construction distributed around a central line and constructions facing south are all Erlitou characteristics repeated by later dynasties. Four roads—each between ten and twenty yards wide—enclose the palace area, creating a transportation network for the central region, and a city wall was constructed along the inner sides of these roads.

A British marine archaeologist named Graham Hancock believes a thriving civilization existed in a now-submerged city on the eastern coast of India's Tamil Nadu state. Not only does he theorize that the civilization predates the Sumerian stronghold of Mesopotamia in present-day Iraq but possibly even the Harappan civilization India and Pakistan.

Underwater explorations conducted in 2001, Hancock said, corroborated Tamil mythological stories of ancient floods, and he believes tidal waves of four hundred feet or more could have swallowed this flourishing port city any time between seventeen thousand and seven thousand years ago. Hancock's theory is strengthened by findings of India's National Institute of Oceanography, which has explored the site since the 1980s.

Life at Stonehenge

In January 2007, archaeologists unearthed an ancient settlement that they believe is connected in some way to the legendary monument on England's Salisbury Plain, Stonehenge.

The village uncovered, referred to as Durrington Walls, is believed to have housed a vibrant ancient community. The settlement is located near the banks of the Avon River, nearly two miles from Stonehenge, the circle of massive stones enclosing a series of concentric rings.

Some twenty-five houses have been excavated, but archaeologists believe that is only the beginning. Based on carbon dating, scientists approximate that construction of the Durrington Walls dwellings occurred sometime around 2600 BC.

Both the stone wonder and the wooden community include large paths leading to the Avon River. Trenches dug by archaeological teams indicate the Neolithic-era houses at Durrington Walls had clay floors, and they theorize that the dwellings housed the builders of Stonehenge.

Oddly, the larger wooden city appears at odds with its neighboring engineering marvel in several ways.

For instance, the ancient monument faces the midsummer sunrise and the midwinter sunset, making it invaluable to solstice buffs through the ages, yet Durrington Walls boasts the exact opposite solstice orientation and has gone unnoticed for millennia.

Archaeologist Mike Parker Pearson of Sheffield University at Stonehenge is quoted in news accounts of the discovery as saying he and his colleagues uncovered evidence of forty-six hundred–year–old debris in the huts.

"That consists of broken pots, chips, flint, burnt stones used in cooking, and vast quantities of animal bones," he said. "And what's really interesting about these is that many of these were thrown away half eaten. This is what we would call conspicuous consumption. It's an enormous feasting assemblage. People were here to have a really good time."

Yet frolicking and feasting appear to be foreign concepts to nearby Stonehenge, where cremated remains are the most common discoveries.

Into the Russian Deep

In December 2007, the Russian News and Information Agency reported the discovery of an ancient civilization of the bottom of Lake Issyk Kul, high in the Kyrgyz Mountains.

The international archaeology team that made the discovery contends the find proves the existence of an advanced civilization twenty-five centuries ago, equal in development to the Hellenic civilizations of the northern coast of the Black Sea and the Mediterranean coast of Egypt. Among the finds was the discovery of major settlements submerged in the lake.

At depths of sixteen to thirty-three feet underwater, the search team found "formidable" walls, some of which stretched as far as 1,640 feet, indicating organized city walls. In addition, Scythian burial mounds—eroded by waves over the centuries—were found, as well as well-preserved bronze battle-axes, arrowheads, self-sharpening daggers, objects discarded by smiths, casting molds, and a faceted gold bar, believed to have been currency.

According to the Russian article:

Because Lake Issyk Kul lies at the crossing of Indo-Aryan and other nomadic routes, archeologists have found traces of many religions over the years, including Zoroastrianism, Buddhism, Judaism, Christianity, and Islam.

The great Silk Road lay along the lake's coast. Even today, the descendants of caravan drivers recollect their ancestors' stories about travelling from Asia to Europe and back.

Tamerlane built a fortress on one of the lake islets to hold aristocratic captives and keep his treasures.

The famous Asian expeditions of Russian explorers Dmitry Przhevalsky and Pyotr Semyonov-Tianshansky started from that spot.

The article also outlined numerous artifacts found in the lake's depths by the partnership of Russian and Kyrgyzstani archaeologists in the years leading up to the most recent revelation that support its veracity. Some of these items include:

- A 2500–year–old ritual bronze cauldron found on the bottom of the lake.

- Bronze mirrors.
- Festive horse harnesses.
- Gold wire rings used as small change and a large hexahedral gold piece believed to be among the world's oldest extant coins.
- Ritual complexes of times immemorial.
- Homes and ancillary buildings.

Fact, or Just a Bunch of Bull?

Although colorful, the tale of the Minotaur does little more than illustrate the power of Minos's reign, especially in securing the exchange of cargo with neighboring cities.

In fact, the Greek historian, Thucydides, credits Minos as the first ancient king to raise a navy who "made himself master of what is now called the Hellenic Sea." In doing so, Minos also successfully stamped out the rampant piracy in the area, allowing the island people to truly settle in and amass wealth. As a result, trade flourished, construction abounded, and the arts reached new heights of sophistication.

Excavation of the site at Knossos has revealed that what archaeologists call the "Bull Courts" does, in fact, reveal a winding network of hallways, stairs, and doors opening onto the courts. Evidence of ritual feeding on the dead has also been uncovered at the site.

Age and beauty

Taking into account the above archaeological evidence, dating the world's oldest cities is obviously a continuous practice that involves a certain degree of flexibility.

The nice people at www.wisegeek.com took a stab at it based strictly on continuously populated areas. The following cheat sheet is the result of their research:

- Byblos in present-day Lebanon may date back as far as 5000 BC and is considered by many to be the oldest continuously populated city.
- Medinat Al-Fayoum in Egypt is possibly dated at 4000 BC.
- Gaziantep in Turkey dates to 3650 BC.
- Hebron in Israel is dated at 3500 BC.
- Varansi in India also dates back further than 3000 BC.
- Damascus in Syria has existed at least since 3000 BC.
- Athens in Greece dates to about 3000 BC.
- Arbil and Kirkuk in Iraq have dates of 2300 BC and earlier than 3000 BC respectively.
- Hama in Syria was established before 2000 BC.
- Both Adana in Turkey and Jerusalem in Israel were established around 2000 BC.
- Thebes in Egypt also dates to 2000 BC.
- Israel's Jaffa and Syria's Aleppo are both about thirty-eight hundred years old.
- Some dispute exists about excluding Jericho from the list. In its present location, it is about thirty-four hundred years old, yet it is routinely cited as one of the oldest civilizations, with settlements dating back as far as 11,000 BC.
- Catal Huyuk in Turkey is another potential candidate for the list, dating either to the founding of Jericho or 3,000 years later, depending on the source of the information.

King Minos

Sometime around 1720 BC, man and myth began to overlap on the island of Crete. Greek myth holds that a man named Minos, stepson of a Cretan nobleman, wanted so badly to ascend the throne, he told the people of Crete he could prove his reign was ordained by the gods. Specifically, he claimed whatever he prayed for—no matter how preposterous—would be delivered. To prove this claim, he asked Poseidon for a bull to sacrifice, and the hoofed creature appeared almost immediately out of the surf. The problem was that the creature was so magnificent Minos couldn't bear to have it slaughtered, so he hid the bull in his own herd and sacrificed a less impressive specimen.

The Cretans, so overwhelmed by what they witnessed, immediately declared Minos king, but Poseidon wasn't fooled—or pleased—by the act of insubordination. Enraged by Minos's greed, the water god cursed the new king's wife, Pasiphae, with an uncontrollable lust for the bull. And because it never hurts to have a legendary architect on staff—in this instance Daedalus—Pasiphae acted upon her urges with a little help from a contraption involving a large wooden cow on wheels.

It's no surprise, then, that when Pasiphae's son, Asterius, was born with the face of a bull, King Minos connected the dots and banished the deformed child to a prison beneath the palace. Of course, Daedalus couldn't very well deny his role in the fornication, so Minos gave the architect the job of designing the bastard child's lair, known as the Labyrinth, a maze of winding passages so complex the child-bull could never escape. Myth also holds that Minos fed the creature, which he called the Minotaur, human flesh in the form of seven young men and seven young women each year as tribute from the Greek mainland following a shameful defeat.

Early Bronze Age, 2900–2000 BC

Colonies during this period ranged from about three hundred to a thousand people, and it is through the remnants of their architecture, burial rituals, and everyday practices that this information has been pieced together.

The period obviously gets its name from the introduction of the metal bronze into everyday life around 3000 BC, but it was a slow process in a simpler time.

The most common use for the metal was in the forging of knives and swords because it was more malleable than stone, bone, or wood.

And because gold and silver debuted at the same time as bronze, so too did the class system.

And because the principles of supply and demand existed millennia before they had a name, commerce was born of necessity. The barter system emerged with stone, pottery, textiles, and metals driving the fledgling economy.

For all of its simplicity, the Early Bronze Age set the stage for the opulence of the Minoans and the Mycenaean Greeks.

Minoan Age, 2000–1400 BC

The island of Crete is actually geographically closer to Asia than Europe, yet for almost two thousand years it was the epicenter of Greek culture.

Named after the notorious King Minos—who some historians believe was an actual person and others believe to be an entire line of kings—the Minoan culture was trade oriented with scarce evidence of a military presence.

Ironically, it appears the civilization's lack of a military presence coupled with its mercantile base most likely led to its undoing.

It was not until Heinrich Schliemann excavated Troy between 1870 and 1890 that any record of the places mentioned in Homer's epic poems existed. Driven to uncover the real Troy and the battlefield of the Trojan War, Schliemann stumbled upon evidence of Mycenae and Tiryus. Those discoveries led an explorer named Arthur Evans to begin his own excavation on Crete, where he found the Minoans.

The Screw

The first recorded use of a screw mechanism in history dates to Greek mathematician Archimedes's visit to Egypt, when he engineered a means of raising water on a scale large enough to allow irrigation of crops from the Nile.

True, the water wheel already existed, but only Archimedes's design allowed for the volume of water necessary for mass irrigation, and by the first century AD, wooden screws were adopted by winemakers for smoother, more even presses of the fragile grapes. The same concept was applied to olive oil production, and trade boomed. In time, the process was adopted by textile manufacturers, and that meant togas for everybody.

The product resembling modern day metallic fasteners didn't emerge until the fifteenth century.

Mycenaean Age, 600–1100 BC

The Mycenaean Age derives its name from the city of Mycenae, situated in southern Greece on the site where palace remains were found. Athens, Thebes, Pylos. and Tiryns also figure prominently into this period.

The civilization is believed to be built upon the adoration of King Agamemnon, who led the Greeks to victory in the Trojan War. In fact, the palace unearthed at the site of Mycenae mirrors Greek poet Homer's description of the king's domicile in his epic poems. It is during this period that class distinction solidified, and trade flourished with both European and Mediterranean countries. There is also evidence of significant engineering and architectural prowess based on the remnants of elaborate tombs, bridges, and palaces.

Politically, the wanax, or king, reigned and was flanked by administrative chiefs and financial wizards.

The working class fell into one of two groups: those who worked for the ruling class and those who were self-employed. Scribes served, in effect, as chief operating officers, overseeing production, financial transactions, and work assignments.

The Mycenaeans also revolutionized the agricultural process by creating storage centers and absorbing surplus as a form of taxation.

The first known textile mills actually sprang up in Pylos, employing around 550, and almost twice that in Knossos. Metallurgy and perfume production also thrived alongside pottery, stone carving, and ivory carving.

Historians offer two theories for the evaporation of the Mycenaean civilization with the simplest explanation being that they simply imploded. The more popular theory is that they were attacked from within by the Dorians from the north or possibly the Sea People.

Of course, it is quite possible that an uprising by the lower classes over the injustice of wealth distribution toward the end of this period set the stage for a violent revolt.

Either way, archaeological evidence suggests both Mycenae and Tiryus were leveled, and the Greek Dark Ages began.

Greece

The Mycenaeans alphabet consisted of about two hundred symbols. The alphabet, known as Linear B, built upon the foundation of Linear A created by the Minoans. The most prolific writers, at least based on archaeological finds, were found in Knossos and Pylos. The oldest known Mycenaean writing is believed to date to the seventeenth century BC.

Just to be clear, calling the cities discussed in this section Greek is just a tiny bit inaccurate because the region's name wasn't coined officially until the classical civilization of Greece was born centuries later. There is also some speculation that the people Homer calls the Achaeans, or earliest Greek heroes, in his epic poems, are actually Myceneans, that mainland bunch forced by Minos to sacrifice fourteen youths each year to the Minotaur. Because these cities lie on what is commonly referred to as the Greek peninsula, we'll let it slide.

The Dark Ages, 1100–750 BC

For some inexplicable reason, the Mycenaean culture fell off the map sometime between 1200 and 1100 BC.

Urban centers dwindled, craftsmanship vanished, and trade with Asia Minor, the Middle East, and Egypt fizzled. Most startlingly, though, writing flat out stopped, and that's the real kicker.

Nothing kills a traipse through time faster than a five hundred–year gap in the historical record.

Best guesses and a great deal of deductive logic conclude that an economic decline coupled with the systematic migration of northern neighbors quietly snuffed them out.

Of course, some historians believe this blip on history's timeline was actually a hibernation period before a great awakening could come to pass. Homer is the greatest argument for this last comment, because his epic poems, the *Odyssey* and *Illiad*, were born as the Greek Dark Ages waned. And this poetry becomes arguably the culturally defining factor in Greek progress as a faint light begins to flicker signaling the rebirth of culture.

ARCHAIC PERIOD, 750–500 BC

The first monumental stone sculpture and naturalistic representations of the human form hit the scene. The polis, or city-state, is born. Aristocracies emerge and colonization of Italy begins.

CLASSICAL PERIOD, 500–336 BC

Nothing brings a little life to the party like good old fashioned carnage, and this period is highlighted by fierce conflict between the Greeks and the Persians to the East. It's the time of Alexander the Great's quest for world domination and Athens's political and cultural zenith. Pericles unveils the democratic system of government, and the Parthenon is perched atop the Acropolis.

HELLENISTIC PERIOD, 336–146 BC

This height of Greek enlightenment, sandwiched between Alexander the Great's ravaging of the Persian Empire and the looming iron smackdown that will be Rome, stressed the importance of education and cultural identity. Literature, poetry, drama, art, and philosophy flourished.

The Greco-Persian Wars, 527–479 BC

The Greeks might have given the world logic, democracy, and hydraulics, but they didn't arrive at those concepts in a vacuum.

Time and again the desire to protect and maintain sovereignty clashed with the lust for domination, and the result is a litany of power struggles and carnage.

In a nutshell, the Greco-Persian Wars waged for decades as Darius, king of the Persian Empire, failed to take Athens, and his son, Xerxes, proved no match for a united Grecian front.

The Ionian Revolt

Hungry to prove himself as a military leader, Darius set his sights on the Scythians and chased the nomadic tribe through the woods for a while but could never get them to stand still long enough for a real fight.

Bored—and more than a little humiliated—he retreated south and ordered his men to capture Thrace as a consolation prize on the long walk home to Persia.

Ironically, the other Greek states took Darius's aggression against the Scythians—failure notwithstanding—as a warning shot, and Macedonia was the first in line to negotiate peace, but the Ionian city of Miletus wasn't far behind with tyrant Aristagoras at its helm.

In an attempt to endear himself to Darius, Aristagoras offered to conquer the Cyclades on Persia's behalf if the king would only provide soldiers and ships.

Aristagoras failed in his quest, but being a good student of Athenian politics, cut his losses and promptly offered his services as the leader of rebellion forces against the Persians along the Ionian coast.

The unsuccessful revolt began officially in 500 BC, but lasted only six years. It did, however, whet the appetites of the Greeks for military clashes.

The First Persian War

Darius enjoyed the spoils of war briefly by gobbling up everything in his path.

With the exceptions of Athens and Sparta, the Greek states wasted little time surrendering, and Darius accepted graciously. He also acquired the islands of the East Aegean and Propontis and appointed his son-in-law, Mardonius, to re-establish order in the Ionian cities he had razed.

Darius then joined his army in Hellespont—after brief detours to capture Thrace and Macedonia—and was on his way to put Thassos in its place when a karmic little thunderstorm wiped out about twenty thousand of his men. He rallied, though, to pay a little retribution on Eretria for having sided with Ionia during the revolt.

The Battle of Marathon

Darius knew from day one that Athens was the key to dominating Greece, and his attempt is chronicled by eye-witness reporter—er, historian—Herodotus.

According to Herodotus's writings, Darius understood the power of alliances, so he accepted the assistance of exiled Athenian Hippias who was desperate to make a triumphant homecoming.

The march toward Athens began around 490 BC with tens of thousands of soldiers demolishing everything in their paths.

The Athenians appealed to Sparta for help, were denied and aligned, instead, with the Plataeans. The plan worked.

Miltiades, commander of the Greek army, ordered his eleven thousand troops to attack the Persians on sight, preventing the aggressors from finding a rhythm. With their superior weapons designed specifically for hand-to-hand combat, the Greeks flanked the Persians.

Casualties of the Battle of Marathon ran about 30-to-1 in Greece's favor.

Leonidas at Thermopylae

When Darius died in 486 BC, any hope of a kinder, gentler Persian Empire fizzled when his oldest son Xerxes took the throne.

In less than two years, Xerxes stamped out rebellion in Babylon and captured Egypt. Greece was next, and he took his time.

Rested, intimidating, and ready to avenge his father, Xerxes trampled Thrace and Macedonia before heading for the mainland around 480 BC He gravely underestimated the resolve of the Spartans, however.

The mountains at Thermopylae, the only thing standing between Xerxes and Greek domination, created a narrow pass through which the Persian king would have to lead his army. Leonidas and his Spartan army waited in the pass but quickly realized they were grossly outnumbered. But Spartans being bred from birth for battle saw no greater honor than death in combat, and history was made.

Leonidas sent all but three hundred of his troops away from certain death. Those who remained fought fiercely but in vain, and their heroism has earned an unparalleled place in history. No other battle in Xerxes's reign claimed so many Persian lives.

The acts of bravery that day rallied Greece, and within one year, Athenians and Spartans united to overtake the Persians at Platae and Mycale. The victories sparked the first true sense of unity in Greece as a culture, established Grecians as capable warriors, and signaled the Persian Empire's decline.

The Peloponnesian War, 431–404 BC

Divided into three phases, the Peloponnesian War was the twenty-five–year conflict between the Athenian Empire and the Peloponnesian League. Led by Sparta, the league also included Thebes and Corinth. The war ended when Athens surrendered and effectively restructured the Greek state. Democracy was restored, and the Spartans got theirs thirty years later at the Battle of Leuctra.

Greek Architecture

- Greek structures typically fall into one of three categories:
  - Doric, or sturdy columns with no decoration.
  - Thinner Ionic columns topped with swirly accents.
  - Ornate Corinthian columns with leaves carved into the design.
- The Parthenon, the most famous Doric temple, was built in the fifth century BC to honor of Athena, the Greek goddess of wisdom. It sits on the Acropolis in Athens.
- The Temple of Apollo at Didyma was built in Turkey around 300 BC, and was considered the epitome of Ionic design. The temple actually boasted two sets of columns encasing the statue of Apollo.
- Although more commonly used by the Romans, the Greeks did use Corinthian style in their temple of Zeus at Athens.
- And then there's the Acropolis:
  - Acropolis means "the sacred rock, the high city."
  - Sometime during the thirteenth century BC, a wall was built to enclose it.
  - The fortress withstood the attack by the Dorians.
- When the Athenia Polias, or "Bluebeard temple," was built in the sixth century BC, the Acropolis became an official shrine.
- Later that century, Peisistratos built the "Old Temple" on the Acropolis, and the area became the cultural and religious focal point of the community.
- The Bluebeard temple was destroyed when Athens prevailed at the Battle of Marathon in 490 BC, and it was replaced by the "Older Parthenon." It was never completed because the Persians attacked again ten years later.
- Pericles was responsible for the majority of construction on the Acropolis during the Golden Age of Athens between 460 and 430 BC.
- When Christianity swept the area, the Acropolis structures were converted into churches and cathedrals, and by the Middle Ages they were used as political headquarters by Frankish and Turkish leaders.

The Parthenon

Pericles commissioned the Parthenon in 447 BC, to replace another temple decimated by the Persians in 480 BC.

Pericles paid 469 silver pieces for the project and had sculptor Phidias construct it from ivory and gold.

Of course, the renowned statesman couldn't have been luckier—or more strategic—in how he financed the project.

The Persian War had ended two years before construction began, but rather than disbanding the Delian League of anti-Persian interests, he funneled the remaining defense funds into the project and gave the league new treasury offices in the completed Parthenon.

Did you know?

- Ictinus and Calibrates were the architects for the Parthenon.
- An estimated 13,400 stones were used in the building after being transported from Mount Pantelakos.
- The Roman library at Ephesus incorporates elements of the Parthenon's design.
- The statue of Athena was stolen in the fifth century, taken to Constantinople and destroyed during the crusades.
- Byzantine Christians converted the temple into the Church of the Theotokos for 250 years.
- When the Venetians attacked the Ottomans in Athens in 1687, the Acropolis took a direct mortar hit, obliterating a large part of the structure that still stands in ruins today.

The Olympic Games

- The first Olympic Games date back to 776 BC, maybe even earlier. As an honor to the Greek god Zeus, the early Olympic Games were held once every four years in Olympia, Greece.
- The first female to win an Olympic gold medal was Charlotte Cooper from Great Britain. She competed in women's single tennis in 1900, the first year women were allowed to compete in the games.
- The modern torch relay began in 1936, when a torch was lit at the original site of Olympia and carried in relay to Berlin.
- In 1924, the first Winter Olympics were held in Chamonix, France. Only events performed on ice or snow can be a part of the Winter Games. Since 1994, the Winter and Summer Games have alternated even-numbered years. Vancouver, Canada, will host the Winter Games in 2010, and London, England, will host the 2012 Summer Games.

Only one person has won gold medals at both the Winter and Summer Olympic Games. Edward Eagan, from the US, captured the gold for light-heavyweight boxing in 1920 at Antwerp, Belgium, and was on the winning four-man bobsled team at the 1932 games in Lake Placid, New York.

Top Winners

- Five individuals share the distinction of winning the most gold medals in Olympic competition: Paavo Nurmi of Finland, Larisa Latynina of the Soviet Union, and Mark Spitz, Carl Lewis, and Michael Phelps.
- Michael Phelps holds the record for the most gold medals (eight) won at a single Olympics. The woman with the most gold medals in one year is Kristin Otto of East Germany with six.

EVERYDAY HISTORY

EYEGLASSES

The Venetians developed the reading stone, a precursor to the modern-day magnifying glass, sometime around AD 1000, and the concept has remained relatively unchanged.

In its earliest form, this reading aid consisted of a piece of glass placed flat on texts, effectively enlarging the words for the reader. At some point, the Venetians fashioned frames to hold the magnifying lenses, but they were clumsy and often cumbersome for the wearer.

It wasn't until the late thirteenth century that spectacles were referred to by a proper name when scientist Roger Bacon defined them for the express purpose of examining tiny letters or objects through a transparent substance that magnified them.

Oddly, the actual mechanism of improving sight through this invention proved far less troublesome than figuring out how to keep them from falling away from the face. It actually took more than 350 years to solve that little problem.

Edward Scarlett, an English optician, introduced sturdy earpieces in 1730, and finally man had a reliable means of hooking the spectacles over his ears so that the lenses rested squarely in front of the eyes. And it certainly was not uncommon to find colored lenses—even turquoise or yellow—for fear that clear glass allowed too much direct light to pass through.

Culturally, eyeglasses have always carried a certain degree of stigma among some groups, while others embraced spectacles as a sign of enlightenment and knowledge. Spaniards, for instance, adored the look as dignified, while the French and English banished the objects' wearing to behind closed doors so as not to invite criticisms of weakness or inferiority.

Of course, given their expense, eyeglasses were typically available only to upper class residents who could afford the equivalent of a $1,000 indulgence in present-day dollars.

Greek Art and Sculpture

- Western art was most heavily influenced by the Roman Empire, but Alexander the Great's conquests inspired Greco-Buddhist art, reaching as far east as Japan.
- The Greeks used everything from stone and marble to limestone to express themselves through sculpture, the preferred medium for preserving tributes to gods, heroes, and events alike. These monuments are divided into seven main periods:

  - Mycenaean
  - Dark Age
  - Proto-Geometric
  - Geometric
  - Archaic
  - Classical
  - Hellenistic

- The technologically advanced Mycenaeans flaunted their skilled artisans with works such as the Cyclopean Wall of Mycenae (masonry) and Agamemnon's Death Mask (goldsmithing). When Troy fell around 1200 BC, though, Mycenaean art declined.
- Understandably, very few artistic remnants have been found dating to the Dark Ages, and what has been discovered is fairly uninspiring.
- By 1025 BC, however, the Proto-Geometric era had begun, and simple pottery appeared to coincide with the rekindling of civilization.
- Geometric art, dating from 900 to 700 BC began to document the rise of the Greek city-state. Trade routes emerged, colonization flourished, and art became an export. Of course, the Greek's were ever mindful of their roots, so temples and sanctuaries to the gods who blessed them began popping up, and the statues inside were adorned with the intricate trappings of heroic figures.
- During the ensuing Archaic period, Asian influence began to infuse Greek art, most likely as a direct result of trade. Animals debuted as well as "composite beasts" such as the part bird-part

lion griffin and the part female-part winged lion sphinx. Marble statues, gold jewelry, and bronze armor also emerged. But gigantic stone statues were the coup de gras.

- Freedom of movement revolutionized sculpture during the Classical era, and The Discus Thrower remains the most celebrated example. The human form also went on display for all to see, but the gods were not forgotten. Some of the most heralded works from this period include Zeus at Olympia and Athena at the Parthenon.
- The death of Alexander the Great in 323 BC marks the beginning of the Hellenistic era when artists started taking risks. A few examples include:

    - *Charioteer of Delphi*
    - *Colossus of Rhodes*
    - *Dying Gaul*
    - *Venus de Milo*
    - *Winged Victory of Samothrace*

Alexander the Great: Scholar and Military Leader

Military intelligence might sound like an oxymoron, but no other phrase quite fits when a twenty-year-old hotshot mounts an army and invades the Persian Empire.

Born in Macedonia in 356 BC, Alexander the Great assembled his army in Corinth and began cutting his bloody swath, but he made it only as far as Thrace when rebellion began in some of the Greek cities to the south. Not fond of distractions, Alexander promptly captured the city of Thebes around 335 BC and leveled it as a deterrent to other Greek cities even considering resisting his reign.

With everything under control at home, Alexander set his sights again on Syria and resumed his power grab. He defeated the Persians at the Granicus River, followed by Darius III at Issus; he then marched into Egypt a hero and a liberator.

But the son of Philip of Macedon wasn't quite finished.

In 331 BC, Alexander shifted north through Syria and Mesopotamia to Gaugamela and trounced Darius, who then fled and was murdered by his own army. With the entire Persian Empire, including Susa and Persepolis, under his control, he figured there was nothing to stop him from conquering the world.

He methodically trampled through what is now Afghanistan to the Indus River Valley, occupying Punjab by 326 BC.

To his credit, he did manage to dominate every known metropolis in the civilized world in less than thirty years, but his vision for creating a world monarchy driven by divine ordination ended with his death at thirty-three, of a fever.

Alexander the Great was the first military leader to conquer Greece, Egypt, Asia Minor, and Asia. The process expanded the Greek presence and influence into Syria, Iran, and Egypt. His reign is considered the foundation of the Hellenistic Age.

Archimedes: Mathematician and Philosopher

Born in Sicily, in 287 BC, Archimedes studied in Egypt. He seems to have been quite a practical joker. In some of his writings, he tells about sharing his theories with friends in Alexandria. When he caught on that his friends were claiming his theories as their own, he sent them two false theories.

Perhaps best known for his principle of the lever—"Give me where to stand, and I will move the earth"—Archimedes invented many things that were used as weapons of war for his government. He invented the compound pulley, hydraulic screw, and the odometer and gave mathematics numerous theorems.

Archimedes eureka moment came with his discovery that a body immersed in fluid loses weight equal to the weight of the amount of fluid it displaces. Today, this is known as the Archimedes's principle and is found in his book titled *On Floating Bodies.* This work also contains his notes on other principles of hydrostats relating to floating bodies of different shapes and different specific gravities.

As the story goes, Archimedes began thinking about hydrostatics when he stepped into a bathtub and noted the displacement of the water. At this point, he is said to have exclaimed, "Eureka!" and run naked into the streets.

With his country involved in war and taken over by the enemy, Archimedes met his death when confronted by a Roman soldier. It is said that he was working on calculations and angered the soldier by not telling his name. His only words to the soldier—"Don't disturb my circles"—were for naught as the soldier slashed the famous mathematician with his sword and the work of Archimedes was destroyed.

Pericles: Statesman

Born in 495 BC, Pericles was bound for greatness from day one with a name that translates literally to "Surrounded by Glory." He began his political career as a celebrated prosecutor. He is credited with leading the charge that got Cimon, his chief political rival, ostracized from Athens in 461 BC. Interestingly, his remaining competition, Ephialtes, was murdered that same year.

With no one standing in his way, he ascended to the top of the statesman food chain and also commanded the military during the Peloponnesian Wars.

Despite his rough exterior, he did appear to have a soft spot for the masses and passed laws that not only allowed the underclass to attend the theater free of charge but paid citizens for jury duty. He also used surplus Peloponnesian War funds to pay for Athens's 448 BC facelift, including refurbishing the Acropolis and building the Parthenon.

Pericles died from the plague in 429 BC, but not before he played an integral role in the transformation of the Delian League into an empire whose members paid tribute to Athens.

World Literature

The Greeks

Aeschylus

Born in the city of Eleusis in 525 BC, Aeschylus is widely recognized as the Father of Greek Tragedy.

He revolutionized theater by introducing the second actor and making the chorus an active participant in productions. It is believed he wrote close to one hundred works, the majority of which were tragedies performed around 500 BC.

Despite his poet's soul, Aeschylus fought victoriously at Marathon and Salamis and also traveled frequently. He died at Gela during his third trip to Sicily in 456 BC, and the locals honored his genius and memory with a monument.

Aristophanes

The specifics of Aristophanes's life (c. 448–c. 388 BC) are a bit fuzzy, but the prolific writer of comedies had a penchant for stirring controversy. Only about one-quarter of his forty plays have survived and most focus on the political climate of Athens at the time.

To says his earliest recovered work, *The Acharnians*, was not well received in 425 BC is an understatement. Aristophanes took aim at the woes of Attica, where incessant raids and invasions became a way of life, but his own people thought it disrespectful to tackle such a touchy subject with the Peloponnesian War and statesman Pericles's death so fresh.

The Knights, written one year later satirized the tyrannical stylings of then Athenian ruler Cleon. The playwright also made a point to ridicule Cleon's boozing ways. Ever the diplomat, though, he personally took on the role of Cleon, and the gamble worked. He took top honors at the festival that year.

In 423 BC, Aristophanes veered sharply from politics to explore the cultural impact of Socrates with *In the Clouds*, but the diversion didn't last long. *The Wasps* (422 BC) lampooned the fledgling justice system, and *The Peace* (421 BC) tackled the treaty negotiated to end the Peloponnesian War and the terms reached between Athens and Sparta.

There is a seven-year gap in Aristophanes's known writings before *The Birds* took the stage in 414 BC, and this time the target was the lawsuit-happy Athenians.

The playwrights most celebrated work, however, remains *Lysistrata*, written around 411 BC, and the first known public anti-war statement. The G-rated synopsis simply highlights the efforts of women to spread peace and prevent the deaths of their husbands and sons. But where's the real fun in that?

In *Lysistrata*, the women literally conspire to end war by withholding sex until peace reigns, and lo and behold, it works. Talk about a universal truth.

Euripides

In his 74 years, Euripides was one of those rare presences, beloved not only by his audiences and contemporaries, but insightful enough to have his work transcend cultural barriers and influence Roman dramas before trickling into English, German, and even French tradition.

A philosopher and scientist in his spare time, Euripides epitomized the well-rounded intent of the enlightened age in which he lived. Most notably, he captured quite eloquently this cultural shift that began to trade blind faith in divinity for science and critical thinking.

Sophocles

Born in 496 BC, this educated and affluent pillar of the Golden Age burst onto the scene at the tender age of sixteen. His good looks and poise secured him the lead in a celebrated boys choir performance following the victory of Salamis in 480 BC.

His greatest coup came just twelve years later when he unseated Aeschylus as the king of tragedy in competition. Over the next twenty-seven years, Sophocles won first prize almost two dozen times and a slew of second-place nods.

Of course, Euripides upstaged him in 441 BC, but the enlightened Sophocles, who lived to be ninety and to hold two military offices, was undeterred.

He wrote more than one hundred plays, introduced the revolutionary third actor and broke away from the trilogy format.

Homer: Greece's Favorite Son

The legend of Homer, ancient Greek poet and author of the *Iliad* and *Odyssey*, is almost as dramatic as the epic tales he is credited with spinning.

The truth is, no one is really certain if Homer actually existed.

If he did, is one single blind man really responsible for the momentous works that chronicled the history of the Trojan War and, in effect, ancient Greece?

Was he a marketing genius who collaborated with dozens of other wordsmiths, yet somehow walked away with all the credit and the glory?

Or was Homer—blind by all accounts—a majestic creation of an age starved for explanation and identity?

If he did exist, he would have roamed sometime around the eighth century BC, and is believed to be the son of Epikaste and Telemachus. The dialect of his poems indicate that he lived in Ionia, and he was an all-out ham, vying for constant attention as a storyteller and court singer.

Interestingly, there is absolutely no evidence that Homer himself could physically write. The Greek alphabet didn't debut until sometime around the turn of the eighth century. It's a stretch, but it is possible that Homer dictated his masterpieces to scribes, but no one knows for certain.

Historians have also argued for millennia over whether one man could possibly have written both works, citing differing styles and improbable lengths in the age of oral tradition when poetry was memorized and recited.

As far as the lengths are concerned, some experts believe there is enough consistency of style to indicate a single author, but some concede it is likely an ancient editor actually compiled a series of fragmented stanzas into epic form.

As for inconsistencies between the two works, most critics believe it's simply a matter of the author's style maturing. Longinus, an ancient Greek critic, argued that the *Iliad* was composed by Homer the young man, but the *Odyssey* sprang from the inspirations of a seasoned poet.

And as for people believing that ridiculously long stanzas cannot be memorized and recited, try to remember life before calculators, the Internet, and smart phones turned our brains to mush.

Regardless, it is also widely recognized that Hipparchus, a particularly nasty tyrant of Athens, had a hand in tweaking the original material sometime during the eighth century. Hey, if King James can do it, who are we to judge?

Iliad

This epic tale chronicles the sack of Ilion by the Greeks and provides the play-by-play for the Trojan War. Ilion is believed to be the first city in the state of Troy.

Talk about history repeating itself, both sides believed adamantly that they were guided by their gods toward victory, so religious and supernatural nuances dominate the narrative.

Of course, the poem addresses only the final decade of the siege.

Odyssey

This work tracks the ten-year journey of Greek hero Odysseus from Troy following its defeat home to Ithica. With the paterfamilias away, gentlemen callers are swarming his presumed widow, Penelope. Odysseus makes it home, reclaims his wife, and takes care of those pesky suitors, but it's more about the getting there than the actual destination.

Plato

The birth date of Plato is estimated at around 428 and 427 BC, and he was likely born in Athens. Plato was probably educated in grammar, music, and gymnastics by the best teachers of his time.

At age forty, Plato established in Athens one of the earliest known organized schools in Western civilization. The Academy was closed in AD 529, when Justinian I of Byzantium saw it as a threat to Christianity. Many intellectuals studied at the Academy, including Aristotle.

Although philosophers existed before Plato, some scholars call philosophy his invention because of the way in which he approached issues and influenced the world. As a matter of fact, his writing has influenced every era forward, even today. Few thinkers have come close to his understanding and ability. Aristotle, his student, Aquinas, and Kant are counted among those few.

Plato's works have influenced many contemporary thinkers including Albert Einstein, Friedrich Nietzsche, Karl Popper, and Leo Strauss to name a very few. Some agree with Plato's assertions, while others use his philosophy as a point of argument.

Although some scholars have tried to classify Plato as a historian, the time frame of his depictions are not consistent with known historical events. Therefore, he was probably not intending his dialogues to be used as historical accounts.

The Dialogues

Scholars have attempted for years to determine the order in which Plato wrote his dialogues. Currently, the dialogues are grouped into three periods, with a few considered transitional works.

Early Dialogues

Called the Socratic dialogues, these are considered indirect teachings. Most of them employ Socrates discussing a subject such as friendship, piety, and so forth with another person. Through a series of questions he explains the topic to his opponent. This period also includes several dialogues related to the trial and execution of Socrates. They are:

- *Apology*
- *Crito*

- *Charmides*
- *Laches*
- *Lysis*
- *Euthyphro*
- *Menexenus*
- *Lesser Hippias*
- *Ion*

Transitional dialogues:

- *Gorgias*
- *Protagoras*
- *Meno*

Middle Dialogues

Plato's own views come into the middle dialogues. In these works, he allows Socrates to answer some of his own questions. Some of the topics in this period include immortality, justice, truth, and beauty. They are:

- *Euthydemus*
- *Cratylus*
- *Phaedo*
- *Phaedrus*
- *Symposium*
- *Republic*
- *Theaetetus*
- *Parmenides*

Late Dialogues

These reveal Plato's mature thought on most of the issues he dealt with in his earlier writing. Scholars are still working to decipher these views. Although these later works are difficult and challenging, they are more logical than his earlier works. They are:

- *Sophist*
- *Statesman*
- *Philebus*
- *Timaeus*
- *Critias*
- *Laws*

ARISTOTLE

Born in 384 BC at Stagirus, a Greek colony and seaport on the coast of Thrace, Aristotle travelled to Athens, the intellectual center of the world, when he was seventeen years old. He joined the Academy and studied under Plato, attending his lectures for twenty years. When Plato died, Aristotle moved to Mysia and then on to Mytilene. At Mytilene, Aristotle began tutoring the thirteen-year-old Alexander, later known as Alexander the Great. He eventually set up his own school at the Lyceum in Athens.

Known as the founder of logic, Aristotle practiced what is today called inductive reasoning. He conducted detailed observations and documented his findings. He is said to be the first to classify animals into two groups—a task that could not have been accomplished without inductive reasoning.

Aristotle wrote dialogues for his students and composed many other philosophical treatises. Out of an estimated one hundred fifty works, only thirty survive. His writings touch on a myriad of topics including biology, politics, physics, and mathematics.

When Alexander died, the government in Athens was overthrown, and Aristotle was forced to flee to Chalcis where he died in 322 BC.

That's What He Said: Aristotle

- All virtue is summed up in dealing justly.
- Dignity consists not in possessing honors, but in the consciousness that we deserve them.
- Education is the best provision for the journey to old age.
- Happiness depends upon ourselves.
- Pleasure in the job puts perfection in the work.
- Law is mind without reason.

Herodotus

"The most hateful human misfortune is for a wise man to have no influence."

Born in Halicarnassus sometime in the fifth century BC, Herodotus's claim to fame was writing *The Histories,* which chronicled the rise and ultimate defeat of the Persian Empire at Salamis in 479 BC.

Perhaps the first reporter in history, his travels made possible on-the-scene accounts of the Nile, Sicily, and Babylon and earned him the title the Father of History.

Greek historian Herodotus would be quite jealous of the technological advances the Renaissance made possible. It was during this period, you see, that a little thing called the broadside was introduced, allowing eye-witness accounts of daily life—not to mention notes for posterity—to be recorded in written form. Not to disrespect the power of oral tradition, but the broadside, a rudimentary version of the modern-day newspaper, revolutionized the exchange of ideas. Much as the Internet in the late twentieth century compacted world views into idiot-friendly search engines, the broadside erased geographical boundaries—at least for the literate—that had kept the masses ignorant of the world around them for centuries.

Epicurus

Solitude, obviously, has its place, but no philosopher embraced the idea as fully as Epicurus, born in 341 BC.

Epicurus's sole purpose in life was to attain a happy and satiated life in the absence of pain or fear. But he believed firmly this could be accomplished only by living in "seclusion." By this he meant man should avoid politics and the trappings of wealth.

In contrast to Aristotle, Epicurus believed pleasure and pain were no more than measures of good and evil, so he theorized that fearing death was illogical because the absence of life meant the absence of sensation. Or maybe he was just rationalizing the agonizing—and recurring—kidney stones that ultimately led to his death in 270 BC.

"For I have been attacked by a painful inability to urinate, and also dysentery, so violent that nothing can be added to the violence of my sufferings. But the cheerfulness of my mind, which comes from the recollection of all my philosophical contemplation, counterbalances all these afflictions."

Thucydides

Thucydides wrote *The History of the Peloponnesian War,* which details the fifth-century smack-down between Sparta and Athens.

Thucydides's graphic descriptions also depicted the Athenian plague of 430 BC, that snuffed out about one-third of the population.

"Externally the body was not very hot to the touch, nor pale in its appearance, but reddish, livid, and breaking out into small pustules and ulcers. But internally it burned so that the patient could not bear to have on him clothing or linen even of the very lightest description; or indeed to be otherwise than stark naked. What they would have liked best would have been to throw themselves into cold water; as indeed was done by some of the neglected sick, who plunged into the rain tanks in their agonies of unquenchable thirst; though it made no difference whether they drank little or much. Though many lay unburied, birds and beasts would not touch them, or died after tasting them."

Socrates

Born in 469 BC, Socrates laid the foundation for modern Western philosophy and is considered the father of political and moral philosophy.

He also introduced a little concept called pedagogy, the process by which a teacher extracts the proper answer from students by asking the right questions in the right way.

His Socratic Method placed the burden back on the afflicted. Essentially, if you ask enough questions of your own situation, the needed answer will reveal itself.

And given the legacies of some of his star pupils—most notably Plato and Aristotle—the approach carried some water.

Oddly, the majority of what is known about the philosopher's life is recounted in *The Apology* of Plato, as well as the works of Aristophanes and Xenophon. According to Plato's writings, Socrates served in the Athenian army, serving in at least three large-scale battles, and refused payment for his teaching.

His political views on Athens, however, were a bit more heated.

Given that he abhorred absolutely everything political in Athens, it's no surprise he stood trial for corrupting the minds of its youngest citizens. Yet even then, he used the opportunity of his cross-examination to rail against his accusers for ignoring the "welfare of their souls."

Even more reviled were his beliefs that virtue cannot be taught, success is not innate, and moral superiority was left entirely to the gods.

Ultimately sentenced to death, Socrates died in 399 BC from ingesting hemlock when all he had to do was renounce everything he believed to appease those who found his teachings uncomfortable.

Crash Course

Greek Society

- For all of its enlightenment, Greek society was composed of two main classes: free people and slaves. Free men in Athens fell into one of two categories: citizens or metics. Citizens were born with Athenian parents, held all the power, and were required to participate in government following compulsory service in the army.
- Metics were foreign born but had migrated to Athens for economic reasons. Metics paid taxes, and military service was sometimes required, but they could never achieve full citizen status. They could not own homes and were not allowed to speak in court.
- Women took their social and legal status from their husbands and were barred from government participation.
- The word "aristocrat" is derived from *aristoi*, meaning best people, but literally meant wealthy landowners who governed the Greek states for about fifty years beginning in 800 BC.
- An aristocratic ruling class is called an "oligarchy," meaning rule by the few.
- In 500 BC, Cleisthenes, an aristocrat, introduced democracy.
- Aeolic, Doric, and Ionic were the three major dialects in Ancient Greece. Aeolians lived in the Aegean islands. Dorians hailed from the Peloponnesus coast. Ionians originated on the west coast of Asia Minor.

Pop Quiz #3

1) Which king of ancient Greece asked the gods to deliver—and received—a bull from the surf surrounding Crete as a symbol of his worthiness to rule?
a) Leonidas
b) Minos
c) Darius
d) Gracchus

2) According to Greek myth, the Minotaur was a gruesome beast that lived in a labyrinth beneath the castle. The Minotaur was what sort of hybrid?
a) Dragon and bull
b) Goat and man
c) Wild boar and goat
d) Bull and man

3) Xerxes was the leader of which empire bound and determined to conquer the entire world during his reign?
a) Persian
b) Roman
c) Egyptian
d) Mesopotamian

4) Who was the Spartan military leader who faced Xerxes's mighty army valiantly enough that even though all three hundred men perished on the battlefield? The Battle at Thermopylae became the rallying cry necessary for the Athenians and Spartans to unite one year later and defeat the Persians at Mycale.
a) Mardonius
b) Herodotus
c) Leonidas
d) Aristagoras

5) With its sturdy columns and minimalist design, the Parthenon is the classic example of which type of Greek archticture?
   a) Doric
   b) Ionic
   c) Corinthian
   d) None of the above

6) Who was the scholar, gentleman, and military genius who conquered most of the known world and invaded the Persian Empire all by the age of twenty-two?
   a) Marc Antony
   b) Archimedes
   c) Philip of Macedon
   d) Alexander the Great

Answers:

1) b
2) d
3) a
4) c
5) a
6) d

The Roman Empire

The ancient Roman monarchy was toppled in 509 BC.

The new republican government was threatened by neighboring tribes who sought to take advantage of a weakened state. Two hundred years of constant warfare led to Roman control of the Italian Peninsula. Some of the more memorable moments during this rise to power included:

496 BC: Tusculum signs a treaty with Rome after a bloody battle.

471 BC: The Sabines are defeated and assimilated.

415 BC: The cities of Aricia and Lavinium sign treaties with Rome, sealing Rome's ties with the Latins.

396 BC: Rome's closest neighbor, the city of Veii, is sacked after a grueling siege led by Marcus Furius Camillus. This victory doubled the size of Roman territory. The remaining Etruscan city-states could be picked off one by one.

387 BC: Thirty thousand Celtic Gauls, led by King Brennus, marched down the peninsula and burned Rome after routing its forces. The Gauls left the peninsula hastily to defend their homeland soon after. They never returned. The Etruscan city of Caere was awarded legal equality with Roman citizens for helping fight the Gauls. The Romans built a fortified wall around their city hoping to avoid future embarrassment.

381 BC: Tusculum challenges Roman authority. The Romans simply conferred full citizenship upon the Latin city. Peace was restored.

338 BC: The Volsci are destroyed.

The Rise Continues

Through a series of treaties and assimilations, Rome gradually gained control of the Italian Peninsula. They started founding purely Roman colonies. Towns of three hundred families were built at strategic locations. These settlements tripled the city's territory to fifty thousand square miles.

Secure in expansion trend, Rome turned its attention to the Samnites. The Samnites controlled the center of the peninsula, and its territory was twice the size of Rome.

After three wars that spanned thirty years, the Samnites gave up their independence. Italy, with the exception of Greek holdings in the south, was unified under Roman leadership.

The Greek city-state of Tarentum began to feel threatened. It boasted the largest fleet in the country and had a standing army of fifteen thousand men. After a local outbreak of hostilities, Rome sent a garrison and a fleet to deal with the Greeks. Both were destroyed.

Tarentum, fearing Rome's two legions, sent abroad for help. King Pyrrhus of Epirus invaded Italy with an estimated twenty thousand soldiers, three thousand cavalry, and twenty Indian war elephants. After winning two costly victories, King Pyrrhus sued for peace. The Romans refused, and Pyrrhus was forced to withdraw to Sicily in 279 BC.

Three years later Pyrrhus returned to Italy intent on victory. Two years passed without decisive results. Discouraged, Pyrrhus returned to Epirus. The Tarentines had to accept a Roman alliance. Rome now controlled all of Italy.

Sicily became the next target.

Syracuse and Carthage held control of the island. The harbor city of Messina, originally a Greek city, had fallen under the control of Syracuse. Messina had been taken over by Italian mercenaries from Campania. Messina appealed to both Carthage and Rome for help.

Carthage arrived to find that King Hiero II of Syracuse was encamped and ready to drive out the Italian upstarts. Carthage joined forces with Hiero and occupied Messina. Roman forces showed up shortly after and attacked the occupying forces. They took Messina and spread over the countryside claiming control of Carthaginian land and attacking Syracuse. Thus began the First Punic War, lasting from 264 to 241 BC.

Plumb Brilliant

From the shores of Minoan Crete to the mighty Roman Empire, archaeologist have unearthed evidence of plumbing dating as far back as the second millennium BC.

- The legendary King Minos had his own flushing water closet as far back as 1700 BC.
- The Sea Kings of Crete flaunted their opulent baths, hot and cold running water systems, and bejeweled fountains.
  Carthage, Athens, and Jerusalem all boasted water supplies and sewage systems well before their times.
- Yet Rome holds the title of Historical Hygiene Head Honcho for developing elaborate sewage systems, ornate public baths, and massive aqueducts capable of carrying millions of gallons of water daily.
- More impressively, the Romans exported their plumbing prowess to the far-reaches of their territories.
- But don't give them too much credit. It certainly doesn't take a genius to figure out that people are happier—and more productive—when they can bathe and flush freely. Not only did they fail to make that "eureka!" connection between sanitation and improved public health, they literally flushed their future down the toilet.

Down the Drain

Give the Romans credit for trying, but innovation in the absence of common sense ultimately doomed the short-sighted sanitation pioneers.

With a population of more than one million people at its height, Rome relied on a mixture of groundwater and rainwater to serve the masses. This required constructing an intricate series of underground channels to drain swamps for irrigation, but they also considered this water safe for drinking.

Meanwhile, the great Roman baths accommodated thousands of sweaty, stinky souls at a time without filtration or circulation systems. Besides creating this veritable petri dish on a daily basis, it raises the question of exactly where that water was dumped each day and where the contamination spread.

The public restrooms offered a communal bucket of saltwater with a sponge on a stick for personal cleansing after relieving oneself. Is it really necessary to delve any further? We didn't think so, although it is interesting to note that several historians credit this particular practice with the origin of the expression "getting hold of the wrong end of the stick."

To their credit, the Romans did employ public works administrators, called aediles, who were charged with keeping the streets clear of garbage and the rivers clear of trash and debris.

Political Poison

Just as Rome wasn't built in a day, it certainly didn't fall overnight, and some historians argue Roman plumbers played as significant a role in the empire's demise as the corrupt leaders.

It's no secret that lead was a primary ingredient in Rome's complex sewage and plumbing systems, so it doesn't require brilliant powers of deduction to reason that lead poisoning probably played a role in the highly public—and often entertaining—meltdowns of Roman emperors such as Caligula and Nero. One can also argue that it certainly contributed to the general apathy of the masses after a few generations of the gene pool were contaminated.

Mother Nature and invaders took care of the rest. Earthquakes, volcanic eruptions, and epidemics—helped along by rampaging barbarians—plunged the once great empire into the Dark Ages. Filth, famine and brutal violence set the stage for unparalleled plague.

The Nail

Evidence of the first nail dates to 3000 BC, and by the time the Romans flourished its hand-made cousin was all the rage. The hobnail, used to join strips of leather, was a particularly popular version, and its use endures today.

The mechanism of the nail really hasn't changed since the first ships were made seaworthy and hovels became less vulnerable to the elements. Like many of man's most steadfast inventions, the lion's share of "improvements" have come on the production and distribution sides.

The process was revolutionized in 1565 with the introduction of the slitting mill, designed specifically for the mass production of nail-making components, yet blacksmiths and nailers still did the majority of the finishing work until the early twentieth century.

Machine production rapidly overtook handmade versions of the nail as the world exploded in a flurry of industrial activity, but the work of nailers has endured through the past century as renovation projects often require original materials for authentic completion.

Hannibal Rising

247 BC: Rome controlled most of Sicily and had landed troops in North Africa. Carthage removed the commander of the Roman army and appointed Hamilcar Barca to replace him. Hamilcar Barca captured a base in Sicily with a force of ten thousand men and seventy war elephants.

242 BC: A costly stalemate on Sicily and in Carthage had drained both nations' resources. Rome had stopped supply ships from reaching Hamilcar Barcas forces in Sicily.

241 BC: Hamilcar Barca surrendered. Carthage gave up control of Sicily and paid a heavy fine over the next ten years.

236 BC: Hamilcar led an expedition to Spain in order to start new colonies and make up for the losses in the Mediterranean. Spain would also be a convenient place to launch raids against Rome. His son, Hannibal, accompanied him to Spain. Hannibal was taught his father's hatred of Rome.

229 BC: Hamilcar was slain in battle.

221 BC: Hannibal was given control of the colonies in Spain. He wasted no time attacking Rome.

218 BC: Hannibal led as many as one hundred thousand troops, twenty thousand cavalry, and thirty-seven elephants into the Alps. Rome responded by sending two fleets to attack Carthage. One was sent to North Africa and the second was sent to Spain under the command of Publius Cornelius Scipio. Scipio's forces sailed to the mouth of the Rhone in an attempt to intercept Hannibal's forces. They were three days late. This was the beginning of the Second Punic War.

Fifteen days, twenty-four thousand troops, and thirty or so elephants later, Hannibal made it across the Alps. Scipio had sailed back to Italy with part of his army to intercept Hannibal. The Senate recalled the African fleet to defend Rome when news reached them of the crossing.

The two armies met at the Ticino River in November of 218 BC. Scipio's forces were quickly defeated. What was left fled south to join with the returning African forces. The combined army was savagely beaten at the Trebia River. Panic swept through Rome.

217 BC: Hannibal marched steadily south destroying everything in his path. Gaius Flaminius led a fresh Roman force against the Carthaginians at Lake Trasimene. Fifteen thousand Roman soldiers died fighting in a thick fog. Hannibal was unstoppable as he pushed southward. He bypassed Rome in order to subjugate the lands to the south.

216 BC: Two new consuls, Paullus and Varro, raised an army of some one hundred thousand men and sought battle with Hannibal. The Roman army engaged a force of fifty thousand Carthaginians at Cannae. They were defeated. A quarter of the Roman army was slaughtered.

Rome entered its darkest hour.

Rome Emerges Victorious

Carthage sent a fleet to Greece in order to aid King Philip V in driving the Romans out. The First Macedonian War had begun. Rome was faced with a two-front war.

In 211 BC, Rome recaptured part of Sicily following a two-year siege of Syracuse. The Greek mathematician Archimedes died when the city fell in 212. Publius and Gnaeus, members of the Scipio family, died fighting Hasdrubal in Spain.

Hannibal's brother was unable to push the Romans out of Spain.

Two years later, Publius's son, Scipio, marched to Spain and defeated Hasdrubal's forces. Hasdrubal fled across the Alps in his brother's footsteps. He was intercepted and wiped out by a Roman army. The Romans kept his head, and later threw it into Hannibal's camp. Spain became a Roman territory.

By 207 BC, the Macedonian War began to wane.

The majority of Rome's troops were called home to defend the city and mount a possible expedition into North Africa led by Scipio.

In 205 BC, King Philip V signed the Peace of Phoenice. Macedonian peace allowed Scipio to assemble an invasion force. He was hoping to draw Hannibal out of Italy.

The following year he landed in North Africa with a combined force of Romans and North African mercenaries. Panic-stricken Carthage sent for Hannibal. A bitter Hannibal returned to a country that was no longer his home. He recruited an army of Carthaginians and North African mercenaries, having left most of his army in Italy.

After two years of bloodshed, Scipio and Hannibal met for peace talks at Zama.

Scipio had sent for reinforcements and was waiting for their arrival. These were men whose fathers had died at Cannae fourteen years earlier.

Personal rancor simply would not allow for peace.

Roman forces routed the Carthaginian army at Zama. Hannibal fled to Carthage. He convinced the Senate that victory was impossible. Carthage surrendered to Scipio earning him the title Scipio Africanus.

The Carthaginians were forced to give up their navy. Roman officials towed five hundred ships into the sea and burned them. The Second Punic War had come to an end.

A dispirited Hannibal stayed in Carthage and joined the Senate. He was not well received. Six years later he discovered that his fellow senators were planning to turn him over to Rome as a goodwill gesture. Hannibal boarded a ship and never saw his home again.

Plumbing Points

It's easy to see why plumbing might be considered a marvel of modern ingenuity, what with outhouses disappearing and flushing toilets appointing a king in every castle during the twentieth century.

But plumbing actually dates back at least to ancient Greece. Archaeologists on island of Crete unearthed crude—yet apparently functional—water pipes and forced elimination channels at the palace of Knossos.

Roman sanitation workers were known as plumbers (from the Latin plumbum, meaning lead) and are responsible for crafting a complex water-supply and waste-elimination system throughout the empire, totaling one hundred fifty toilets, thirteen hundred public fountains and about nine hundred baths—some public and some private.

The unparalleled engineering feat created an aqueduct network stretching two hundred sixty miles and delivering an estimated fifty million gallons of water to the empire every day.

When Rome fell to the barbarians, though, maintaining the intricate system wasn't high on the survival priority list, and the world was plunged back into its unsanitary ways.

Toilet Training

The single most important invention responsible for improving public health was the toilet.

But much like the four-year-old bed wetter, the history of sanitation is a story of one step forward, two steps back.

Toilets connected to drains via clay were all the rage in India circa 2500 BC, yet in Europe chamber pot surprises tossed out open windows were the only way to go during the Dark Ages almost four thousand years later.

The Englishman John Harrington is credited with inventing the water closet, the precursor to the modern-day toilet, in 1596, but it took almost two centuries for his insight to hold water with the masses.

Beginning in 1738, a series of innovators improved upon the flushable toilet design. By 1890, the only tweaking that remained was aesthetic.

Of course, it was almost another seventy years before Joseph Cayetty introduced the United States to toilet paper.

Potty Humor

Present day Romans call public toilets vespasiano in honor of Emperor Vespasian, who introduced pay toilets to Rome as a means of raising public revenue. Upon learning the idea didn't sit well with the underclass, Vespasian is said to have held a coin under his nose and declared that "money doesn't stink."

We know when you gotta go, you gotta go, but Emperor Caracalla certainly picked a piss-poor time to get caught with his pants down. The ruler—famous for building the opulent Baths of Caracalla—was ambushed by his own henchmen and murdered while using the facilities.

The Macedonian Wars

The Second Macedonian war was like driving through a small town: Blink and it's over.

In 200 BC, Macedonia and the Seleucid Empire formed an alliance of mutual protection. Philip V wanted muscle to prevent Roman invasion, and Antiochus III wanted a reason to attack Rome.

Rome and the Seleucids were expanding toward one another, separated only by Macedonia. Rome took the offensive and attacked Macedonia.

Within three years, Roman troops, led by Flaminius, routed the Macedonian army at Cynoscephalae. Philip V was forced to surrender his warships, withdraw all troops from Greece, and pay a large fine.

The Greeks were all too happy to sign any anti-Macedonian treaty with Rome.

But peace was a fleeting concept in Rome.

In 196 BC, Antiochus III breezed through Asia and took Thrace. Now he hovered over Greece and sat poised to take on Rome.

By this time, Hannibal had joined the Seleucid war party as chief adviser to the king. He figured the Seleucids were the only nation powerful enough to defeat Rome. Both parties began amassing troops at opposite ends of Greece.

In 191 BC, the two armies collided at Thermopylae. The Seleucid army was driven back losing thousands of soldiers. Antiochus III fled north through Asia Minor, losing most of his holdings in that region as he ran. This was the beginning of the end for Antiochus III.

Roman forces then pushed into Seleucid territory.

Hannibal was given command of a navy, while Antiochus III led the land defense. Hannibal's fleet surrendered off the south coast of Asia Minor. Antiochus III's army suffered a humiliating beat down at Magnesia.

As a parting gift the Romans took all of Antiochus's territory north of the Taurus Mountains and most of his navy. Philip V surrendered his entire navy, all of his border cities, and his son, Demetrius. The kid was held hostage in Rome to ensure that Philip V stayed on his best behavior.

In 187 BC, Antiochus III was slain while attempting to quell a hometown rebellion. His son, Seleucus IV, inherited the throne, and was forced to send *his* eldest son to Rome as a hostage. Hannibal ran away to live out his life in paranoid seclusion. He chose a lovely town on the coast of the Black Sea as his home. He dug seven tunnels from his house that ran in all directions. The original Boy Scout, Hannibal was prepared to run on a moment's notice if the Romans ever came knocking.

But the plan backfired in 182 BC, when a visiting Roman senator recognized Hannibal as a fugitive.

Local authorities quickly sealed all seven tunnels and trapped the disgraced leader in his house. He drank a vial of poison to avoid the shame of capture.

Meanwhile, Macedonia teetered.

King Philip's son, Demetrius, was sent home from Rome. His younger son, Perseus, was no longer next in line for the throne. Anger and jealousy grew in his heart.

Perseus turned his father against Demetrius with a web of lies. Philip succumbed to the deceit and poisoned his eldest son, who died cursing his father's name. Philip V died two years later, and Perseus took the throne.

Drunk with power and totally unqualified, the conniving king decided, unwisely, to take Greece back. For three years he traveled throughout Asia Minor and northern Greece trying to peacefully win cities over to his rule.

Eventually the ruler of Pergamum, King Eumenes, traveled to Rome to lodge a complaint. The assassin that Perseus sent after him failed to kill Eumenes and served only to strengthen his word.

In 171 BC, a Roman force of forty thousand soldiers headed for Macedonia, and so began the third and final Macedonian War. Much like the previous two wars, this one was short and sweet.

Within three years, the Macedonian army was annihilated at Pydna. Perseus was taken back to Rome as a captive, and his country was absorbed into the Roman Empire.

Cusp of Greatness

Trade had resumed with Carthage. North Africa was an excellent source of gold, silver, wine, and figs. An uneasy peace was kept to the mutual advantage of both cities. The treaty resulting from the Second Punic War left Carthage weak and vulnerable.

The Kingdom of Numidia was slowly taking bits and pieces of the Carthaginian territory. As if that wasn't bad enough, Numidia was an ally of Rome, and thereby untouchable by Carthage.

In 157 BC, Rome sent a delegation to North Africa to tell the Numidians to leave Carthage alone. The delegation was led by Marcus Cato, an elderly senator, who despised Carthage.

Apparently, the city-state was too prosperous for his tastes. He felt the citizens were too rich and found evidence of armament that alarmed him.

Cato rushed back to Rome and demanded that Carthage be put down before they became too powerful. His fellow senators brushed him off, dismissing him as a deluded, crotchety old man. The man would not be dissuaded from his belief that Carthage should be wiped off the map.

By 149 BC, the Senate began demanding that Carthage prove its loyalty to Rome. They eventually ordered the Carthaginians to desert their city and relocate ten miles inland from the coast. Scipio Aemilius led the fleet that Rome sent to Carthage.

Meanwhile, Greece was rapidly becoming a political hotbed.

Sparta had lost dominance in the Achaean League and resented being pushed around by neighboring city-states. The Spartans wanted to appeal a league decision directly to Rome, but the league voted that an appeal could be made only by the body as a whole.

Sparta flew off the handle and threatened military action.

In 147 BC, Roman diplomats called a conference in Corinth to mediate the dispute. When they ruled in favor of Sparta, all hell broke loose.

The Corinthians rioted and assaulted Spartans and Romans alike.

The diplomats returned to Rome and wove a tale of a deadly uprising.

Twenty-six thousand troops and thirty-five hundred cavalry sailed for Corinth led by the consul Mummius.

The Achaean League attempted to put up a fight. They soon broke and fled to Corinth.

Mummius set fire to the city and it fell shortly afterwards.

Greece was annexed into the Empire and lost all independence.

In that same year, Scipio and his men captured and burned Carthage.

It took two weeks for Carthage to burn. After the flames had died, the Romans ceremoniously plowed the fields with salt ensuring that nothing would ever grow there. The area once ruled by Carthage was now a Roman province.

Latin

By the second century BC, Latin culture and language were spreading throughout the empire. Many small kingdoms adopted Latin as their official language while retaining cultural independence. The adoption of Latin as a commonly observed official language gave the empire a greater sense of unity. Citizenship was readily bestowed on any kingdom willing to adopt the language, but that little perk created its own red tape. Voting laws had to be passed to keep the immigrants in Rome from controlling the Senate.

Crash Course

Rebellion Remorse

Rome had conquered all of the ancient powers within easy reach. Egypt, Parthia, and the remnants of the Seleucid Empire were all that remained.

Troubles at home prevented the start of new campaigns.

As the empire had grown, thousands of slaves were introduced to the population. The slaves had zero rights and were treated brutally. Once freed, they gained full citizenship and rights.

The freed slaves rapidly assimilated to Roman society since they came from the same stock as their masters. Slaves who were savagely abused realized how fragile the barrier separating them from their masters was.

So what followed should not have been shocking:

In 136 BC, Sicilian slaves organized a revolt.

Four hundred slaves banded together in the city of Enna. They murdered a notoriously cruel slave owner and his entire family with the exception of his only daughter.

A slave named Eunus was appointed their leader. He was a charismatic man rumored to possess magical powers.

In three days time, Ennus had armed six thousand men. He recruited so many slaves that he was able to defeat Roman generals. His ranks rapidly grew to more than ten thousand slaves.

Slave leaders from other locations joined his ranks and became his generals.

It is estimated that seventy thousand to two hundred thousand slaves joined the revolt, which became known as the First Servile War. Sympathetic revolts flared up in Rome and Greece.

But the rebellion was short lived.

In 139 BC, Consul Publius Rutilias crushed the rebellion on Sicily, and trapped the rebellion's leaders in the town of Tauromenium. When conditions in the town became unbearable, Publius refused to end the siege.

DARK DAYS

As supplies vanished the inhabitants began to eat one another. They started out with the children and eventually ate the women as well. The slaves that did surrender were thrown off a cliff without the benefit of being deceased. Eunus was captured and thrown in a prison where Diodorus reported that "his flesh disintegrated into a mass of lice."

Rome had entered into a period of social upheaval.

Hundreds of thousands of soldiers were returning home to rundown farms, crumbling houses, and debt. Many suffered from serious injuries and none had been well paid for their military service.

The merchant classes became rich profiting from newly opened trade routes. Newly taxed lands proffered higher salaries for the public officials. The government had no time to provide for the fair distribution of land conquered by fast moving armies.

The policy was simply to let anyone who worked the land have a share of the annual produce. The rich pounced on huge tracts of unclaimed land, often using bribery and force to steal small farmsteads.

The labor demands to work the huge tracts of land were enormous. Wealthy land owners became increasingly dependent on slave labor because hired freemen were subject to compulsory military service.

The citizens of Rome spent years abroad fighting wars of conquest. They returned home to find no jobs, no land to work, and no voice in an increasingly corrupt government. The rich became more powerful, and the slave population exploded while the average citizen was left with nothing but an empty belly and a sense of abandonment.

A Republic Vanishes

The displaced masses found a voice in Tiberius Sempronius Gracchus.

He had fought under Scipio Aemilius at Carthage and won the honor of being the first man over the enemy's wall.

During his military service abroad, Gracchus witnessed small farmers and herders thrown off their land by the rich. He returned to Rome intent on reforming the system.

Unfortunately, the upper crust resented this encroachment on their monopoly. They convinced his fellow consuls to veto any bills he tried to pass. Gracchus believed that they had been bribed and took matters into his own hands.

He organized his supporters and shut down many public services in an attempt to push the bill to a popular vote. Breaking the law turned many of the cities politicians against him. Using his popularity with the people to get his way was setting a dangerous precedent.

Bypassing the authority of the tribunes to pass his bill caused fear and worry among the community. Even his supporters worried that he had gone too far.

In 132 BC, Gracchus sought reelection. The Senate, gathered for the election, was taut with tension as wild rumors circulated. And then the fighting began.

Senators and supporters armed themselves with clubs and the legs of benches. They beat Gracchus to death along with three hundred of his followers. The bodies were unceremoniously dumped into the Tiber River.

Gracchus's law breaking and the murders that followed were seen as the death blow of the republic. The structure of law that held the republic together had been torn apart.

Eight years later his brother, Gaius Gracchus, ran for office and attempted to pass reforming legislation. When riots broke out this time, the participants were prepared. Swords replaced clubs and three thousand corpses clogged the Tiber.

The politicians and commoners alike understood that no amount of new laws could solve the class struggles of Rome. The law was too easily subverted by bribery and violent action spurred on by charismatic leaders.

Greed, corruption, pride, and moral decay had overcome the Republic.

Delusions of Grandeur

- The Jugurthine War exemplified all that was wrong with Rome as the republic imploded.
- King Masinissa of Numidia had left his throne to his son Micipsa. Micipsa was now growing old and had two sons in line for succession. He also had a nephew, Jugurtha, who he decided should be a military man. Jugurtha was to lead Numidian troops under the command of Scipio Aemilius. Roman officers assured him that their government could put him on his uncle's throne. They told him that in Rome money could buy anything.
- Micipsa died in 118 BC, and Jugurtha went to work.
- His thugs killed one of his cousins, and the other fled the country. He sent ambassadors to Rome, laden with gold and jewels, to buy official recognition of his crown. Adherbal, his cousin, showed up to make his claim.
- Rome gave each of them half the country. Jugurtha declared war on his cousin. He trapped Alherbal in his capital city and tortured him to death.
- The public was outraged. In 111 BC, a consul was sent to Numidia with an army to punish Jugurtha. The new king sent a sizable bribe to the consul, who promptly went home. The next official managed to drag him back to Rome, but Jugurtha bribed a tribune to call the trial off.
- The Senate sent him home. The streets thundered with righteous indignation.
- An honest man, Gaius Marius, was sent to Numidia with an army. He fought well for two years and was elected consul in 107 BC. He continued to fight for three more years. His senior officer, Lucius Cornelius Sulla, aided in the capture of Jugurthga. They took him back to Rome in chains.
- Honesty had bested the corrupt aristocracy.

- Marius was declared Rome's champion. He was elected five years in a row, but this was against the law. When questioned he said, "I'm sorry, but the noise of fighting prevented me from hearing the law."
- Rome's sweetheart was allowed to set an alarming precedent. After six years Marius decided to step down.
- Meanwhile, the subject cities on the peninsula had been asking Rome for years to make them full citizens. They wanted a vote and to share the power of Rome. The Senate had been putting them off, wanting to keep the power centralized.
- Anti-Roman sentiment swept through the Italian cities. They formed an association called Italia. In 91 BC, a Roman officer was killed by an angry mob in Asculum. The Social War had begun.
- The Senate offered citizenship to any city that did not join the revolt. The hostile cities were attacked.
- Marius, now seventy, came out of retirement to lead the campaign. The trappings of old age are ill suited for war, and his role was a brief one.

Sulla and Marius

Lucius Cornelius Sulla took charge of the campaigns and quickly restored order. The Social War ended in 88 BC. The Italian cities had gained full Roman citizenship, and Sulla was elected consul.

Around this time, the king of Pontus, Eupator Dionysius, was conquering territory in Asia Minor. Sulla wanted to lead the legions into Asia Minor and take control of Pontus.

Sulla was preparing some forty thousand troops to lead into Asia Minor when Marius asked the Senate to give him control over the fighting force. Many Romans felt this course of action was insane. Marius was old, bloated, and slow. His pillaging days were over.

Marius would not be swayed by public opinion or reality. He bribed the tribune Sulpicius to support his generalship. Sulpicius gathered an armed mob, called the Anti-Senate and forced the Senate to give Marius what he wanted.

He sent two tribunes to take control of Sulla's army. The army stoned these men to death. Civil war erupted. Marius and his goons set about killing Sulla's friend in Rome.

When word reached Sulla, he summoned the legions and asked them to march on Rome, but invading the city's boundry, the pomerium, was forbidden by the Roman constitution.

The walled inner city of Rome was the sole domain of the Senate. No consul with military authority was to ever march troops within those walls. Technically, Marius had already broken that law, and Sulla felt he must breach the city's walls in order to restore order.

Sulla burst into Rome with torches and burned the houses of his enemies. Marius fled to North Africa, and Sulpicius was captured. Both men were sentenced to death.

Sulla, in an attempt to restore order, had assumed the role of military dictator. He stepped aside and allowed a free election for consul.

Lucius Cinna was elected, and Sulla swore loyalty to both Cinna and the Senate. He then collected the troops and made ready to invade Asia Minor.

Soon after Sulla's departure, Cinna was thrown out of Rome. Cinna raised an army in order to force his way back in. Marius got news of the civil discord and went straight to Rome to join Cinna. He brought with him an impressive force of North African mercenaries.

Meanwhile the remaining consul lost popularity suddenly—one can only assume through the strategic use of bribes—and the Senate invited the two back into Rome. Cinna and Marius marched through Rome's gates at the head of a sizeable force, but it wasn't all fun and games.

Marius had become deranged. His personal bodyguard killed anybody that Marius pointed at. Marius later simplified matters. Anyone who spoke to him and got no reply was killed. Instantly.

Sulla got word of the calamity that had befallen Rome and headed for home. The news of Sulla's eminent return poisoned Marius's mind further. He succumbed to alcohol poisoning and pleurisy in 86 BC.

Sulla did not return to Rome for another three years. During this time many prominent citizens fled the city and joined his forces on the road. Cinna gathered an army and marched to meet Sulla outside of Rome. His own men killed him before he reached Sulla.

There was fighting ahead for Sulla. Marius's son had control of his mercenaries and fought a savage resistance. With the help of two officers, Pompey and Crassus, Sulla was able to breach the walls of Rome. As he addressed the Senate his men butchered several thousand prisoners in the Circus.

In 82 BC, Sulla was made dictator. He began killing his enemies real or imagined. Friends and relatives of Cinna and Marius were murdered or fled the country. Cinna's son-in-law, Julius Caesar, was among the lucky escapees.

Enter Spartacus

When Sulla began killing people to seize their property, Pompey was sent abroad to hunt and kill escaped traitors. But Crassus stuck around Rome and helped Sulla steal property from helpless citizens. He would set fire to a house, buy it at a discount, and summon hidden firemen to douse his new acquisition.

Sulla eventually grew tired of destroying Rome and retired to the country in 80 BC. He took a wife and a male lover and died two years later from cirrhosis of the liver and complications arising from sodomy.

The Roman army was spread thin during the time after Sulla's death. Pompey was fighting in Spain. Another contingent was wrapping up the war against Pontus, and there was an ongoing conflict with pirates in the Mediterranean.

The Italian peninsula was shorthanded. This void in manpower led to a slave revolt.

Gladiatorial combat had been a spectator sport for hundreds of years in Rome. Warriors not killed in battle were taken as slaves. Many were forced to fight in death matches to entertain the public. These slaves were then assigned to training camps where brutality reigned.

In 73 BC, seventy-eight gladiators escaped from a training school in the city of Capua. The escapees looted a butcher shop for weapons and fled to the hills. They killed the troops sent to capture them and took their weapons and armor. The Gladiator War would last for two years.

A Thracian gladiator-slave, Spartacus, was elected as their leader. He proved to be a brilliant strategist.

Some three thousand Roman soldiers drove the gladiators up a mountain and had them trapped between a heavily guarded pass and a cliff. Spartacus had his men weave ladders from vines and rappel down the cliff. Once on the ground, they attacked and wiped out the unsuspecting Roman camp.

Spartacus and his army defeated several Roman forces sent to stop them. Their confidence and numbers grew. It is believed that Spartacus commanded over seventy thousand men.

Tradition holds that Spartacus tried to convince his men to cross the Alps and return to Gaul and Thrace. They decided, instead, to stay in Italy and have some fun.

Rome quickly realized the severity of the revolt as the gladiators went about destroying everything in their path.

The Senate was so alarmed that they sent both consuls out to meet the gladiators in battle. Crassus was appointed to defeat the slaves when both consuls failed.

The first clash resulted in a Roman retreat. Crassus assembled the five hundred foot soldiers who had been in the front of the battle and killed fifty of them by lottery.

This "decimation" was done in front of the entire army as a motivational exercise. It got results. The gladiators were driven to the end of the Italian peninsula.

Spartacus arranged to have pirates ferry his men to Sicily. They took his money and left him trapped on the shores of Rhegium. Crassus built a wall across the narrow peninsula and trapped the army, but Mother Nature intervened, and a snow storm provided enough cover for the army to escape.

A concerned Senate sent Pompey into the fray. He had just returned from Spain with his army and wanted to steal Crassus's glory.

As Crassus was preparing for an assault, the gladiators executed an ill-advised attack and were defeated. Spartacus was deserted on the field and slain.

Pompey's army showed up in time to capture the six thousand slaves who had fled. The slaves were crucified along the road leading from Capau to Rome.

Pompey's Prowess

In 70 BC, Pompey and Crassus were elected as consuls.

They fought constantly and achieved little. The people's loyalty was bought with free grain, and Crassus stopped ripping people off. A new politician named Cicero had even prosecuted a senator for corruption.

It appeared that honesty was making a comeback.

When Mediterranean pirates became a big problem it seemed reasonable to put Pompey in control of the entire navy and one hundred thousand troops. His victory was fast and decisive. Pompey's popularity soared, and his family became one of the most powerful in Rome. Julius Caesar pressed Pompey to agree to marry his daughter. Pompey assented and left immediately on a new campaign. He had been given command of the ongoing conflict with Pontus in the east.

Pompey brought an end to this war in 66 BC and swept down the Mediterranean coast. He took control of Syria and stopped with the capture of Jerusalem. Jerusalem was made a part of the Roman province of Palestine.

He returned to Rome crowned in glory.

That's What He Said: Pompey

- A dead man cannot bite.
- More worship the rising that the setting sun.
- Stop quoting laws, we carry weapons! To the defenders of a besieged city who were crying outrage

Back in Rome

- Meanwhile, Cicero and Caesar had risen to political prominence by 63 BC.
- Cicero became the first consul elected in thirty years whose family had no prior connection to politics.
- Caesar was a financial officer and the high priest of the state religion. He was also in debt from expensive campaigning and needed an out. He pulled some strings and was appointed governor of Hispania, but not quickly enough. As he was boarding the ship his creditors caught him and seized his luggage.
- Crassus insured Caesar's debt and allowed him to go to Spain. Caesar made enough money to pay off his debt and returned to Rome. He talked Crassus and Pompey into bankrolling his campaign for consul in 59 BC. In return he would ensure their control of lawmaking to further their personal agendas.
- The deal was sealed when Caesar let Pompey marry his daughter. The campaign was a success, and the three enjoyed a year of prosperity. When Caesar's term ended he had himself appointed governor of western Gaul.
- Celtic tribes had been pushing into his western frontier and Caesar set out to banish them and began the conquest of the Germanic people. He sent regular reports to Rome to cement his glory at each new victory.
- Of course, the conquest of Germany did not distract from his political ambitions. Caesar continued to buy votes in the Senate and conspire with his partners. In a nutshell:
- It was decided that Crassus and Pompey would buy the 55 BC election for consul and extend Caesar's governorship for five more years. Once the term was up Crassus would be appointed general in the East and gain military glory fighting the Parthians. Pompey would be appointed governor of Spain and profit enormously.
- Caesar landed a force on the shores of Britain as Pompey and Crassus won their election. Two years later Caesar had subjugated the southern portion of the island and returned to Gaul.

- Crassus began his campaign against Parthia the same year. He led a force of thirty thousand foot soldiers and a thousand cavalry towards the Euphrates River. The Parthian army met them outside of the town of Carrhae.
- The Romans could not defend against the Parthian archers. The army had no experience against long-range weapons and was cut down quickly. Crassus regrouped and sent his son, Publius, to lead a charge against the Parthian line.
- Publius and his troops were slaughtered. Crassus and most of his men were killed two days later. The eastern frontier of Rome's empire had been closed. Parthian troops laid siege to Syria and failed only because they lacked experience in this type of warfare.
- Parthia, ruled by King Orodes, now stretched from the Euphrates River to the Chinese border.

Caesar's Fifteen Minutes

One year after the Parthian victory Caesar headed for Rome. He had just put down a major rebellion in Gaul and intended to march victoriously into Rome.

Pompey's relationship with Caesar had become strained. Pompey was envious of Caesar's glory and feared his army. He wasn't the only one.

The Senate feared Caesar would march into Rome and take control of the government. Word was sent that Caesar was not to enter Rome with his army. He offered several compromises to the Senate, but Pompey persuaded them to refuse. Caesar decided to march on Rome and take the city by force.

Panic seized the city as Caesar's army grew closer. Pompey fled to the south to the city of Brundisium, taking part of the Senate with him. He sent his army to Greece to prepare for war. This delay in confronting Caesar gave Pompey time to build a large army and amass a strong navy.

Caesar marched into Rome and assumed control with little resistance. After two years of bloody fighting, Caesar defeated Pompey on the plain of Pharsalus.

Pompey slipped away in the confusion following the battle and headed for Egypt.

Caesar was proclaimed dictator in 48 BC, and named Marc Antony his deputy. Antony took over daily control of the city, and Caesar chased down Pompey.

Egypt was a plum ripe for the falling. It was a large state that had lost its former greatness.

Ptolemy XIII was at war with his sister Cleopatra VII over the throne. His advisers learned that Caesar was coming for Pompey and decided to capture him as a show of good faith. Ptolemy's men met Pompey's ship in the harbor and cut him down as he was disembarking.

Caesar was given Pompey's head as a welcome gift when he arrived in Egypt, but Ptolemy did not receive the reaction he expected.

Caesar was furious as he had only wanted to humiliate Pompey and bring him back to Rome. Deep down—somewhere—they were still buds, and all is fair in love and war, right?

Always the opportunist, though, Caesar used this act of aggression as an excuse to take over Egypt. He ordered Ptolemy and Cleopatra to Alexandria where he would appoint one of them to rule under his direction.

Cleopatra promptly won Caesar's heart, so Ptolemy lost the throne. Ptolemy died fighting Roman troops sent to enforce Caesar's will.

Cleopatra had been crowned and married her younger brother in accordance with Egyptian custom. She didn't let a little thing like marriage prevent her from shacking up with Caesar for several months.

He left a pregnant Cleopatra behind and went on a military tour around the edge of the republic. He destroyed the armies of Pontus and returned to Rome by way of Africa and the Iberian Peninsula. During his travels he had been elected consul four times to keep up a legal pretence of power.

In 46 BC, his supporters and many who feared him decided to throw a victory parade in celebration of his return. Statues of him were erected all over the city, and he was allowed to wear a purple robe in the parade.

He was given the ceremonial title of Imperator.

The parade was fronted by a banner that read "*Veni, vidi, vici*!" or "I came, I saw, I conquered."

Crash Course

Caesar's Fall

Caesar took over sole responsibility for running the government with Rome divided into two camps: one that supported him and one that feared his retaliation.

He had the full support of the people, who saw him as their guardian, and a well-seasoned army to enforce his will. His unfortunate fate unfolded rather quickly, though:

In 44 BC, he was made dictator for life. This was not good enough for Caesar, who aspired to wear a crown.

Marc Antony experimentally crowned him at a religious festival. The crowd showed little enthusiasm, and Caesar pushed the crown away to thunderous applause. The idea of a king was repugnant to the pride of the republican.

Caesar had no son other than Caesarion, the illegitimate one he had with Cleopatra.

Caesar disregarded Caesarion and named his eighteen-year-old nephew, Octavian, his heir.

The Senate did agree to let him wear a crown when he was in Parthia fighting. There was an old legend that said only a king could conquer Parthia.

Even though the coronation was only for show, it made some of the Senators fearful for the fate of the republic. A group of them decided to kill Caesar when he made his next appearance at the Senate on March 15, 44 BC.

Caesar's cousin, Marcus Brutus, was one of the ringleaders.

The senators knew Marc Antony would not betray his general and devised a plan to keep him out of the way.

When Caesar entered the Senate they jumped him from all sides and killed him in a frenzy of violence.

After he had died the senators involved took turns stabbing him to show that they had all shared in the murder. He was stabbed thirty-five times.

Rome After Caesar

The people wanted to believe that Rome was still a place where the people still had power, even though that had not been true for decades. The ambition of power-hungry men could not be stopped by a constitution. This lie of empowerment was the cornerstone of Rome's national identity.

When Marc Antony shoved his way into the Senate and found his friend lying prone on the floor, his first act was to prevent the conspirators from chucking his mentor's body unceremoniously into the Tiber.

The senators began marching through the streets, inviting the citizens to resume their liberty.

Marc Antony disguised himself as a slave and fled the city. Brutus and Cassius made speeches to the effect that Caesar's death had been born of tragic necessity.

They convened the Senate the next day and said that Caesar should be given a ceremonial funeral and be honored as divine.

The public was appeased, and Marc Antony was encouraged to come out of hiding.

Things stayed calm until the reading of Caesar's will. He had left his vast fortune to the citizens of Rome.

Caesar's body was carried through the streets in the funeral procession, and people took notice of his mutilated body.

An angry mob started to form, and Marc Antony fueled their anger with his funeral speech. He had brought an armed guard with him.

Marcus Aemilius Lepidus had been raising an army for his new command in Gaul. Caesar had appointed him, and he was sympathetic to Marc Antony.

Lepidus surrounded Antony with troops as he waved Caesar's bloody toga in front of the mob. The mob went into a frenzy and sought to kill Brutus and Cassius, but the traitors had been smart enough to leave early on in the riot, fleeing to Antium.

Antony took control of the government and gave Lepidus the office of pontifex maximus.

Octavian in the House

- But Antony's hold on the city was precarious at best. Not only did he lack Caesar's charisma and natural leadership abilities, it was feared he would become a tyrant by overcompensating for his shortcomings.
- A bitter campaign to win public approval began.
- Brutus wooed the people from afar by sponsoring lavish public festivals.
- Antony was viewed in an increasingly bad light as the people came to see Brutus as the answer to their troubles. Brutus was on the verge of a triumphant return when Caesar's adopted son and heir returned to Rome.
- Octavian had been abroad on military duty and heard of his uncle's murder. Cicero rallied behind Octavian to take Antony out of power. Brutus was outraged at being knocked out of the race but was powerless without Cicero's voice. He relocated to Athens to live with a friend.
- Antony, as a supporter of Caesar, could not oppose Octavian's claim to leadership. He did perceive Octavian as a threat to his power and treated him with disdain.
- Octavian befriended all of Antony's enemies, and the two became bitter rivals. Antony got wind of an assassination attempt and it was on.
- Both men scoured the country gathering old soldiers and recruiting fresh troops.
- Cicero convinced the Senate to vote Antony an enemy of the people and order the army to run him out of the country.
- Antony retreated to the north with his army.
- Octavian followed close behind with his army and the two consuls in his camp.
- They collided at Modena in 43 BC, and the battle was a costly one.

- Both consuls and most of Octavian's men were killed before Antony's forces broke rank and fled.
- Antony made it over the Alps and recruited Roman soldiers stationed in Gaul.
- Octavian finally caught on and realized that Cicero was using him to run Antony off, so he (Cicero) could restore the Republic.
- Octavian had no interest in giving up the power his uncle had won. He sent envoys to Antony's camp and proposed a meeting.
- The two met at Bologna, deliberated for three days and decided to form a Triumvirate, or three-way partnership of rule.
- Lepidus became their third man and was named pontifex maximus, controlling several legions as governor of Gaul and nearer Spain.
- The empire was carved into three equal portions to be governed by each man. They compiled a list of people they wanted killed during the takeover.
- The trio returned to Rome with a large force and brutally murdered more than three hundred people.
- Octavian got the western part of the empire, while Antony was given the eastern portion. Lepidus got the short end of the stick with Africa, but he was appeased by being granted control of Rome while Antony and Octavian went after Brutus and Cassius.

Crash Course

Bloodbaths and Peace

The beat-down and ensuing chaos was amusing to say the least. Try to keep up:

- Cassius and Brutus divided their army in Macedonia and made a stand.
- Octavian and Antony split their forces and attacked the opposing armies.
- Antony quickly defeated Cassius and went to Octavian's aid.
- Octavian had fallen ill and could not lead his men. Brutus was finished off by Antony.
- Octavian headed for Rome as his sickness worsened.
- Meanwhile, the province of Syria was under attack.
- King Orodes II was amassing an army for invasion.
- The governor of Syria, Antipater, had been poisoned and his son, Herod, was now in charge. He was new to the office and not likely to be much help.
- In 41 BC, Cleopatra came to meet Antony and seduced him away to Alexandria.
- In 40 BC, the Parthians attacked Syria and took Palestine.
- Herod fled to Rome, and the Parthians captured and mutilated the high preist, Hyrcanus.
- Having been Herod's second-in-command, Hyrcanus could not remain a priest after having both his ears cut off. Jewish law would not allow priests to be disfigured.
- King Orodes II was murdered by his son, Phraates IV, shortly after this victory.
- The bloodthirsty Phraates also killed his brothers and eldest son in an effort to eliminate rivals.

- Antony pulled out of Cleopatra—er, Egypt—and returned to Rome to discuss strategy with a newly recovered Octavian.
- Antony marched east with a fresh army and Herod in tow.
- He drove the Parthians out of Palestine in 37 BC and installed Herod as the secular king of the Jews.
- Lepidus decided he was tired of being the weak link and took Sicily by way of expanding his territory and power.
- Octavian landed on Sicily and talked his troops into avoiding civil war and deserting Lepidus.
- Lepidus surrendered to Octavian, who took his army, his provinces, and his title. He was forced to live under house arrest for the rest of his life.
- Octavian and Antony now shared the empire, but not on equal footing.
- Antony's position grew weaker as his campaign against Parthia fell apart. He went on the offensive after reclaiming Syria and met with disaster.
- Antony was forced out of Media losing twenty thousand infantry and four thousand cavalry.
- In 34 BC, Antony gave up and returned to Cleopatra's side in Egypt.
- Octavian used this lustful desertion as an excuse to have Antony declared an enemy of the people, but to do so he would have to win over Antony's supporters in the Senate.
- In 32 BC, Octavian read Antony's will aloud to the Senate. When they realized that he intended to leave his wealth to Cleopatra and their children, the Senate declared war on Antony.
- Antony quickly assembled an army of a hundred thousand foot soldiers and a navy of five hundred warships at Ephesus. He also recruited several allies including King Herod.
- Octavian sailed toward Egypt with a sizeable force. After several close battles, the two navies met off the northern coast of Greece.

- After losing three hundred ships, Antony and Cleopatra sailed back to Egypt. Most of their troops deserted to Octavian's army. Octavian decided to wait out the winter and go after Antony to remove any future threat from Egypt.
- Antony ran himself through with a sword when he heard of Octavian's plan to return. Cleopatra poisoned herself soon after. (Note the conflicting versions of this part of the tale when reading about Egypt.)
- Octavian had their son put to death to prevent any future retaliation. It was now 30 BC, and Octavian had control of the Roman Empire.
- Octavian returned to Rome triumphant. He threw a victory parade and gave money away to the people. He ordered the doors to the Temple of Janus closed to signify a new peace.
- The people rejoiced that the wars were over, but Octavian had to allow the Senate to remain intact in order to keep the peace at home.
- Likewise, the Senate had to enforce its will from time to time to prevent Octavian from seeming like a monarch.

THE FIRST CITIZEN

The power given Octavian by popular mandate was no longer needed now that he had restored peace. The Senate returned the favor by allowing him to remain consul and giving him direct control of the armies in the outlying provinces.

He was also allowed a personal army to act as his bodyguard. The Praetorian Guard was his private army that would be kept near at hand. He kept the title imperator and took the name Augustus.

Augustus meant he was above everyone and everything, including the laws of the republic.

In 23 BC, he declined to run for consul. He had contracted an illness and felt that not allowing other men to run for office might harm the illusion that the republic was still ruled by the people.

The Senate had made him proconsul for life. He could pass any law he wanted and direct governmental policy. He also had a standing army in the capital to enforce his will.

He was royalty in everything but name. He was the First Citizen.

In 20 BC, Augustus made peace with Phraates IV, king of Parthia. The gesture was quite important for Rome's economy. Peace meant trade routes to India and China were now accessible.

Antony's defeat was an embarrassment for the republic, though.

Parthia had taken prisoners of war and had captured Roman standards. The republic needed to get them back. Phraates gave the men and standards back in return for seemingly little.

The only thing known for certain is that he got a slave girl. He did give all four of his sons as hostages to Rome. This may have been to his advantage. Patricide was an accepted custom among Parthian royalty. Rome could now teach the Parthian princes how to be Roman.

The illusion of a functioning government was crumbling quickly.

Crash Course

Topsy-Turvy

- Senators were coming to vote later and later. They felt they were wasting their time passing impotent laws. Augustus needed the forms of government in place to keep the people happy, and in 17 BC he started fining tardy senators.
- Lepidus died in that same year, and Augustus assumed the title of pontifex maximus. He was in charge of political affairs and head of the state religion. His power grew considerably and a precedent was set. The Senate became completely irrelevant.
- Augustus passed several laws to streamline the legislative process. The appearance of government remained intact, while he assumed total control of the republic. It was time to find an heir and start a dynasty.
- Augustus considered letting his son-in-law be his successor, but his daughter gave him no heir. After burying two husbands, Julia was forced to marry Augustus's stepson, Tiberius.
- Tiberius was cold hearted and had no social graces. It was hoped that he would give Julia a son who would become the heir. Cold-hearted bastards often have trouble getting laid, and Tiberious was no exception.
- Herod the Great died in 4 BC, and Augustus split Palestine into three states each ruled by one of Herod's sons.
- Phraates IV's slave girl gave him a son who grew up and murdered him.
- Phraates V was highly unpopular in Parthia. It probably had something to do with his queen and co-ruler, his mother.
- The happy couple were slain after six years on the throne.
- One of Phraates IV's romanized sons took the throne next. Vonones I was disliked for his Western lifestyle by his court.

- He was deposed four years later by Artabanus II. Parthia stayed at peace with Rome, tentatively.
- Augustus still had not found a suitable heir by AD 4.
- He formally adopted Tiberius as his ward. Hereditary rule remained an impossibility. so Augustus gave Tiberius control of the Roman army. He may as well have given him a crown.
- The Senate made Tiberius proconsul and priceps alongside Augustus in AD 13.
- Augustus died of an illness in AD 14.
- Tiberius did not have the personality to lead Rome. He appointed his nephew, Germanicus, as his heir.
- Germanicus was made governor of Syria. He died soon after his arrival and was survived by his wife and young son, Caligula.
- Tiberius named his son, Drusus, as his heir. Drusus died in AD 23. Tiberius lost heart and left Rome never to return.

Shenanigans

The Senate was less than happy. They had given up their power, so a single presence could prevent civil war and revolt.

Tiberius, however, was more concerned with fulfilling his twisted sexual desires than governing the empire.

The Senate was running the city, and civil war was in the air. The commander of the Praetorian Guard, Lucius Aelius Sejanus, was looking to seize power as soon as Tiberius was dead. Tiberius learned that Sejanus was conspiring to poison him.

In AD 31, he had his nemesis sentenced to death. He then went on a rampage and killed hundreds of citizens who may have been involved with Sejanus. He ordered the deaths of his own children and the son of Germanicus.

While Tiberius was cleansing Rome, a wandering prophet was stirring trouble in Jerusalem.

Jesus had offended a large and powerful group of priests. They needed Roman authority to silence him. They appealed to vassal king, Herod Antipas. He feared drawing attention from Rome and turned Jesus over to the Roman procurator who had replaced his brother. Pontius Pilate, fearing Tiberius, did not want to be responsible for anything that undermined Rome's power. He agreed to execute Jesus and ordered him crucified, the standard punishment for revolutionaries.

He put a group of Samaritans to death in AD 36 for similar reasons. His actions caused much unrest among the Palestinians. Pilate was removed from office by his superiors and returned to Rome in disgrace.

In AD 37, Tiberius died of a lingering illness. Caligula, young son of Germanicus, was to be his heir.

Caligula had not been made joint proconsul or been given any title prior to Tiberius's death. The Senate gave him the title of princeps, made him the pontifex maximus, and gave him control of the army.

Caligula began his rule with a reasonable tone. He pardoned all prisoners, invited exiles back to the city, and made tax reforms. Things changed.

He murdered his cousin, his grandmother, and his father-in-law.

Caligula slept with other men's wives, sought male and female prostitutes, and slept with all three of his sisters. He had a Senator torn to pieces and paraded through the streets. He fired the consuls and stipped the Senate of its power in AD 39.

Rome was now ruled by an autocracy. The republic had fallen. Caligula gave wealth and title to those who stayed on his good side. Others, not so fortunate, were tortured and killed. Everyone lived in fear of what he would do next.

Caligula declared himself divine in AD 40 and issued gold statues of himself to be worshipped. The Praetorian Guard killed him a short while later.

Claudius Conquers Britian

The Senate wanted to abolish the office of princeps and take back control of the republic.

Caligula's uncle, Claudius, wanted the power of state and bribed the Praetorian Guard to ensure that he got it. The guard had become a powerful voice in Roman politics and stood to lose its power if the Senate regained control.

Claudius took power in short order and paid off the guard. He had Caligula's murderers executed and issued a series of pardons. His mercy lasted less than a year.

From AD 41 to 42 he executed countless senators and citizens. Anyone he perceived as a threat was destroyed.

He did achieve the full conquest of Britain in the process, though.

Roman legions had been helping small kingdoms defend against a local king whose power was growing. King Caratacus had begun to threaten Roman control of the channel.

Insanity Reigns

Claudius sent four legions and overwhelmed the British forces. Rome now had full control of Britain.

Meanwhile, his wife defiantly married her lover. This could only be interpreted as a play for the throne, and Claudius had them killed. He married his niece, Agrippina, and adopted her son whom he gave the family name of Nero.

He named Nero his heir in AD 51. Agrippina started plotting his death immediately and poisoned Claudius in AD 54.

Nero was made princeps at age sixteen. He, of course, bribed the Praetorian Guard.

His lack of experience and youth made the whole thing smack of monarchy.

Nero did promise to return some of the Senate's powers in his first speech. He even kept the "purging" to a minimum. The first six or so years of his reign were benign.

Nero made the rapid transition from overindulgence to insanity soon after his twentieth birthday. He had his mother and wife killed. He stole his good friend's wife. Taxes were raised to fund his debauchery, and he held countless treason trials.

In AD 64 a fire destroyed a fourth of Rome, and severely damaged almost the entire other three-fourths. It was rumored that Nero ordered the fire. This rumor would haunt him.

A group of senators planned to assassinate Nero in AD 65. The plot was discovered, and they were executed.

Nero's paranoia worsened. Of course, if they really are out to get you…

He began persecuting Christians at this point. He felt that they were to blame for the fire.

In AD 66, Nero appeared to give up the border city of Armenia to Parthia, by crowning a Parthian prince as king of Armenia. In actuality , he was fulfilling a treaty obligation and establishing Armenia as a "clinet kingdom," but the move was widely misinterpreted.

Rome was embarrassed when four thousand Parthian troops came to witness Nero handing the crown of Armenia over.

Musical Chairs

The next three years were a rather bumpy ride:

Nero's behavior had deteriorated. He kicked his pregnant wife to death. He then ordered the castration of a young boy, who resembled his dead wife, so he could marry him in a public ceremony.

The captain of the Praetorian Guard offered to make Galba, governor of Hispania Tarraconensis, princeps and supreme ruler of Rome. The man had plenty of support.

Nero attempted to flee but was cornered outside of Rome and forced to commit suicide.

Galba was installed as the leader of the empire.

The princeps derived their power from the armies at their command. The rulers relied on the support of the Praetorian Guard. These men controlled the state.

Galba refused to pay the Praetorian Guard for their services.

They slew him seven months later in the Senate and made Otho the supreme ruler of Rome. Galba's body was thrown in the road. His head was stuck on a pole.

As Otho was being sworn in, the army stationed on the Rhine announced that they wanted Vitellius declared princeps. He commanded all of the German forces.

They marched on Italy and scattered Otho's small army. Otho committed suicide the next day to spare Rome a civil war.

Vitellius marched in and assumed control. He abolished the Praetorian Guard and replaced them with his own men. The rest of the army resented the preferential treatment given the German legions.

They decided to put Vespasian, govenor of Syria, in power. Vespasian was in Syria dealing with a revolt.

In AD 66, the Zealots had declared war on Roman soldiers in Jerusalem. The Zealots managed to defeat the local governor's army and take control of the city. In 67, Vespasian marched to Jerusalem to clean up the mess. His forces quickly drove the rebels into Jerusalem and laid siege to the city.

Back on the ranch, Vitellius dove into excess in Rome as his army prepared to defend the capital from Vespasian's supporters. The initial fighting took place at Cremona. Vespasian's troops claimed victory and went on a four-day rampage. The fires reached the outskirts of Rome. The capital and the Temple of Jupiter were engulfed in flames as fighting broke out in Rome.

Vitellius was slain in 69 and his body thrown in the Tiber.

Hadrian the Boring

Hadrian's biggest war was the result of poor judgment.

He decided to build a new capital on the ruins of Jerusalem, complete with a temple of Jupiter on the site of the burned Second Temple.

The Jewish uprising was speedy and violent. Hadrian sent his best generals to put down the rebellion. They wiped out individual guerrilla groups across the country. Fifty fortified towns, and 985 villages were completely destroyed. The battles killed 580,000 men, and countless others died of famine, disease, and fire.

Judea was reduced to ashes.

Hadrian made no attempt to conquer Parthia or extend the empire. He built a wall across Britain to mark the stopping point of the empire.

Hadrian's Wall took ten years to build and cut the island in two. It stood twenty feet high and stretched from the Irish Sea to the North Sea.

Tangled Web

The Senate quickly made Vespasian princeps before his supporters burned anything else. Vespasian assumed control of the empire without setting foot in Rome.

It was obvious that a group of elite generals was calling the shots. They put men in power and removed them from office at their whim. The republican ideal had given way to brute force.

Vespasian broke the rebel Jewish army in AD 70 and went to Rome. He understood the importance of military control and reorganized the command structure of local troops. Once the loyalty of the troops had been assured he settled into a ten-year reign.

He lowered taxes and held no treason trials. The last Jewish stronghold, Masada, fell in AD 73, and Palestine was absorbed into Syria.

Vespasian died of the flu in AD 79. The Senate confirmed his son Titus as his heir.

Titus assumed office in the level-headed manner of his father. Then disaster struck. Mount Vesuvius erupted in August of AD 79. Titus mobilized a relief effort and visited the ruined city twice. During his second tour of Pompeii, a fire consumed much of Rome. An epidemic swept through the tightly packed refugees in the city and claimed countless lives. Titus died of a fever in AD 81. His three-year reign had been a string of disasters.

The Praetorian Guard chose his brother Domitian to be princeps. Domitian took over the government. He assumed the title dominus et dues (Lord and God).

Domitian did not use his godhood to break the law, and there was no public outrage. His strict and harsh enforcement of the law made for an uneasy atmosphere. Informants were rewarded, while lawbreakers were persecuted.

Tired of living in fear, his own family had him killed. His wife, niece, chamberlain, and several Praetorian Guards, stabbed him to death in his bed. The Senate proclaimed a consul, Nerva, princeps soon after.

Crash Course

Trajan's Legacy

The people were pleased by Domitian's death, but not the army.

In AD 97 the Praetorian Guard locked Nerva in his bed chambers and killed the chamberlain responsible for Domitian's safety.

Nerva quickly named Trajan as his heir. Trajan was a general stationed near the Rhine River and popular with the military. Nerva died of fever soon after, and Trajan assumed leadership.

Trajan is celebrated as a great leader.

He repaired roads and sewers, built libraries and harbors, and personally led Roman legions to victory.

By 106, he had added the Sinai and the lands north of the Danube to the empire.

Trajan was a fair and respectful administrator. The Senate received the best treatment they had seen in decades. The empire reached its greatest size under Trajan's rule.

In 113, he turned his attention to Parthia.

Trajan marched his troops into Armenia and then across the Euphrates River. Following retreating Parthians, he took Babylon and finally the Parthian capital, Ctesiphon. He remained in Mesopotamia until 117 fighting a stubborn resistance.

At the same time, the Jews had decided to start a rebellion. They wanted God's Promised Land back.

As the situation grew serious Trajan allowed the non-Jewish inhabitants of the region to slaughter their neighbors. This decree quieted things down temporarily.

Trajan died of a stroke in 117 while returning from Parthia. His legal ward, Hadrian, was appointed heir quickly to avoid civil war. He bought the support of the guard and entered a twenty-one year reign of mediocrity.

Marcus Aurelius

The empire was now a unified country. Client kingdoms no longer existed. You were either a full Roman citizen or an enemy.

In 138, Hadrian adopted Antoninus Pius as his heir. Pius ruled for twenty-three uneventful years. He adopted two heirs. Marcus Aurelius, his nephew, and a younger boy named Lucius Verus.

Marcus Aurelius was made emperor when Pius died in 161. Marcus disliked politics, and the Senate pushed the office on him.

He turned around and made his brother, Verus, co-emperor. The two faced war with Parthia, who had invaded Syria.

In 162, Verus led an army into Syria and drove the Parthians out. He took Armenia and captured the Parthian capital, Ctesiphon. Verus returned victoriously to Rome in 166, bringing a plague with him.

The plague swept through Rome for three years. At its height, two thousand people died every day. Body disposal was a nightmare, and Marcus outlawed the digging of graves in Rome. The bodies were removed to the surrounding countryside.

Rome's weakened state encouraged the tribes along the Danube to attack border outposts. Both emperors marched out to push the tribes back. They arrived to find the situation under control and headed for Rome.

Verus fell ill on the way home and died before he reached Rome. Marcus buried his brother in Rome and returned to the Danube to fight the invading tribes.

He spent the remainder of his reign fighting the widespread encroachment of the Germanic tribes. Marcus Aurelius died of chicken pox in AD 180. His son Commodus became emperor.

Commodus

- Full name: Lucius Aurelius Commodus
- Commodus took power when he was nineteen. He skipped the usual niceties and went directly to insane.
- He had a harem of three hundred women and three hundred boys.
- He murdered one of his sisters and forced one to sleep with him.
- One of his sisters conspired against him.
- The man liked to participate in gladiatorial games.
- He compared himself to Hercules and ordered statues to be made with this likeness.
- He was a skilled archer.
- He held the Plebian Games and participated in many of the events, often winning them.
- He liked to run around in women's clothes, draped in a lion's skin, and club random citizens.
- His popularity plummeted, and he was poisoned in 192.
- His death brought an end to the Nervan-Antonian dynasty.

CARACALLA

- Four different men tried to get the support of Praetorian Guard.
- In 193, Septimus Severus won the prize and marched his army toward Rome. The Senate made him emperor before he got to Rome.
- Upon his arrival he ran off the part of the guard that did not support him. The rest of his career was spent securing the borders of the empire.
- He appointed his son, Caracalla, as his heir in 198. Caracalla soon proved that he was not the man for the job. He killed his father-in-law, threatened to kill his wife, and tried to murder his father.
- Severus made his younger son, Geta, co-heir in 209.
- Severus died two years later, and his sons were forced to rule together.
- Caracalla had Geta killed and his body burned. He then spent an enormous amount of money winning the Praetorian Guard to his side. Having secured his power, he went on a killing spree. Anyone suspected of supporting Geta was cut down.
- By 212, Parthia was embroiled in civil war.
- King Artabanus V had been forced out of the capital by a relative claiming the throne. He was desperately fighting to retain his position.
- Caracalla saw weakness and pounced on the chance to make Parthia a vassal of Rome. King Artabanus V refused to deal with Caracalla, who promptly invaded Parthia in 216. He fought until winter and made camp to wait for spring. Before hostilities resumed in 217, Caracalla's bodyguard killed him while he was squatting in the woods.
- It should be noted that another account of Caracalla's death has him murdered by his own men while relieving himself in the infamous bathhouses bearing his name. Either way, he was obviously caught with his pants down.

CRASH COURSE

DEATH AND DESTRUCTION

- In Caracalla's absence, the eastern legions appointed their general, Macrinus, emperor, and he led them against Artabanus V. The Romans were forced to retreat, and Macrinus paid off the Parthians rather than risk another assault.
- Caracalla's first cousin, Elagabalus was made emperor, but like many before him, he went crazy.
- He was assassinated by the Praetorian Guard in 218, and his body was thrown in the Tiber only after being terribly desecrated.
- In the same year, Artabanus V won his capital back. Two years later he was killed in battle against the Persian prince, Ardashir. The Parthian empire collapsed.
- Persia had gained control of the region. The new Persian king left his son, Shapur, a strong, organized empire. He marched into Syria in 241 and was repulsed.
- Rome was under considerable strain at this time.
- The Goths, a Scandinavian people, had overrun Europe and were streaming into the northern part of the empire. They have been grouped into two separate political entities. The Ostrogoths held the east and the Visigoths held the west.
- Military history was made.
- In 249, the Visigoths crossed the Danube and laid waste to the country. Emperor Philip had stopped paying them their tribute.
- The army deposed him and installed Decius on the throne.
- He died in battle in 251. He was the first emperor to die in battle.
- Shapur I started his second assault on Syria in 252.
- Rome could not man a two-front war. The drain of men and supplies eroded at the army's strength.

- The eastern front buckled, and Syria was lost to the Persians.
- Shapur sacked Antioch in 253.
- Valerian was made emperor in the same year. He took control of the eastern army and won much of Syria back.
- His plague-ridden army was forced to retreat in 260, and Shapur I took him prisoner. He was degraded and paraded around like a slave.
- The barbarians in the north took heart and overran the northern arm of the empire.
- Gaul declared itself an independent kingdom,
- The Germanic Alemanni tribe had invaded the Italian peninsula, and the Franks rampaged through Spain.
- Valerian remained a Persian slave, and his son Gallienus had control of the empire. Gallienus was slain in 268 by an insubordinate field commander.
- Valerian was slain by his captors. They took his skin as a trophy and displayed it in a temple.
- The Roman Empire was teetering on the brink of destruction.
- The Emperor Aurelian launched a series of campaigns that reclaimed much of the lost territory.
- He built the Aurelian Walls around Rome and was slain five years into his reign.
- Over the next nine years six men were made emperor and killed.

The Empire Falls

Diocletian took the throne by force and took steps to secure the future of Rome.

He realized quickly that one man could never effectively rule so large an empire. The soldiers were too far removed from the capital and, therefore, loyal to their commanders. He declared an officer, Maximian, to be co-emperor and divided the empire in two. Each half had an emperor who would remain with his respective army.

Diocletian declared in 293 that each man would have an appointed heir. Constantius and Galerius were forced to marry the emperors' daughters to seal the arrangement. Diocletian stepped down from power in 305 and forced Maximian to do the same.

Constantius inherited Gaul, Italy, and Africa. Galerius took command of the east. Constantius died in 306 and the system fell apart.

The western army wanted Constantius's son, Constantine, to inherit the throne. Galerius insisted that Severus, the appointed heir, was to be emperor. Maximian came out of retirement and marched against Severus with Constantine's help. Maximian's son, Maxentius and Constantius's son, Constantine set their sights on the throne.

Civil war tore the empire apart.

Maximian commited suicide when it became apparent that he would never reclaim his throne. Maxentius seized power in Rome, and Constantine led an army just north of the capital in 312.

Constantine had a vision before the battle, however, and converted to Christianity. He destroyed Maxentius's plague-ridden army and took Rome. Christianity unified the empire in a way that no ruler or idealized form of government could do.

The old Rome was gone.

Ungodly Interesting

Quetzalcoatl was the Aztec spirit of the winds, depicted most commonly as a feathered serpent. Tradition holds that he was the child of the earth and the sun.

The original Father Time, Itzamna was the creator-god of the Mayans and was typically portrayed as wrinkled and toothless, and he is often credited with inventing the calendar.

Chac was the Mayan agricultural god, most often depicted as the weeping warrior.

Chacmool was the attendant god who held the bowl to catch vital organs from human sacrifices to the Aztec gods. Sounds gross, but since, as a people, they believed only sacrificed human hearts and blood could prevent the death of the universe, it was kind of an important job.

In Greek mythology, Jason, whose famous quest was the Golden Fleece, was the son of King Aeson

Nox was the Roman god of night, and Cura is credited with the creation of man from clay.

In Norse mythology, Hel is the goddess of the underworld, but Odin is the god of gods.

Turn of Phrase

The Romans certainly had a way with words, so much so that several of their everyday practices have wiggled their way into the modern conversation. Did you know:

The term "dog days" actually refers to the stars and not the animal. During Roman times it was believed that Sirius, the Dog Star, lent its heat to the sun for an almost six-week period spanning July 3 to August 11. The almost unbearably hot temperatures were referred to as *des caniculres,* or "days of the dog."

Despite their brutal reputation, wrestling matches in Ancient Rome weren't exactly no holds barred. The single rule during matches was "No eye gouging," and poking someone's eye out was the only way to get bounced from competition. And that is where we get, "It's all fun and games until someone loses an eye."

Rome

Tradition holds that the first engineer known to have constructed a bridge across the Tiber River in ancient Rome was called Pontifex, meaning "bridge builder." As time progressed, the title shifted from the literal to the figurative, and a pontifex became the accepted moniker for any person with the ability to "connect" people. The symbolism became so powerful that high priests—Julius Caesar among them—eventually adopted the title pontifex maximus. The title eventually passed from Roman rulers to leaders of the Roman Catholic Church, explaining why the pope still includes pontifex maximus in his title.

For more than two thousand years, the Pantheon's domed ceiling held the world record as the largest unsupported concrete span. The CNIT building in Paris took the honor when it was completed in 1958.

Even though there is zero hard evidence supporting the theory that the Romans persecuted Christians in the Colosseum, the venue has long been recognized as a site of Christian martyrdom. As early as the sixth century it was converted into a shrine, and the Vatican still holds its Good Friday services live and on location—minus the lions, of course.

Roman influence is hard to deny in American architecture. The Jefferson Memorial in Washington, D.C., is almost identical to the Pantheon, Penn Station—before its resurrection—brought a taste of the Baths of Caracalla to New York City.

Emperor Nero certainly knew a little something about ambiance. Seutonius wrote that Nero's Domus Aurea boasted a circular main dining room with a roof that revolved with the sun and stars. Modern archaeologists believe a large octagonal room—complete with dome and oculus—to be that room. Some historians have even argued that the snazzy structure was actually the inspiration for the celebrated Pantheon. Tradition holds that when slaves cranked a cloaked system of pulleys, the ceiling beneath the dome actually rotated in time with the sky. But leave it to Nero to take things up a notch. Guests were then showered with rose petals and perfume from above while they dined.

No one's really sure when Emperor Nero officially left the building, but he was rumored to have stabbed himself to death while in hiding outside of Rome. So it's no surprise that even in death Emperor Nero commanded the spotlight, and his antics from the beyond are more than a little reminiscent of at least one modern icon. For years following his apparent suicide people across the Roman Empire claimed to catch glimpses of their former ruler. No word on how he felt about peanut butter and banana sandwiches.

Apparently there's a lot in a name when it's Trajan, emperor of Rome for almost twenty years beginning around the turn of the first century. Even though his reign was short, his influence appears immense because the Roman senate reportedly honored all newly anointed emperors with the prayer *felicior Augusto, melio Traiano*, or "may he be more fortunate than Augustus and better than Trajan." Renowned author Dante took his idolization one step further. In his celebrated *Divine Comedy*, Dante allows only Trajan into heaven.

Even Roman emperors needed someone to look up to, and they found their inspiration in Alexander the Great. In fact, Julius Caesar reportedly suffered a minor nervous breakdown upon seeing a statue of the great conqueror while in Spain. Caesar, who was only a thirty-three-year-old general at the time of the epiphany, was simply overcome by the realization that Alexander had taken over the world by his age.

But Caesar wasn't alone in his idolization of Alexander. Emperor Caracalla attempted to retrace the master's battle plan across the east before visiting Alexander's tomb in Alexandria. But Caligula took his hero worship to the extreme. He is said to have built a bridge across the Bay of Naples just so he could traipse across it wearing armor he pilfered from Alexander's tomb.

Some of the strongest evidence suggesting that Columbus—or even the Vikings—was not the first European to visit the New World lies in Roman coins that have surfaced in excavations across the Americas. From Texas and Maine as far south as Venezuela, the currency has resurfaced intermittently. A mound dig in Round Rock, Texas, actually uncovered a stash dating to AD 800, but Oklahoma holds the record for oldest find. A bronze coin sporting Nero's profile was unearthed in Heavener sometime around 1976. Archaeologists estimate it dates to AD 63 and probably hails from Antioch, Syria.

The U.S. railroad system draws its standard width from Roman chariots because it was designed by English expatriates. The designers based their system on England's system of tramways that predate railroads, and those tramways were built using wagon tools. Wagons had historically been built to the 4-foot, 8.5-inch width to prevent them from bouncing apart on long trips across jagged English country roads. Those same roads had been built by the Romans and had been rutted by Roman chariots. Because all Roman chariots had been constructed to a standard width of 4 feet, 8.5 inches, the English wagons followed suit in order to fit into the ruts.

Hygiene High Jinks

The glitter eye shadow that was all the rage in Egypt around 4000 BC was made from the crushed shells of beetles.

The modern world might have "heroin chic," but rail-thin runway supermodels can't hold a candle to the eighth-century European "It" girl. Powder might have been a wig mainstay, but those pale complexions were all natural. Their secret? Aresenic Complexion Wafers made with traces of the actual toxin.

Cologne is named for its German birthplace. The original recipe called for alcohol, orange bitters, mint oil, and lemon spirits.

It didn't take a bunch of rocket scientists to figure out the Black Death was contagious, but medieval physicians would have done the CDC proud. Rather than waste a lot of time trying to pinpoint the origins of the sickness responsible for wiping out one-third of Europe's population between 1347 and 1351, these quick-thinking docs fashioned the first-known biohazard suits. An admitted fashion faux pas, the protective suits made the medicine men inside look an awful lot like gigantic birds, but the beak portion of the ensemble was filled with oils and vinegar to mask the stench of rotting flesh.

The first U.S. city to put fluoride in its water was Grand Rapids, Michigan, in 1945.

Bow and Arrow

Simple. Convenient. Effective. Deadly.

The bow and arrow revolutionized life from the moment the first thwack sounded and something big and meaty fell to the ground without the predator receiving so much as a scratch.

This little low-tech gem provided man with the means for stalking large prey—from a safe distance—and providing sustenance. It also changed the face of warfare for the same reason.

Given that the bow appears on thirty thousand-year-old cave drawings, it's difficult to pinpoint the weapon's exact genesis, but they are believed to date to the days of Stone Age hunters.

Although modern-day composite bows and arrows are veritable engineering marvels, their rudimentary ancestors consisted of nothing more than some form of flexible material—usually sinew or cord—strung tightly between the two ends of a narrow shaft of wood.

And miracle of miracles, it worked.

The only real requirement for bow ingredients were that they be available and effective, meaning bone and wood were the most popular varieties. Arrowheads evolved from charred wood to stone and bones and finally metal.

Because of its portability, the bow and arrow became the preferred weapon of nomadic tribes. It eventually infiltrated more organized warfare, though, because of its rapid-fire capabilities and accuracy long after gunpowder debuted on the battlefield.

The bow and arrow has proved a tried and true wartime companion of Assyrian charioteers, Mongol cavalry, English marksmen, and advanced infantry soldiers. From treetop perches to open battlefields, this weapon has proved its worth time and again.

And when the machines finally rise up to stamp out their creators, it will most likely be these little suckers that pierce the motherboards and send them packing.

Ah, the circle of life.

The Wheel

There's no denying that without the wheel there would be no agriculture, economic structure, transportation, or warfare.

From the first rock sanded to roll, mankind's destiny has been lurching toward the next great advance, and it's the very simplicity of the discovery that makes the wheel so revolutionary.

No doubt this innovation has been refined and recrafted throughout millennia to steer man farther—and faster—into new frontiers, but it's very creation is a marvel unto itself.

The oldest recorded image of a wheel dates to ancient Sumer around 3500 BC, but within fifteen hundred years that design had been revolutionized with the introduction of the spoke—most notably on chariots in Asia Minor. The chariot alone is credited with mobilizing armies and changing the face of warfare from Egypt and India to China and Greece.

But it was the Romans who crafted roads to support transportation and, in turn, encourage communication and effective land-based trade.

The design itself has improved through the ages, thanks in large part to innovations such as the hub for stability and the tire for increased traction.

But do not overlook the wheel's less commercial applications.

The first potter's wheel—vital to the production of pottery—dates to around 3500 BC in Mesopotamia. The ability to mass produce what had once been built slowly by hand not only allowed civilizations to store and ship their goods from one locale to another, but it also established the finished products themselves as economic commodities, historical markers, and vessels for cultural exchange.

Face it, until the day that first log rolled down an embankment gaining moment as it spun, man had no inkling of the power he stood to harness from a simple spinning motion.

Of course, brakes are an entirely separate chapter.

Pop Quiz #4

1) What nasty little bug invaded Europe in the mid-fourteenth century via trade ships from China carrying flea-infested rats?
   a) Black Death
   b) Bubonic Plague
   c) Cholera
   d) Both A and B

2) Who wrote the famous *Canterbury Tales* in the fourteenth century?
   a) Geoffrey Chaucer
   b) William Shakespeare
   c) Leonardo da Vinci
   d) L. Ron Hubbard

3) Which Norman leader seized control of Britain in 1066 following the death of Edward the Confessor?
   a) Edward Longshanks
   b) Robert the Bruce
   c) William the Conqueror
   d) Charles de Gaulle

4) What was the name of the ledger commissioned by William I in 1085 to account for his holdings and national production capacities?
   a) The Domesday Book
   b) Laws of Accountancy
   c) It's All Mine
   d) None of the above

5) What is the name of the historic sixty-three-clause document signed in 1215 by King John I and his revolting barons that established checks and balances, preventing even the king from ignoring the law and customs of the feudal system of government.
   a) Treaty of Gant
   b) Magna Carta
   c) Treaty of Versailles
   d) The Domesday Book

6) The Peasants' Revolt of 1381 succesfully achieved which of the following?
   a) Excommunication of the Archbishop of Canterbury
   b) Capture of the Tower of London
   c) Formal recognition of guild influence
   d) All of the above

ANSWERS:

1) d
2) a
3) c
4) a
5) b
6) b

Papal Powerhouses

Two hundred sixty-three men have held the title pope, the highest position in the Roman Catholic Church, since St. Peter assumed the post in AD 33. Here are a few of the papal movers and shakers through the ages:

Leo the Great, 440–461

St. Leo I called the papacy "a burden to shudder at," and his words proved prophetic.

Leo was actually in Gaul when St. Sixtus III died and knew nothing of his promotion to pope until he returned to Rome. It became his purpose in life to stamp out heresy.

It would appear that Eutyches, a Constantinople monk, aligned with Dioscorus, the patriarch of Alexandria, in teaching that in Christ only one nature exists.

St. Flavian, the patriarch of Constantinople, was so unnerved by the popularity of this way of thinking that he asked Leo to intervene, prompting the pope to pen his famous letter to Flavian condemning this Monophysite heresy.

But the upstarts persisted—driving Flavian to his grave—and in 451 Leo convened a historical meeting of the minds at Chalcedon, formally eradicating the Monophysite influence over the Eastern Church.

Leo then set his sights on the West and the barbarians threatening the Christian way of life.

The invincible Leo requested and was granted a sit-down with Attila the Hun and negotiated a peaceable outcome for Rome.

He stepped up again three years later when the Vandals threatened the empire from the shores of the Tiber. Leo met with the Vandal king, Genseric, who agreed to spare the lives of the Romans, but the price was high this time. The pact allowed Genseric's men two full weeks of plundering.

St. Gregory I, 590–604

Gregory the Great was born in Rome sometime around 540 to a wealthy family with strong Christian beliefs. In fact, his mother, Sylvia, and two aunts were honored as saints.

Although he became prefect at a young age, he shed public life for a career as a monk and founded monasteries on his six Sicilian estates. His home at Coelian Hill was converted in the same vein in honor of St. Andrew.

When Pope Pelagius II died in 590, Gregory was the unanimous choice as successor, and he served for fourteen years. He worked diligently to protect Rome from the threatening Lombards—paving the way for their conversions—and helped persuade the conversion of the Arian Visigoths in Spain.

His writings were less lofty, but no less inspiring, than the works of Cicero or Augustine, and his homilies, dialogues, and pastoral care helped shape prevailing philosophies of the early Middle Ages.

He died in 604 with the conversion of Spain complete and the one in England just beginning.

Leo III, 795–816

Leo III was born into a humble family, but his path had been set in youth, and he made his mark on the papacy early as well.

One of his first acts was to demonstrate his intent to maintain friendly relations with Charlemagne, strengthening foreign policy but fanning fires closer to home.

In 799, a nephew of the late Pope Hadrian led a revolt against Leo, who was attacked by armed men who attempted to blind him and cut out his tongue. Leo not only survived the brutal attack but regained both his vision and speech.

He sought Charlemagne's assistance and was obliged when the Frankish ruler visited Rome in person the next year to help clear Leo's name. In fact, Charlemagne ordered the pope's conspirators executed, and Leo actually commuted their sentences to exile.

Two days later, Leo placed a jeweled crown on Charlemagne's head during the Christmas Mass, restoring the empire in the West.

St. Leo III died in June 816. His feast is kept on June 12.

John XII, 955–963

The original "poor little rich boy," John XII's papacy was secured by his father, Alberic, who greatly miscalculated his son's virtues.

Born Octavian, John XII had a far from godly reputation.

His missteps began when he called on King Otto I of Germany to free Italy from the tyrannical hold of King Berenger. Otto did not disappoint.

He chased Berenger into the mountains, and John crowned Otto emperor for his promise to vanquish the cowering despot. Yet while Otto chased Berenger, John conspired with Berenger and his son to prevent Otto from wielding too much power over Rome.

When Otto returned to Rome to deal with John at the request of the people, the humiliated pope fled. The council appointed Leo, who served until Otto left the city, antipope.

John returned triumphantly, excommunicated everyone in sight and pretty much made Rome a living hell for those who remained.

According to at least one report, John died in 964 while committing adultery and was denied Holy Viaticum.

St. Gregory VII, 1073–1085

Born Hildebrand in Tuscany, Gregory VII entered the monastery at a young age and became Pope Gregory VI's protégé. The young monk's first directive was to clean up the lawlessness devouring Rome in Benedict IX's wake. When Gregory the elder resigned, Pope Leo IX took the monk back where the people finally won his consecration as pope in 1073.

He faced the abuses of the church head on, barred usery, and awaited the fallout from King Henry IV. It came during Christmas Mass when Gregory was carried to Henry's tower. The angry masses swarmed, and Henry relented.

Gregory ordered Henry to answer to synod charges; Henry's bishops condemned Gregory, and Gregory had Henry excommunicated.

The German nobility saw its chance to attack, but Gregory persuaded them to at least allow Henry to repent before they took his throne.

Shenanigans ensued, and Gregory was forced to absolve the king, who then defeated the German nobles, captured Rome, and wreaked general havoc.

Gregory died in Salerno in 1085.

Blessed Urban II, 1088–1099

Born Odo in Lagery, he founded the great Carthusian order before becoming a canon and archdeacon of Reims, but shed it all for monastic life at Cluny.

Sent by St. Hugh to Rome to aid Gregory VII in his campaign against Henry IV, Odo helped Gregory achieve significant reforms and secure the election of worthy bishops.

When elected to the papacy by acclamation in 1088, he took the name Urban II.

He is best remembered for organizing a crusade that would change the face of the church by ending the Eastern Schism, and he did so in a quite politically correct fashion.

He absolved Emperor Alexius's excommunication in a move he hoped would reunite the Eastern Church with Rome and give the Western warriors a noble enough reason to put aside their petty conflicts.

In November 1095, Urban assembled thirteen archbishops, 225 bishops and ninety abbots in Clermont who passed reform decrees, leaving him to proclaim, "God wills it."

Urban achieved the desired effect.

His fiery rhetoric and impassioned leadership resulted in the assembly of able knights led by Godfrey of Lorraine, Robert of Nomandy, Hugh of Vermandois, Raymond of Toulouse, and Bohemond of Norman Italy; and Urban appointed Adhemar, bishop of Le Puy, to oversee their exploits.

Urban dedicated his life to the Crusade, and Jerusalem did fall to the Christian army before his death, but the good news never made it to his pious ears. Urban II died on July 29, 1099.

Innocent III, 1198–1216

Born Lotario de' Conti, Innocent III was a young intellectual when he assumed the papacy and became one of the greatest medieval popes.

Born in Gavignano, near Anagni, around 1160, the future pope received a classical education abroad in Rome, Paris, and Bologna, through which he became a canon lawyer and was appointed cardinal by his uncle, Clement III.

He retired from the papal court during the pontificate of Celestine III to write spiritual works. In all honesty, he wasn't exactly pleased to ascend the papal throne in 1198, but he recognized opportunity when it knocked.

Innocent III empathized with the Italian patriotism that spawned rebellion against German influence in Italy. Henry VI's death left Otto of Nordheim and Philip of Swabia vying for the crown of a divided nation, and Innocent saw his chance to reassert papal independence and extend papal influence.

He failed.

Innocent III crowned Otto of Nordheim Otto IV, and the monarch promptly turned on the church. Being the eternal optimist, Innocent bided his time and groomed his ward, Frederick II, to set things right.

Frederick was the son of Constance and the late Henry VI. His mother had entrusted the child to papal oversight, and Innocent reciprocated by preserving Sicily as Frederick's birthright.

Of course, Innocent was by no means an idle pontiff.

On the contrary, he became feudal overlord of Aragon and England when Pedro II and John abdicated their thrones as fiefs. Sure, John lost face with this sneaky little maneuver, but he also freed himself from rebelling barons, aggressive French adversaries and the shame of excommunication.

Case in point, viewing the Magna Carta as the extortion of the vassals, Innocent ultimately declared the historic contract null and void.

A tactician, however, he was not. In his attempt to rid the Papal States of the Manichean heretics, Innocent III encouraged a crusade against the threat, effectively launching the Fourth Crusade. He underestimated the cunning of the Venetians, though, and watched in horror as his own soldiers of God attached the Catholic city of Zara followed by the Christian stronghold of Constantinople.

Fortunately for the faithful, Innocent's true strength laid in his spirituality.

In 1215, he convened the renowned Fourth Lateran Council and condemned the heretical Albigensians, the term used by the French for Manichean heretics.

This twelfth ecumenical council also encouraged learning, set penalties for abuses of Church power and established the rule still practiced that every Catholic must receive Holy Communion as part of the Easter observance.

The measure also called for a new Crusade, but Innocent died at Perugia on July 16, 1216.

The Anti-Pope Clement VII, 1523–1534

Born in Florence in 1478, Giulio de' Medici was created cardinal in 1513 and pope ten years later, but he proved ultimately ill-equipped to manage the tumultuous times he inherited.

As pope, two major tragedies defined his reign: the sack of Rome and the loss of England.

He failed at brokering peace between the emperor and Francis I, and then proceeded to align foolishly with the French.

The emperor was understandably displeased.

In his defense, Clement assisted in forming the League of Cognac, but the feeble act could not deter the imperialists from sacking the Vatican and desecrating St. Peter's in 1527.

Only one year later, the disgruntled imperialist army in northern Italy—angered by lack of pay and impatient for plunder—headed south.

Clement's Cognac League managed to protect Florence from their wrath, but Rome itself was the actual target.

A massacre ensued, and Rome fell.

And yet Clement's trouble's were only beginning.

Despite his pro-papal leanings, England's Henry VIII became infatuated with Anne Boleyn and stalked the pontiff to grant him an annulment from his marriage to Catherine of Aragon.

Clement's denial only angered Henry who, in 1534, broke away from the Church.

Clement died in September of 1534.

Dark Days

Imagine clustered communities of dirt-floor shacks. More precisely, imagine one-room dirt-floor shacks with thatch roofs and vermin-ridden straw floors. Imagine entire families sharing one chamber pot or trekking out into the elements for a moment's privacy.

Imagine water being in such short supply it was reserved for cooking and drinking only. Imagine changing clothes only occasionally and bathing less often than that.

They weren't called the Dark Ages for nothing, and Black Death was the reward for surviving.

No one blames plumbing alone for the public health disaster that single-handedly wiped out one-third of Europe's population, but it certainly played a role in the plague's swift and merciless spread.

England was first ravaged by the epidemic in 1348.

It rode in on flea-bitten black rats and was carried by lice that thrived in such close quarters. The rats then fed on the garbage and waste cast about so freely in the streets of London and the city was largely abandoned for the countryside where residents attempted to flee their puss-swollen glandular demise.

The poor were left behind to die, and even the rats stowed away on the very trade ships on which they arrived and which they bound for far-away places, carrying their little secret with them.

"Men and women carried their own children on their shoulders to the church and threw them into a common pit. From these pits such an appalling stench was given off that scarcely anyone dared to walk beside the cemeteries, so marked a deficiency of labors and workmen that more than a third of the land in the whole realm was left to," wrote William of Dene, a monk from Kent.

And the misery continued for almost three centuries.

The Great Fire of London in 1666 is actually regarded as a blessing in disguise by many historians because it might have killed thousands of people but it also eviscerated rats, garbage, and the last remnants of the plague.

Black Death

The Black Death left an indelible mark. Some twenty-five million Europeans died between 1347 and 1352, alone, decimating almost four centuries of steady population increases. Estimated European population levels between 1000 and 1352 are as follows:

- 38 million in 1000
- 48 million in 1100
- 59 million in 1200
- 70 million in 1300
- 75 million in 1347
- 50 million in 1350

In case you've ever wondered why people proclaim it's "raining cats and dogs," you should know it's really not just a random metaphor. Despite all the philosophical and scientific enlightenment beginning to take hold during this period, drainage in seventeenth-century England remained more than a bit primitive, and city streets were quite prone to flooding. Given the Brits of the age knew nothing of spaying and neutering stray animals, it's no wonder the streets were often overrun with furry little refugees. When floodwaters rose, however, those poor creatures couldn't find shelter and often drowned, and it was not uncommon to see them floating among the runoff. No one truly believed they really fell from the sky, but the phrase has been passed along often enough the saying finally stuck.

WESTERN PASSAGE

Printed literature infiltrated the West via vice, and then the life's work of Johann Gutenberg changed everything.

Ironically, "Bible thumpers" have maligned playing cards for millennia, yet without gambling there would be nothing to thump!

In fact, gambling led directly to the mass reproduction of the Bible, but first things first:

Because the West had no interest in eastern religious literature, the printed word arrived under much less enlightened pretenses. Printed playing cards spread like wildfire in Western Europe. By 1377, printed cards were so popular in Germany and Spain that the Synod of 1404 forbade the clergy to play cards.

In 1423, St. Bernard of Siena encouraged listeners from the steps of St. Peter's to collect and burn their playing cards.

Before Gutenberg was printing books, playing cards were made in Venice, Augsburg, and Nuremberg. The Council of Venice passed a law in 1441 to protect domestic card printers. It is speculated that Gutenberg got his start printing cards.

Gutenberg spent decades developing and perfecting his moveable-type printing press. Materials for the project cost large sums of money. Investors often waited years for a return that was never realized. His secretive nature and unwillingness to sell less-than-perfect products landed him in court on more than one occasion. All that is known about the man comes from the legal records of the many lawsuits filed against him by investors.

In 1445, he lost a lawsuit to an investor named Johann Fust. Fust was awarded a large sum of cash and all of Gutenberg's materials and equipment. The firm of Fust and Schoeffer marketed Gutenberg's Bible the same year. They quickly followed with the Latin Psalter and a book titled *Catholicon.* These were printed using two different fonts Gutenberg had cast.

World Literature

- The world's oldest complete novel, *The Tale of Genji*, was written in Japan in the eleventh century.
- The youngest author is Dorothy Straight, who wrote *How the World Began* at the ripe old age of four.
- The largest library is the Library of Congress in Washington, D.C. It has more than one hundred thirty million items, including books, recordings, photographs, maps, and manuscripts. It was established in 1800 as a reference library for the U.S. Congress. When the British destroyed it during the War of 1812, Thomas Jefferson helped rebuild it by selling his personal literary collection.
- The longest novel is *A la recherché du temps perdu* (*Remembrance of Things Past*) by French author Marcel Proust. It contains more than 9.6 million characters.
- The most translated author is L. Ron Hubbard. His books have been translated into sixty-five languages.
- The oldest surviving biblical texts are dated 587 BC, and were found on two silver amulets under Jerusalem's Scottish Church in 1979.
- In 1945, various papyrus texts were discovered at Nag Hammadi, Egypt, including Gnostic gospels, or secret books, ascribed to Thomas, James, John, Peter, and Paul. They were buried around AD 350, but the originals are thought to have been written some two hundred years earlier.
- The world's best-selling fiction author is Agatha Christie. Her seventy-eight mystery novels have been translated into forty-four languages and have sold roughly two billion copies.

Midterm

1) Cleopatra was of what nationality?
   a) Egyptian
   b) Macedonian
   c) Sumerian
   d) Assyrian

2) Who established the first dynasty in China, the Xia, which lasted from 2205 until 1766 BC?
   a) Mao
   b) Yu
   c) Yao
   d) Shennong

3) Egyptian Pharaoh Khufu commissioned which monument during the Fourth Dynasty— around 2560 BC—to serve as his own burial tomb in what is today part of greater Cairo?
   a) The Parthenon
   b) The Sphinx
   c) The Great Pyramid of Giza
   d) None of the above

4) Who commissioned the Hanging Gardens of Babylon?
   a) Alexander the Great
   b) Hammurabi
   c) Xerxes
   d) Nebuchadnezzar

5) When Hannibal set out to conquer Rome after his father's death in 221 BC, what did he take with him across the Alps?
   a) 100,000 troops
   b) 20,000 cavalry
   c) Thirty-seven elephants
   d) All of the above

6) King Maussollos of Carina gave us the name for which final resting place?
   a) Mausoleum
   b) Tomb
   c) Crypt
   d) Pyre

7) Who was proclaimed dictator of Rome in 48 BC?
   a) Julius Caesar
   b) Marc Antony
   c) Both A and B
   d) Neither A nor B

8) Who was the father of Cleopatra's children?
   a) Julius Caesar
   b) Marc Antony
   c) Both A and B
   d) Neither A nor B

9) Ptolemy Soter commissioned which of the Seven Wonders of the Ancient World for a practical, life-saving purpose in 290 BC?
   a) Lighthouse of Alexandria
   b) Colossus at Rhodes
   c) Hanging Gardens of Babylon
   d) None of the above

10) What name is used interchangeably to refer to the Indus River civilization in present-day India.
   a) Inca
   b) Harappa
   c) Anasazi
   d) Buddhist

11) How many men have held the title of pope?
   a) 203
   b) 252
   c) 263
   d) 278

12) What brought the Black Death to England?
   a) dogs
   b) cats
   c) birds
   d) rats

13) About how many Europeans died as a result of the Black Death?
   a) 12 million
   b) 25 million
   c) 35 million
   d) 50 million

14) The Synod of 1404 forbade the clergy to do what?
   a) Marry
   b) Smoke
   c) Play cards
   d) Drink alcohol

15) What was found at Nag Hammadi?
   a) Papyrus texts
   b) Dinosaur fossils
   c) A pharaoh's tomb
   d) An ancient civilization

ANSWERS:

1) b	6) a	11) c
2) b	7) a	12) d
3) c	8) c	13) b
4) d	9) a	14) c
5) d	10) b	15) a

CRUSADES

Warfare is as old as mankind, and ironically, some of the bloodiest and most gruesome clashes in history have been waged in the name of spiritual enlightenment.

Take, for example, the Crusades of the Middle Ages.

This series of military campaigns was fought by medieval Europeans against the Muslims of the Middle East, and not unlike most modern conflicts, it was a battle for real estate.

Jerusalem, the most holy city of cities for Christians, fell to the Muslims in 1076.

Given that Jesus—believed by Christians to be the son of God—was born in nearby Bethlehem, spent most of his life in Jerusalem, and was crucified on the city's famed Calvary Hill, Jerusalem was heralded by Christians as the "City of God."

But when Muhammad, the founder of the Muslim faith, made his pilgrimage to Jerusalem, the city became the center of the religious universe for his devoted followers as well.

In fact, when the Muslims captured Jerusalem in the late eleventh century, an awe-inspiring dome—known as the Dome of the Rock—was constructed on the very rock where Muhammad was said to have communed and prayed.

What ensued was almost two centuries of Christians fighting to reclaim the City of God and Muslims fighting to maintain their conquered stronghold. They went something like this:

- The First Crusade, 1096–1099
- The Second Crusade, 1147–1149
- The Third Crusade, 1189–1192
- The Fourth Crusade, 1201–1204
- The Children's Crusade, 1212
- The Fifth Crusade, 1219–1221
- The Sixth Crusade, 1228–1229
- The Seventh Crusade, 1248–1254
- The Eighth Crusade, 1270

First Crusade

Following the Muslim capture of Jerusalem in 1076, Christians wishing to pay a pilgrimage to their City of God met with Muslim soldiers and more than a little hostility. But the problems were not limited to the city walls.

Alexis I of Constantinople feared that his proximity to Jerusalem made his territory ripe for plunder by the Muslims and appealed to Pope Urban II for intervention.

In 1095, Urban spoke frankly to the French crown at Clermont, making his case for war:

"Christians, hasten to help your brothers in the East, for they are being attacked. Arm for the rescue of Jerusalem under your captain Christ. Wear his cross as your badge. If you are killed, your sins will be pardoned," Urban proclaimed.

And thus, the First Crusade—intended solely to reclaim Jerusalem—was launched.

Volunteers cut red crosses and sewed them on their tunics. The Holy War began.

In fact, the term crusade is actually derived from the Latin word *croix*, or cross.

And people fought for a variety of reasons:

Devout Christians sought to reclaim Jerusalem.

Others sought forgiveness for past sins, and the pope himself told them that if they died, heaven would be their reward.

As usual, some fought for profit and were eager to plunder the riches they thought they'd find on the other side of Jerusalem's walls.

Of course, claiming one was on a pilgrimage was the ultimate "get out of jail free" card. Pilgrims were not only protected by the church but were not required to pay taxes.

Pilgrim's Progress

Just to be clear. The trek to Jerusalem was no cake walk.

Because the Crusaders controlled none of the Middle Eastern ports, they were forced to make the perilous journey across land, beginning in France before trudging through Italy and Eastern Europe before finally arriving in what is now modern-day Turkey.

Ironically, the pilgrims—at least, those who survived the harsh conditions—were often forced to pillage and plunder for food and water. Disease was rampant, and it was an equal opportunity offender.

By 1097, almost ten thousand people had gathered at Constantinople in preparation for the journey to the Holy Land, but they lacked a clear leader. Urban II had appointed Bishop Adbenar commander, but more often than not he deferred to anyone else willing to make a decision. While there were, in fact, four primary armies dispatched for the offensive, communications were nonexistent. And so it went:

The fortress city of Nicea became the first target, and it fell easily because its own leader was off to war elsewhere.

Crusaders then set their sights on Antioch in Turkey and fought for seven months before prevailing and turning their attention to the real business of the day.

The attack and capture of Jerusalem began in 1099.

A monk named Fulcher provided one of the few remaining eyewitness accounts of Jerusalem's siege. According to Fulcher, once the Crusaders actually made it over the well-defended walls of the city, the Muslim protectors scattered. The city streets ran ankle-deep with blood, and then the gates to the city were opened and the remaining Crusaders swarmed Jerusalem.

Fulcher's writings indicate that the Muslims who were spared were forced to collect the bodies of the dead and dump them outside the city walls.

The Muslims claimed some seventy thousand were killed, and that the Crusaders pillaged the Dome of the Rock in their zealous attack. It was only the beginning.

Richard the Lionheart and Saladin

What is known about the Third Crusade is usually recounted in the chronicling of the conflict's two larger-than-life leaders: Richard the Lionheart and Saladin.

R. Unstead wrote in 1962: "Richard of England, a red-haired giant, generous, incredibly brave, hot-tempered and tactless, won a great reputation in the capture of Acre but quarreled with his allies who left him and went home."

L. Du Garde Peach was less kind, writing in 1965: "Richard was not a good king. He cared only for his soldiers. But he was brave and loved a brave man."

The keepers of Saladin's legacy were actually far more flattering of Richard with Baha' ad-Din Ibn Shaddad, a Muslim writer who lived in Saladin's court, writing, "(Richard) was a very powerful man of great courage and spirit. He fought great battles and showed a burning passion for war. The king was indeed a man of wisdom, experience, courage, and energy…excitable, brave, and clever."

Shaddad's portrait of Saladin was equally balanced.

"Out of his desire to fight for God's cause he left behind his family, children, country, home, and all the towns under his control. Saladin was well-mannered and entertaining. If anyone was sick, he would ask about their illness, his treatment, food and drink, and whether there was any change in his condition. I never saw him insult anyone. He always stuck to his word and was loyal. No orphan ever came to him without Saladin offering to provide the same amount of care as his father had done," he wrote.

According to the much more recent historian (1989) Elizabeth Hallman, "Saladin used the idea of a holy war to bring the Muslims together. His popularity with the poor people increased when he survived several assassination attacks. Friends and enemies saw Saladin as a man of honor. Even the Crusaders praised him. However, he was criticized for fighting against his fellow Muslims and for failing to capture Tyre."

Children's Crusade

Faith in the plight of the Crusades began to wane after the turn of the thirteenth century.

The Fourth Crusade had failed miserably, and morale was low. The Children's Crusade in 1212—if nothing else—reminded people what they were fighting for.

In that year, two groups made up entirely of children left from France and Germany bound for the Holy Land. Convinced they would be protected by God, it was a show of hope and innocence the movement desperately needed.

Unfortunately, it failed more miserably than its predecessor crusades.

By all accounts, a youngster named Stephen of Cloyes led the offensive even though he was nothing more than an illiterate shepherd boy of twelve.

Tradition holds that Stephen approached King Philip II,of France directly in May of 1212, telling the regent he had a letter from Christ ordering him to lead a crusade. Philip told him to come back when he could shave.

Stephen preached that crossing the Mediterranean would be a cinch because—given their protected status—the waters would simply part and grant their passage. By June 1212, he had amassed a children's army thirty thousand strong.

The Roman Catholic Church never officially ordained the Children's Crusade, but neither did it prevent it from happening.

The children who did not die of exhaustion walking from Vendome to Marseilles arrived at the shores of the Mediterranean to find the seas had no intentions of parting. Undeterred, they boarded boats and were never heard from again.

Meanwhile, a boy named Nicholas led a German Children's Crusade that same year, but they were accompanied by religious men and unmarried women.

Those who survived the trek across the Alps proceeded to Rome, where the pope intervened, applauding their bravery but telling them to return home knowing their hearts were most definitely in the right place.

Spoils of the Crusades

While the Crusades lasted for 174 years combined, only twenty-four of those years saw actual fighting and most of that was comparatively minor compared to modern standards.

Western Europe benefited greatly, however, from expanded trade routes and the introduction of previously unknown or exotic items into everyday life. For example:

New food products included rice, coffee, sherbet, dates, apricots, lemon, sugar, ginger, melons, and dates.

New household items included mirrors, carpets, cotton clothing, compasses, writing paper, wheelbarrows, mattresses, and shawls.

New ideas included Arabic numerals and the zero digit, painkillers, chess, algebra, chemistry, irrigation, and water wheels.

In turn, the Muslim world was introduced to linen and woolen cloth.

The British, it seems, were a little numerically challenged, or at the very least subscribed to a unique form of rounding off numbers. We only mention this oddity because the 100 Years War really wasn't. In all actuality it was waged from 1337 until 1453—intermittently, of course—making its duration 116 years. But we understand. Who in their right mind would read about the Century and a Score Minus Four Years War? By contrast, the shortest known war in history lasted only thirty-eight minutes between Zazibar and England—the victor—in 1896, so no one can ever accuse the British of lacking balance.

Major Christian Pilgrimages

Jerusalem

Jerusalem is a major destination for pilgrimages today, as it is the location of the crucifixion and resurrection of Jesus. According to Christian beliefs, Jesus was brought to Jerusalem not long after his birth, and was cleansed in the Second Temple later in his life. The Last Supper is believed to have been held in Jerusalem, atop Mount Zion. Golgotha, the site of the crucifixion, is thought to be the main reason why Jerusalem has been a major Christian pilgrimage site for two thousand years.

> The Church of the Holy Sepulchre in Jerusalem, known as the Church of the Resurrection to Eastern Orthodox Christians, stands on a site that encompasses Calvary, where Jesus was crucified, and the tomb (sepulchre) where he was buried. A marble slab marks the place where Jesus' body was believed to have been laid.

Rome

Ancient roads such as the Via Francigena are important pilgrimage routes connecting Western Europe and Rome with harbors near Jerusalem. During medieval times, the Via Francigena was a major pilgrimage route to Rome. Many pilgrims still use this route today on foot, horseback, or by bicycle. Of course, a most popular pilgrimage spot for Catholics is Vatican City, located in Rome. These locations make Rome the most visited Christian pilgrimage site in the world.

EXTRA CREDIT: Vatican City is a landlocked territory made of a walled enclave inside Rome. It is the world's smallest independent state.

> St. Peter's Basilica, designed and decorated by Michelangelo and other great artists, contains the relics of Saint Peter (the first pope), is the ceremonial center for the Catholic Church, and is located in Vatican City, Rome.

Lourdes

Nestled in the foothills of southwestern France, Lourdes is the second most visited Christian pilgrimage site, following Rome. With a population of about fifteen thousand inhabitants, Lourdes accommodates close to five million pilgrims and tourists each season. From March to October, the Sanctuary of Our Lady of Lourdes is the site of mass pilgrimages. The spring water found in the grotto there is believed to have healing properties, and miracles have been reported in the sanctuary.

Canterbury Cathedral

The Canterbury Cathedral, one of the oldest and most famous Christian structures in the world, was the site of many famous events, including the assassination of Thomas Becket. Becket was an archbishop of Canterbury who was murdered under the arguably misinterpreted orders of King Henry II. Many Christian pilgrims visit the cathedral to see Becket's shrine, believed to be a place of healing.

Did You Know?

The second largest pilgrimage in the history of Christendom occurred in April of 2005, after the death of Pope John Paul II. It was estimated that four million people traveled to Vatican City to attend the funeral, adding to the near three million people already in Rome who ventured to see the pope's body.

Crash Course

The Dead Sea Scrolls

Discoveries throughout time have confirmed the Bible's authenticity. The most recent of these discoveries is the Dead Sea Scrolls. They were first discovered in 1947 when a goat-herder threw a rock into a cave and broke open a clay pot that contained scrolls wrapped in linen. Excavations until 1956, to find additional scrolls continued in eleven caves located on the northwest shore of the Dead Sea near the ancient site of Qumran. Over 800 scrolls were found covering both biblical and non-biblical topics. The Scrolls are believed to be written as early as the second century BC thru first century AD. This makes the Dead Sea Scrolls the oldest biblical manuscripts known to date. The majority are written in Hebrew, but some are in Aramaic and Greek. Copies of a portion of every book of the Old Testament have been found, with the exception of Esther. This includes almost forty copies of Psalms, over thirty copies of Deuteronomy, and over twenty copies of both Genesis and Isaiah. The scroll containing Isaiah is over a thousand years older than any other known copy. A large portion of the scrolls are written on animal hide, others on papyrus (paper-like material), and one is on joined together copper sheets. This Copper Scroll is a list of hiding places in Israel that some believe are the locations of hidden treasure of the Temple at Jerusalem. The longest of the scrolls was found in cave 11 and is referred to as the Temple Scroll. It presently is 26.7 feet long, but was originally over twenty-eight feet. Numerous scrolls have been displayed in various locations all over the world, but most are kept in the Shrine of the Book at the Israel Museum or in the Rockefeller Archaeological Museum; both are in Jerusalem. Thousands of books and publications have been written not only containing the text of the scrolls, but also their impact on history, society, and religion. The discovery of the Dead Sea Scrolls has been regarded as the greatest biblical and archeological find in the twentieth century.

Judaism at a Glance

Judaism is one of the three major Abrahamic Religions. Worldwide more than 18 million people consider themselves Jewish. Unlike most religions, Judaism does not have a strict outline of beliefs, but most Jews follow the Thirteen Principles of Faith as outlined by twelfth century Rabbi Maimonides:

1. God exists.
2. God is one and unique.
3. God is incorporeal.
4. God is eternal.
5. Prayer is directed to God alone.
6. The words of prophets are true.
7. Moses' prophecies are true and he was the greatest of the prophets.
8. The Written Torah and Oral Torah were given to Moses.
9. There will be no other Torah.
10. God knows the thoughts and deeds of men.
11. God will reward the good and punish the wicked.
12. The Messiah will come.
13. The dead will be resurrected.

Judaism focuses on relationships and a person's actions. Jews also believe that everything was created by God; that one shouldn't spell the name or title of a deity in full; that God is neither male nor female and is omnipresent, omnipotent, omniscient, just, merciful, holy, and perfect; and that we are all God's children and were created in his image.

Judaism teaches that the Messiah, or Moshiach, will eventually come. Unlike Christianity, Jews do not believe that Jesus was the Messiah. Some see him as a moral leader, while others insist he was a false prophet.

The Jewish texts are made up of the Tanakh and the Talmud. The Tanakh, which is made up of the Torah, the Nevi'im, and the Ketuvim, contains the Jewish scriptures. The Talmud is comprised of the

Mishnah and the Gemara and contains Jewish stories, laws, medical knowledge, and other material.

Jewish Holy Days

- Days of Repentance
- Hanukkah
- Passover
- Purim
- Rosh Hashanah
- Sabbath
- Shavuot
- Sukkkot
- Tisha B'av
- Tu B'Shevat (Tu Bishvat)
- Yom Hashoah
- Yom Kippur

> Children are considered adults when they reach a specific age. Boys enter Bar Mitzvah on their thirteenth birthday, and girls enter Bat Mitzvah at twelve.

World Literature

The Nibelungenlied

This famous German epic poem was written around 1200 and inspired much of Wagner's opera *Der Ring Des Nibelungen.* In a nutshell, the hero, Siegfried, travels to Worms to win the hand of the lovely Kriemhild. Her three brothers get the skinny on Siegfried—turns out he is a war hero, he owns a cape of darkness which makes him invisible, and he is thick-skinned, literally, because when he killed a dragon, its blood washed over him, making him a bit scaly and horny. Not the prettiest complexion, perhaps, but a darn useful one in battle. They approve of him as a spouse for their sister, but first one of them needs a favor.

Brother Gunther is in love with Queen Brunhild of Iceland, but he needs help in winning her love. Siegfried agrees to help him in exchange for his sister, Kriemhild. Brunhild will be no easy catch for Gunther, however. She has sworn that she will only marry a man who can throw a spear farther than her. Siegfried, in his invisible cape, helps Gunther pull off the stunt. Gunther marries Brunhild; Siegfried married Kriemhild. However, Brunhild suspects that her darling Gunther really isn't as strong as she is. So, like so many brides, on their wedding night she ties little Gunther into a knot and hangs him on a wall like a picture. This was not Gunther's idea of fun. In a kinky display of heroism, Siegfried arrives in his invisible cloak and wrestles Brunhild into submission. He steals her girdle and ring and gives them to Kriemhild. Later, in a catfight between the two brides, Kriemhild shows Brunhild that she now has her girdle and ring, thus proving that Siegfried fooled the hefty Brunhild.

From this bizarre episode, the plot takes numerous turns. Kriemhild betrays Siegfried and he gets killed by her brothers. She remarries and kills her brothers, but then gets killed herself proving a story that is truly the stuff of opera.

Lighting the Fire

From the French meaning "rebirth," the Renaissance refers to the period of European history beginning around 1450 when scholars, philosophers, artists, and the like began to realize that a great big world existed outside their own little bubbles.

This period is generally accepted as the jumping-off point for modern history, and it's no wonder. This unprecedented period of discovery, innovation, and cultural enlightenment began in northern Italy before sweeping Europe.

Trade between Europe and the Middle East flourished via Italian hubs including Naples, Genoa, and Venice. Arab scholars began preserving ancient texts, most notably those of the Greeks, in their libraries, encouraging the exchange of ideas as well as goods along these routes.

The shift was so profound that when the Byzantine Empire fell in 1453 to Turkish control, Christian scholars left Greece in droves for Italy.

Literature abounded. Artists traded religious themes for subjects of the human spirit.

But what exactly had changed after eleven centuries?

Quite simply, the Renaissance is the result of realization.

Crusaders returned en masse with a greater understanding of the world far beyond Europe's grasp.

The invention of the printing press spawned a surge in widespread literacy and the relatively free exchange of ideas.

Wealthy families—not to mention the church—had finally squirreled away enough money to become patrons of the arts.

Merchants flourished with new systems of bookkeeping and credit.

Art 101

- The Louvre in Paris houses the *Mona Lisa.*
- Monet, Renoir, and Degas were all prolific during the Impressionist period. Degas, by the way, was best known for his portraits of ballet dancers.
- The paintings on the ceiling of the Sistine Chapel are called frescoes.
- Norman Rockwell is the artist renowned for his illustrations in *The Saturday Evening Post.*
- The painting most commonly referred to as *Whistler's Mother,* was actually titled *Arrangement in Black and Gray.*
- Domenikos Theotokopolius is the real name of the painter popularly referred to as El Greco. A true renaissance man, he lived from 1541 until 1614.
- Painter Piet Mondrian refused to use the color green in his work.
- French artist Yves Klein is said to have had women smear their naked bodies with paint and imprint themselves on paper. Seems to beg the question, what sort of artist was he exactly if they were doing all the work?
- Giotto is considered to be the grandfather of the Renaissance.

Michelangelo di Lodovico Buonarroti Simoni

Born to an upper class Tuscan family in the fifteenth century, Michelangelo produced at least two relief sculptures—the *Battle of the Centaurs* and the *Madonna of the Steps*—by the age of sixteen. He then traveled to Venice, Bologna, and Rome where he studied classical statues and ruins. His first large-scale sculpture, *Bacchus*, is one of the master's rare non-Christian pieces.

In 1948, Michelangelo was commissioned to sculpt the *Pietà*, which was to become one of his most famous works of art. Completed in 1500, the masterpiece is still in its original place in St. Peter's Basilica. After it was placed in St. Peter's, Michelangelo overheard an admirer say the sculpture was the work of another artist. That night, in a fit of anger, Michelangelo inscribed Mary's sash, saying in Italian, "Michelangelo Buonarroti, Florentine, made this." The act of egotism explains his only signed work in existence.

The great statue of David was Michelangelo's next project, and it took him three years to complete. Because he believed David to be a model of heroic courage, he insisted that the statue be placed before Florence's Palazzo Vecchio to serve as a warning that "whoever governed Florence should govern justly and defend it bravely."

Four year later, in 1508, Michelangelo was in Rome working on Pope Julius II's tomb when the pope requested that the artist turn his attention to painting the ceiling of the Sistine Chapel. He was given free reign over the project, and by October 1512, he had painted more than 300 figures on the chapel's ceiling.

After a day's work painting the ceiling of the Sistine Chapel, he could not read a piece of paper without tilting his head back and holding it close to his eyes. More than twenty years later, Michelangelo painted the fresco of the Last Judgment in the Sistine Chapel. He worked seven years on this massive project that spans the entire wall behind the altar. It was completed to the sound of public outcry, as many people believed that the nude characters that made up the fresco were inappropriate for a church. The pope fended off the critics; however, after Michelangelo's death, he did agree to have the paintings touched up.

Poet in Hiding

When Florence was under siege, Michelangelo hid for a time in a small room underneath the church of San Lorenzo. Today, tourists can still see some of Michelangelo's sketches on the wall there.

In addition to painting and sculpting, Michelangelo served as architect for many projects in Florence and Rome, including St. Peter's Basilica, the Palazzo Farnese, and the Sforza chapel.

When he wasn't painting, sculpting, or designing, Michelangelo was writing poetry. He is considered one of the great Italian lyric poets of his time. In the mid-1530s, Michelangelo met poet Vittoria Colonna. He and the widow wrote sonnets to each other for many years.

Michelangelo was once described as inventor delle porcherie, or an inventor of obscenities.

EXTRA CREDIT: Michelangelo's sculpture *David* is 14.24 feet high.

Renaissance Timeline

The period referred to broadly as the Renaissance actually swept systematically through Europe, following this approximate timeline:

- Italy: 1300–1600
- Spain: 1350–1650
- France: 1350–1700
- Netherlands: 1400–1750
- England: 1500–1700
- Russia: 1550–1750

LEONARDO DA VINCI

Born on April 15, 1452, near Vinci, Italy, Leonardo da Vinci was sent to Florence in 1466 to study painting under Andrea di Cione, better known as Verrocchio. His earliest known work is a pen-and-ink drawing of the Arno valley drawn in 1473. Between 1476 and 1478, Leonardo did several commissioned pieces, including an altarpiece for the Chapel of St. Bernard and *The Adoration of the Magi* at Scopeto, which was never completed.

Leonardo had a brilliant sense of observation and perception evident in his painting and in the pages of his notebooks. He wrote about and drew detailed designs of machinery five hundred years ahead of his time. Along with drawings of a bicycle, airplane, helicopter, and a parachute, he also recorded observations on subjects including geology, anatomy, flight, and gravity.

Many of the thirteen thousand pages of his notebooks are written in mirror image. Although many scholars believe that Leonardo used this means for writing to ensure privacy; another school of thought says that since Leonardo was left-handed, he probably found it quicker to write from right to left.

Leonardo's notebooks are kept in various locations including the Louvre, the national library of Spain, the British Library in London, and others. There is one privately owned notebook, the *Codex Leicester*, owned by Bill Gates.

Leonardo was a master of anatomy. He made detailed drawings of muscles and tendons as a part of his study under Verrocchio. He was so good at what he did that he was allowed to dissect human corpses at several hospitals, drawing the human skeleton, the heart, and vascular system, as well as other organs. Several of his drawings show comparisons of human organs with the corresponding organs of birds, frogs, bears, and other animals.

Several people have used the specifications in Leonardo's notebooks to construct working machinery. In 2000, Katarina Ollikanen built Leonardo's parachute, and skydiver Adrian Nicholas proved that it worked. Two years later, British hang-gliding champion Judy Leden successfully flew a fixed-wing glider that had been built following Leonardo's instructions.

In addition to the parachute and several flying contraptions, check out a few other innovations credited to Leonardo da Vinci:

- Flying machines
- Submarines
- Underwater rebreathing devices
- Self-flotation and ocean rescue devices
- Swimming fins
- Pumping mechanisms
- Dredging systems
- Steam calorimeters
- Water-well drills
- Swing bridges
- Canals
- Leveling and surveying instruments
- Pulley systems
- Cranes
- Street-lighting systems

That's What He Said: Leonardo

- Art is never finished, only abandoned.
- He who is fixed to a star does not change his mind.
- For once you have tasted flight you will walk the earth with your eyes turned skywards, for there you have been and there you will long to return.
- I have been impressed with the urgency of doing. Knowing is not enough; we must apply. Being willing is not enough; we must do.
- Where the spirit does not work with the hand, there is no art.

Other Renaissance Men and Women

Vasco Núñez de Balboa crossed the Isthmus of Panama and claimed the Pacific for Spain.

Sandro Botticelli, recognized widely for his Madonnas, painted the celerated *Birth of Venus* and other scenes from classical mythology.

Robert Boyle was the founder of modern chemistry.

Pedro Alvarez Cabral, claimed Brazil for Portugal.

John Calvin broke away from the Catholic church, defined his new religion, emphasized predestination, and created a new church in Switzerland

Jacques Cartier, voyaged up the St. Lawrence River, allowing France to claim eastern Canada.

Catherine the Great was the Romanov ruler of Russia who continued Peter the Great's expansion policies and dealt severely with Poland.

Charles V was a Hapsburg who reigned as king of both France and Spain.

Christopher Columbus landed on a tiny island he named San Salvador.

Nicolaus Copernicus is the Polish scientist credited with theorizing that the sun sits at the center of our universe, known as the Heliocentric theory.

Hernán Cortés defeated the mighty Aztec ruler Montezuma.

Ferdinand II led the Spanish Inquisition.

Frederick I was named by the Holy Roman Emperor as the first king of Prussia."

Frederick II (the Great) expanded Prussian territory, transforming the region into a world power.

Galileo, proved that the earth rotates on its axis.

Johannes Gutenberg invented moveable type.

Henry VIII was the English monarch who established the Anglican Church.

Robert Hooke is the renowned scientist who first identified cells.

Isabella I ruled Castile, manipulated her marriage to Ferdinand II, and forged the country to be called Spain.

Johannes Kepler discovered that orbits of the planets were ellipses.

Antoni van Leeuwenhoek discovered bacteria.

Louis XIV ruled France and declared himself the divine monarch.

Martin Luther protested against the corruption of the Catholic Church. He challenged the church by posting his ninety-five theses on the church door, sparking the Protestant Reformation.

Niccoli Machiavelli wrote the book *The Prince*, emphasizing control of the people by a ruler to establish a society where people would be best served by the ruler.

Ferdinand Magellan was the first explorer to circumnavigate the globe.

Michael Romanov established the Romanov dynasty that was in control in Russia for more than three hundred years until the last czar abdicated in 1917.

Peter the Great attempted to westernize Russia.

Philip II centralized the Spanish government

Francisco Pizarro conquered the Incas.

Juan Ponce de León explored Florida.

Prince Henry of Portugal established a school for navigators.

Cardinal Richelieu was Louis XIII's chief minister who strengthened the power of the king by appointing special officials that undermined the local power of the nobles. He also weakened the power of the Hapsburgs throughout Europe as well as that of the Huguenots, or French Protestants.

Sir Thomas More wrote *Utopia,* which described both social problems and possible solutions.

Vasco da Gama sailed around the Cape of Good Hope at the southern tip of Africa and brought back spices and jewels from India.

Geography 101

- Reykjavik, Iceland, is the northernmost capital city in the world.
- Finland holds the world's record for country with the most number of islands: 179,584.
- Vatican City—located inside Rome—is the world's smallest independent state.
- Portugal is the world's largest producer of cork. Wine aficionados everywhere couldn't be happier.
- Mount Vesuvius is mainland Europe's only active volcano, but at 4,190 feet tall it has proven before to be the very definition of destruction. When it erupted just after the turn of the second century it buried the city of Pompeii under a thirty-one-foot wave of molten mud and volcanic ash.
- Long before Paris became the City of Light, it went by another name: Lutetia.
- Roughly 40 percent of the Netherlands lies below sea level.
- The Ural Mountains separate Europe from Asia.
- The Cathedral of Augsburg in Germany boasts possession of the world's oldest stained-glass window, dating to the eleventh century.

Everyday History

Pen and Pencil

Writing utensils have existed for thousands of years in a variety of forms, but that which is most closely linked to what is known as a modern-day graphite pencil appeared in Borrowdale, England, in 1564.

Tradition holds that a curious bloke observed what would later be identified as graphite growing on a felled tree and realized the black material could be used to write and draw quite nicely.

The problem wasn't the graphite itself but how to hold it without creating a horrible mess.

Rudimentary pencils consisted of graphite sticks wrapped in string but those quickly evolved into hollowed out wooden sticks into which the graphite could be inserted.

Pens enjoy a much more storied history and hail from ancient Egypt when scribes used reeds filled with ink to chronicle the whims and fancies of pharaohs and high priests.

The construction of pens grew gradually sharper until the use of feather quills became common in the sixteenth century, improving the quality of writing and legibility. Not only could a quill be sharpened but it was less likely to break under pressure.

Within three hundred years the fountain pen was born when industrious artisans and writers began using metals to craft the tools of their trade.

The pen's eureka moment came in 1884, though, when businessman Lewis Waterman discovered how to control the flow of ink and rid the world of messy and inconvenient ink wells. Coexisting chambers allowing both ink and air to flow simultaneously made this possible.

With ink flow mastered, the only problem remaining was the issue of a method for writing without smudging wet ink, and the ballpoint pen was born.

The mechanism of a ballpoint pen is actually quite similar to rolling paint on a wall. The ink is directed toward the paper—straight down in flow with gravity—allowing the ink to dry almost as quickly as it hits the paper.

René Descartes

"I think, therefore I am."

French philosopher René Descartes actually began his studies in law at the University of Poitiers in 1614, but philosophy, theology, and medicine quickly trumped that stodgy career path. Four years later, he joined the military and spent another four years traveling and studying what he deemed "the great book of the world."

Because he believed that everything in the natural world could be explained by science and mathematics, he combined his philosophical ideas with those disciplines and wrote extensively on the overlap.

Descartes is probably most celebrated for developing a set of principles asserting that a person can know certain truths without any doubt. He then used methodological skepticism—a doctrine that rejects any idea that can be doubted—and arrived at a single idea: that thought exists, thus, "I think, therefore I am."

He also incorporated the principles of deduction and perception into his work, spawning what he called the Wax Argument. In observing that every single property about a piece of wax—its color, shape, and smell—changed completely when acted upon by heat, he reasoned that only deduction—and more specifically the use of judgment rather than perception—could be considered reliable knowledge.

Descartes also believed the human body was in constant motion except for the brain. He reasoned that because the brain was a nonmaterial entity it was immobile.

He took the relationship between mind and body further, though, by theorizing that they were inextricably linked by a dualistic purpose. Specifically, Descartes believed that the mind controls the body but that the body also influences the mind, and he pointed to man's reaction to cold and heat to prove this relationship.

Descartes combined the principles of algebra and geometry into analytical geometry, known today as Cartesian geometry. His idea of using intersecting lines to identify a point is called the coordinate system.

Descartes's Three Most Celebrated Works

- *Discourse on Method*, published in 1637, described the universe as a giant mathematically designed engine.
- *Meditations on First Philosophy*, published in 1641
- *Principles of Philosophy*, published in 1644.

Did You Know?

- Descartes's works were banned by the pope in 1663.
- His coordinate system eventually enabled the development of global positioning system instruments.
- He is credited with inventing graph paper and the use of exponential numbers, or superscript.

Philosophy 101

- Neoplatonism, or the belief that an individual could achieve a unity, or oneness, with God, was the school of thought that emerged to bridge the gap between Greek and early Christian philosophy.
- In *Critique of Pure Reason*, German philosopher Immanuel Kant attempted to prove what one can and cannot know.
- Hedonism is the belief that pleasure is the highest good.
- Utilitarianism, the dominant philosophy in England during the nineteenth century, was developed by Jeremy Bentham and John Stuart Mill.
- Plato was the author of *The Republic.*
- Laozi is considered the founder of Daoism.
- The German philosopher Friedrich Nietzsche wrote *Thus Spoke Zarathustra* in only ten days.
- Epicureanism, the namesake of Greek philosopher Epicurus, encourages one to cast off material possessions and live a simple life that embraces health and inner peace.
- Humanism is the school of thought characterized by the belief that goodness and inherent nobility are present in man at birth and should, therefore, be the guiding principles of all human action.
- And just to prove philosophers are not above hypocrisy, Frenchman Jean Jacques Rousseau penned a famous edict on the proper way to raise children yet dumpted all of his own—illegitimate—spawn in orphanages.

Protestant Reformation (1500–1650)

This movement began around 1500 in the Germanic principalities that were only beginning to form their own city-state form of government.

Disillusioned by the rampant abuses of power by officials within the Roman Catholic Church, revolutionaries began rebelling against the establishment with a force and determination that would ultimately splinter factions into myriad Protestant faiths.

In an act of what centuries later would be called civil disobedience, Martin Luther is credited with launching the Reformation by posting his ninety-five theses protesting the church's indulgences.

Luther's contemporary, John Calvin, pioneered the idea of predestination and took his beliefs to Switzerland where he established his own theocracy, or church-centric government.

Meanwhile, England's King Henry VIII wanted a divorce that the Catholic Church would not grant, so he took his self-serving cue from his principled brethren and broke away, forming the Anglican Church so he could sever ties legally and move on to the next young thing. And other movements were afoot as well:

Of course, the Catholics weren't exactly accustomed to being questioned—much less defied—and they launched the Counter Reformation (1550–1600) in an attempt to clean their own house.

The Scientific Revolution (1200–1700) actually coincided with—and was arguably one of the primary causes of—the Renaissance. This period, also in direct contradiction to the teachings of the Catholic Church, was fueled by kindled curiosity in the mechanics of life and nature, and encouraged the questioning of accepted fact.

The Age of Exploration (1400–1600) was spawned by all of the above. New ways of thinking bred insatiable curiosity for world at large. As questioning attitudes prevailed, the Scientific Revolution yielded the necessary technology to venture forth, providing the means for acquiring exotic products while satisfying the unrelenting need to spread religion.

Reform Roots

The Renaissance did not occur in a vacuum, so it is no surprise the church grappled with the marriage of technical advances such as the printing press and the rediscovery of the ancient world and its influences in a less open-minded fashion than its intellectual counterparts.

Christian humanists—particularly around the end of the fifteenth century—sought to strike a balance and apply this new approach of scholarly study to scriptures in their original languages and possibly discover the true original teachings and intentions of their ministry.

In fact, they began translating the Bible into vernacular tongues—meaning everything other than Latin—in an effort to spread the word more vigorously. This widespread introduction of the masses to the written word also kindled a spiritual revival of more mystical works as well, including Thomas à Kempis's *Imitatio Christi.*

What followed was anything but shocking.

The proliferation of reading material among the masses led to new thoughts and new ways of thinking. New ways of thinking led to questioning the old ways of thinking. Questioning the old ways of thinking put the church and its rampant abuses of power under a powerful microscope.

For instance, the Renaissance popularized the belief that man could be perfected and fueled a frenzy to improve life in the here and now, rather than sacrificing it all for the promise of a blessed hereafter. The corruption of the church became more apparent with each passing day as its leaders held enormous wealth, exercised sweeping political power and even waged war, all in the name of God.

The christian humanists seized the opportunity to purify the Church while lessening its stronghold over the masses.

Exception to the Rule?

In every conflict, there are those who march to their own drumbeat, and in this particular case it was the French, who had maintained a unique relationship with the church since the days of Pope Clovis.

Because of this peculiar relationship, France exercised no inkling of a separation between church and state. French kings were consecrated by the pope with the title "Most Christian King," after which the monarch agreed to eradicate all heresy in his kingdom.

As a direct result of this relationship, the Gallican church in France operated outside the stronghold of the central church's pecking order.

In fact, the Concordat of Bologna in 1516 confirmed the right of Francois I to make church appointments, yet gave the pope veto power over unqualified candidates as well as the authority to collect one year's royalties—no pun intended—from each post.

In the end, a balance was maintained.

The pope enjoyed tremendous power, but the king reigned supreme—a novel concept for its day.

Of course, if the travails of Spiderman have taught us anything, it's that with great power comes great responsibility.

The king of France was free to distribute the church's wealth almost at will, but it was expected he would do so for the benefit of the masses. For anyone who believes that's how things went down, we at On the John University would like to discuss the sale of a bridge when you've got a minute.

Despite the blurring of lines between responsibility, reward, and obligation, the Gallican church did at least appear to exercise objectivity over its dealings. The University of Paris—known also as the Sorbonne—operated as what some scholars consider to be one of the first think tanks in modern history, and it was charged with arbitrating the complex church-state relationship of the era.

MARTIN LUTHER

"I would never have thought that such a storm would rise from Rome over one simple scrap of paper..."

Martin Luther was born into a world dominated by the Catholic Church and vowed at an early age to become a monk to ensure he received the church's promise of eternal salvation.

The idealistic Luther was devastated, however, when after entering the monastery and trekking to Rome he discovered that the world of Catholicism was rife with corruption. Disillusioned, he threw himself into the study of the Bible and in his self-directed study made a revelation that would change the world.

Luther decided upon reflection that his own personal faith—and not any intangible promise of the church—would guarantee his personal salvation.

The rest is history.

Luther penned his famous treatise, known as the *Ninety-five Theses,* which in actuality was more of a detailed list of grievances against the church. At its core, the work criticized the church's practice of selling indulgences, sparking a revolution in religious thought.

Like all successful revolutionaries, Luther used the technology of the day to his advantage and in this particular case pounced on the power of the recently adopted process of printing to spread his word to the masses. Within months, Europe was literally blanketed with copies of the *Ninety-five Theses.*

Although not solely responsible, Luther's courageous act took on the Catholic Church—the empire that had ruled unquestioned for a thousand years—and laid the foundation for a movement that would ultimately haul Western civilization out of the Dark Ages.

The Day of the Placards

Luther—with his *Ninety-five Theses*—had drawn a line in the sand so prominent even the blind had no trouble making a distinction.

Just after daybreak on October 18, 1534, Parisians and their countrymen to the north awoke to find their city walls plastered with placards denouncing the Catholic Mass as an "insufferable abuse."

The broadsides not only condemned the very sacrament of the Eucharist but charged the priesthood with "disinheriting" the royal lineage of kings and their sons in the name of piety.

Up until this point, the Most Christian King of France had been relatively accommodating of the spirit of inquiry spreading across his enlightened kingdom. In fact, he had intervened on numerous occasions when the scholars at the Sorbonne sought retribution for anyone questioning their authority on such issues.

But on October 18, 1534, a placard denouncing the church was nailed to the king's own bedroom door.

He took it a little personally and declared it an attack on mankind's fundamental social fabric.

He discarded quickly his earlier view that Lutherans were nothing more than zealous theological scholars cruising for a worthy war of words. He deemed them heretics, rebels, and traitors.

And, thus, began the inconsistent treatment of French Protestants.

Several supposed ringleaders of the Day of the Placards were burned, but Francois I stopped far short of a full massacre.

Instead, as head of both church and state he ordered a massive procession of the Holy Eucharist through Paris, requiring all members of the royal and parliamentary institutions to take part.

From that point forward, Protestants were persecuted sporadically at best.

John Calvin

Born the son of a lawyer in 1509, John Calvin abandoned his own legal studies the year his father died to attend the College de France in Paris—known for its humanistic teachings—to study Greek and religious studies.

Sometime between 1528 and 1533, he experienced a "sudden conversion" to Protestantism, describing the experience by saying, "God subdued my soul to docility."

Given the recent occurrence of the Day of the Placards, Calvin knew his criticism of the French Catholic Church's abuses would be considered heresy, yet he was firm in his belief that he was one of God's "chosen instruments in the spiritual regeneration of the world." Smartly, he fled Paris and floated between France, Italy, and Switzerland.

In 1536, he published *Institutes of the Christian Religion*, explaining his beliefs and ultimately outlining his prescribed reorganization of the church.

Calvin was residing in Geneva when the city adopted mass religion reform in 1536:

Monasteries were dissolved.

The Mass was abolished.

Papal authority was renounced.

Then the real fight began—who had the best ideas regarding how to enact reform?

The Libertines, who favored mild reform such as abolishing mandatory church attendance, won the battle, and Calvin, who favored a theocracy, didn't stick around for a war.

By 1555, the Libertines had fallen from power, and Calvin—who had dedicated his life to religious reform—was finally free to impose his own approach, and it was as bare bones as it gets.

Sermons took center stage, and he banned musical instruments from the services, even though he personally enjoyed the occasional melody. Likes and dislikes had nothing to do with it, though, as Calvin argued that they were distractions from the purpose at hand. He did allow parishioners to sing hymns, and the practice was wildly popular. Calvin was pleased because it was yet another way to spread the word.

The Counter-Reformation

In 1521, a Spanish soldier was wounded in battle and found solace in religion.

Ignatius Loyola founded the Society of Jesus, or Jesuits, who adopted a military approach to spirituality. They answered only to the pope and emerged by 1959 as the A-Team of the Counter-Reformation.

Meanwhile, Vincent de Paul and Francis de Sales chose to stand with the meek and humble who appeared to be lost in the shuffle. They founded charitable orders at a time when an emerging capitalist economy was wreaking social havoc by inflating the occurrences of homelessness and poverty.

And in direct response to the growing desire for a more personal relationship with God, there was also a Counter-Reformation revival of Catholic mysticism. St. John of the Cross probed *The Dark Night of the Soul*, and St. Theresa of Avila explored *The Interior Castle* where God dwelt.

But who exactly were these measures enacted to combat?

Protestants in France, the Huguenots, were typically city dwellers, except for those living in the southern countryside who were famous for thumbing their noses at the crown. City folk drawn to the practice tended to be artists and intellectuals.

It's no surprise Protestantism appealed to the literate classes, given the emphasis it placed on Bible study.

Skilled craftsmen and tradesmen of the emerging technologies of the day—particularly printers, booksellers, painters, goldsmiths, and even silk makers— tended to be more open to Protestantism than older, more traditional laborers.

By the mid-sixteenth century, however, large numbers of noble elites began gravitating toward Protestantism, greatly increasing its chances of survival beyond artisan communes.

Protestant Tenets

Justification by faith: Human actions have no bearing on salvation. Believing in Christ and his sacrifice for their sins is all it takes.

The priesthood of all believers: All people have a direct line to God. Go-betweens are not necessary.

The scriptures are the only source of true doctrine, meaning everyone should read them, and widespread translation was part of the ministry.

The sacrament of Holy Communion is figurative, not literal. because there is no need to repeat the sacrifice.

Protestants did not reject the idea of the Virgin Mary, saints, and angels as residents of heaven, but they objected to their use as intermediaries to God and especially of the creation of images in their honor, believing it to be idol worship.

Predestination: Human actions have no bearing on one's fate because God is all powerful, and his plan is already in motion.

The Bible mentions only two sacraments: Baptism and the Last Supper.

Dismas and Gestas

You won't find the names Dismas and Gestas in the Bible, but don't go assuming that means they didn't exist. Believers in the lost gospel of Nicodemus believe not only that these "hidden" chronicles of Pontius Pilate exist but that they name the common criminals—Dismas and Gesta—who were crucified alongside Jesus Christ. Specifically, this disputed gospel claims Dismas was on Christ's right and Gestas was on his left. The story holds that because of Christ's unyielding faith and ultimate sacrifice, Dismas repented of his sins while on the cross and was allowed to pass later through the Pearly Gates, but Gestas cursed God's name and suffered the fiery consequences of Hell.

Catholic Tenets

Faith alone won't earn salvation. Good works (i.e., acts of devotion, charity, sacraments, etc) are required to improve one's chances.

The Catholic priesthood is necessary because only men of the cloth are divinely allowed to perform the sacraments, oversee spiritual health, and interpret the scripture.

Scripture is only one means of receiving doctrine. The priestly order reveals the rest.

The Eucharist reenacts spiritually the consumption of Christ's body and blood.

The Catholic Church is clear that **angels and saints** should not be worshipped, yet it holds that their use as intermediaries, especially the Virgin Mary, is a vital component for achieving salvation. Images of these intermediaries are not to be worshipped but should inspire devotion.

God's omnipotence does not nullify free will, so people are still responsible for their own salvation.

There are **seven sacraments**: baptism, Eucharist, penance (confession and absolution), confirmation, marriage, holy orders, and last rites. Except for marriage and baptism, a priest must perform these rites.

Three Wise Guys

Just in case you never caught their names, the Three Magi, or Wise Men, mentioned in the Bible were Melchoir, the "king of light," Gaspar, the "white one," and Balthazar, the "lord of treasures," and they delivered respective gifts of gold, frankincense and myrrh to the Nativity.

Laws of Necessity

Puritan laws might seem strict, but they were actually rooted in practicality. Consider the following:

- Smoking was banned, but the gesture was more out of necessity than moral disdain. The farmers in question simply saw no need to waste time, energy, and resources cultivating anything—including tobacco—that didn't directly sustain the settlement.
- Cooking was banned on Sundays, not out of religious observance but to prevent homes from burning while families spent hours—literally hours—in church.
- Hunting was prohibited among young men not to oppress their free, frontiersman spirits but to prevent hostile neighbors from overpowering them and taking their loaded weapons.

The End is Clear

Even non-Christians know that the last book of the Bible, Revelation, foretells the end of the world as humankind knows it, and its authors did so with some colorful and thought-provoking language. There's a lot of burning and smoke and smoldering and general destruction that's the clear favorite for fire and brimstone sermons. But just to be clear for anyone not really big on imagery and metaphors, the scribes in question really spelled it out quite bluntly, giving the Four Horsemen of the Apocalypse the names Conquest, Slaughter, Famine, and Death. So much for poetic ambiguity.

What Did They Say?

If you take a minute to consider that the Bible was written by more than fifty men over the span of hundreds of years, it should come as no shock that many scholars believe a great deal has been lost in translation. For instance, consider that ancient Aramaic—the language in which it is believed the Bible was penned—does not provide a simple translation for the phrase "many things." For literal lack of a better word, the original Aramaic phrase has been manipulated over time—some believe—and has evolved over time to mean "forty." Not to burst anyone's bubble, but if this theory is true, then Noah and his brood were afloat on the Ark for "many" days, but there's no physical proof the rains lasted for exactly forty days.

Movie "Real"

We all saw the movie, but just in case you were sleeping when Morgan Freeman tutored Brad Pitt on the unnerving themes of John Milton's *Paradise Lost* and Herman Melville's *Moby Dick* as they apply to a gruesome serial killer creating his own "master work," the widely accepted Seven Deadly Sins frowned upon in the Good Book are:

- Lust
- Pride
- Anger
- Envy
- Sloth
- Avarice
- Gluttony

Crash Course

Archangels

The archangels get a lot of ink in the Bible, most notably Gabriel and Michael who appear from time to time and interact with the common folk on earth.

In addition to these two, there were actually five other archangels, including Raphael, Uriel, Chamuel, Jophiel, and Zadkiel. And unless you've been under a rock, you know that Lucifer, the Fallen Angel, was once God's go-to guy until he got too big for his breeches and decided to incite mutiny out of jealousy for the creator's visible affinity for humans.

But just so you understand how deep this thing goes, there are actually nine choirs of angels sprinkled throughout Christianity, and the archangels and angles comprise only the two bottom rungs. The other seven, from lowliest to most revered, are:

- Principalities
- Powers
- Virtues
- Dominions
- Thrones
- Cherubim
- Seraphim

If you're not thoroughly confused yet, remember there are seven virtues:

- Charity
- Hope
- Faith
- Courage
- Temperance
- Prudence
- Justiceß

William Shakespeare

Shakespeare and his works were most closely associated with the Globe Theatre.

- He died at the age of fifty-two.
- The fairer namesake of *Rome and Juliet* is set to turn the ripe old age of fourteen. Where the hell is *Dateline*'s "To Catch a Predator" when you really need it?
- Richard III uttered the famous line, "A horse, a horse! My kingdom for a horse!"
- In *The Merchant of Venice* Lorenzo falls for Shylock's daughter, Jessica.
- An original bad boy, Iago plays the villain in *Othello*.
- It's bad enough that Hamlet's uncle was his stepfather and was known to talk to himself, but the poor, misunderstood prince saw ghosts, too. The spookiest of them all, his dead father's apparition, told him to "revenge his foul and most unnatural murder."
- Goneril, Cordelia, and Regan were King Lear's three daughters.
- *Twelfth Night* opens with the memorable line, "If music be the food of love, play on."

Shakespeare's Poetry

It is widely believed that Shakespeare wrote poetry before plays. He used several poems within his plays.

- *Love's Labour's Lost* contains three of his sonnets.
- *The Passionate Pilgrim*, a collection of 20 poems published in 1599, was attributed entirely to Shakespeare; however, after much scholarly study, only five of the poems are now said to have been written by Shakespeare.
- Shakespeare's sonnets were first published in 1609, and were probably written during the 1590s. The first 126 of the 154 sonnets speak to a man whose identity continues to intrigue scholars. And sonnets 127 to 152 hold an equal mystery as to the identity of the Dark Lady.

Measuring Hot and Cold

Metals and liquids change when subjected to heat and cold. Thermometers are instruments used to gauge those changes. In a mercury or alcohol thermometer, the liquid expands as it is heated and contracts when it is cooled. Modern thermometers are calibrated in standard temperature units such as Fahrenheit or Celsius.

- Galileo created a basic tool to measure the temperature of water in 1593, allowing temperature variations to be measured for the first time.
- Early thermometers were called thermoscopes. Italian inventor Santorio Santorio was the first to put a numerical scale on the instrument.
- German physicist Daniel Gabriel Fahrenheit invented the alcohol thermometer in 1709. Five years later, he improved his invention by using liquid mercury as the heat indicator.
- Swedish-born Anders Celsius developed the Celsius scale (or centigrade scale) for measuring temperature in 1742. This scale is divided into segments from 0 to 100, with 0 being the freezing point of water and 100 being the boiling point.
- Lord William Thomson Kelvin invented the Kelvin scale in 1848 to measure the extremes of temperature. His scale is based on absolute zero, the temperature when all molecular motion ceases.

0° vs Absolute 0

- 0° Fahrenheit is the temperature derived by mixing equal amounts of snow and common salt.
- Absolute zero is actually -459.6° Fahrenheit and -273.1° Celsius. This is theoretically the lowest temperature possible.
- 0° Kelvin is absolute zero.

SIR ISAAC NEWTON

Born in Lincolnshire, England, on January 4, 1643, Isaac Newton was reared by his grandparents. Because he was a frail and sickly child, he was rarely allowed to play with other children. The solitude transformed him into a toymaker, a pastime that progressed quickly to more practical—and less childish—pursuits. Among his most prized creations were a clock, a sundial, and a mouse-powered mill.

In 1661, he entered Cambridge University, where he studied mathematics, optics, physics, and astronomy. He said the period when the school was closed because of the plague (1664–1666) were "the prime of my age for invention." During those eighteen months, he developed theories regarding gravity and light, and invented calculus.

High school students across the globe continue to curse his name.

Although his theories caused controversy early on, Newton became the most highly esteemed natural philosopher in Europe. For thirty years—while carrying out his official duties at the Royal Mint—he spent time revising his earlier works, studying ancient history, and defending himself against his critics.

Newton died on March 31, 1727, and was buried in Westminster Abbey.

Literary Trail

The Wren Library in Trinity College at Cambridge, has Newton's own copy of the first edition of *Principia*, containing handwritten notes for the second edition.

The Martin Bodmer Library in Switzerland has the original first edition that was owned by Gottfried Wilhelm Leibniz. In it are handwritten notes by Leibniz concerning the controversy over the discovery of differential calculus.

PHYSICS 101

LAWS OF MOTION

In 1668, Newton constructed the first reflecting telescope, which he used to study the universe. As he gazed at the stars, he wondered what kept them from falling to earth. This curiosity led him to develop the laws of motion and theory of gravitation. He could then predict the locations of stars and planets around the sun. Here are the Laws of Motion.

Law of Inertia
Every object persists in its state of rest or uniform motion in a straight line unless it is compelled to change that state by forces impressed upon it.

Law of Acceleration
Force is equal to the change in momentum (mV) per change in time. For a constant mass, force equals mass times acceleration, $F = ma$.

Law of Action and Reaction
For every action, there is an equal and opposite reaction.

In 1696, he became warden of the Royal Mint, and within three years he was appointed master of the mint. He remained in this office until his death.

He was elected a fellow of the Royal Society of London in 1671, and in 1703 he became president. He was annually reelected for the rest of his life.

He was knighted in Cambridge in 1705.

In 1727, Newton became the first scientist buried at Westminster Abbey.

To Shed Some Light...

Newton drew inspiration from other great thinkers. He studied the works of Robert Boyle and Robert Hooke on optics and light; Rene Descartes's work on mathematics and physics; and the works of many other great scholars.

He observed the refraction of light by a glass prism and developed a series of elaborate experiments that led him to the conclusion that white light is made up of all the colored rays found in the rainbow. He said that light consisted of streams of minute particles.

His unconventional ideas were strongly rejected, causing Newton to delay the publication of *Opticks* for twelve years, until 1704.

MATH 101

CALCULUS

Newton is also credited with inventing integral and differential calculus. He shared credit—begrudgingly—for the latter with Gottfried Wilhelm Leibnitz.

Newton had developed the idea of differential calculus early in his studies, but did not publish it until after Leibniz had already published his findings. Leibniz claimed to have no prior knowledge of Newton's work, yet documents discovered after Leibniz's death seem to indicate that the mathematician was—at the very least—aware of Newton's mathematical theories.

In 1687, Newton published his greatest work, the *Philosophiae Naturalis Principia Mathematica*, or *Mathematical Principles of Natural Philosophy.* This three-volume work attempts to organize scientific and mathematical principles.

Did You Know?

Several of Newton's writings were published posthumously including the *Observations upon the Prophecies of Daniel* and the *Apocalypse of St. John* in 1733.

Islam

Islam at a Glance

There are at least 1.3 billion followers of Islam on the planet.

The major sects and denominations of Islam are the Sunni and the Shiite. Sufi is a mystical branch of Islam, not a major denomination.

Religious professionals of Islam are known as sheikhs. In the Shiite denomination, they are known as imams.

Muslims are strict monotheists, as they only believe in one god, whom they call Allah. Allah is the same God worshipped in Christian and Jewish faith.

The Five Pillars of Islam are:

- Confession of faith—*shahada*
- Daily prayer—*salat*
- Tax—*zakat*
- Pilgrimage—*hajj*
- Fasting—*sawm*

Qu'ran

Muslims follow the Qu'ran, a sacred text they believe to be the divine word of Allah as written by the prophet Muhammad. The origin of the name Quran comes from the text itself, and though it has many translations, it is loosely translated to "recitation".

The text has 114 chapters, and each is called a *sura*. Each sura is given a title which comes from a name or value discussed within the chapter. Muslims believe that Muhammad gave the suras their name under the command of Allah.

Major Islamic Holidays

Ramadan

Similar to the Jewish holiday Yom Kippur, Ramadan is a period of atonement and obedience to Allah. During Ramadan, Muslims are required to resist evil thoughts or actions, food and drink, and sexual intercourse from dawn until dusk.

Eid al-Fitr

The holiday is translated to mean the Festival of Fast-Breaking. It is similar to Christmas in the way it is celebrated, but has strong religious significance. Gifts are given, along with donations to charity, and Muslims typically take off from school or work for the celebration, which lasts three days.

Eid al-Adha

Also known as the Festival of Sacrifice, Eid al-Adha celebrates Ibrahim's (Abraham's) willingness to sacrifice his son Ishmael to Allah. In the ancient story, Ibrahim is allowed to save his son and sacrifice a goat instead. It begins the day after the pilgrims descend from Mount Arafat in their annual pilgrimage to Mecca.

Fond Farewells

Bloodlines for millennia have built and destroyed empires—and waged their fair share of wars in the name of family and all that is right and just— because, well, it really is the way of the world. Blood really is thicker than water, unless we're talking about the ports that dominate trade routes and drive economies, but we've already told you about those. Instead, let's stroll—in no particular order—through some of the last known political powerhouses of the past few thousand years. And yes, this will be on the final exam, so pay attention.

Yeah, yeah, we know. She wasn't truly Egyptian, but Cleopatra with her Macedonian heritage was, in fact, the last of the Ptolemy line to rule the Nile before she took her own life in 30 BC.

Montezuma II's 18-year reign as the last Aztec emperor ended in 1520.

In 1533, Spanish conquistador Francisco Pizarro ordered the death of Atahualpa, the last Inca king in Peru.

Poland hasn't had a king since Stanislaw II August Poniatowski's thirty-one-year reign ended in 1795.

The Qing Dynasty was the last imperial dynasty to rule China, and its last emperor, Henry Puyi, ended his four-year reign in 1912.

Charles I had the distinction of being both the last emperor of Austria and the last king of Austria, but the stress got to him after only two years, and he abdicated in 1918. Apparently, it was a popular year for deposing monarchs—and you'd know that if you've been reading carefully—because Germany forced its last kaiser, Wilhelm II, from the throne that same year. But none had it quite as bad that particular year as Nicholas II, a Romanov and the last of the Russian czars. He was executed alongside his family in 1918, ending three hundred years of dynastic rule in Russia.

Napoleon Bonaparte might not have had the staying power he would have liked as the despotic ruler of France—and self-proclaimed ruler of the world—but his offspring certainly kept the family name going. His last known descendent, Jerome Napoleon Bonaparte lived until 1945.

Afghanistan's shift from monarchy has been relatively recent. Its last king, Mohammed Zahir Shah, passed away in July 2007 at the age of ninety-two.

PHOTOGRAPHY

Joseph Nicéphore Niépce is said to have made the first successful photograph in 1826. He exposed pewter coated with a chemical substance to eight hours of sunlight. The chemical reaction to the sun produced a permanent image of a building and tree. Because the earth and sun were moving over the course of the eight hours, the picture is somewhat blurred. This photograph is on display at the University of Texas, Austin.

1727: Professor J. Schulze mixed chalk, nitric acid, and silver. He noticed a darkening effect on the mixture when it was exposed to sunlight. He had accidentally created the very first photosensitive compound.

1826: Nicéphore Niépce created a permanent image using photosensitive paper.

1834: Henry Fox Talbot created permanent negatives by using paper soaked in silver chloride and fixed with a salt solution.

1861: James Clerk-Maxwell, a Scottish physicist, demonstrated color photography in an experiment that involved three black and white photographs taken through a red, green, or blue filter.

1888: The first Kodak camera was produced. It contained a 20-foot roll of paper and could produce 100 circular photographs, all 2.5 inches in diameter.

The word photography comes from the Greek words meaning "light" and "writing." Sir John Herschel is credited as being the first to use the term in 1839; however, photography historian Robert Leggat says that astronomer Johann von Maedler used the term in a lecture before the Royal Society a few month's ahead of Herschel.

Daguerreotypes

Louis Daguerre discovered a way of projecting an image onto glass plates and reduced the exposure time from eight hours to ten to fifteen minutes. He also found that the image could be made permanent by immersing it in salt. He called this process, which took the world by storm, the daguerreotype.

Some people thought the daguerreotype was an instrument of the devil. They believed no manmade machine should attempt to fix an image created by God. Others thought the invention would put an end to painting and artists would be without jobs. However, one of the features of daguerreotypes was the ability to color them. Many artists of the day took on jobs hand-painting the photographs.

Autochrome to Kodachrome

Auguste and Louis Lumière made photography plates that could reproduce color in 1907. The pastel colors made photographs look dark, but the novelty was still received well by consumers. The Lumières called their process autochrome.

Almost thirty years earlier, Louis Ducas du Hauron came up with an idea of coating film with thin layers of dye. When processed, the photographs would be in full color. The only drawback was that the emulsions in the late 1800s were not perfected enough for the process to be accurately tested until the 1930s. The Eastman Kodak company produced a film based on Hauron's idea in 1935 and called it Kodachrome.

When Thomas Edison saw Eastman's cellulose film, he thought of a way to use it to make motion picture film for his Kinograph and Kineoscope.

BERNOULLI'S PRINCIPLE

Bernoulli's Principle is one that can help illustrate how pressure affects velocity of liquids. The principle, in part, explains the way water moves through a pipe, the way an airplane's wings rely on pressure, and the way airflow and pressure systems relate to one another. In simple terms, the principle states that when velocity of a fluid is increased, the pressure the fluid releases is decreased.

The principle comes from Bernoulli's equation, which shows that the sum of energy of fluid flowing on an enclosed path, or streamline, is the same at any point on the path. Consider water moving through a pipe: If the diameter of the pipe decreases, the speed of the water flow must increase, and vice versa.

Bernoulli's Principle only applies to incompressible flow, such as liquids, which have constant densities and are unaffected by pressure. This is untrue of gases. Bernoulli used liquids in all of his experiments, and therefore his equation can only be applied to incompressible flow with constant density.

Bernoulli's Equation

$p + \frac{1}{2} pV^2 + pgh = \text{constant}$

where *p* is the pressure, *p* is the density, *V* is the velocity, *h* is elevation, and *g* is the gravitational acceleration

Many textbooks falsely attribute the cause of an airplane's lift to Bernoulli's Principle. While the principle does lay the groundwork to understanding pressure and velocity, it does not explain the airflow above and below the wings of a plane. Newton's Third Law of Motion is actually a better explanation of airplane lift, since Bernoulli's Principle is only an explanation of liquids. Newton's Third Law of Motion holds that in order for an airplane to lift, the wing must push air down.

Pop Quiz #5

1) Who fought in the Crusades?
   a) Christians vs. Muslims
   b) Muslims vs. Jews
   c) Jews vs. Hindus
   d) Hindus vs. Christians

2) Who was the pope during the First Crusade?
   a) John Paul II
   b) Leo III
   c) Urban II
   d) Innocent III

3) Richard the Lionheart was the leader of which Crusade?
   a) First
   b) Second
   c) Third
   d) Fourth

4) When did the largest pilgrimage of Christendom occur?
   a) December 1761
   b) May 1859
   c) September 1908
   d) April 2005

5) *The Nibelungenlied* inspired what composer?
   a) Beethoven
   b) Bach
   c) Wagner
   d) Verdi

6) How tall is Michelangelo's *David*?
   a) 12.3 feet high
   b) 14.24 feet high
   c) 16.07 feet high
   d) 20.5 feet high

ANSWERS:

1) a 3) c 5) c
2) c 4) d 6) b

Crash Course

American Revolution

The American Revolution—known also as the American War of Independence—was the struggle through which the thirteen colonies along North America's Atlantic seaboard won their independence from Great Britain to form the United States.

It began April 19, 1775, with the "shot heard round the world" fired at Lexington, and ended more than eight years later with the Treaty of Paris, signed September 3, 1783.

The Thirteen Colonies adopted the Declaration of Independence in 1776, signifying formally their break from the mother country and the formation of the United States. They were New Hampshire, Massachusetts, Rhode Island, Connecticut, New York, New Jersey, Pennsylvania, Delaware, Maryland, Virginia, North Carolina, South Carolina, and Georgia.

Of course, revolution takes a little stoking, so consider the chain of events responsible.

Like a child off to college, experiencing his first taste of freedom, the colonists grew accustomed to life with its absentee parent, Great Britain. Local political institutions and social practices operated outside the British norm. Throw religious and economic strife into the equation, and the melting pot began to boil.

Like most imperial powers of the eighteenth century, Britain favored a mercantilist economy and passed the Navigation Acts to regulate the commerce of its colonies in the British interest. But decreeing it be so without strict enforcement, left the colonies, by and large, to their own devices, and its inhabitants began questioning why their toils should benefit a government half a world away.

In 1763, the Treaty of Paris ended the French and Indian War, effectively eliminating a long-running thorn in the side of the colonies. And then a shift in Britain's domestic policy tightened the political reins on the colonists, forcing them to begin earning their keep.

Conflict Commences

The first official shots of war were fired on April 19, 1775, and a revolution began.

On May 10, 1775, Ethan Allen and his Green Mountain Boys—flanked by Benedict Arnold and his troops—wrested control of Fort Ticonderoga from the British. Two days later, Seth Warner captured Crown Point, and Boston found itself under siege.

The British might have won the costly Battle of Bunker Hill on June 17, 1775, but they were unaware of the political strategizing taking place. Two days earlier, the Second Continental Congress had selected George Washington commander in chief of the Continental Armed Forces.

It was officially on. And yet indecision within the Congress ran rampant, pitting fierce revolutionaries against pro-British Loyalists. The schism was personified in the public split between patriot Benjamin Franklin and his Loyalist son, William.

In early 1776, Thomas Paine penned *Common Sense*, a fiery little pamphlet championing the colonial cause. The pen was obviously still mightier than the sword, though, as Paine's writings did indeed stir the emotions of his countrymen, but militarily they remained an untrained brood of farmers and merchants.

And despite its widespread historical significance, Thomas Jefferson's Declaration of Independence actually elicited little more than ripples in the wider world the day it was signed, July 4, 1776.

Realizing the uprising represented more than a few rogue ideas, the British government sent General William Howe and his brother, Admiral Richard Howe, to New York to negotiate peace. The colonists wouldn't have it, and the British retaliated with force.

Washington was defeated at Brooklyn Heights, retreated north and was forced to retreat again at Manhattan's Harlem Heights as well as at White Plains.

Demoralized, Washington and his troops fled to New Jersey.

Re-energized—and bolstered by popular support kindled by Thomas Paine's newest pamphlet, *The Crisis*—Washington crossed the Delaware River during the merciless winter of 1776–77, and captured small victories at Trenton and Princeton.

Help and Resolution

While war waged, the exhausted Middle Atlantic colonies finally received foreign aid thanks to the tireless wheeling and dealing of diplomats such as Benjamin Franklin, Arthur Lee, Silas Deane, and—not to give anything away—even the second president of the United States, John Adams.

In 1777, diplomat Pierre de Beaumarchais succeeded in arranging for the delivery of arms and supplies for the colonials just in time to win the Battle of Saratoga. The victory was enough for France to cautiously enter into an alliance with the fledgling country, and Benjamin Franklin is recognized for negotiating a treaty to that effect with the French foreign minister in 1778. The Spanish entered the fray one year later on the side of the colonials, but it was the French funding and supplies that proved crucial to a successful outcome.

In 1783, the Treaty of Paris recognized formally the sovereignty of the new nation, but the war-torn country now had to grapple with its own rebuilding efforts. A postwar depression gripped the economy, and the new administration proved politically wobbly in achieving the administrative benchmarks outlined in its own Articles of Confederation.

Wartime and political heroes—Washington, Adams, and Jefferson—understandably served as the first three presidents of the burgeoning nation, and their governing styles proved far less impressive to the salt-of-the-earth farmers-turned-revolutionaries who longed for more aggressive measures.

And yet, the American tenets of liberty and democracy had been embraced unequivocally, so no one complained too loudly.

France's middle class even took a few notes, but we'll get to that in good time.

Lexington and Paul Revere

On April 19, 1775, British General Thomas Gage deployed some seven hundred British troops commanded by Lieutenant Colonel Francis Smith to Concord, Massachusetts, just northwest of Boston, and ordered the brood to seize munitions that the colonists had been stockpiling. Word of the British departure from Boston spread like wildfire, thanks to patriot Paul Revere—along with William Dawes and Samuel Prescott—and his famous Midnight Ride.

When the British reached Lexington, they were met by seventy Minutemen under the command of Capt. John Parker.

The colonial militia was ordered to disperse, and the famous "shot heard round the world" rang out, signifying the launch of a revolution.

The Minutemen lost eight in the battle, with a ninth suffering severe wounds.

One British soldier was wounded in the skirmish, and they powered on the six miles to Concord.

The British contingent did accomplish its primary objective of seizing the stockpiled gunpowder, but some outlying bands encountered several hundred more Minutemen.

This time, three British soldiers fell, and only one patriot was lost.

Before the British retraced their steps to Boston, Minutemen inflicted some 273 casualties on their trained and seasoned adversaries.

Treaty of Paris

Signed September 3, 1783, between the American colonies and Great Britain, the Treaty of Paris ended the American Revolution and formally recognized the United States as an independent nation. It also brokered peace between Great Britain and its European adversaries, France and Spain.

Preliminary articles had been drafted almost one year earlier by John Adams, Benjamin Franklin, and John Jay, and they took their time negotiating the finer points of the contract to ensure the United States enjoyed the strongest foundation possible.

In addition to Britain recognizing the independence of the new nation, the diplomatic trio were also quite adamant regarding the delineation of boundaries that would allow for future western expansion of the former colonies.

David Hartley signed the document on behalf of Great Britain.

France and Spain signed separate preliminary documents with Great Britain on January 20, 1783, with the Dutch following suit on September 2 of the same year.

And per the negotiations of Adams, Franklin, and Jay, the treaty did, in fact, delineate the new nation's boundaries.

In the Northeast, the line extended from the source of the St. Croix River due north to the highlands separating the rivers flowing to the Atlantic from those draining into the St. Lawrence River, thence with the highlands to forty-five degrees north latitude, and then along the forty-fifth parallel to the St. Lawrence.

From there, the northern boundary followed a line midway through contiguous rivers and lakes (especially the Great Lakes) to the northwest corner of the Lake of the Woods, then due west to the sources of the Mississippi River, although no one yet knew where it was.

The Mississippi, south to thirty-one degrees north latitude, was made the western boundary.

On the south the line followed the thirty-first parallel east to the Chattahoochee River and its junction with the Flint River, then took a straight line to the mouth of the St. Marys River, and from there to the Atlantic.

Benjamin Franklin

Born in Boston in 1706, Benjamin Franklin was the tenth son of a soap and candlemaker. A true self-made man, he served an apprenticeship with his father between the ages of ten and twelve and then went to work for his half-brother James who ran a print shop.

James Franklin founded the *New England Courant* in 1721, only the fourth newspaper in the colonies. It was through the *Courant* that Benjamin Franklin secretly published his first writings under a pseudonym. But Ben and James parted ways in 1723, with the younger Franklin moving to Philadelphia and taking a job with another printer.

After two years in Philadelphia, Franklin worked his way up in the printing industry and published the *Pennsylvania Gazette* from 1730 to 1748, but it was *Poor Richard's Almanac* that gained the newspaperman widespread popularity with its pearls of frugal wisdom. He used his hard-won wealth to support libraries, hospitals, and an array of colleges and universities.

It was science and politics, however, that would ultimately endear him to the annals of American history. His was truly a life of service.

- He served as a clerk and member of the colonial legislature.
- He served as deputy postmaster of Philadelphia and deputy postmaster general of the colonies.
- He represented Pennsylvania at the Albany Congress, convened in 1754 to unite the colonies during the French and Indian War.
- He served as agent for Pennsylvania and later Georgia, New Jersey, and Massachusetts until 1775, when his English sensibilities were compromised by an illogical tax.
- In May 1775, Franklin returned to Philadelphia and immediately rose through the ranks of the Continental Congress. Only thirteen months later, he served on the committee that drafted the historic Declaration of Independence.
- Perhaps his greatest service was abroad, however, as a statesman who directed negotiations of the treaties of commerce and alliance with France and ultimately the resolution of the war for American independence.

- After returning to the United States in 1785, Franklin became president of the Supreme Executive Council of Pennsylvania and was a vocal participant in the Constitutional Convention.
- In his sunset years, he was elected in 1787 as the first president of the Pennsylvania Society for Promoting the Abolition of Slavery, a cause he had championed for some fifty years. He went so far as to sign a memorial to Congress recommending the abolition of the disgraceful practice.
- He died in 1790 at the age of eighty-four and was laid to rest in Christ Church Burial Ground in Philadelphia.

That's What He Said: Benjamin Franklin

- A good conscience is a continual Christmas.
- If you know how to spend less than you get, you have the philosopher's stone.
- A slip of the foot you may soon recover, but a slip of the tongue you may never get over.
- He that falls in love with himself will have no rivals.
- Early to bed and early to rise makes a man healthy, wealthy, and wise.
- Wish not so much to live long as to live well.
- A countryman between two lawyers is like a fish between two cats.

Thomas Paine

"I am certain that when opinions are free, either in matters of government or religion, truth will finally and powerfully prevail."

The Age of Reason, 1794

Thomas Paine, who became one of the most celebrated political theorists and writers of the colonial period was born in Thetford, Norfolk, England, to Quaker parents.

Although he began his adult career in the military, he was dismissed in 1772 after leading the call for higher pay. Two years later, he set sail for what—with his help—would become the United States. Benjamin Franklin provided his letters of introduction.

In 1776, he penned *Common Sense*, arguing the colonies had outgrown the usefulness of Britain's oversight and calling for recognition of their independence.

In December of that same year, he wrote the first in a series of sixteen follow-up pamphlets, collectively called *The Crisis,* that proved quite effective in keeping the fires of revolution stoked.

Immediately following the war, he returned to his homestead in New Rochelle, New York, but he departed for England in 1787, where he wrote the two-part *The Rights of Man* (1791 and 1792), defending the French Revolution in reply to Edmund Burke's *Reflections on the Revolution in France.*

The Rights of Man, at its core, argued that men possess natural rights common to all men and that only democratic institutions are able to guarantee these rights.

It's certainly not surprising that the English took exception to Paine's opinions, and he fled to Paris in 1792. It was there—as a member of the National Convention—he injected himself into the fray of the French Revolution. He was imprisoned by the Jacobins during the Reign of Terror which gave him ample opportunity—and inspiration—to write his famous *The Age of Reason.*

When Paine returned to the United States in 1802, he found himself a pariah for having written a fiery criticism to the new nation's commander in chief and first president.

He died a pauper in 1809.

THOMAS JEFFERSON

Despite Thomas Jefferson's lengthy and distinguished resume, his tombstone reads simply:

"Author of the Declaration of American Independence, of the Statute of Virginia for religious freedom, and Father of the University of Virginia."

Apparently his stints as governor of Virginia, U.S. minister to France, secretary of state under George Washington, vice president under John Adams, and president of the United States from 1801 to 1809.

Elected to the Second Continental Congress, Jefferson was appointed to lead a committee responsible for drafting the Declaration of Independence for which he served as primary author.

He later proved instrumental in revamping the State of Virginia's criminal code, but his plans for tax-supported elementary education and modernized curriculum for the College of William and Mary failed.

His introduction in 1779 of a bill on religious liberty literally reshaped political lines in Virginia. It stated simply "that all men shall be free to profess, and by argument to maintain, their opinions on matters of religion, and that the same shall in no wise diminish, enlarge, or affect their civil capacities."

Eight years of arguing ensued because many Virginians regarded the bill as an attack upon Christianity, but it did pass in 1786, due to the diplomacy of James Madison.

In June 1779, Jefferson was elected governor of Virginia, and his political adversaries gave him poor marks as a wartime leader. He retired after only two years in office.

In 1796, Jefferson lost the presidency to John Adams by a slim three-point electoral college vote and, instead, assumed the vice presidency before becoming president four years later where he faced stiff opposition from the Federalists. The people, however, loved his simple and frugal politics:

- Internal taxes were slashed.
- The military budget was cut.

- Alien and Sedition Acts were allowed to lapse.
- And a plan was put in place to eliminate national debt.
- What wasn't to love?

His successful negotiation of the Louisiana Purchase in 1803 sealed his bid for a second term, and he swept every state except Connecticut and Delaware. But trouble was brewing, and Aaron Burr conspired unsuccessfully to create an independent republic in the new territory and mount an invasion against the Spanish in Mexico.

Jefferson, who ironically had little stomach for insubordination, had Burr arrested in 1807, but he was ultimately acquitted.

Jefferson turned his sights to foreign policy and found his popularity didn't serve him nearly as well overseas. He enforced economic pressures on Britain and France to avoid both war and cowardice. The Embargo Act of 1807, was designed to force British and French recognition of American sovereignty by prohibiting practically all exports and many imports.

He somehow miscalculated how many feathers this action would ruffle at home, and the Federalist party soared to newfound popularity. He repealed the widely unpopular measure shortly before his retirement in 1809.

Jefferson spent his retirement focused on pet projects such as founding the University of Virginia at Charlottesville in 1819. It wasn't just his idea. He actually planned it, designed it, and supervised its construction as well as faculty hiring.

On July 4, 1826—the fiftieth anniversary of the signing of the Declaration of Independence—Jefferson died at his personal estate, Monticello. His lifetime had been dedicated successfully to attaining American freedom from Britain, freedom of conscience (i.e., religious liberty), and the freedom only formal education can ensure, an enlightened people.

Cholera in America

The arrival of cholera in America bore striking resemblance to the spread of the Black Death in Europe. The ports might have welcomed wealth and prosperity to the fledgling nation with open arms, but they also accepted death and destruction with equal abandon.

Embracing the tired and huddled masses meant exposing the rest of the country to the virulent ailments that plagued trade and immigrant ships from the corners of the earth.

Ireland posed a particular threat on the cholera front. It cost only three pounds to gain passage to America, and the Irish fled their homeland's potato famine in droves.

And that's where the real fun started.

Immigrant ships were literal petri dishes of disease and vulgarity.

Imagine five hundred people crammed into a space big enough for one hundred fifty, sharing slop buckets and contaminated water. Those who survived the treacherous trip quickly infected their new homes. The results were unequivocally disastrous, and the United States wasn't the only North American locale impacted. In the summer of 1832 some 2,200 new arrivals died in Quebec along with another 1,220 in Montreal.

Residents of Detroit were smart enough not to draw their water from the river, but they weren't quite smart enough to set up their outhouses far enough away from their wells to avoid contaminating the water supply.

Quarantine efforts in New York, Vermont, and along the Erie Canal failed, and at least one businessman—banker John Pintard—asked incredulously whether the physicians causing the mass hysteria with their daily cholera reports had any idea the repercussions it could have on trade.

CRASH COURSE

THE U.S. PRESIDENCY

One of the coolest things about being president of the United States—especially in the early days—was that most everything one did was considered a first of its kind. Of course, sometimes that could just as easily be a curse. For instance, Thomas Jefferson might have had a distinguished career as secretary of state, vice president, and eventually president before wielding his real power as a foreign diplomat, but another line on his lengthy resume notes that he was also the first presidential candidate to ever lose a bid for commander in chief. It certainly didn't help things that he lost to John Adams by only a three-point margin in the largely untested Electoral College. Remember, no one quite had the chutzpah to challenge General George Washington when he "ran," so somebody had to be the first to lose.

Of course, making history is all part of being president of the United States. Consider Grover Cleveland, who remains the only U.S. president to serve nonconsecutive terms, and Andrew Johnson, who was the first president impeached. In 1972, Richard Nixon earned the distinction of being the first U.S. president to visit China, igniting a trend that continued without incident for two decades until George H. W. Bush became the first U.S. president, we believe, to vomit on a Japanese prime minister. Bad sushi was ruled the culprit in that one. Even Bill Clinton—full name William Jefferson Clinton for anyone taking notes and enjoying the historical reference—was continuing to make history years after he left office. Due to a recent tweak to the law, you see, Clinton will be the last president to receive the courtesy of lifelong Secret Service protection. The cost-cutting and security-conscious measure states that presidents elected after January 1, 1997, and their spouses will receive protection for only a maximum of ten years after the conclusions of their terms.

The U.S. President's cabinet includes: the attorney general and the secretaries of state, Treasury, defense, agriculture, interior, commerce, health and human services, housing and urban development, labor, transportation, Energy, veterans affairs, homeland security, and education.

Crash Course

American History

- The city of New Orleans likes to take the credit for launching the biggest annual party in the country—Mardi Gras, or Fat Tuesday—but the Carnival celebration in Mobile, Alabama, actually predates the festivities in the Big Easy by more than a hundred years. Indeed, the first known Mardi Gras celebration occurred in the Alabama port city in 1703, one full year before New Orleans was even founded, giving it exclusive rights to the French inspired celebration that precedes the forth days of the Christian season of Lent beginning on Ash Wednesday. New Orleans didn't adopt its raucous festivities until 1826, making Mobile the true birthplace of Mardi Gras. Laissez les bon temps rouler!
- When South Carolina became the first state to secede officially from the Union on December 20, 1860, the stage was set for what remains the bloodiest campaign ever to involve American soldiers: the U.S. Civil War. In fact, more than twenty thousand soldiers were killed, wounded, or declared missing in action during the Battle of Antietam alone, waged on September 17, 1862, and recorded as the most gruesome one-day skirmish of the war.
- On February 24, 1924, the state of Nevada became the first in the country to use the gas chamber to execute a prisoner, but it was Texas in 1977 that first administered capital punishment via lethal injection.
- If there's one thing for which Americans have a penchant it's innovation in transportation, and for the longest time the adage held that bigger was better. Built by eccentric billionaire Howard Hughes, the Spruce Goose flew for one mile on November 2, 1947, and remains the largest aircraft ever built. Because it was originally designed as a prototype for troop transport for the military, the eight-engine seaplane boasted a wingspan of 320 feet. But because of its grandiose design, the 140-ton Spruce Goose—with aviator Hughes himself at the wheel—managed to fly for only one mile on its virgin and only flight in 1947.

- Architectural prowess—again, subscribing to the bigger–is-better school of thought—is another mark of distinction for the United States over the past two centuries or so. Consider the following:
- New York City is home to the Cathedral of St. John the Divine. At 601-feet long and 146-feet wide, the Amsterdam Avenue marvel is the largest documented cathedral in the world.
- Queens, New York, is home to the largest known stained-glass window in the world. The masterpiece—300 feet long by 23 feet high—can be glimpsed at Kennedy International Airport by any travelers who arrived the full two hours before departure and have a little time on their hands.
- St. Louis's famed Gateway Arch is perhaps one of the greatest optical illusions ever constructed. Although it appears taller than it is wide, the architectural gem is actually an identical 630 feet in height and width.
- Frederic-August Bartholdi sculpted the 225-ton Statue of Liberty. It arrived in New York City in 1885 aboard the Isere.

WESTERN CIVILIZATION 101

FRENCH REVOLUTION

The French monarchy underestimated terribly the power of a disgruntled middle class in 1789. Don't worry if you get a little confused. King Louis XVI lost his own head trying to keep up:

On July 14 of that year, the Paris prison, the Bastille, was stormed.

Three months later, Louis and the royal family were removed to Paris.

In June of 1791, Louis attempted unsuccessfully to flee to Varennes.

In September 1792—under immense pressure of the advancing armies of Austria, Holland, Prussia, and Sardinia—the Legislative Assembly was replaced by the National Convention.

The National Convention proclaimed France a republic.

Three months later, Louis stood trial and was executed on January 21, 1793.

That same month, the French revolutionary government declared war with Britain—wanting only to rule the entire world—and the conflict continued for another twenty-two years.

The Committee of Public Safety and the Revolutionary Tribunal were instituted immediately after Louis's execution.

The resulting Reign of Terror began in September 1793 and lasted until Robespierre's fall ten months later.

The brutal period in French history was punctuated by the particularly gruesome acts of its final six weeks—known as the Red Terror—during which almost 1,400 people met their fates at the guillotine.

In October 1795, the Directory replaced the Convention, but it was short lived.

In 1799, the Consulate replaced the Directory.

Napoleon Bonaparte appointed himself emperor in May 1804.

Liberty, Equality, and Fraternity

The French Revolution is undoubtedly one of the defining periods of Western history, and while its parallels with the almost simultaneous American Revolution will be explored, there's a larger implication to consider first.

The revolution's impact on nineteenth-century British political, philosophical, and intellectual thought was monumental, especially on English radicals such as Thomas Paine, William Blake, and William Godwin.

The reason was simple.

The movement resonated as the triumph of reason over irrationality and the status quo.

It's no surprise then that English revolutionaries such as Paine, Blake, and Godwin saw it as mankind's golden opportunity to reclaim perfection.

The masses embraced for the simplicity of its battle cry of "Liberty, equality, and fraternity."

The revolution's descent into carnage via the Reign of Terror, however, swayed many observers—including English poets William Wordsworth and Samuel Coleridge—to reconsider their convictions.

Of course, England's old guard never drank the Kool-Aid.

Instead, the establishment clung to the rational ideologies of philosopher John Locke and physicist Sir Isaac Newton.

In fact, Edmund Burke denounced the uprising with such vehemence in his 1790 *Reflections on the Revolution in France* that England's King George III is said to have bound countless copies for his friends because he believed it a book "every gentleman ought to read."

In case you're interested, Burke's premise was that buying into the revolution's hype was short sighted because it was launched by a bunch of zealots who preyed on the religious anguish of a downtrodden people. Burke argued that these upstarts weren't just out for blood in their own country, but that they wouldn't be satisfied until all of Europe—and ultimately the entire world—lay at their feet.

Paine answered Burke's intellectual challenge with *The Rights of Man* in 1791, and, the debate continues today.

Peas in a Pod

So what was the common denominator between the American and French revolutions? Their economies.

Take one oppressed and abused majority being bled dry by the elite minority. Throw in incalculable examples of exploitation and incessant political manipulations. Stir, and heads begin to roll.

- Britain's economic dependence on the American colonies—and, thus its continual taxation—drew the appropriate line in the sand for revolt.
- Of course, the taxes themselves weren't the problem. The problem was that Britain finally stopped even trying to formulate reasonable explanations for the incessant demands for new revenue streams.
- In turn, cries arose of "taxation without representation" because the colonists themselves had seated members of Parliament who weren't the ones responsible for levying the new tariffs.
- In the end, it wasn't an issue of inability to pay but rather unwillingness to be extorted.
- The situation in France was a bit more complicated.
- Trade alone didn't raise enough funds to pay off the second-tier nation's debts, so the king levied arbitrary taxes to make up the difference, and it was the lower-class residents who bore the brunt of the bill.
- Complicating the issue was the fact that nobles were exempt from taxation, and the king delighted in selling titles when it suited him. The practice served, however, to only worsen the nation's economic stability and drive a more divisive wedge between the peasants and the nobility.
- It wasn't just a case of the rich getting richer.
- In France, the peasants were literally starving to death while the king's pets flaunted their status with flagrant disregard.
- In this context, one can see that both the American colonists and the French peasants had no choice but to revolt as a means of survival.

Napoleon Bonaparte

Born into an upper crust family in Corsica on August 15, 1769, Napoleon Bonaparte began his despotic exploits in military school, where he showed promise and was rapidly promoted.

In 1796, he was appointed commander of the French army in Italy and promptly forced Austria and its allies to make nice.

Just two years later, Napoleon set his sights on the strategic—and profitable—British trade routes with India and conquered Ottoman-ruled Egypt in short order. The maneuver backfired.

Napoleon's fleet was obliterated by the British during the Battle of the Nile, and the fracas gave France's chief adversaries—Austria and Russia—a new ally in Britain.

Disgraced, Napoleon returned to Paris only to discover its government crumbling.

Never one to let an opportunity slide, Napoleon became consul, was made consul for life in 1802 and, by 1804, had proclaimed himself emperor.

And in many rights, he was a highly effective leader: He centralized the government, established the Bank of France, reinstateded Roman Catholicism as the national religion, and initiated widespread legal reform through the adoption of the Napoleonic Code.

He was also a force to be reckoned with militarily.

- In 1800, he defeated the Austrians at Marengo.
- He negotiated a sweeping European peace, establishing France as the continent's true power.
- But war resumed with Britain in 1803—joined later by Russia and Austria—and the tide shifted.
- Napoleon's forces suffered a humiliating defeat by the British navy at Trafalgar in 1805.
- Recognizing—to some degree—his weaknesses, Napoleon opted to attack the Austro-Russian forces rather than invade England per his original plan.
- He dealt the Austro-Russian armies a swift defeat at Austerlitz in 1805, and gobbled up annexed Prussian lands as his spoils.

He now fancied himself emperor of Europe, and many signs bolstered his argument:

- The Holy Roman Empire dissolved.
- Holland and Westphalia were created.
- Napoleon's supporters assumed positions of power across the continent from Holland, Westphalia, and Italy to Naples, Spain, and Sweden.
- Eager for an heir, Napoleon had his marriage to Josephine de Beauharnais annulled in 1810 and married the daughter of the Austrian emperor. His new bride bore him a son the next year.
- It was a day late and a dollar short, however.
- The Peninsular War had begun in 1808, and by 1813 France's military budget had been tapped.
- Napoleon invaded Russia in 1812, but was forced to retreat.
- Within two years, Paris fell and Napoleon went into exile on the island of Elba in the Mediterranean.
- Never one to know his limits, the despot escaped from the island in 1815 and waged the Battle of Waterloo. He failed.
- He was captured, imprisoned by the British and held until his death on May 5, 1821, on the island of St. Helena in the Atlantic.

That's What He Said: Napoleon

- Glory is fleeting, but obscurity is forever.
- A celebrated people lose dignity upon a closer view.
- Courage is like love; it must have hope to nourish it.
- A revolution can be neither made nor stopped. The only thing that can be done is for one of several of its children to give it a direction by dint of victories.
- France has more need of me than I have need of France.

THE INDUSTRIAL REVOLUTION PHASE I: ENGLAND

Originating in England, at a time when great changes occurred in economic practices, transportation, and social structures, and in agricultural, textile, and metal manufacturing technologies. Agricultural economies became industrial. The nature of production was itself changed, impacting what was produced where and in what manner. Items historically made in homes or small shops began to be produced in factories, in mass quantities. As technical efficiency increased through applications of both scientific and practical knowledge of the manufacturing process, productivity increased dramatically.

The Industrial Revolution saw the growth of cities as people moved into urban areas from rural communities searching for work. These changes overturned not only economies, but societies as a whole, following the availability of a variety of material items and new business practices. This was the beginning of modern economic growth and development expansion.

Changes in Agriculture

Agriculture was prominent in English life not only for sustaining the population but also as a source of raw materials for the textile industry. Wool and cotton production for cloth manufacturing increased annually. This yield was the result of improved techniques such as cultivating clover and other legumes to restore soil fertility rather than allowing the land to lie fallow after being exhausted of nutrients during cultivation. This increased the amount of food available to sustain livestock, which increased the size of herds for meat and allowed farmers larger spring herds.

Sturdier farm utensils created from metal aided the agricultural changes and increased the efforts in livestock breeding, insect control, irrigation and farming methods, new crops, and the use of horsepower for cultivation. These changes and advances in agriculture supported the growing industrial areas. With the means to sustain its workforce, England was prepared for further expansion of its economy.

Changes in the Textile Industry

The manufacture of cloth had occurred in the home. Beginning with the raw product shorn from the sheep, the wool would be sorted, cleaned, and dyed before being combed and spun into thread to be woven into cloth. Typically these tedious tasks were performed by the hands of women and children. Prior to machines such as John Kay's flying shuttle and Lewis Paul's roller spinner, the textile industry was too inefficient and complex. Other advances with similar machines allowed for the creation of factories that could utilize the machines to increase output. Again, women and children could be employed in these factories at far lower wages than men. Working conditions within the factories were not regulated and were often dangerous.

Changes in Coal Mining

An industry struggling with unsafe working practices and conditions, coal mining faced hazards that predated the Industrial Revolution. Different methods of mining were used in different areas, but all required use of manual labor. Children were often used due to their size. Coal was mined and moved through tunnels to a shaft to the surface. Carts on rails pulled by mules or ponies were later used to speed the process, which increased steadily. Other improvements in the industry were in the form of improved tunnel ventilation and illumination systems, surface and underground transportation, the use of gunpowder to blast seams, and safety lamps.

Changes in the Iron Industry

Major improvements in the iron industry came in the eighteenth century, most notably with Abraham Darby's invention of pig iron smelted with coke as opposed to charcoal. Where charcoal was an excellent source of energy for smelting, it was depleting the forests. Darby's process grew in popularity in spite of issues with brittleness and impurities, so pig iron could not sustain being forged into implements. This type was limited to use in castings. Other improvements would occur to produce higher quality materials and better techniques for fashioning.

Transportation by Rail

Improving transportation stimulated the progress of the Industrial Revolution. Raw materials, finished goods, food, and people all needed a quick, reliable, and cost efficient manner of transportation. Rivers and streams had long been used for internal transport, but moving bulk goods could be problematic. Backed by merchants and industrialists, canals were built to aid in the overland transport of goods. The emergence of the railroad made canals obsolete. Cast-iron rails had been servicing mines with trams, and a number of engineers were searching for a way to apply the steam engine in an application for rail. A few initial developments of locomotives were made by Richard Trevithick, John Blekinsop, and William Hedley. The first public railroad to use locomotives and carry passengers in addition to freight was the Stockton to Darlington line, but the equipment was too costly. Railroads came to dominate transportation throughout England and serve as another example of economic challenges sparking industrial innovation, this time to create an effective rail system crucial to the growth not only of industry but the economy as a whole.

Transportation by Steam

Steam power is touted as the greatest technological advance of the Industrial Revolution. The development of the steam engine is attributed to James Watt, whose engine was an improvement upon a development of Thomas Savery and Thomas Newcomen. Watt's engine was more efficient than Newcomen's and used the cannon-boring technique developed by John Wilkinson to create the large cylinder he needed for the steam engine. Applying an efficient steam engine to industrial and transportation needs accelerated industrialization.

Population Explosion

The population rates began to grow at a faster rate than ever known. This can be attributed not only to a decline in the death rate and a simultaneous rise in birth rates, but also the elimination of disease and an increase in availability and access to foods that provided a healthier diet and lifestyle. Increased wages were provided by industries. This increase in wealth by working these positions instead of apprenticeships gave people the means to marry and have children at earlier ages as well as provided improved clothing and housing for their families.

As factories became more widespread, settlements grew up around them. Some factory owners provided housing for their employees. Other factories started up in existing towns with an available labor pool.

Location, Location, Location

The primary factor in locating a factory was power. and as early forms of power hinged on moving water so factories would develop in the hills around streams and rivers. As steam power developed, and various applications for its use were improved, proximity to water was not as critical. The steam engine could drive machinery and free mill owners from being saddled with property close to moving water. Location near natural mineral sources was also key to minimizing the cost and effort in moving bulk materials. This allowed factories to be located closer to population centers and seaports, thereby fulfilling both labor and transport needs.

Complications of Growth

Unfortunately, growth in northern cities was so rapid that crowding, filth, and lack of regulations were rampant and besides, no one took the time to consider the impact of these conditions. Little was known about the impact of public sanitation or public health on the human population. As hygienic conditions began to decline in heavily populated areas, outbreaks of disease such as typhoid and cholera would appear.

Money, Money, Money

Progress is expensive. In the era before the Industrial Revolution, land was a source of wealth and power among aristocrats in the feudal system. With the ownership of factories and machinery, that began to change. Investors in factories and machines came from all backgrounds and did not belong to any single class but shared a desire to invest in new ventures and thereby speed the growth of the revolution. Initially investments were made in a field close to that of the investor's primary business, but as opportunities brought profit, these same entrepreneurs would invest in ventures they knew far less about.

There were two types of capital in play here, long-term capital to expand current business and short-term capital to purchase needed materials, maintain inventories, or pay wages. Long-term capital needs could be met by mortgaging buildings, factories, and machines. The short-term capital was more problematic as the need for raw materials and maintaining stocks was crucial. This was often financed by extensions of credit to manufacturers, producers, and dealers, and the supplier of the raw materials would often wait months to be paid by the manufacturers following their receipt of payment for products sold.

Paying employees presented additional problems as there were often insufficient stores of money with which to pay the wages. Employers might alter the days on which employees were paid or pay some early in the day allowing the money to circulate through shops and stores as purchases were made. The money would make it back to the hands of the employer through these purchases, and he would be able to pay more employees. All of these practices were ineffective and unacceptable. The true cause of the matter was an inadequate banking system in remote industrial areas, nor was the Bank of England, with its attention on affairs of state and the financial center of London, able to accommodate the needs of the manufacturers.

Cholera's Calamity

Stunning in its speed to spread and grow virulent, cholera claimed hundreds of thousands of lives, but it also helped epidemiologists identify the link between sanitation and public health. Its wrath really did lay the foundation for modern water and sewage systems.

But the silver lining pretty much ends there.

The malady strikes with staggering swiftness. Acute diarrhea, cramps, vomiting, fever, and—ultimately—death typically occur within twelve to forty-eight hours. It is caused by ingesting water, food, or any substance contaminated by the feces of another cholera victim, and casual contact with chamber pots, soiled clothing, and even bedding were also thought to contribute to its spread.

Cholera reached pandemic status in the nineteenth century.

For centuries, the illness had incubated along the Ganges River in India; then a grand-scale outbreak decimated Calcutta in 1817. The great Kumbh festival at Haridwar in the Upper Ganges was ground zero, and because the festival lasts three months—drawing pilgrims from across the country—the aftershock was devastating.

It is believed that inhabitants of the Lower Bengal unknowingly carried the disease into festival camps, and then the illness spread exponentially after folks returned to their homes. Hundreds of thousands nationwide succumbed.

And then trade routes fanned out the epidemic to Iran, Baku, and Astrakhan and up the Volga into Russia. These northern neighbors then repeated the very same faux pas and carried cholera into their own autumn merchants' fair in Nizhny-Novgorod.

The cycle repeated. When the businessmen returned to their homes across Russia and Europe, cholera made the trips with them.

Expanded trade routes and the advent of steam engines might have brought the world a little closer together, but it also hastened the spread of global killers such as cholera, leaving death and destruction in their wake:

In 1832, a New Yorker said he literally fell out in the street "as if knocked down with an ax. I had no premonition at all."

Harbor quarantines proved futile.

There appeared to be little or no pattern among the stricken.

Acute dehydration was one of the more grotesque symptoms. The skin would become discolored, taking on a bruised appearance, while the hands and feet were drawn and puckered.

In a letter to a friend, the German poet Heinrich Heine offered the following characterization of an outbreak in Paris: "A masked ball in progress...suddenly the gayest of the harlequins collapsed, cold in the limbs, and underneath his mask, violet blue in the face. Laughter died out, dancing ceased and in a short while carriage-loads of people hurried from the Hotel Dieu to die, and to prevent a panic among the patients were thrust into rude graves in their dominoes (long, hooded capes worn with a half-mask). Soon the public halls were filled with dead bodies, sewed in sacks for want of coffins...long lines of hearses stood in queue."

As stated earlier, the Industrial Revolution hastened cholera's spread and, in turn, spawned the world's first slums to house its less fortunate victims and survivors.

The first-recorded tenements began dotting skylines in what some historians contend was a pathetic attempt to live as far above the ground-level cesspools as possible.

Of course, until the 1840s sewers were nothing more than oblong cesspools with an overflow engineered at one end. It was the lucky job of "night men" to climb into the cauldrons of waste and shovel them out by hand.

In fact, it was actually a common practice to empty one's chamber pot out an open window directly onto the street below.

It was under these circumstances that cholera first struck England in the town of Sunderland on October 26, 1831.

Tradition holds that a citizen by the name of William Sproat died from the malady that day, even though everybody from his family to random merchants tried to explain away his death to any number of unrelated factors. Their ulterior motive, of course, was to avoid a forty-day maritime quarantine of the ports.

Luckily for them—in the short term, anyway—the medical profession of the day did not yet consider cholera contagious. Little did the esteemed physicians know there were already two infected households just doors away.

Sproat didn't learn of the "coincidence" for three months.

Edison and the Lightbulb

Thomas Edison didn't invent the lightbulb—he just made it work. More than a dozen people were working on their versions of the lightbulb. Joseph Swan had already placed lightbulbs in homes in England. And American inventor Hiram Maxim had a bulb that would burn for 24 hours straight.

So what was the big deal for Edison? He developed a total electric system—the bulbs, the wires, the fuses—all the elements necessary to satisfy customers. He had a plan to install underground wires and light up all of lower Manhattan.

New and Approved

Edison improved on Alexander Graham Bell's telephone by designing a carbon transmitter (mouthpiece) that improved the sound of the speaker.

Lightbulb Trivia

- Macy's department store in New York City became the first store to use incandescent lamp lighting in 1883.
- In 1888, the Hotel Everett on Park Row in New York City became the first hotel to be illuminated by electric light. There were 101 electric lightbulbs.
- New York theaters were the first to take advantage of using lightbulbs to spell out messages on their marquees.
- The world's largest lightbulb is in Edison, New Jersey. The lamp shaped like a lightbulb stands on top of the 131-foot Edison Memorial Tower. The tower itself stands on the site of Edison's famous Menlo Park Lab.

Edward Jenner: Father of Immunology

Born in Gloucestershire, England, Edward Jenner was the son of the local vicar. When he was 14, he began training to be a physician.

- In 1796, already a well-established doctor, he experimented on an eight-year-old boy by inserting cells from a cowpox lesion into the boy's arm.
- Jenner's experiment was successful, and he proved that a mild case of cowpox would prevent children from getting smallpox.
- The Royal Society said this was not proof enough, so Jenner experimented on other children, including his 11-month-old son.
- Finally with enough proof, Jenner's discovery was published, but the general public did not accept it. Many people, especially the clergy, thought it was repulsive and ungodly. Eventually, people understood the protection Jenner's vaccines could provide.
- Smallpox vaccinations were being used in many countries around the world before Jenner's death in 1923.

Annihilation

It was Jenner's hope that someday the smallpox virus would be annihilated. It took 180 years, but today, according to the World Health Organization, smallpox exists in only two university research laboratories.

The last case of smallpox occurred in Somali in 1977.

PHASE II: AMERICA

The Industrial Revolution began to impact America on a socioeconomic level as it grew into a modern, more urban and industrial nation. The United States began as a rich but sparsely populated continent completely open to exploration. As the populations grew, Americans explored the territory and applied business and manufacturing processes for their needs.

The fact that Americans were far more literate than their European counterparts aided in their efforts, because they could read and apply new industrial techniques as they became available in print.

They worked quickly to adapt and provide more efficient and cost-effective methods of creating goods as well as moving them, as well as people and capital cross country. The stability of the government and its willingness to aid these processes and encourage progress in enterprise helped tremendously.

Growth became noticeable following the Embargo Act of 1807 as well as the War of 1812. The Embargo Act ceased the export of American goods and the import of goods from other countries. During the War of 1812 against the British, it was exceedingly obvious that the United States needed a more effective system of transportation and greater economic independence. The two factors served to expand manufacturing throughout the country.

The United States is credited with what has been deemed the "Second Industrial Revolution" due to the wave of additional inventions developed to benefit textiles, centrally powered factories, iron making and structuring businesses.

Location, Location, Location

The United States had abundant natural resources. The key was to establish your business close enough to make use of them without great cost and delays in production times. For example, wood, because of its availability, was used more in the United States than in Europe as fuel as well as for machinery and in construction. Americans were able to construct world-renowned woodworking machines. Mills and other factories began to emerge close to rivers and streams, for water fuels power.

Complications of Growth

As seen in England, people in the United States also began moving from rural communities into cities in pursuit of work within growing industrial factories. The complications witnessed in America also mirrored those of England—crowded cities, poor sanitation, and disease. Advances in technology allowed for good production levels to increase, often in factory settings, and meet the demand of the growing populations. Again, as in England, these new factories needed workers and with no trained adults, child labor was abundant and cost effective. The economical workforce faced environments with little or no regulation and conditions that were often dangerous.

Changes in Agriculture

The majority of the labor force, almost 75 percent, worked in agriculture in the United States. Advances in agricultural technology provided better equipment to more efficiently perform tasks. Cyrus McCormick invented a reaper which could provide a less expensive yet more efficient manner of harvesting grain. John Deere's metal plow produced a similar effect on cultivation techniques.

Changes in Manufacturing

The development of continuous-process manufacturing in the United States enabled large quantities of the same product to be made in a nonstop operation. Stopping only for repairs and to maintain the equipment, the process would run continually. The process was applied to flour production in water-powered mills with grain literally entering at the high end of the mill and leaving as flour at the other. The process minimized the need for manual labor and lowered mill production costs. Mills for grinding snuff and other tobacco products adopted this process as well. The meatpacking industry also found ways to apply this process to improve their production, as did distilling and refining processors of kerosene and other petroleum based products. Automated processes gave the added benefit of a uniform product and reduced human labor.

The American system of production, using specialized machines to produce mass quantities of interchangeable parts for assembly into a final product, was adopted and applied throughout various industries that continued to impact the labor force needed to supply demand. The process first appeared in the manufacture of axes, shovels, clocks, and locks but would also become critical in producing large numbers of firearms, as seen in Samuel Colt's application in the manufacture of pistols.

Changes in Textiles

Eli Whitney invented a machine able to separate cotton seeds from fibers much faster than manual labor. The cotton gin allowed the South to increase cotton supplies and support the economy of the North. where they processed the raw cotton into cloth. Francis C. Lowell's investment in this manufacturing venture was a result of the destructive impact of the War of 1812 on his business. By combining spinning and weaving in a factory based on successful models in England, he was able to revitalize his business. Factories of this type expanded the textile industry in the northern states. Isaac Singer utilized the American system in his development of sewing machines. The application of mechanized sewing in factories delivered the ability to meet the ever increasing demand for goods.

Changes in Communication Methods

The invention of the telegraph and its transmission network by Samuel F. B. Morse provided communication from the East Coast to through the Deep South. This allowed messages to be sent over long distances via electronic pulses transmitting the code through a wire. As the use of the telegraphs expanded, a national market was created.

Changes in Iron

Iron and steel production welcomed the application of newer processes in the late 1800s, which revolutionized the industry.

Transportation

Unlike England, the United States is a vast country, presenting a challenge in tying together resources, markets, and people. Where private entrepreneurs made initial progress in transportation efforts, the government was active in the process as well. Their impact was most noted in the development of roads and in canal construction. With the development of rail and engines, substantial amounts of money were invested in applying the technology and practices to the needs and landscape of the country.

Poetry

- Li Po of China's Tang Dynasty is best known among Westerners for "The River-Merchant's Wife," written during the eighth century.
- Edgar Allen Poe published his first volume of poetry in 1827.
- Thomas Hardy's "Ah, Are You Digging on my Grave," was published in his 1913 collection *Satires of Circumstance: Lyrics and Reveries with Miscellaneous Pieces.*
- If only he'd turned out to be an assassin, the world might have known sooner that Robert Frost's middle name was Lee. Regardless, his first book actually published was called *A Boy's Will.*
- Poet Robert Burns moved to Irvine in Ayshire in 1781 to learn the flax business. He was plowing on Mossgiel Farm, however, when disturbing a mouse nest prompted him to write "To a Mouse."
- It has been argued that Rita Dove's "Geometry" contends rational thought and imagination intersect at a point called enlightenment.

Crash Course

All Employees Must Wash Hands

From the inconvenient to the catastrophic, as long as there have been people there has been disease.

Ironically, the very civilizations that bred progress—and more people—are to blame for the infections that have periodically thinned the population. Indeed, communal water, unwashed food, and overwhelmingly unsanitary conditions conspired against the folks who fancied themselves civilized for planting roots.

It certainly didn't help that urine was a common ingredient in everyday products such as bleach, hair dye, and—more ironically—antiseptic. It was only a matter of time under these close quarters and questionable conditions before disease began running rampant.

Thomas Sydenham, England's first recognized physician and medical authority, lived in the sixteenth century and was himself a medical historian, so much of the earliest disease classifications on record are based on his work.

According to Sydenham, typhus was the most common malady of early history, followed by typhoid fever and relapsing fever, plague and other insect-borne ailments, smallpox, and ultimately dysentery and cholera.

Of course, it never occurred to most ancient folks that their hygiene habits had any bearing on their health. It made much more sense in those days to write off illness as the wrath of vengeful gods or even the alignment of the stars.

It bears repeating that these people actually thought urine counteracted germs.

In fact, Hippocrates was the first to recommend boiling water for purification, and that wasn't until about 350 BC. It's no wonder he's considered the Father of Medicine.

Sadly, sanitation didn't progress much past Hippocrates's revelation until the nineteenth century.

Johann Wolfgang von Goethe

Born in 1749, in Frankfort, Germany, Johann Wolfgang von Goethe is most known for his work *Faust,* a poetic drama that he worked on for nearly sixty years. At the prompting of his father, Goethe finally passed his law exams at age twenty-two and began practicing law while working on his first novel, *The Sorrows of Young Werther* (1774).

In 1775, he was invited to the court of Duke Karl August in Weimar where he worked in several governmental offices, including being a council member and member of the war commission; director of roads and services; and managing the financial affairs of the court. He later became manager of the court theater. He died in Weimar in 1832.

But Goethe was also a student of natural science. He wrote the book, *Theory of Colours,* which presented theories contrary to the understanding of the day. They are believed to have influenced the painting of artists such as Mondrian and Kandinsky.

Extra Credit: Early on, Goethe, who took lessons in everything from fencing to dancing, thought painting might be his true calling.

The Sorrows of Young Werther (1774), which some call the world's first best-seller, recounts an unhappy romantic infatuation that ends in suicide, a writing process Goethe admittedly used to quell his own issues involving obsession. The book itself, which appeared to glorify suicide, was quite controversial at the time, when Christian doctrine denied burial of those who committed suicide.

Blissful Ignorance

Renowned British physician Dr. John Snow actually traced all of the cholera cases in a district of central London to a single contaminated water supply. Sixteen years later he was awarded a prize by the Institute of France for his discovery that cholera was indeed water borne.

Pity his own peers and colleagues refused to listen.

Rather than embrace the logical theory, Snow came under fire for being unable to aptly identify the nature of the contamination. Never mind that people were dropping dead, and he—at the very least—had isolated the source and understood how they were contracting the disease. He was dismissed and ridiculed for failing to identify the mechanism at work behind the pathogen's wrath.

Sadly, sanitation improved very little following the first cholera epidemic, despite well-documented links between infection rates and the dirty, poor-draining portions of town.

And yet what is known about people who fail to learn history the first time around?

The second cholera epidemic hit England in 1854, and Snow called it "the most terrible outbreak" to ever occur in the kingdom. He set out to make people listen.

His research indicated more than five hundred cases occurred over the span of ten days and within a 250-yard radius of London's Broad Street. Using his theory that cholera was spread by ingesting the excretions of cholera sufferers, he sought out contaminated water lines and found exactly what he suspected.

A workhouse in the area with a private well reported only five deaths among 535 inmates. Likewise, a Broad Street brewery that never used the public pump reported zero cholera cases among seventy employees.

A single water line running to the Broad Street pump from one of several water companies was contaminated.

Finally, the tenacious Snow had been vindicated.

CRASH COURSE

RELUCTANT REFORM

- Class structure played a significant role in the spread of cholera because outbreaks were worst in areas where crowded conditions and poor drainage overlapped. As a result, slums were harder hit than the swanky districts.
- The rich saw cholera as a scourge on the poor.
- The poor believed the outbreaks were mass poisonings orchestrated by the aristocracy.
- Time bridged the gap, though, and it didn't take long for the open sewers in the slums to overflow, polluting the groundwater, nearby wells, and eventually the rivers.
- Curiously, once the wealthy began falling ill, the push for government reform got a bit more aggressive.
- The majority of municipal water mains and sewer systems were built during the nineteenth century in direct response to cholera epidemics. Public health agencies were not only formed but funded, and building codes and ordinances found their way onto the books and into the hearts of inspectors across the globe.

Friedrich Nietzsche

Born on Oct. 15, 1844, near Leipzig, Prussia, Friedrich Nietzsche got his start in a stuffy boarding school near Naumburg. During his six-year stint at Schulpforta that ended in 1864, he worked primarily on poems and musical compositions. By the age of twenty-four—after formal training in philology at the universities of Bonn and then Leipzig—he became a professor of classical philology at the University of Basel.

Philology is the study of literary texts and of written records, the establishment of their authenticity and their original form, and the determination of their meaning. He spent a fairly unassuming ten years teaching, and then the horrors of war changed his entire world view.

Nietzsche spent only a few months serving as an orderly in the Franco-Prussian War, but apparently it was long enough. He witnessed the traumatic effects of battle, contracted diphtheria and dysentery, and some scholars believe he damaged his health irreparably.

As a philosopher:

- Nietzsche challenged the foundations of traditional morality and Christianity.
- He introduced the idea that "God is dead."
- He identified the difference between "master" and "slave" moralities with the former celebrating life and the latter resenting those who celebrate.
- A frequently recurring theme in Nietzsche's work is the "will to power," which links to his concept of *Übermensch*— traditionally translated as "overman."
- He claimed the *Übermensch* as a goal that humanity can achieve for itself or that an individual can set for himself.

Nietzsche's downfall began around 1887. Until this point, he had managed to maintain a close friendship with the German composer, Richard Wagner, but it ended abruptly.

It was also around this time that Nietzsche experienced a public breakdown followed by his sending short letters, called "madness letters," to several of his friends. Realizing that he was in need of help, his friends took him to a psychiatric clinic in Basel. His mother and sister took care of him until his death.

Nietzsche's Controversial Career

- In 1872, Nietzsche published his first book, *The Birth of Tragedy Out of the Spirit of Music.* When his colleagues expressed little enthusiasm over the work, he said he felt isolated within the philological community.
- Beginning with *Human, All Too Human* in 1878, Nietzsche published one book—or major section of a book—each year for ten years.
- In 1888, he actually completed five books.
- *The Gay Science* was published in 1882, followed by *Thus Spoke Zarathustra,* which he wrote in only ten days.
- In 1885, he printed only forty copies of the fourth part of Zarathustra and distributed them to close friends only.
- He self-published *Beyond Good and Evil* and revised some of his earlier works.
- *Twilight of the Idols* and *The Antichrist* were both written in 1888.
- On his forty-fourth birthday, he began the autobiography, *Ecce Homo.*

EXTRA CREDIT: Nietzsche is pronounced *Neech-uh.*

CRASH COURSE

FAMOUS FIRSTS

- Ivan IV, better known as Ivan the Terrible, was the first czar of Russia, beginning his rule in 1547.
- The first book published in America was Steven Day's *Bay Psalm Book.*
- Henrietta Johnston, a portrait artist active in Charleston around 1707, was the first known professional female artist in America.
- André-Jacques Garnerin was the first person to parachute jump. He dropped from a balloon over Monceau Park in Paris in 1797.
- The first known architect was Imhotep, chief architect to the Egyptian Pharaoh Djoser.
- The first paper mill was established in North America (near Philadelphia) in 1690. At this time, paper was made from old clothes and rags.
- In 1809, Mary Kies became the first woman to receive a U.S. patent. She received the patent for her idea of weaving straw and silk to make bonnets.
- In 1867, Sir John Alexander McDonald became the first prime minister of Canada.
- Lucy Walker, in 1871, became the first woman to completely climb the Matterhorn.
- In 1902, Vida Goldstein was the first woman within the British Empire to run for a national office. She ran for senate in Australia.
- The first handheld electronic calculator was invented in 1967 by Jack Kilby, Jerry Merryman, and Jerry Van Tasael.
- Martha Washington was the first woman pictured on a U.S. postage stamp. She was printed on the eight cent stamp in November 1902.

SIGMUND FREUD

Born on May 6, 1856, in Moravia (now the Czech Republic), Sigmund Freud grew up in Vienna. The future father of psychoanalysis entered the University of Vienna, were he worked closely with physiologist Ernst Wilhelm von Brücke. He received his medical degree in 1881, specializing in neurology and psychiatry.

Freud opened his own medical practice in neurology in 1886. He began treating his neurotic patients with hypnosis; however, he soon changed to the "talking cure," or having the patient talk through a problem. He believed this approach provided a more effective treatment.

In researching neurophysiology, specifically cerebral palsy, Freud concluded that William Little, the man who first identified the disease, was incorrect in his theory that the disease was caused by complications during the birth process. Freud believed that the complications were merely a symptom.

Freud's most celebrated contribution to the psychiatric field was his development of a method for studying the subconscious mind. Researchers prior to Freud had documented the concept of an unconscious, or subconscious, mind, but Freud believed vehemently that dreams were the "royal road" to reach it. He believed that people who experience painful thoughts and feelings cannot banish them from their minds but that the memories can be pushed into the unconscious. He said that this repression in itself is an unconscious act.

Freud identified three concepts of the unconscious:

- The **descriptive unconscious** contains memories of which the person is simply not subjectively aware.
- The **dynamic unconscious** comprises memories that are actively removed from consciousness as a result of conflict.
- The **systemic unconscious** is the organizational zone, but Freud soon replaced the idea of the systemic unconscious with the concepts of the ego, superego, and id.

In *Beyond the Pleasure Principle* (1920) and *The Ego and the Id* (1923), Freud proposed that the psyche could be divided into three parts: Ego, superego, and id. He believed each stage is a progression into adult sexual maturity.

Psychosexual development and awareness are the motivators for all aspects of a person's life, according to Freud. He presented this theory as the Oedipus complex—a sexual fixation on the mother—and the Electra complex—you guessed it, a sexual fixation on the father.

Freud's theories were controversial during his day, and little has changed in that regard.

In 1930, he received the Goethe Prize in appreciation of his contribution to psychology and to German literary culture. Then three years later, the Nazis ceremoniously burned his books.

Onta' Something

Freud was an early user and proponent of cocaine as a stimulant and analgesic. He wrote several articles on the antidepressant qualities and believed that cocaine would work as a cure-all for many disorders, including "nasal reflex neurosis."

The ashes of Sigmund Freud and his wife, Martha, are kept in a Greek urn that Freud received from Marie Bonaparte.

Jane Addams: Activist Extraordinaire

Born in Cedarville, Illinois, in 1860, Laura Jane Addams was the first woman to win a Nobel Peace Prize. She grew up with the town's library in her home, so it's no surprise she was incredibly well read long before she attended the Rockford Female Seminary.

While at the seminary, Addams developed her leadership skills and was named valedictorian of her class. After graduation, she traveled to Europe, where she became familiar with the idea of socialized housing, which eventually led her to be a founder of the U.S. Settlement House Movement.

In 1889, she and friend Ellen Gates Starr opened a social settlement, Hull House, in Chicago. Women—and a few men—came from across the nation to live and work at Hull House.

Addams's efforts led to garbage collection, a kindergarten, and the first playground in Chicago. Hull House grew to include an art gallery, a public kitchen, a gym and swimming pool, a bookbindery and library, an employment bureau, and much more.

Addams became a respected public philosopher and social leader. She drew the attention of the day's philosophers, John Dewey, William James, and George Herbert Mead. Throughout her lifetime, Addams authored or coauthored a dozen books and more than five hundred articles for both scholarly and popular periodicals. A dynamic speaker, she traveled nationally and internationally to make presentations that supported her progressive values.

In 1905, Addams was appointed to Chicago's Board of Education and subsequently became chairman of the School Management Committee. But she was one busy lady:

- She became the first woman president of the National Conference of Charities and Corrections in 1909.
- She led investigations on midwifery, narcotics consumption, milk supplies, and sanitary conditions.
- In 1910, she received the first honorary degree ever awarded to a woman by Yale University.

- She lectured at the University of Wisconsin, and later published a book, *Newer Ideals of Peace*.
- She spoke in 1913 at a ceremony commemorating the building of the Peace Palace at The Hague, and for the next two years spoke out against America's involvement in World War I.
- In January of 1915 she became chairman of the American Women's Peace Party and then president of the International Congress of Women.
- She went on to serve as president of the Women's International League for Peace and Freedom until 1929, when she was named honorary president for the remainder of her life.
- One of the most recognized and admired figures in the United States, Addams was instrumental in the establishment of the National Association for the Advancement of Colored People, the American Civil Liberties Union, and the Women's International League for Peace and Freedom.
- After experiencing a heart attack in 1926, Addams's health continued to decline. She was admitted to a Baltimore hospital on Dec. 10, 1931, the very day the Nobel Peace Prize was being bestowed upon her. She died of cancer four years later.

Did You Know?

Addams's outspoken opposition to war caused her to be expelled from the Daughters of the American Revolution, which most likely served to only encourage her campaign. She began providing food to the women and children of the enemy nations.

Steel Reshapes the Scene

Factories began to increase their output by either building larger facilities for their needs or boosting production levels in their existing ones. The growth was aided by a number of factors that included not only technological and scientific advances but also improvement in management styles and expanding markets to meet the demands of a larger, growing population with rising incomes.

Iron and steel manufacturing was completely transformed with a more innovative approach known as the Bessemer process which used an open-hearth furnace. Developed by British inventor Henry Bessemer, the process enabled more efficient steel production by using blasts of air in the conversion of crude iron to steel. The open-hearth furnace also allowed higher temperatures to be reached, which allowed impurities to be burned away from the crude iron.

Andrew Carnegie built an empire in the iron and steel industry by utilizing new, larger plants. John D. Rockefeller applied similar techniques to his petroleum refining business. As the advances in science-based machines continued to emerge, their applications in the industry were introduced just as quickly. This continued to stimulate economic growth.

Crash Course

The American Civil War

- **Battle of Gettysburg, July 1-3, 1863, Gettysburg, Pennsylvania:** Confederate General Robert E. Lee attacked Gen. George G. Meade's Army of the Potomac. Lee's forces numbered some 83,000, Meade's 75,000. The Confederates succeeded in driving the Union soldiers back the first day, but both sides sent in reinforcements that night. On July 2, Union forces began repelling the Confederate attack. Lee began withdrawing his men on July 4. The total number of casualties was estimated at 51,000, or 23,000 for the Union side and 28,000 for the Confederates. Gettysburg is generally accepted as the tipping point of the war.
- **Battle of Antietam, September 17, 1862, near Sharpsburg, Maryland:** Lee had won the Second Battle of Manassas August 28-30, 1862, and intended to press his advantage northward. Lincoln tasked General George B. McClellan with responding to Lee's advances. The Battle of Antietam began at dawn on the seventeenth. General Joseph Hooker, General Joseph Mansfield, and General Edwin Sumner led Union assaults on Confederate forces. Twelve hours after the battle began, the single bloodiest day of battle in American history ended with 23,000 casualties. By comparison, in World War II, American casualties on D-Day would number 2,510.
- **Battle of Chickamauga, September 18-20, 1863, Catoosa and Walker County, Georgia:** Union General William S. Rosecrans was seeking to capture the strategically important rail hub and river shipping city of Chattanooga, Tennessee. Rosecrans was convinced that Confederate General Braxton Bragg was continuing to retreat from the area, but Bragg had in fact begun to advance toward Chattanooga. Over the course of three days, Bragg's forces managed to repel Rosecrans' forces. Union casualties numbered 16,170, while the Confederates had 18,454 casualties.

- Abraham and Nancy Todd Lincoln had four sons, but only the first, Robert Todd, lived into maturity. Edward Baker Lincoln died before his fourth birthday from what was thought to be diphtheria. William Wallace Lincoln died at eleven from an acute malarial infection. Thomas (Tad) Lincoln died at eighteen from pleurisy.
- Jefferson Davis, president of the Confederacy, also had his share of family tragedy. Davis married Sarah Knox Taylor on June 17, 1835. The couple left on a trip to see members of Davis' family, first brother Joseph E. Davis and then sister Anna Smith, of West Feliciana Parish, Lousiana. The newlyweds both came down with either malaria or yellow fever. Davis survived, but his bride died on September 15, two days from the couple's three month anniversary. Davis married Varina Banks Howell in 1826, and their first child, Samuel Emory, died before he was two from measles. Their fourth child, Joseph Evan, died at age five after falling from a porch on the White House of the Confederacy. Their fifth child, William Howell, died at eleven from diphtheria.
- Hire badges were metal badges worn by slaves who had been "rented out" for day labor. The badges served several purposes, from identifying the slaves to providing tax revenue to preventing slave labor from competing with white laborers. (Slave labor was cheaper than white labor, so badges for occupations more likely to be done by whites were limited) Although several cities, including Mobile, Alabama, New Orleans, Louisiana, and Savannah, Georgia issued badges, only those from Charleston, South Carolina are known to exist today.
- Mary Virginia Wade had no intention of becoming part of history on July 3, 1863, but then, few historical figures ever do. All "Jennie" wanted to accomplish was the baking of some bread for Union soldiers near her sister Georgia McClellan's Baltimore Street house. But while Wade was kneading dough in McClellan's kitchen, a bullet penetrated two wooden doors, striking Wade in the back and killing her instantly. Wade had become the only civilian killed during the Battle of Gettysburg.

Wash, Rinse, Repeat

Waves of changes in the manner in which businesses were structured and work organized created as strong an impact as that of the manufacturing and technology changes themselves. Business leaders learned to simultaneously operate and coordinate many different activities spread across geographic areas.

Factories had grown exponentially but had lacked the capability to coordinate production and marketing across multiple business units and territories. Carnegie and Rockefeller were two leaders in this arena, and under their models firms grew in many different industries as solid corporations.

But perhaps the most revolutionary innovation of this revolutionary period was the automated assembly line. The automotive industry utilized the continuous-process methods and the American system in combination for a success unlike any seen before.

Henry Ford applied both systems to his business when he founded the Ford Motor Company. His innovative approach is now known as the assembly line which brought many mass-produced parts together by manual labor in the process of building an automobile.

The moving assembly line proved its effectiveness and reliability while maintaining efficiency. This production levels in the second decade of the twentieth century proved the long-term success rate of the process. But automotive leaders weren't the only beneficiaries of this new way of thinking.

Americans continued to innovate the manner in which work was organized by studying and modifying production to utilize the most efficient ways of designing a factory, move materials, route job processes, and control the flow and pace of work with precise schedules.

Frederick W. Taylor, an industrial engineer, created scientifically tested management principles which measure and analyze each aspect of a job and provide the workers more efficient and enjoyable methods of completing their tasks. His 1911 book, *The Principles of Scientific Management,* is regarded as one of the most influential texts of the Industrial Revolution.

It's no surprise that the guidelines and directives of Ford and Taylor came to symbolize the leadership of America as an industrialized nation.

Workforce Leap Frog

Industrialization brought many changes to American society, just as it had in England. As industrialized cities grew, the influential nature of rural communities declined and understanding of the economic importance of agriculture began to diminish.

Where the amount of land cultivated and the numbers of citizens earning a living based in agriculture had increased, the parallel growth in commerce, manufacturing, and service industries had surpassed it.

The ratio of workforce in agriculture steadily declined after the late 1700s and by the late 1800s had reached 40 percent.

New technology had entered agriculture in large part due to the scarcity of labor and the ever-increasing growth of markets and demand for agricultural goods.

Machinery on farms increased productivity, so fewer labor hands were required to produce more food per square acre.

Technological advances applied to implements, including plows, seed drills, cultivators, mowers, threshers, and reapers were all in use by the late 1800s.

Harvesters and binding machines were developed into a single unit appropriately named combines.

Steam power inventions of the last nineteenth century aided farm work, as did the use of gasoline-powered tractors.

Science and technology were not limited to farm implement applications but also impacted the applications for plant breeding through genetics and the use of fertilizers and pesticides which increased farm production.

Urban centers of the nation began to grow in record numbers, with the shift of labor to the manufacturing and textile industries. The cities were found to be highly crowded and poorly cared for in respect to public health.

Many of the industrial and commercial centers exploited workers and forced dank—often inhumane—conditions on them.

No matter the negative consequences, urban sprawl was unstoppable in the United States due to the movement of rural residents to these locations in tandem with the growing influx of immigrants from Europe. This trend is quite common in societies undergoing industrialization and is still evident worldwide, notably in areas of Asia and Latin America.

Workers in skilled trades and those with a stake in the traditional economy found their status, income and way of life under attack each time new technology would provide another mechanized tool.

Slowly, mechanized production replaced the household-centered productions of the past. Businesses began to relish their power over their workforce as they grew.

To counter that power and ease exploitation, workers tried to form unions within their trade to represent them and negotiate on their behalf. Skilled craft workers were the only group to note success in this arena until the time of the Great Depression. The most successful unions were in the American Federation of Labor and did not seek fundamental social or economic change, rather accepting industrialized society and focusing on improving wages and working conditions for their members.

Big Brother from Way Back

The U.S. government began to create regulations and antitrust laws in response to the worst excesses of big businesses.

Monopoly enterprises were being formed to reduce competition and effectively gave a single large firm control enough of the market to control pricing.

Laws such as the Fair Labor Standards Act were enacted to mandate worker protection, including establishment of the now-traditional maximum eight hour workday and forty hour workweek.

Material progress and excess convinced most Americans that the industrialization boom had been positive for the nation as a whole. Still, seeking balance between business growth and worker rights remained a critical issue and it remains important even in today's economic circles.

CRIMINAL JUSTICE 101

LOOPS AND WHORLS: FINGERPRINTING

Copying fingerprints—and footprints and handprints—dates back 4,000 years. Ancient prints have been found in Egypt and China. In fact, it was common for the Chinese to use fingerprints as signatures on legal documents such as deeds and loans. Then in the late seventeenth and early eighteenth centuries, philosophers began contemplating skin, its surface, and the arrangement of friction ridges on fingers. In the nineteenth century, Sir William Herschel, an administrator in India, started requiring thumbprints and palm prints on legal documents.

In 1880, Henry Faulds, a missionary and physician, wrote a paper for Nature magazine discussing the unique properties of the loops and whorls of his patients' fingerprints. He noted that cuts and abrasions on fingers did not change the fingerprint pattern. He even asserted that "fingermarks" left on objects by bloody or greasy fingers might lead to identification of criminals.

The first conviction of a person by means of fingerprint evidence occurred in Argentina in 1892. A woman accused a ranch hand of killing her children, and indeed, investigators found bloody fingerprints on the doorpost of her home. However, upon examination, the fingerprints were not those of the ranch hand but of the mother herself. When confronted, she confessed to the crime.

The National Institute of Standards and Technology developed standards for fingerprint collection. Currently, along with the FBI database, all states and some major cities maintain their own system of criminal fingerprints. These records are shared among law enforcement agencies.

DNA Fingerprinting

DNA fingerprinting begins by extracting DNA from the cells in a sample of blood, saliva, or other body fluid or tissue. This genetic screening is used in forensic science to match suspects to evidence found at crime scenes. It has also led to several acquittals of formerly convicted suspects.

People other than law enforcement are using DNA tests. Coroners use DNA tests to identify human remains. Family court judges order paternity testing using DNA screens. Physicians match organ donors by using DNA samples. Wildlife conservationists use DNA to study populations of wild animals. Archaeologists use DNA in studying human existence during prehistoric times. At this time, list for the potential use of DNA fingerprinting seems limitless.

Going the Extra Mile

Although DNA fingerprinting is close, it is not 100 percent exact. Court trials have questioned not only the scientific principle but also the human factor involved in collecting and processing samples. However, criminals will go long ways to try to ensure that DNA screening doesn't convict them.

NDNAD

The United Kingdom currently has the most extensive DNA database in the world. As of 2007, the National DNA Database (NDNAD) has well over 4 million records. Given the size of this database, and its rate of growth, civil liberties groups in the UK have begun to raise questions related to the right of privacy. Reportedly, British police are able to take DNA samples of anyone arrested and retain the records even in the event of acquittal.

The First Catch

In 1988, Colin Pitchfork of Narborough, Leicestershire, England, became the first person to be convicted of a crime because of evidence provided by DNA fingerprinting.

Fyodor Dostoevsky

Born on Nov. 11, 1821, in Moscow, Russian author Fyodor Dostoevsky enrolled in the Military Engineering Academy in St. Petersburg as a teenager. His hatred of math—his expected course of study—drove him to write in his spare time, and the course of literary history was altered forever.

- His first novel, *Poor Folk*, written while he was at the academy, was published in 1846, and marked his entry to the literary elite at the tender age of twenty-five.
- Being young and full of oats, however, he joined a literary discussion group that examined Western philosophy, a topic that was banned in Russia. His participation in the group led to imprisonment, mandatory military service, and a mock execution. He was released from prison in 1858, and what followed was a period of intensive writing and publishing.
- During this time, he wrote: *The House of the Dead* (1862), *Notes from the Underground* (1864), *Crime and Punishment* (1866), *The Idiot* (1868), and *Devils* (1871).
- Considered by many people as a precursor of twentieth-century existentialism, Dostoevsky used his novels to explore human psychology in the political, social, and spiritual turmoil of nineteenth-century Russian society.
- Outside of literature, he is said to have influenced the modernist movements in philosophy and psychology.
- He died on February 9, 1881.

Read It and Wheat

The epigraph of Dostoevsky's final novel, *The Brothers Karamazov*, is also the epitaph on his tombstone—"Verily, Verily, I say unto you, except a corn of wheat fall into the ground and die, it abideth alone: but if it die, it bringeth forth much fruit."

Global Influence

The Industrial Revolution in England and the United States spread globally, particularly in Western European nations. British workers and entrepreneurs would move into other areas and teach the practices they had acquired in Britain. Change happened differently in each setting due to differences in available resources, political situations, as well as socioeconomic conditions.

France experienced a delayed industrial revolution due to political turmoil and a lack of coal but indusdry did benefit from the support of its government in the growth process. The French government funded most of the endeavor to build railways, where Britain's had been financed predominantly by private investors. Production of craft materials also remained a sought-after element of the French economy; therefore, without the extent of mechanization infiltrating the industry, the French did not experience industrialization as quickly as did the British.

The German government also played a more prominent role in the industrial development of its nation in an effort to hasten the process to match that of Britain. The rich iron and coal resources of the nation were used to develop heavy industrial facilities for the manufacture of iron and steel. Big business, large firms, and a large banking sector all aided rapid industrial development in Germany.

Repeated efforts to heighten industrialization were made by the Russian government, often employing foreigners to not only build but manage entire factories. The Russian economy was overwhelmingly agricultural, so the entire process spread far more slowly than in other nations.

Japan was the first Asian nation to become industrialized, and that feat was an achieved goal of the central government. Other Asian nations, including China, South Korea, and Taiwan would not begin the process until the early to mid-twentieth century.

The effects of colonialism in various parts of Southeast Asia, Africa, and India, as well as Latin America delayed the industrialization process even further for these corners of the globe. Their dependence on parent countries made change difficult due to the lack of control.

Lasting Impact

Although the variations of success experienced by different cultures in the process of industrialization are notable, the similarities are just as prominent.

Urbanization and mechanization were key in each area of success in connection with the tensions and disruptions that the advancements and growths created. For the first century of the Industrial Revolution, the changes made were truly revolutionary.

The modern societies created through the Industrial Revolution came at a cost, however.

The nature of work became more demanding and placed stress upon the family as people began to work outside the home.

The distance—both economically and socially—between groups of people could be very wide within an industrialized society and often created tensions between neighboring countries where one could be substantially more or less affluent than the other.

The impact of the Industrial Revolution on natural resources is apparent through the destruction of animal and plant habitats pushing many species to the brink of extinction. Perhaps the most well-received benefit of the industrialization process, however, is improved health care and the material well-being it has afforded.

Modern industrial life continues to provide new goods and services giving consumers a variety of choices of products and price points.

CRASH COURSE

NOTABLE ENGINEERS: CONTRIBUTORS TO THE INDUSTRIAL REVOLUTION

Edwin H. Armstrong	1890–1954	Superhetrodyne receiver and FM radio
Werner von Braun	1912–1977	Rocketry
James Brindley	1716–1762	Canal engineer
I. K. Brunel	1806–1859	Railway engineer, steamship pioneer
M. K. Brunel	1767–1849	Civil engineer, Thames tunnel
Gotteib Daimler	1834–1900	High-speed IC engine
Abraham Darby	1677–1717	Production of pig iron
Rudolf Diesel	1859–1913	Diesel engine
John Presper Eckert	1919–1995	ENIAC and UNIVAC computers
Thomas Alva Edison	1837–1931	Phonograph, dc power supplies
Michael Faraday	1791–1867	Electo-magnetic induction
Sebastian de Ferranti	1864–1930	High voltage ac generation/transmission
Henry Ford	1863–1947	Assembly line production
William Jessop	1745–1814	Civil engineer (Aberdeen Harbour)
Robert Fulton	1765–1815	Steamboats
Gulglielmo Marconi	1874–1937	Radio
Henry Maudslay	1771–1831	Machine tools, screw cutting lathe
William Murdock	1754–1839	Gas lighting
Thomas Newcomen	1663–1729	Atmospheric engine
Charles Parsons	1854–1931	Steam Turbine

Sir Joseph Paxton	1801–1965	Pre-fabricated buildings, Crystal Palace
Charles William Siemens	1823–1883	Electrical engineering, telegraphy
George Stephenson	1781–1848	"Father of the railways"
Osborne Reynolds	1843–1912	Hydraulics and fluid mechanics
Thomas Telford	1757–1834	Civil engineer, bridges and canals
Nikola Tesla	1856–1943	AC induction motor
Richard Trevithick	1771–1833	Steam engines and locomotives
Leonardo da Vinci	1492–1519	Dynamics, architecture, military engineering
Barnes Wallis	1887–1979	R100, Wellington bomber, bouncing bombs
James Watt	1736–1819	Steam engine
George Westinghouse	1846–1914	Westinghouse brake, founder of Westinghouse Electric
Frank Whittle	1907–1996	Turbojet and turbofans
Joseph Whitworth	1803–1887	Uniform system of screw threads
Vladimir Kosma Zworykin	1889–1982	Iconoscope (TV), electro microscope
Ferdinand von Zeppelin	1838–1917	Airships

Pop Quiz #6

1) Who invented the first steam engine in 1689 to pump water from mines?
   a) Thomas Savery
   b) Thomas Newcomen
   c) William Seward
   d) James Watt

2) Which company was formed following the forging of a 1775 partnership and became a pivotal engineering powerhouse?
   a) Boulton and Watt
   b) Watson and Savery
   c) Carmichael and Bell
   d) Adams and Reese

3) Who revolutionized textile manufacturing by creating in 1733 what would become known as the flying shuttle?
   a) James Hargreaves
   b) Richard Arkwright
   c) John Kay
   d) Samuel Crompton

4) In 1791, which U.S. official called for the new nation's own industrial revolution to establish itself as a world economic power in his Report on Manufactures?
   a) Benjamin Franklin
   b) John Adams
   c) Alexander Hamilton
   d) Thomas Jefferson

5) In what year was the first World's Fair held at the Crystal Palace of London to give inventors and diplomats an international stage for their industrial triumphs?
   a) 1851
   b) 1855
   c) 1860
   d) 1862

6) Industrial engineer Frederick W. Taylor wrote which famous work in 1911 that became the most influential book of the Second Industrial Revolution and became Henry Ford's textbook for mass assembly production.
   a) *Macroeconomics*
   b) *The Principles of Scientific Management*
   c) *A Guide to Econometrics*
   d) *The Wealth of Nations*

ANSWERS:

1) a
2) a
3) c
4) c
5) a
6) b

BIOLOGY 101

CHARLES DARWIN

Luckily for mankind, Charles Darwin was easily distracted.

The Shropshire, England, native—born February 12, 1809—attended Edinburgh University to study medicine, but his medical pursuits fell by the wayside when he became enthralled with natural history.

Darwin's father was less than pleased with the scholarly detour and enrolled his son, instead, at Cambridge University to study theology. To say the tactic backfired is an understatement.

While he graduated tenth in his class with a degree in theology, Darwin still made time to study naturalism.

EXTRA CREDIT

The grandson of china manufacturer Josiah Wedgwood, Darwin married a cousin, Anne Wedgwood, in 1839 after finishing at Cambridge, and the pair had ten children, only seven of whom survived to adulthood.

> ***Slow and Steady Wins the Race***
>
> Harriet, a Galápagos tortoise, died in 2006 at an estimated age of 175. She lived at a zoo in Australia.

EVOLUTION OF A THEORY

Darwin began working on his theory of evolution in 1836, yet the idea was not entirely his own. His research extended from two environmental observations of well-known and respected scholars.

Darwin's work expanded on geologist Charles Lyell's theory that fossils found in rocks were from animals that had lived thousands or millions of years ago. It focused specifically on the varieties of finches found on the Galápagos Islands.

Darwin melded Lyell's theory with the ideas of Thomas Malthus, who examined man's struggle for existence and put forth the Principle of Population.

Two decades after beginning his scholarly journey, Darwin and naturalist Alfred Wallace, who had been working independently on the same theory, in 1858 proposed a theory of evolution occurring by the process of natural selection. In 1859, Darwin published *On the Origin of Species by Means of Natural Selection.*

The theory of evolution has remained controversial since its inception based, primarily, on the theory's contention that humans are simply animals.

The theology student had theorized that thousands of years of religious creation tales were no more than convenient folklore. He believed that humans most likely descended from apes, and the church remains displeased to this day..

But Darwin could never be accused of being a one-trick pony. He also studied a variety of animals and plants during his lengthy career, and his research—along with Gregor Mendel's breakthrough research in genetics—is the foundation for modern biology.

And because astute documentation played such a crucial role in his research, it's no surprise that Darwin was a prolific writer, penning works that include the following:

- *The Voyage of the Beagle*
- *The Origin of Species*
- *The Descent of Man, and Selection in Relation to Sex*
- *The Expression of Emotions in Man and Animals*
- *The Power of Movement in Plants*
- *The Formation of Vegetable Mould Through the Action of Worms*

THE TITANIC

The RMS Titanic was an Olympic-class steam-powered passenger ship built and owned by the White Star Line in England. The ship was touted as being the largest of her kind and unsinkable as a result of the design and construction of the vessel.

This claim was tested on April 14, 1912, however, during her maiden voyage. The luxury liner clipped an iceberg, tearing small holes in the hull. Two hours and forty minutes later the ship sank beneath the Atlantic Ocean surface.

The disaster resulted in the reported deaths of 1,517 passengers and crew members, making it one of the worst maritime disasters in recorded history.

The media descended on the Titanic survivors in an attempt to chronicle the series of events happening on board the ship during the sinking, including legends and tales of musicians playing until the end, literally going down with their instruments in hand, in an attempt to calm the passengers.

In the end, it was determined there were not enough life boats on the vessel in case of an emergency of this nature. It was one of many flaws in design and operation that resulted in the disaster.

The cause and effects of the sinking have remained in public view since the discovery of the wreckage on the Atlantic Ocean floor in 1985. Technology has advanced enough that robotic exploration devices have been used to tour and recover items from the wreckage, nearly one mile beneath the ocean surface.

The tragedy has inspired several movies and touring exhibits.

Political Science 101

Sociopolitical Systems

Marxism

Marxism is the ideology born from following the theories of Karl Marx and Friedrich Engels, two political scientists of the 19th century. The main ideas of Marxism involve the production of society and the class systems. Marxism argues that the labor force drives the means of production and ought to control it.

Communism

The final stage of Marxism, communism seeks to create a classless society based on common ownership of a state's means of production. It is said to date back to hunter-gatherer times, when food was gathered and divided among a society and when work was distributed according to ability and efficiency.

Socialism

Socialism, a transitional system between communism and capitalism, encompasses all doctrines or political movements that argue for a socioeconomic system in which all wealth and property is controlled by the community in an equal distribution. Socialists strive to increase equality and community cooperation and raise the welfare of the state as a whole.

Capitalism

Capitalism refers to the common economic system of private ownership and a competitive market economy. Common practice in capitalism is for individuals and groups to act as corporations or legal entities that produce, sell, and trade goods. Corporations and persons abide by a system of pricing that is dictated by the market, instead of the state or central government. Since the disappearance of feudalism, capitalism has been prevalent in Western society, and the free market system has continued to shape politics and economics.

Czar Nicholas II (May 18, 1868–July 16, 1918)

Life

The last emperor of Russia was Czar Nicholas II.

The reserved and shy gentleman found himself ascending the throne at the age of twenty-six, following his father's death. Within that same year, Nicholas married Princess Alexandra of Hesse-Darmstadt, granddaughter of England's Queen Victoria.

Nicholas was a nationalist, and Alexandra's autocratic predisposition was a complement to his tastes, even in opposition to the growing interest in democracy by the people.

The couple had five children: Olga, Marie, Tatiana, Anastasia, and Alexi, the sole male heir. Alexi was also a hemophiliac, quite sensitive and prone to infections.

The family preferred to keep to themselves, rather than be out among the people. This, and the noticeable influence Alexandra held over their leader, fueled the declining public opinion of and confidence in the czar.

Alexandra was also known to seek guidance from Grigory Rasputin for matters of policy as well as healing for her son. The power Rasputin seemed to possess over the royal family ultimately led to his murder.

Impact on WWI

Russia had unsuccessfully engaged in war with Japan from 1904 to 1905, the same time in which workers in St. Petersburg went on strike in protest of declining wages. An appeal was made to the czar to reduce working hours and improve both pay and working conditions. When a march of protesters at the Winter Palace met an armed response, killing more than one hundred, the day was dubbed Bloody Sunday, with the czar portrayed as a murderer, and the 1905 Revolution began.

The response nationwide? Strikes and mutiny within the army and navy swept the country.

The czar responded by issuing the October Manifesto, granting freedom of conscience, speech, meeting, and association, as well as prison confinement without a trial. A consultative body known as a duma was created and charged with overseeing any new laws. The duma made demands for release of political prisoners, improvement of union rights, and land reform during its first meeting—all of which were swiftly rejected by Nicholas, who responded by dissolving the body entirely.

Following Germany's entrance into an alliance with Italy and Austria-Hungary, Germany was viewed as the main threat despite Nicholas being cousin to the German kaiser, Willhelm II. Russia entered into its own alliance with Britain and France—each vowing to aid the others in the event of attack by the Triple Alliance. At the time Russian came to the aid of the French during summer of 1914, most of the workforce in Russia had been on strike. The war served to end industrial problems momentarily and united the support behind the czar.

Nicholas became dissatisfied with his army in the war and took over command. The lack of success on the Eastern Front elevated the levels of dissension at home. The continued failures were attributed directly to the czar rather than the actions of the army, and the czar's popularity continued to fade. In late 1916, the czar was warned of potential revolution unless constitutional reform was pursued. Nicholas refused to sanction such reform.

Mystery

The czar abdicated his throne on March 15, 1917, and sought exile in England, the land of his cousins. The request was denied, and the royal family was forced to remain in their castles until the were physically removed by the Bolsheviks, who relocated them to a small farm house in Ekaterinburg, Syberia.

They believed naively they would be safe and eventually returned to power but remained cautious of their caregivers and surroundings. The family was gathered under the ruse of a portrait during the night of July 16–17, 1918, only to learn they truly faced an execution order.

It is reported that death was not swift for some of the children of the czar as they had lined their clothing with royal jewels, effectively bulletproofing their garments. The bodies of the royal family were removed from the farm house and buried elsewhere. Fearing discovery, the bodies were moved to a second location, some burned, and the others doused with lye and buried in a mass grave.

Rumor speculated that two of the children, Anastasia and Alexi, had survived the execution. Several laid claim to these titles for generations, but none have been scientifically linked with the royal family. The most well known claimant was Anna Anderson, who was proven through DNA analysis after death to be a Polish commoner.

The burial location has in recent years been fully excavated and all remains identified by use of facial reconstruction and DNA comparison to descendants of other members of the royal family. Each family member has been interred in the Peter and Paul Fortress in St. Petersburg.

Even Dictators Need to Wet Their Whistles

This little tidbit might not date to antiquity, but it certainly falls under the category of history revisited. It is a news item, but the source was not clearly identified: In early 2008, hundreds of former patrons protested the closing of Mexico's oldest cantina, El Nivel, in Mexico City. The small bar, which received the first cantina license in 1855, closed on January 2 after losing a seventeen-year legal battle against the owners of the building, the National Autonomous University of Mexico. Demonstrators—many drinking beers—protested outside the bar's padlocked door on a side street near the National Palace. They called for the university to renegotiate a deal with the bar owner or for the city to expropriate and reopen it. Mexican presidents from the 1870s to Ernesto Zedillo in the 1990s called in for a drink while in office. And when the exiled Cuban revolutionary Fidel Castro lived in Mexico in the 1950s, he frequented the bar with his fellow revolutionary Che Guevara.

THE CURIE FAMILY

Pierre and Marie Curie developed an extensive study of radioactive isotopes during their careers, and their oldest daughter and her husband followed in the study.

Marie Curie

Maria Sklodowska was born in Warsaw, Poland, in 1867. She went to Paris in 1891 to study at the Sorbonne. There she received licenciateships in physics and mathematical sciences. She married physics professor Pierre Curie in 1895. She received her Ph.D. in 1903.

After her husband's death, Marie took his place as professor of general physics at the Sorbonne, becoming the first woman to hold the position. She was also appointed director of the Curie Laboratory in the Radium Institute of the University of Paris.

Together, the couple achieved isolation of the radioactive substances polonium and radium. Marie played the major role in developing methods for the separation of radium from radioactive residues in sufficient quantities to allow for its characterization and study.

The United States backed the Curies' study. In 1921, US President Warren Harding, on behalf of the women of America, gave Marie one gram of radium in recognition of her service to science. And, in 1929, US President Herbert Hoover gave $50,000, on behalf of American friends of science, to purchase radium for use in the Curie Laboratory.

Marie received numerous awards during her career. With her husband, she was awarded half of the Nobel Prize for physics in 1903, for their study into the spontaneous radiation discovered by Becquerel, who was awarded the other half of the Prize. In 1911, she received a second Nobel Prize, this time in chemistry. She also received, jointly with her husband, the Davy Medal of the Royal Society in 1903. Marie Curie died in 1934 after a short illness, likely caused by overexposure to radiation during her research.

Pierre Curie

French-born Pierre Curie received his licenciateship in physics in 1878 and his Ph.D. in 1895 at the Sorbonne. He worked as faculty at the Sorbonne for his entire career.

His early interest was in crystallography. Together with his brother Jacques, Pierre discovered piezoelectric effects. Later, he turned his attention to magnetism, where he showed that the magnetic properties of a given substance change at a certain temperature—this temperature is now known as the Curie point.

After marrying Marie, Pierre began helping with her study of radioactive substances. Their work formed the basis for research in nuclear physics and chemistry. Pierre Curie was killed in a carriage accident in Paris in 1906.

Irène Joliot-Curie

Irène Curie, the oldest daughter of Pierre and Marie Curie, was born in Paris in 1897. She studied at the Faculty of Science in Paris and served as a nurse radiographer during World War I. She received her Ph.D. in science in 1925. A year later, she married fellow scientist Frédéric Joliot.

Throughout her career, Irène researched natural and artificial radioactivity, transmutation of elements, and nuclear physics. Together, she and Frédéric were awarded the Nobel Prize in chemistry in 1935 for their work with the synthesis of new radioactive elements. The next year, Irène was appointed Undersecretary of State for Scientific Research.

In 1946, Irène became director of the Radium Institute. She took part in the creation and construction of the first French atomic pile in 1948. She was also instrumental in the establishment of the center for nuclear physics at Orsay.

In addition to science, Irène promoted the social and intellectual advancement of women. She was a member of the Comité National de l'Union des Femmes Françaises and of the World Peace Council. Frédéric and Irène had two children. Irène Joliot-Curie died in Paris in 1956.

Jean-Frédéric Joliot

As assistant to Marie Curie, Jean Frédéric Joliot not only studied science but also found his wife, Marie's daughter Irène. Frédéric was born in 1900, in Paris, where he attended the Ecole de Physique et Chimie. In 1925, he joined the Radium Institute as assistant to Marie Curie. He received his Ph.D. in 1930.

While serving as a lecturer in the Paris Faculty of Science, Frédéric joined Irène in studying the structure of the atom. Together, they also discovered artificial radioactivity, perhaps their most important work. They produced the isotope 13 of nitrogen, the isotope 30 of phosphorus, and, simultaneously, the isotopes 27 of silicon and 28 of aluminum. For this significant work, the couple received the Nobel Prize for chemistry in 1935.

In 1937, he became a professor at the Collège de France and left the Radium Institute. For his new laboratory, he commissioned the construction of the first cyclotron in Western Europe.

Frédéric also took an active part in political affairs and served as president of the World Peace Council for a time. When Irène died in 1956, he assumed her position as Chair of Nuclear Physics at the Sorbonne, while retaining his professorship at the Collège de France. He died two years later.

On a humanitarian note, Pierre and Marie's second daughter, Eve, married American diplomat H. R. Labouisse who became director of the United Children's Fund and received on its behalf the Nobel Peace Prize in 1965.

Leo Tolstoy

Born on Aug. 28, 1828, in Tula Province, Russia, Lev Nikolayevich Tolstoy moved to Moscow with his family in 1836 to attend school. A year later, Tolstoy's father died and the young Leo returned to the family estate, Yasnaya Polyana, in Tula Province. He lived there until he enrolled at Kazan University at age sixteen to study Arabic, Turkish, Latin, German, English, and French.

Although he dropped out of the university after only a few months, Tolstoy developed an acute interest during this period in the works of leading authors such as Charles Dickens, Jean Jacques Rousseau, and Francois-Marie Arouet Voltaire. While he did not excel as a student, Tolstoy possessed a true gift as a wordsmith, and it shows in his prolific works.

In 1852, he published his first book, *Childhood*, the first in an autobiographical trilogy. It appeared as a series in the magazine *Sovremennik.*

While fighting in the Crimean War, Tolstoy was inspired to write another serialized work, *Sevastopol Sketches.* This time *The Contemporary*, another magazine was his vehicle for publication.

In 1862, at age 34, Tolstoy married Sofia "Sonya" Andreyevna Behrs, with whom he had thirteen children. Sonya helped her husband with the business side of writing and managing the estate. She organized his notes, copied out drafts, and handled correspondence. This enabled him to begin writing *War and Peace*, which resulted in six volumes of commentary on the absurdity, hypocrisy, and shallowness of war and aristocracy. The six volumes were published over a period of six years, between 1863 and 1869.

Anna Karenina is considered by many scholars—not to mention the masses—to be the greatest novel ever written. In fact, Tolstoy called it his first real novel. Cleverly weaving fiction and real events, he created one of the earliest examples of stream-of-consciousness writing.

Tolstoy's biting commentary was certainly not restricted entirely to fiction. He also wrote numerous nonfiction articles criticizing the government and church. His outspoken judgment led to his excommunication by the Russian Orthodox Church; but it only increased his popularity with the public. By the turn of the twentieth century, Tolstoy had a large following of adoring readers.

In the latter part of his life, Tolstoy turned to pacifism and embraced the teachings of Christianity. He gave up meat, tobacco, alcohol, and eventually his ancestral estate.

In 1893, he wrote commentary based on the Gospel of Luke. The resulting *The Kingdom of God Is Within You* began a friendship between Tolstoy and Mahatma Gandhi.

By 1910, Tolstoy had adopted extreme beliefs and alienated the majority of his family. In October, he set out to make a new life for himself. The attempt was short-lived. He died one month later—on November 20, 1910—of pneumonia.

Did You Know?

In January 2007, two of Tolstoy's novels, *Anna Karenina* and *War and Peace*, were named to *TIME* magazine's list of the ten greatest novels of all time.

The play *The Power of Darkness* was banned in Russia, yet it was the first successful production of a Tolstoy play in the United States. A 1920 English-language Broadway production of the play ran for more than eighty-five performances.

Diseases

Dysentery

Characterized by painful diarrhea and body-wracking cramps, dysentery is linked more directly to human waste than most ailments and is considered to be at least one contributing factor to the ultimate defeat of the Crusaders.

English historian Charles Creighton wrote, "The Crusaders of the eleventh–thirteenth centuries were not defeated so much by the scimitars of the Saracens as by the hostile bacteria of dysentery and other epidemics."

A major flaw of waging a holy war is relying on a higher power to ensure the safety and well-being of the righteous. Dysentery apparently answers to no such deity, and the result wasn't pretty.

Although women and children typically developed symptoms first, the scourge spread quickly to troops, and more than a hundred thousand—plus about 2,500 German reinforcements—died.

Typhus Fever

Typhus fever is another malady born of close quarters and poor sanitation. Transmitted by lice that set up shop in human feces, this particular ailment is frighteningly contagious and has pervaded jails and sailors for thousands of years. Napoleon lost thousands of his men to typhus in Russia, and his enemy wasn't spared either.

Typhoid fever actually involves a salmonella bacillus found in human excrement. Because of the similarity in symptoms, the two ailments were not distinguished professionally until 1837. England's Prince Albert succumbed to typhoid in 1861.

Although Queen Victoria did not fall ill, her son Edward came close ten years later, prompting an astute plumber to identify—and address—the source of the contamination: the lines of a new water closet.

By the time the two-year Boer War erupted in 1899, not only were typhoid vaccinations available, but common sense had revealed the malady to be a waterborne illness. Boiling and filtering water became a common practice. British troops stationed in South Africa didn't get the memo, though, and drank directly from rivers. An estimated 43,000 of the 400,000 troops contracted typhoid.

Typhoid reared its ugly head in America intermittently, but its last appearance came in the early 1900s with Typhoid Mary. A cook for several influential families, Mary Mallon, never fell ill herself, but she is unofficially blamed for the typhoid epidemic which infected around 1,400 people in Ithaca, New York, in 1903.

Malaria

Like a parasite, malaria attacks the liver and red blood cells, causing nausea and flulike symptoms and, if untreated, even seizures, coma, kidney failure, and death. Transmitted by mosquitoes, the disease infects between 350 and 500 million people every year. Because of new vaccines and medicines, the death rate for malaria has dropped over the last 100 years. While each infection used to be fatal, now only around 1 million cases per year are deadly.

H. Flu

H. flu, also known as Hib disease, is caused by the Haemophilus influenza type B bacteria. The infection is not related to any type of the influenza virus, but it can lead to bacterial meningitis, pneumonia, and serious infections of the bone, blood, and pericardium. A vaccine for the Hib disease was introduced in 1990 and achieved worldwide success. Even so, the disease is still responsible for 2 to 3 million infections each year, around 450,000 of which are fatal.

Before the advent of antibiotics, tuberculosis claimed the lives of many famous writers, including Jane Austen, Aubrey Beardsley, Anne Brontë, Charlotte Brontë, Emily Brontë, Stephen Crane, Franz Kafka, John Keats, D. H. Lawrence, Katherine Mansfield, and George Orwell.

WORLD LITERATURE

FRANZ KAFKA

The Story Behind the Stories

Franz Kafka was born in a Jewish neighborhood in Prague in 1883. As a Jew with German-Austrian ancestry, he encountered hostility all of his life. He studied law and then worked for fourteen years as a bureaucrat in a job he hated, all the while living with his domineering father, whom he described as huge and overbearing. Throughout his life, he suffered from tuberculosis, depression, and anxiety, which helps explain the troubled tone and religious and psychological questions of much of his writing. He never married, but was twice engaged to a woman named Felice Bauer. He only published a few stories during his lifetime. In fact, he left instructions to his friend Max Brod to burn all of his unpublished material after his death, including three novels. When he died in 1924, Brod disobeyed Kafka's wishes and published his fiction and diaries.

Critics debate whether Kafka's symbolic, surreal, Freudian works are religious allegories or representations of his own troubled mind. He is often aligned with the Existentialists because of the absurdity and hopelessness that permeates his fiction. His style is precise, dream-like, and even humorous at times. He is the master of weird, so that even if people have never read any of his stories, they usually know what the word "Kafkaesque" means.

The Stories

- "A Hunger Artist"—The title of this short story refers to a man whose craft is starving himself to the brink of death. In the good old days, crowds used to gather around him as he wasted away in a cage. As the years go by and people lose interest in his art form, he has to come to terms with suffering, art, and what it means to sell out to the public. (Ironically, Kafka himself died from starvation as he was being treated for tuberculosis. His throat was so sore he could no longer eat).

- "A Country Doctor"—This surreal tale describes the events of one night as a rural doctor tries to find a horse to make a house call. Mysterious horses appear, but as he rides off, his maid is placed in danger. He arrives to discover a patient who may or may not be dying. Can he rescue the patient and his maid, or are forces working against him?
- "The Metamorphosis"—Gregor Samsa wakes up one morning to the surprise of his life: he has turned into a giant insect! Will he be squashed underfoot by his family? Will he ever return to normal?
- "In the Penal Colony"—A condemned prisoner is subjected to a unique torture device, a machine that carves the victim's punishment in words deep into his flesh. He is literally "sentenced" to death.

That's What He Said: Franz Kafka

- How can one take delight in the world unless one flees to it for refuge?
- A book must be an ice-axe to break the seas frozen inside our soul.
- Anyone who keeps the ability to see beauty never grows old.
- Don't despair, not even over the fact that you don't despair.
- Writers speak stench.
- Evil is whatever distracts.
- The history of mankind is the instant between two strides taken by a traveler.
- One of the first signs of the beginning of understanding is the wish to die.

Pablo Picasso

Born on October 25, 1881, in Malaga, Spain, Pablo Picasso is considered the co-founder of Cubism.

He learned his craft from his father who was also an accomplished painter, instructor, and museum curator. He attended various art schools and even enrolled in college at Academia de San Fernando in Madrid but stayed only a few months.

He was married twice and had four children by three women.

Picasso lived the stereotypical "starving artist" lifestyle in Spain and France. In his early career, he sold his paintings to pay rent and burned some to stay warm. By the end of his life, his popularity was such that he was able to keep many of his paintings for himself and had even built a substantial collection of other artists' works. At his death in 1973, Picasso had no will, so his art collection went to pay estate tax in France. These paintings are now in the Musée Picasso collection in Paris.

Cubism

In 1901, while living in Madrid, Picasso teamed with a friend to establish the magazine *Arte Joven.* Illustrating the entire first edition himself, the artist started to sign his work Picasso; before he signed his work as Pablo Ruiz y Picasso.

Picasso introduced analytic cubism into his painting in 1909. Using shades of brown, the artist painted pieces of objects and "analyzed" them according to their shapes.

He developed this cubist style further when he added cut pieces of wallpaper and newspaper to his paintings, creating collages. He was the first to use collage in fine art.

Guernica, his depiction of the 1936 German bombing of Guernica, Spain, is said to be his most famous work. It was commissioned for exhibit at the Spanish Pavilion in the 1937 Paris International Exposition.

Picasso During the War

Picasso stayed in Paris when the Germans occupied the city during World War II. Since the Nazis did not like his work, the artist was forbidden to display his paintings. In 1944, he joined the French Communist Party and received the Stalin Peace Prize in 1950 and again in 1961. However, when the party criticized his portrait of Stalin, Picasso lost much of his interest in the Communist Party.

The Blue Period

The most commonly accepted periods for Picasso's work are the Blue Period (1901–1904), consisting of paintings in shades of blue and green and with a recurrent theme of blindness; the Rose Period (1905–1907), characterized with warm colors including oranges and pinks and many times featuring harlequins; the African-influenced period (1908–1909), analytic cubism (1909–1912), using brown monochrome colors; and synthetic cubism (1912–1919), which incorporates bits of paper into the paintings.

Postwar Picasso

After World War II, Picasso is said to have "returned to order" in his painting, joining the neoclassical movement that was prevalent in literature, music, and art.

From 1968 to 1971, Picasso used a mixture of styles and more color in his paintings. During this time he worked fast and produced a number of paintings. Most of them were called incoherent scribbling. It was not until after his death that these paintings were seen for what they were—a new style named neo-expressionism. Even up to his death, Picasso seemed to be an artist before his time.

Pablo Picasso died on April 8, 1973, in Mougins, France.

Workin' It

- Some paintings by Picasso are considered among the most expensive paintings in the world.
- Nude on a Black Armchair sold for $45.1 million in 1999.
- Les Noces de Pierrette sold for more than $51 million in 1999.

- Garçon à la pipe sold for $104 million in 2004.
- Dora Maar au Chat sold for $95.2 million in 2006.

Art-i-Facts

- Pablo Picasso's full name was Pablo Diego José Francisco de Paula Juan Nepomuceno María de los Remedios Cipriano de la Santísima Trinidad Martyr Patricio Clito Ruiz y Picasso.
- Picasso's mother said her son's first word was *piz*, Spanish slang for "pencil."
- Picasso was the first to incorporate collage techniques, using bits of paper in his paintings, in fine art.
- Along with Georges Braque, Picasso is considered the co-founder of cubism.

The Chicago Picasso

Located in Daley Plaza in the downtown Chicago Loop, the Chicago Picasso definitely draws attention. The abstract metal sculpture stands 50 feet tall and weighs 162 tons. It was the first major public artwork in Chicago. Following Picasso's instructions, U.S. Steel Corporation in Gary, Indiana, created the sculpture for $351,959.17. Picasso turned down payment of $100,000, choosing to offer the work as a gift to the people.

ALBERT EINSTEIN

Born in 1879, in Ulm, Germany, Albert Einstein earned a Ph.D. in 1905 from the University of Zurich. As a professor of physics at universities in Zurich, Prague, and Berlin, Einstein became a well-recognized figure in the science community.

In 1916, Einstein published his theory of general relativity. Einstein had earlier theorized that distance and time are not absolute. He believed the rate that a clock ticked depended on the motion of the person looking at the clock. His theory of general relativity said that gravity and motion can affect time and space. In other words, gravity pulling in one direction is equal to acceleration in the opposite direction. This is an explanation of why a person is pushed back against the seat when a car accelerates.

In 1933, seeking to escape political oppression in Germany, Einstein immigrated to the United States. He accepted a position at the Princeton Institute of Advanced Study in New Jersey, where he taught until retirement in 1945.

During his retirement years, Einstein continued to work on his general theory of relativity.

- Einstein received the 1921 Nobel Prize in physics for his discovery of the law of the photoelectric effect and his work in the field of theoretical physics.
- He was instrumental in establishing the Hebrew University in Jerusalem.

EXTRA CREDIT: Einstein was offered the presidency of Israel in 1952. He declined.

WORLD WAR I

Warfare Tactics

Technology improved proven weapons and also brought new tools to the battlefield. However, it took time for tactical warfare to develop and perfect the use of these creations. Many casualties resulted from the combination of new technology with old battle styles.

Machine Guns

Machine guns had been introduced to warfare during the American Civil War, and they continued to evolve during this war. The Vickers Machine Gun was adopted by the British army and coupled with interrupter gear became standard armament for all British and French aircraft after 1916. The Lewis Gun, which was far easier to produce and lighter than the Vickers, was also used by the British army. These could be found with soldiers on the Western Front, along with armored cars and aircrafts as well.

Tanks

Almost a year into the war, a tractor equipped with a caterpillar track, bullet-proof casing, and mounted armor was showcased in England. Prime Minister Winston Churchill was impressed by the machine's ability to cut through a barbed wire entanglement and sponsored a committee to investigate the construction of a new military weapon. The machine resembled a water carrier and was code named "tank." The goal of the tank, based on armored cars heavily used on the Western Front, was a machine possessing two twenty-mile range machine guns, a ten-man crew, minimum speeds of four miles per hour, and the ability to climb a five-foot obstacle and span a five-foot trench, all while being immune to small-arms fire. The result was a three-man sardine can able to move three miles per hour across rough terrain. The first battle-ready British tank did not debut until 1916, and the French unveiled their own in 1917. Mud and rough terrain often left them stranded, and the noxious fumes inside crippled their crews. The successes inspired the German, Austrian, and United States armies to develop their own tanks, and advances continued through the end of the war. By that time, the tank had become a tactical component of warfare, being used in tandem with aircraft and artillery to advance the infantry.

Air Power

The newly emerging airplane took warfare to the skies. Using airplanes allowed gunners to fire from overhead, on and into enemy lines using guns mounted directly to or built directly into the aircraft. Coupling airplanes with the use of poisonous gas-laden artillery shells produced greater damage. The pilots' skill was an art displayed in dogfight battles of enemy pilots pushing their airplanes to their limits and beyond. This technology continued to evolve throughout the war and became an essential component of advancing the infantry.

Gas

Mustard and chlorine gas were introduced during World War I. How was this an effective method of eliminating the enemy? Simple, toss poisonous gas into their trenches and wait. Those able would attempt to escape the trench running into the hail of gunfire awaiting them. Those unable to flee would die a painful, gasping death.

Pillboxes

Pillboxes were small, reinforced concrete shacks with small slits just large enough for machine guns to be aimed and fired. In 1915, the use of safety straps in tandem with existing tactics enabled gunners to fire in multiple directions simultaneously. Use of this tool was quickly abandoned due to the labor costs for construction and maintenance. Generals also feared their troops would lose offensive battlefield techniques by limiting their forces in such structures.

Flamethrowers

Although invented by the German army, the flamethrower was not introduced to the battlefield until World War I. The first such apparatus required two men to operate and would produce a jet stream of fire created by pressurized oil shot through a flame. An enemy trench could be cleared from a distance of about eighty feet but burned for only forty seconds. Advances eventually advanced the distance to about 130 feet. The drawback? Those using the apparatus were instantly the target of the enemy fire and killed.

Trench Warfare

Trench warfare is nearly as old as warfare itself, but it had never been a predominant tactic prior to World War I. Advancements in firepower without means of further mobility resulted in crippling frontal attacks and made outflanking operations essential. By creating a defensive tactic of constructing zigzag trench systems parallel to those of the enemy—just out of enemy weapons' reach and usually heavily enclosed in barbed wire—troops found their positions fortified as the trenches expanded to move troops forward. The open area between trenches was dubbed "no-man's-land," and those within it were subject to open fire with no means of protection.

The Battle of Verdun, 1916

A major military engagement of World War I, the Battle of Verdun was a ten-month ordeal between the French and German armies. The battle was part of an unsuccessful German campaign to take the offensive on the Western Front. Both the French and German armies suffered incredibly, with an estimated 540,000 French and 430,000 German casualties and no strategic advantages gained for either side. The Battle of Verdun is considered to be one of the most brutal events of World War I, and the site itself is remembered as the "battlefield with the highest density of dead per square yard."

In the years preceding World War I, Germany became Europe's leading industrial power. France felt increasingly threatened by German industrialization; and although France ruled the second largest colonial empire in the world (Britain's was the largest), French leaders realized that France could not protect itself on its own from the burgeoning power of Germany.

As a response to the German threat of invasion, France built a continuous line of sunken forts in the hopes that an invading army would not be able to maneuver through it. The line of fortifications extended from the Swiss frontier to the French city of Verdun, thus making Verdun a vital strongpoint for the French war effort.

The German attack began on February 21, 1916, with an intense artillery bombardment of the forts surrounding Verdun. The French army retreated to predetermined positions while the German army pounded through the French lines. On February 25, Fort Douaumont, near Verdun, surrendered to German forces. On that same day, General Joseph Joffre, the French commander in chief, dedicated to ceasing further French retreat, assigned General Henri Philippe Petain to command the French army at Verdun. While the exhausted German army was lingering at Fort Douaumont, Petain restructured his troops and transported reserves to the region continuously.

On March 6, the German commanders ordered an attack, and on March 22, another French fort near Verdun, Harcourt, surrendered to the German army. A week later, on March 22, Malancourt, a French fort near

Verdun, fell to the Germans. Although three French forts near Verdun had capitulated to German forces, Verdun itself remained undefeated.

German attacks ensued, but by April the French Air Force had secured the sky over Verdun, which would help the French to successfully defend the area. However, the French forts of Thiaumont and Vaux had fallen to the German army in June even though the pressure on France had diminished as a direct result of the British attack on German forces near the Somme River. This British attack and a Russian offensive in the east forced the German army to transfer troops away from Verdun. These events put Germany in a defensive mode, and the French quickly took the offensive.

By November, Fort Vaux, Fort Thiaumont, and Fort Douaumont had been reclaimed for France. By December, the French had advanced to their February lines, their original position. No new advantage had been gained for either side.

Women in WWII

Women can be found in almost every effort of World War II. They were found on the front lines, not only as nurses but as scientists, engineers, journalists, and soldiers. They were found in the factories and work places, supporting their families at home and producing the items needed for war. The images of Rosie the Riveter are well known from this era. In the U.S., women even joined the All American Girls Baseball League in an effort to support the troops and boost morale. Tokyo Rose could be heard broadcasting propaganda to Allied troops. That Rose was convicted of treason for her efforts. Other women were exiled to concentration camps and tortured. Most countries around the world contained women who were left to run their households and families while supporting their men who had gone off to war.

The Battles of the Marne, 1914; 1918

On September 4, 1914, the rapid advances of the German army through Belgium and northern France caused panic in the French army, and troops were rushed from Paris in taxis to halt the advance. Facing combined troops of France and the British Expeditionary Force (BEF), the Germans were eventually halted and the war settled into the familiar defensive series of entrenchments. Ironically, by the end of May 1918, the Germans had again reached the Marne after the enormous successes of Ludendorff's offensives of that year. The intervening four years had cost hundreds of thousands of lives and the armies were still, literally, exactly where they had started.

The Battles of Ypres, 1914; 1915; 1917

In actuality, there were three different battles around Ypres Salient in a three-year period of World War I. In 1914, the BEF made an attempt to stop advances of the Germans. In 1915, the battle witnessed the first use by the Germans of poison gas. The battles' name most appropriately should be associated with the last of the three—a-long planned offensive on July 31, 1917. This battle is perhaps the one for which the horrific images of the war are most connected. The weather was horrible, the goals were too ambitious, and misapplied persistence resulted in a loss of approximately a quarter of a million lives from either combat wounds or literally drowning in liquefied mud.

The Battle of the Somme, 1916

The "Big Push" was launched July 1, 1916, as an attack across the River Somme finding the British intending to break through German defense lines quickly and with relative ease. Orders from the high command required the troops to maintain uniformed lines while marching across no-man's-land directly at the enemy. As artillery efforts to dislodge German wire and machine-gun posts failed, the result was one of the largest slaughters in military history, as the Germans were able to man their posts and destroy the approaching infantry.

The Battle of Cambrai, 1917

The British offensive launched to utilize the tank in a surprise artillery assault with 476 tanks moving in a tight mass moved on the German lines on November 20, 1917. The result was an impressive breach of German lines with a depth of penetration much greater than expected. Ultimately shocking not only the Germans but the British as well for its success, Cabrai proved that well planned and executed tank assaults could break the deadlock in the trenches.

World War I Phrases

Several words and phrases that are common place in today's language have their origins from the events of World War I. Some reflected the technical innovations of the time such as *ammo, dogtag, foxhole, parachute, blimp, tank*, and *bomber*, which maintain their military origin. Others have lost almost all military connotation: *ace, chow, slacker*, and *dud*.

Basket case, for instance, was of course a term associated with the mentally unstable, but during WWI, the British used this term for quadruple amputees that were removed from the field in baskets.

Below are other words and phrases you might use on a regular basis:

- *Gives the willies*: be frightened, or shell shocked
- *Go West*: used when referring to a comrade who had died
- *Hayburners*: army horses and mules (U.S.)
- *Kamerad Schnurschuh* or *pal with laced boots:* German nickname for Austro-Hungarian troops
- *Kilometerschwein* or *kilometer pig:* German infantryman (German)
- *Lakenpatscher* or *puddle splasher:* German infantryman (German)
- *Land crabs*: tanks (British)
- *Limeys*: American troops' term for British soldiers based on the lime juice sailors were given for scurvy
- *Leatherneck*: American Marines garnered the name due to the material on their collars
- *Monkey meat*: canned beef and carrot mixture ration from South America (U.S.)
- *Mothers*: 5.7-inch British guns (British)
- *Over the top*: to attack, generally from the trenches
- *Poilu* or *hairy one:* French infantryman.
- *Pozzy*: ration-issue jam (British)
- *Roughneck*: artilleryman (U.S.)
- *Slum* or *slumgum*: a stew of meat, potatos, onions, and tomatos (U.S.)
- *Suicide Ditch*: front line trench (British)
- *Tommy*: British infantryman, from Tommy Atkins, a fictional name used in instructions for filling out British military forms
- *Wives*: nine-inch British guns (British)

Sir Karl Popper: Critical Rationalism

Born in Vienna in 1902, Karl Popper attended the University of Vienna where he earned his Ph.D. in philosophy in at the age of only sixteen. From there he went on to teach secondary school.

His first book, *The Logic of Scientific Discovery*, was published in 1934. In this work he questioned some of the popular thought of the day and introduced his theory of falsifiability.

In 1937, Popper left Vienna to escape political oppression. He accepted a teaching position at the University of Canterbury in New Zealand, lecturing in philosophy.

He moved on to England in 1946 to become reader in logic and scientific method at the London School of Economics.

Popper was among the most influential philosophers of science in the twentieth century. He called his philosophy "critical rationalism," arguing that the positive outcomes that result from experimental testing cannot confirm a scientific theory. His insistence that a theory should be considered scientific only if it is falsifiable led him to question psychoanalysis and quantum mechanics, among other popular theories of the day. Yet he was a staunch proponent of Albert Einstein's theories about the universe.

- Popper died in 1994 at the age of ninety-two.
- He was honored by both colleagues and society throughout his career, including the following nods:
- He was named president of the Aristotelian Society.
- He was knighted in 1965.
- He was elected as a fellow of the Royal Society in 1976.
- He received the Lippincott Award from the American Political Science Association.
- He won the Sonning Prize.
- He received the Grand Decoration of Honour in Gold from Austria.

Personal Protection

Some historians peg the invention of the modern day condom in the early sixteenth century, but records indicate folks have been getting their jollies in a safe—and sheathed—fashion for more than three thousand years.

From Egyptian hieroglyphics to war journals, the history of the condom materialized long before their mass production began around the turn of the twentieth century. And think about this next time you blow a tire: It was Charles Goodyear's revolutionary vulcanization of rubber that not only made the mass production possible but resulted in the most popular alias for the little suckers.

Roman soldiers are believed to have fashioned their condoms from the innards of slain opponents, while Cassanova is purported to have worn a linen variation during his romp through the eighteenth century.

Now keep in mind, disease prevention for the wearer alone was the primary motivation for this handy little contraption, so it's little surprise that some of the earliest versions were reusable, and a few have managed to survive for several centuries.

The shocking revelation is that the practice was resumed in the 1940s when animal intestines replaced rubber as the preferred material, and used condoms were washed, preserved in petroleum jelly, and put away until the need arose.

World War II: Causes

Following their World War I defeat, Germany, Italy, and Japan were ready to regain and increase their power. All three nations adopted various forms of fascism or socialism, whereby, the state was supreme and could call for expansion at the expense of neighboring countries. Each gained some form of tolerance from many nations due to their apparent early efforts to combat Communism. The desire for peace among so many democracies left them lacking in military preparedness. The League of Nations found itself floundering after the departure of the United States and could not promote disarmament. This, with the long economic depression of the 1930's, increased fears and distrust along national lines.

The League of Nations after a string of treaty violations and aggressive acts was unable to stop the Second Sino-Japanese war in 1931. Adolf Hilter rose to power over Germany in 1933, reshaped the German army and began to prepare for a war of widespread conquest. Benito Mussolini conquered Ethiopia for Italy while the forces of fascist Francisco Franco found aid in Germany and Italy. Germany annexed Austria in 1938 while, as a part of the Munich Pact, much of Czechoslovakia was sacrificed to Germany.

During this occupation, as Albania was seized by Italy, Great Britain and France abandoned their policy of appeasement to create a front of opposition in alliance with Turkey, Greece, Romania, and Poland. As a push for rearmament raged, Germany signed alliances with Italy and the Soviet Union. Germany was now poised to invade Poland. That act led Britain and France to declare war on Germany. With the exception of Ireland, all members of the Commonwealths of Nations followed. Germany utilized new techniques in its quick assault on Poland, using new technology and air warfare, effectively completing the conquest before the Soviet forces breached the borders. The Soviets conquered Finland while the British and French contingencies fell into complacency using a sea blockade of Germany.

Using such ignorance to their advantage, the Germans invaded Denmark in April of 1940 with little or no resistance. They overran

Luxembourg to invade the Netherlands and Belgium in May and had conquered Norway by early June. Their armored columns raced to the English Channel and cut off Flanders. The Allied forces evacuated from Dunkirk. France signed an armistice with Germany, followed by an armistice with Italy, and the Vichy government was established in France. Britain—the only remaining Allied power—continued resisting even with Germany bombing it repeatedly.

Shifting sights

The war moved into new theaters with the air assaults, attacks by the Italians on Britain in North Africa, and invading Greek and German submarine warfare in the Atlantic Ocean. Hungary and Romania joined the triple axis in 1940 and after repeated resistance to German pressure, Yugoslavia and Crete fell, followed by Bulgaria in 1941.

After the German invasion of the Soviet Union on June 22, 1941, Great Britain gained a new ally. The hard Russian winter halted the German sweep destroying its army and foiling its attempt to take Moscow.

Until this time, the United States had managed to remain neutral and offered lend-lease aid to Britain to save it from collapse as a part of the Atlantic Charter agreement between President Franklin Delano Roosevelt and British Prime Minister Winston Churchill. In an effort to establish bases to protect its shipping from German submarine attacks, the United States occupied portions of Greenland and Iceland. While attacks continued to strain relations with the Germans, the United States protested the Japanese acts of aggression on China, Indochina, and Thailand.

Crash Course

Pearl Harbor

All efforts of peace and neutrality for the United States came to an immediate halt when the Japanese, without warning, bombed Pearl Harbor, the Philippines, and Malaya on December 7, 1941. The United States, the Commonwealth of Nations, and the Netherlands all declared war on Japan the following day. In response, Italy and Germany both declared war on the United States within days of their declaration against Japan.

This brought World War II to the Pacific theater and the initial phases were a disaster for the Allies, while the Japanese continued to conquer the island countries of the Pacific. Australia became the chief Allied base in the offensive directed by General Douglas MacArthur, Admiral Chester Nimitz and Admiral William Halsey against Japan. The successful Allied maneuvers were seen in the battles of the Coral Sea and at Midway, where U.S. bombers were able to knock out most of Japan's carrier fleet and push Japan into retreat. The battle of Midway was the first real blow to the Axis by the Allied forces. This continued on land in New Guinea and the Solomon Islands.

ELSEWHERE IN WARFARE

While the Allied position was improving in the Pacific, the summer of 1942 was not as positive elsewhere. Axis forces were advancing in North Africa, Egypt, Russia, and in the Atlantic, almost to the shores of the United States in the Gulf of Mexico. German submarines were striking Allied ships at an astonishing rate.

Such aggressive pushes were beginning to wear the Axis, and it was beginning to show. The United States was only beginning to realize its potential, and Russia stretched out with its reserves, lend-lease aid courtesy of the U.S. via Iran.

The major blows felt by the Axis were those in North Africa by the Anglo-American invasion of Algeria in November 1942.

Free French forces and other regular French forces joined the American and British while the surrender of the German Sixth Army occurred in February 1943. following a Soviet stand at Stalingrad.

The Allies successfully conquered Sicily during the summer of 1943, and Italy soon followed in spite of hard-fought battles by the Germans.

Likewise, the threat of submarines in the Atlantic was obliterated by summer of 1944.

Supplied largely by Allied forces, all across German-occupied lands in Europe, underground forces began to fight back.

Through a series of conferences around the world, the Allies signed the United Nations declaration and vowed to continue the war until the complete surrender of the Axis.

An invasion of German-held France was determined and General Dwight D. Eisenhower commanded the effort.

The Aftermath

Air warfare became the overwhelming favor for the Allies who utilized this technology to bring untold destruction on many German cities and transport, and on industries in German-held Europe preparing the pat for Allied forces to land in France. After Normandy and Rhine, most of France and Belgium were cleared of German forces by October 1944.

While the Soviets pressed into East Prussia, Czechoslovakia, and East Germany, the Western Allies overran Western Germany. With the meeting of these armies in Torgau and Hitler's death in a ruined Berlin, Germany finally collapsed and unconditionally surrendered at Reims on May 7. The surrender was ratified at Berlin on May 8, 1945.

The Allies advanced in two lines through scattered island groups en route to Japan. Japan weakened as most of its fleet was sunk. yet refused to surrender. It was not until the United States detonated the first atomic bomb used in warfare on Hiroshima on August 6, 1945, and a second three days later on Nagasaki. With the USSR already invading Manchuria, Japan surrendered on September 2.

Technology

World War II began with armies utilizing the existing technologies of World War I and the nineteenth century. Most of the countries involved were not equipped for the mechanization that would ultimately be necessary to win the war. Where Germany recognized and demonstrated the value of concentrated use of mechanized forces, it could not produce the quantities needed to overcome the Allied forces. The war progressed with rapid change and advancement: ballistic missiles, jet aircraft, and the development and first use of the atomic bomb.

Electronics

Radar and devices created for communication and for the interception of communications became crucial during World War II. These devices were used for code breaking, ballistic tables, and other time-sensitive calculations. Many are predecessors of our modern day computers. The Enigma machine is possibly the most famous of these.

Industrial Boom

Countries with the ability to quickly ramp up their industrial capacity to build and mobilize their war efforts found they could rapidly respond to the needs of the soldiers. This began to fuel the global economy as well. The Allies created synthetic rubber once their access to the rubber trees had been cut off, just as the Germans created an alternative fuel from hydrogen peroxide.

EXTRA CREDIT: The largest advance was the use of penicillin for the combat treatment of wounds, bacterial infection, and disease.

Ships

The aircraft carrier became the elite ships of the navy, while the submarines became more increasingly effective as the war progressed. Most naval advancements, however, were hampered by the length of production time for new vessels, and engaged governments found that retrofitting current ones was equally important to the war effort.

The war was over before many of the more advanced ships were ready for launch, or—more often—navies had lost too many of the experienced men needed to command them. The fleet of any nation became its lifeline: its way to move, feed, and arm troops.

The German U-boats were able to stop and destroy many of the American and Canadian shipments.

Submarines were widely used in both the Atlantic and Pacific for the same purpose.

The destruction of their fleet and their inability to replace aircraft carriers was fatal for the Japanese.

The crucial advances of this war were the widespread use of sonar and the addition of both shipboard and airborne radar equipment.

AIRCRAFT

Air power became a crucial element of the Western European Theater and throughout the war for both strategic and tactical operations. Initially, superior aircraft allowed the Germans to overrun Western Europe quickly.

After World War I, the French Air Force had been neglected and was based in northern France and quickly overtaken by Germany. French aircraft were no match for the Germans. While the British Air Force did possess the same Spitfires and Hurricanes, they were not useful for ground-troop attacks, and their small numbers were quickly destroyed by the Germans.

Using the conquered French areas for bases, the Germans were able to launch raids on London and other English cities with ease and great success. The other European and American air forces had learned the value of strategic bombing from battles fought in the Spanish Civil War and from advanced aircraft bombers.

The speed at which these were built surpassed the bombing technology—which left bombs falling far from their targets. Guidance systems were evolving in the Allied forces that would correct this issue. Jet aircraft were also introduced during the later phases of the war, but the air superiority of the Allies devastated the German airbases. This was due to the aerial combat lessons learned as the war advanced.

Vehicles

The Treaty of Versailles had placed hard restrictions upon Germany and its production of military vehicles. Most of its tanks were developed in secret and took the European countries by surprise.

These tanks had rotating turrets and cannons, not machine guns. This allowed them to fire on other armored vehicles with great penetration. Germans equipped their tanks with radios, giving them the ability to communicate with one another and area commanders.

The innovative use of technologies was crippling to the French tanks of the day. British tanks were well equipped for trench warfare, but this made them too slow for open battlefields. The Americans introduced the first amphibious water vehicle technology in 1941.

Weapons

The actual weapons used in World War II were as diverse as the countries in the war, and as the war progressed, more were developed to meet specific needs. The most profound military advancement of the war—the atomic bomb—also had a great impact on the scientific community.

The weapon was designed to be carried by a single aircraft and yet level entire cities. To launch a war against a country possessing an entire arsenal of them was sheer suicide. The technology was completed too late in the war to be of use in the European Theater, and the Germans had no success with their attempts to build an atomic weapon. The most notable reason for their failure was the anti-Semitism of the day. Most of the first tier of high energy physicists and scientists were, or were married to, Jews.

Crash Course
Weaponry

Infantry weapons: Bazooka, anti-tank weapons, assault rifles, rocket propelled grenades.

Naval Weapons: Eighteen-inch guns, radar, torpedoes with magnetic detonators, compass directed guidance systems.

Armor Weapons: Tanks, tank destroyers, mine clearing Flail tanks, tanks of amphibious design.

Missiles: The Pulse jet-powered V1 flying bomb (the first "cruise missile").

Aircraft: Glide bombs (the first "smart bombs" with wire or radio remote control for detonation), the first jet fighters, jet bombers, military helicopters.

Small Arms: New methods evolved that allowed quicker production of arms in the quantities needed. Stamping, riveting, and welding all played a role. The war also saw the birth of the first reliable semi-automatic rifle and the first real assault rifle, a phrase pioneered by the Germans. Advances in machine-gun technology also made a far more dependable weapon. That technology is still used today.

Battle of Midway

The Battle of Midway was the turning point in the war against Japan because most of Japan's fleet was destroyed. This naval battle was fought in the Pacific Theater June 4-7, 1942. During the battle, the U.S. Navy repelled a Japanese attack against Midway Atoll, losing one aircraft carrier and a destroyer but destroying four Japanese carriers and a heavy cruiser. This victory was decisive for the American forces as it permanently weakened the Japanese Navy. The loss of more than two hundred experienced naval aviators was impossible to overcome.

While both sides of the battle sustained heavy losses, the Americans were able to reconstitute their forces through shipbuilding and training programs. The shipbuilding program had been put in place to expand the fleet to surmount that of Japan. The U.S. Navy was then able to take the initiative offensively in the Pacific.

The last play the Japanese had was to lure the remaining U.S. carriers into a trap and attempt to sink them all. This was not a conquest campaign but an attempt to drive the Americans out of the Pacific so Japan could extend its power and possibly force the U.S. to end the Pacific War in negotiations favorable to Japan.

Normandy

The invasion of Normandy gave the Allies their first strong foothold in Europe by landing on the shores of France during Operation Overlord. It covers the initial landings on D-Day, June 6, 1944, until the Allied breakout in mid-July.

This invasion was the largest ever conducted on the sea as more than 850,000 Allied troops—Canadian, Free French, British, and American—crossed the English Channel into Normandy by the end of June. These countries. along with Poland, Greece, the Netherlands, Australia, New Zealand, and Norway. provided not only ground forces but also naval and air support.

The Normandy invasion began under the cover of darkness by using parachute and glider landings overnight, air attacks, bombings launched from the sea, and early morning beach landings.

Battle of the Bulge

The Battle of the Bulge—the Ardennes Offensive to the U.S. Army—was Hitler's last offensive between December 16, 1944 and January 25, 1945. Hitler planned to capture Antwerp, Belgium, by splitting the American and British line and forcing the Western Allied forces to negotiate a peace treaty with the Axis after being surrounded.

This assault was planned in complete secrecy, and although aware something was brewing, the U.S. Third Army was blindsided by it. The "bulge" was the initial incursion of the Germans into the Allies' line of advance. For the U.S. Army, this battle incorporated more troops than any conflict to that time. The Germans failed to reach any of their objectives, and in the wake of the defeat, their units were depleted of supplies, equipment, and men.

Battle of Stalingrad

The Battle of Stalingrad, deep in Russia, is a common name for several large operations by Germany, its allies, and Soviet forces to possess the city of Stalingrad. These offenses took place between July 17, 1942, and February 2, 1943. The results are considered a turning point in the European Theater, as well as one of the bloodiest battles in history.

Combined casualties exceeded 1.5 million with disregard for military as well as civilian injuries. The German offensive was thwarted by the Soviet counteroffensive and destroyed the Sixth Army and other Axis forces.

Battle of Britain

The Battle of Britain refers to the efforts to gain air superiority over the Royal Air Force's fighter command in the summer and fall of 1940 and finds its name in a speech Prime Minister Winston Churchill gave on June 18 of that year. This was the first major battle to be waged entirely by air. Germany's inability to defeat Britain's air defenses and morale is considered its first major defeat.

Iwo Jima

The Battle of Iwo Jima was fought between the United States and Japan in February and March of 1945. Ground fighting on the Japanese island lasted from February 19 to March 26. The U.S. invasion, known as Operation Detachment, had the objective of capturing the airfields on Iwo Jima. Japanese imperialists defended their homeland from this invasion with some of the fiercest fighting of the campaign.

Of the 21,000 soldiers present at the onset of the battle, only 216 were taken prisoner and 20,000 were killed. One of the most famous photographs of the war was taken on this island. The iconic image captured five U.S. Marines in the second flag raising on Mount Suribachi.

Concentration Camps

Concentration camps are typically known as locations where groups of people are confined, usually for political reasons and under horrific conditions. Incarcerations took place without trial and led to undetermined lengths of confinement. They are also known as relocation centers, corrective labor camps, and reception centers.

During World War II, more than six million people died in German concentration camps. Those sent to the camps were found to be in opposition to the German Nazi movement for any number of reasons: religion, stature, physical description, or profession.

U.S. Army forces placed almost 120,000 Japanese Americans in ten camps in the interior of the nation, referring to them as relocation centers.

Auschwitz

Auschwitz was the largest of all German concentration camps. Located in Poland, this atrocity was actually three camps in one. Those detained here were from countries all over Europe and were Jewish.

The compound housed a forced-labor camp, and once prisoners were too old or weak to work, they were sent to the death camp. Some were also the victims of experimental medical tests and procedures. The massive gas chambers of the death camp used the cyanide-based insecticide Zyklon B.

It is estimated that 2.5 million people died within the walls of this concentration camp.

Bergen-Belsen

Built near the two villages in Germany, this camp was constructed in 1943 as a prison camp and Jewish slave work camp. Originally intended for ten thousand people, the facility ultimately held forty-one thousand. The thirty-seven thousand who died at the camp succumbed to disease or overwork. Anne Frank was one victim of this camp.

Buchenwald

One of the first and largest concentration camps, Buchenwald was built in Weimar in 1937. The twenty thousand prisoners held as work slaves for nearby factories endured medical testing. Most died as a result of disease, malnutrition, and exhaustion, as well as beatings and executions.

Dachau

The first Nazi concentration camp, built in 1933 in Dachau, Germany, was meant to perform medical experiments on prisoners. These left the prisoners disabled, if they survived. Although not designed as a killing camp, it became one of the most harsh due to its living conditions and the experiments performed.

Pop Quiz #7

1) What entity declared war on Japan on Dec. 8, 1941, in direct response to the bombing of Pearl Harbor?
   a) The United States
   b) The Commonwealth of Nations
   c) The Netherlands
   d) All of the above

2) Which battle is considered the first real blow to the Axis powers by the Allied forces?
   a) Battle of Stalingrad
   b) Battle of the Bulge
   c) Battle of Midway
   d) Battle of Pelilieu

3) How many Allied troops were on the beaches of Normandy—establishing the first Allied foothold in Europe—during the D-Day Invasion on June 6, 1944?
   a) 750,000
   b) 850,000
   c) 950,000
   d) 1 million

4) Adolf Hitler's last offensive, waged between Dec. 16, 1944, and Jan. 25, 1945, is known as what?
   a) Ardennes Offensive
   b) Battle of the Bulge
   c) Battle of Britain
   d) Both A and B

5) What was the name of the first concentration camp established by the Nazis during World War II?
   a) Dachau
   b) Buchenwald
   c) Bergen-Belsen
   d) Auschwitz

6) Which of these movies does not involve World War II?
   a) *Flags of Our Fathers*
   b) *Kelly's Heroes*
   c) *Platoon*
   d) *The Longest Day*

Answers:

1) d
2) c
3) b
4) d
5) a
6) c

The Cold War

Following World War II, the United States and the Soviet Union were engaged in intense rivalries involving the two power blocs and their political endeavors. This period, deemed the Cold War, began in the 1940s and endured more than four decades.

During this time, each power shaped policies based upon its own political structures. For the Americans and their allies, including Britain, France, West Germany, Japan, and Canada, the approach was democratic and capitalistic.

For the Soviets, the approach was Communism. Soviet allies included Bulgaria, Hungary, Poland, Romania, East Germany, Czechoslovakia, Cuba, and China.

The term "Cold War" surfaced as a suggestion that relations between the Soviet Union and its former World War II adversaries were at the point of war, just without the use of actual warfare. The following years witnessed the rivalry emerging between the two power blocs become more mutual and hardened to the point of preoccupation and obsession, dominating foreign policy agendas on both sides and leading to the formation of two military alliances.

The North Atlantic Treaty Organization (NATO) was created by the Western powers in 1949. The Soviet bloc established the Warsaw Pact in 1955. The Cold War originated in Europe but eventually drew the United States and the Soviet Union into conflicts around the world, producing intense competition to develop and accumulate advanced military weapons which would allow one superiority over the other.

This competition was dubbed the "arms race."

FROM EARLY FROST TO HARD FREEZE

Although gaining momentum following World War II, the hostility between the Soviet Union and the United States had been festering since the First World War.

The Bolsheviks (who eventually became Communists) had overthrown the czar and the existing government in Russia in 1917, and as the emergent leader, Joseph Stalin sought to have Russia exit the war.

In an effort to restore the collapsing Eastern Front, the United States and its allies staged military interventions in Russia.

Stalin and his colleagues perceived the action as an assault on the new regime. In actuality, the members of the Western alliance did resent the approach of the new leadership, centering on appeals against capitalism and efforts to fuse local Communist groups into a revolutionary movement.

The tactic was successful as Russia and neighboring areas formed the Union of Soviet Socialist Republics under Communist control. Although this occurred in 1922, the United States would not recognize the Soviet state for another eleven years.

The vast differences in ideology were purposefully intensified under Stalin's leadership during his rule of the Soviet Union until 1953. One key issue, which existed prior to the fall of Germany in World War II, was the future of Poland.

Stalin had successfully driven Germans out of Poland and created a pro-Communist government and therefore believed Soviet control of the nation was imperative for the security of his own country. Naturally, the Allies opposed the view and the struggle eventually extended to other Eastern European countries.

This became the first critical phase in the Cold War, with each side believing the growing differences could eventually be overcome in the spirit of wartime cooperation.

The Soviet Union perceived itself as the leader of progressive forces and accused the United States of stalling revolutionary activity wherever it arose and interceded for its own gain. Likewise, the United States accused the Soviets of attempting to expand their communistic reach throughout Europe and Asia.

The U.S. leaders had great foresight, as the Soviet Union did help establish Communist governments in Romania, Poland, Hungary, and Bulgaria. U.S. President Henry Truman created the Truman Doctrine, authorizing the United States aid to any anti-Communist forces in Greece and Turkey; it was later expanded to support any nation the U.S. considered threatened by the Soviet expansion. The containment effort spread worldwide and soon became the official U.S. policy toward the Soviet Union.

The possibility of preserving some level of cooperation quickly deteriorated with the growing tensions and sense of competition. Developments in and around postwar Germany became the new core of the disagreements.

Germany had been divided into four separate zones following the war, with France, Britain, the United States, and the Soviets each maintaining an occupation zone.

Although Berlin was within the Soviet zone, the city was divided into four similarly structured administrative hubs. Inevitably, the four occupying governments could not agree on an economic and political infrastructure for Germany.

The U.S. and British administrative portions were merged, as they believed keeping the segmentation intact could have far more damaging impact upon the Western world as the Soviet and Western regimes drifted along ideological lines. This belief was furthered by concern for the war-ravaged Western countries that faced the economic challenges of a post-war reconstruction leaving them vulnerable to Soviets through European Communist parties already under Moscow's hand.

Under the Marshall Plan, the United States created an economic aid program to help rebuild the Western European economies, and to suppress Soviet expansion to the west.

Political Science 101

Political Musical Chairs

It's right around this point in history when political sciences majors get a little dizzy:

Eventually France merged its administrative area with that of the joint American-British zone establishing a West German state. Fearing this area would be rearmed and become a part of the U.S. led alliance, Stalin opposed the decision. The Soviet response was a land blockade cutting off these governments from their sectors in Berlin. The counteroffensive was a massive airlift of supplies over a period of nearly a year to West Berlin, effectively breaking the blockade.

The Soviet-backed Communists in Czechoslovakia formed a new government, thereby placing all Eastern European countries under Communist control, and completing the Soviet bloc. These actions further convinced political leaders of the U.S. and the Soviet Union that the other power was a fundamental threat to their own nation.

The spread of Communism in Europe garnered negotiations between Western Europe, the United States, and Canada resulting in the North Atlantic Treaty and establishing the North Atlantic Treaty Organization (NATO). The Berlin crisis also furthered the development of the state of West Germany and prompted the allied Western forces to consider arming their areas of Germany.

Elsewhere in Europe

After the death of Stalin in 1958, Nikita Khrushchev sought to ease the rigidness of policies toward the West but did not resolve the issue of a divided Germany in the midst of a divided Europe.

The Western powers approached softening policies toward the Soviets very cautiously, eventually addressing key issues by holding several summit conferences in Geneva, Switzerland. Where the issues began with reunification of Germany, they had grown to include the danger of nuclear attack and the remaining conflicts in Korea and Indochina.

The Geneva Conference gained little momentum regarding the central issues in Germany, Eastern Europe, and arms control. It did result in the signing of the State Treaty between the Allies and Austria, essentially securing Austria's neutrality, removing occupational forces, and ensuring the reestablishment of the Austrian republic.

The one noted change of this time was the realization that nuclear weapons had revolutionized military tactics and made war between the two an untenable action.

The 1950s saw the two powers involved in conflicts in Asia.

Stalin appeared to support Kim Il Sung, leader of Communist North Korea, in a plan to attack South Korea, believing the U.S. and other major world powers would not be involved.

The presumption led to the Korean War, placing American-led United Nation forces against the forces of both North Korea and China. This was the first armed conflict of the Cold War and resulted in major increases in military spending by the United States.

Seeing Stalin's actions as a potential precursor to more aggressive movements in Europe, the Korean War also prompted the United States to see NATO evolve into a more purposeful and permanent structure.

Although conflict would rise again surrounding Vietnam, the Communist world began to change in the 1960s as China and the Soviet Union became divided due not only to ideological issues but out of an emerging rivalry.

Cuban Missile Crisis

In 1962, the United States became aware of the Soviet Union's attempting to locate nuclear missiles in Communist Cuba.

The United States attempted to block the delivery of the missiles on Soviet ships, resulting in a standoff. Khurshchev eventually folded to the demands of U.S. President John F. Kennedy.

The Cuban Missile Crisis was the most serious confrontation between the two powers during the Cold War and taught each side that the risk of using nuclear weapons for political gain was too great. Such a gamble between the two never again occurred.

Although both powers continued to explore their own positions and objectives in regard to furthering and improving their technology, the 1970s became a time in which the two powers sought to control the cost of the nuclear arms race and collaborate on both economic and scientific ventures.

The reunion was short-lived as the competitions resumed over civil war in Angola and the Somali-Ethiopian war. While China allied with the United States, Cuba remained supportive of the Soviet Union.

The final period of friction between the U.S. and Soviet Union occurred in the early 1980s resulting from the 1979 Soviet invasion of Afghanistan to establish a Communist regime. By labeling the Soviet Union an "evil empire" and admiring strength foremost, U.S. President Ronald Reagan only compounded the friction.

Soviet leaders saw Reagan as an unappeasable adversary to their system and questioned his willingness to risk nuclear war as a needed means to defeat it.

The Drake Equation

Developed by Frank Drake in the 1960s, the Drake Equation is a way of estimating the number of civilizations that exist and might be transmitting radio frequencies in our galaxy. The factors of the equation include the number of sunlike stars in our galaxy and the fraction of habitable planets supporting communicating civilizations, along with several other elements of consideration. The result of multiplying these various factors is N, the number of transmitting civilizations. As you might think, many of the factors necessary for the equation are somewhat unknown; therefore, N could range from one (with our civilization being alone in the galaxy) to thousands or even millions. For this reason, the Drake Equation is related to the Fermi Paradox.

The Equation

N = R x fp x ne x fl x fi x fc x L

where:

- **N** is the number of civilizations in our galaxy with which we might expect to be able to communicate
- **R** is the rate of star formation in our galaxy
- **fp** is the fraction of those stars that have planets
- **ne** is the average number of planets that can potentially support life per star that has planets
- **fl** is the fraction of the above that actually go on to develop life
- **fi** is the fraction of the above that actually go on to develop intelligent life
- **fc** is the fraction of the above that are willing and able to communicate
- **L** is the expected lifetime of such a civilization

Warming Trend

It was under the rule of Soviet leader Mikhail Gorbachev in the mid-1980s that this bitter impasse began to dissolve.

Gorbachev was intent on stopping the decay of the Soviet system and reducing the burdens of foreign policy for his country. In three years time he managed to abandon many Soviet assumptions of the West and reach agreements previously believed unattainable.

This altered the dynamic of East-West relationships resulting in a series of summit talks between Gorbachev and Reagan. By 1987, the two agreed to abandon a class of nuclear missiles—long-range weapons that either could use to strike the other.

The Soviet government pulled out of Afghanistan and reduced its forces throughout Eastern Europe.

The year 1989 also saw the destruction of the wall that had physically divided East and West Berlin since 1961; Germany was one country once more.

The Soviet Union dissolved, collapsing into a confederation of independent states and essentially ending the Cold War.

The dissolution of the Soviet Union allowed the overhaul of military and industrial focus and spending, but it left millions of Russians unemployed after cuts were made.

The economic impact upon Russian lives was greater than that endured by the United States or Germany during the Great Depression.

The post-Cold War is a vision of a more unified world with the United States remaining the sole superpower and the number of ethnic and revolutionary wars declining significantly.

The legacy of the Cold War continues to affect global affairs in the wake of its cost over four decades in both monetary and casualty figures.

CRASH COURSE

COLD WAR-INSPIRED FILMS

- *Mission to Moscow*
- *The Day the Earth Stood Still*
- *Red Nightmare*
- *On the Beach*
- *The Manchurian Candidate*
- *Dr. Strangelove*
- *Seven Days in May*
- *Fail-Safe*
- *Point of Order*
- *Red Dawn*
- *Atomic Café*
- *The Hunt for Red October*
- *Are We Winning Mommy?*
- *War Games*
- *Matinee*
- *Nixon*
- *Blast from the Past*

Pop Quiz #8

1) The Cold War refers to post-World War II relations between which two nations?
   a) United States and Soviet Union
   b) Soviet Union and Germany
   c) United States and Germany
   d) Italy and Soviet Union

2) Which journalist popularized the term "cold war?"
   a) Edward E. Murrow
   b) Walter Lippman
   c) Walter Cronkite
   d) Barbara Walters

3) In 1947, what policy did the United States adopt in an attempt to contain the spread of Communism?
   a) Monroe Doctrine
   b) Marshall Plan
   c) Truman Doctrine
   d) Manifest Destiny

4) Who replaced Joseph Stalin as the Soviet leader in 1953?
   a) Mikhail Gorbachev
   b) Fidel Castro
   c) Vladmir Putin
   d) Nikita Khrushchev

5) Aside from the obvious, the Vietnam War was waged in which country?
   a) Laos
   b) Cambodia
   c) Neither A nor B
   d) Both A and B

6) Which world leader was not involved in the 1962 Cuban Missile Crisis?
   a) Nikita Khrushchev
   b) John F. Kennedy
   c) Yasser Arafat
   d) Fidel Castro

ANSWERS:

1) a
2) b
3) c
4) d
5) d
6) c

Korean Conflict

As World War II came to an end, Stalin sent his troops into Korea from the north in an effort to control as much of East Asia as possible after the fall of Japan. The Soviet Union had agreed to receive the surrendered Japanese forces north of the thirty-eighth parallel, and south of that line the Japanese surrendered to the United States.

The agreements held that Korea would become a united country, holding democratic elections, but there were no specified dates, and the Soviets soon established a hold for themselves on the Korean Peninsula at the thirty-eighth parallel.

After the fall of Chiang Kai-shek and the rise of Mao Zedong, tensions rose quickly.

Although the U.S. commitment to securing Japan and Chaing's regime on Taiwan was clearly expressed, support for Korea was not as specific.

North Korea saw this as the time to take control over all Korea and crossed the thirty-eighth parallel on June 25, 1950. Seoul was overrun by early July. This aggression should have evoked a collective response from the United Nations, but as the Soviet Union was boycotting the Security Council on another matter, the United States and others made unsuccessful efforts to persuade the Soviet ambassador to attend the meeting. The remaining council adopted a strong resolution opposing the actions of North Korea and authorized a military response.

Eventually, twenty-two nations contributed troops—the largest being the United States.

The U.S. was stunned by the scale of North Korea's attack, which benefited from Soviet weapons. South Koreans could not oppose them. The U.S. was unprepared for the occupation, irrespective of its troops based in Japan.

MacArthur's Involvement

General Douglas MacArthur sent a minimal contingent of men to battle North Korean forces. American troops fell back due to a flood of refugees but eventually held a line around the city of Pusan, the Pusan Perimeter.

As the perimeter held, MacArthur spotted a weakness in North Korean positions that were vulnerable in the midst of overstretched supply and communications lines.

On September 15, 1950, a counterattack was launched as American and other U.N. troops came ashore at Inchon—Seoul's seaport—and quickly broke through the North Korean lines.

With their positions threatened on two sides, the North Koreans were forced into retreat, allowing the U.N. forces to push North Korean forces from all of South Korea.

MacArthur was not content with this position and pressed onward to gain more ground toward China against warnings of others.

This left the U.N. forces facing masses of Chinese "volunteers" along the front lines.

Using their forces and willing to suffer heavy casualties, the Chinese began to push back their adversaries.

Allied troops retreated under horrid winter conditions.

On January 4, 1951, Seoul was recaptured by Communists.

Operation Ripper pushed them back, and then a stalemate developed with little movement in either direction.

Political Tension

U.S. President Harry S. Truman found himself in a delicate position. Neither the Chinese nor the North Koreans possessed atomic weapons, but the U.S. did.

Using them would most definitely bring the Soviet Union into the war. Victory might be achieved, but at the cost of another world war, no doubt.

General MacArthur did not share Truman's concern. In his view, a war should be waged militarily to the greatest extent possible.

And, quite frankly, damn the consequences.

So it's no surprise that during the early months of 1951, his disagreements with Truman became more public.

Truman felt that his constitutional role as commander in chief was being challenged. On April 11, 1951, he replaced MacArthur with General Matthew Ridgway.

Ironically, a man who had held the rank of captain in World War I had fired a five-star general and war hero.

MacArthur returned to the United States on the crest of widespread support. On April 19, 1951, he addressed a joint session of Congress, where he defended his views and announced his retirement from public life.

Truman kept a low profile for a while, and the furor about MacArthur eventually waned. As the war continued and casualties continued to mount, the American public looked for new directions.

General Dwight Eisenhower entered partisan politics as the Republican candidate for president in 1952. Promising to "go to Korea" to end the war, Eisenhower defeated Adlai Stevenson in the November elections.

He visited Korea on November 29, 1951. A cease-fire was declared on April 1, setting the line between the armies near the thirth-eighth parallel, where it began.

The Korean War cost 54,000 American lives. Chinese and Korean military losses were around a million, with another million civilian deaths. The war was one of the few hot wars during the Cold War period, and its indecisive conclusion stood in stark contrast to the complete victory that ended World War II.

Armored Warfare

North Korea was able to establish dominance using its Soviet World War II-era tanks against South Korea's forces without tanks and with few antitank weapons. The bazooka was still available, but was ineffective against the tanks.

U.S. forces found themselves using light tanks that had been left in Japan for post-WWII occupation duties so as not to destroy the roads. These were totally useless against the North Korean tanks.

Shipments of heavier U.S. and British tanks, coupled with their ground attack aircraft, diminished the North Korean's superiority with tanks. The terrain of North Korea made it difficult to use tanks, and they were effective only in small groups.

Air Warfare

The Korean War was the last major war where propeller aircraft—fighters such as the Mustang and Corsair—were used. Turbojet fighter aircraft such as the Panthers came to overwhelm the skies, dominating North Korea's propeller-driven fleet.

North Korea then began to fly the Soviet MiG jets, which overshadowed the U.N. jets used early in the war. The U.N. forces were reluctant to engage in open war with the Soviet Union and China, many of whose piloted MiGs for the North Koreans.

The war also saw the use of UH-58 helicopters for transport of the wounded.

Nuclear Weapons

U.S. President Harry S. Truman's allusions to the use of nuclear weapons at a 1950 press conference was more a threat than contingency planning. This is perhaps another reason Truman removed General MacArthur; he questioned his reliability should Washington decide to use nuclear weaponry.

Although Truman implied it was under consideration in several press conferences after the Chinese interventions, no such discussions actually took place until months later when the U.N. forces had suffered some major setbacks and were in retreat.

War Crimes

Political killings, supposedly in the tens of thousands, took place in South Korea while it was under North Korean control. The targets were South Korean government officials and any others labeled hostile and a threat to the Communists.

By similar token, South Korean military, police, and paramilitary forces executed leftist inmates and those considered Communist sympathizers. A U.S. diplomat put the number near one hundred thousand.

Both sides would round up men and women for their cause, and thousands never returned home. American troops were also instructed, for a time, to consider any Korean civilians approaching their position on the battlefield as hostile forces and to eliminate them. This led to random killings of many Korean civilians.

Legacy

The war heavily damaged both Koreas. South Korea stalled economically following the war, while North Korea recovered quickly due to Chinese support. A heavily guarded demilitarized zone is still maintained at the thirty-eighth parallel. This war introduced the theory of major world powers waging war in another country that would be left to endure the assault of the combat and death.

POWs

The North Koreans mistreated prisoners of war by imposed beatings, starvation, forced labor, summary executions, and death marches. Brainwashing and reeducation techniques were also employed. South Korea held and repatriated more than seventy-six thousand prisoners, while North Korea repatriated only eight thousand of their seventy thousand POWs.

Korean War: The Real 4077

In today's world, the mention of MASH will conjure images of a beloved movie or television series created in Hollywood depicting the lives and antics of men and women serving in a Mobile Army Surgical Hospital during the Korean War. While many of the skits depicted are fictitious in nature, the entire production was based in truth.

MASH units were introduced by the U.S. Army during World War II, but the concept was overhauled for application to the battlefield during the Korean War because of failures in World War II. The concept: a completely mobile, fully staffed surgical unit and all support staff in large trucks providing immediate care to wounded soldiers and civilians fresh from the battlefield, providing one MASH in support to each major unit in the army. The problems: not enough staff, funds, or time to adequately shape the units.

MASH units were originally restricted to performing surgical procedures but later handled all types of injuries sustained in battle. The soldiers would be evacuated from the field and transported to the MASH via a dedicated ambulance, or a helicopter for the most critical. The patients would be evaluated for care and triaged, or cared for in order, with the more life-threatening injuries at the head of the line. The key was to deliver care quickly, using the latest procedures at hand, and evacuate the soldiers to hospitals toward the rear of the fighting for their recuperation. The units would move monthly but were always kept in such proximity to the front that transport time for patients was minimized.

These units also managed their units with such strict and regimented guidelines that the unit could be completely disassembled and relocated to a new position on six hours' notice. Once at their new base of operations, the unit would once again be set up and operational within four hours. The efficiency of such units exceeded expectations, and many of their triage concepts became standard practice within civilian hospitals. More often than not, the MASH unit would be established within twenty miles of the front line, with care given to remain beyond the range of artillery fire. The concept was successful and helped reduce the fatality rate to less than 2.5 percent.

The Hollywood depiction of the 4077 Mobile Army Surgical Hospital was based on the Forty-third MASH, which comprised one hundred soldiers staffing a thirty-six-bed facility with two operating curtains. Doctors, nurses, and patients from this unit were interviewed and served as consultants on the production of the television series to ensure that the portrayal accurately reflected MASH life. The struggles, triumphs, tears, and laughter were just that—a true, yet often comedic, look at everyday life in war.

The MASH unit of the Korean War era has morphed into the Forward Surgical Teams of smaller, faster and more efficient medical groups utilized by today's army. The last remaining MASH units were phased out of service in the late 1990's.

On the television show *M*A*S*H*, nurse characters who played very small parts were given names such as "Nurse Able," "Nurse Baker," and "Nurse Charlie." These names came from the phonetic alphabet used by HAM operators during the time of the Korean War. In this alphabet the letters A, B, and C were Able, Baker, and Charlie.

Entertainment Bonanza

For the first time in American history, popular culture didn't just embrace the political and military climate, the entertainment industry humanized the efforts from the big to the small screen.

In fact, Hollywood forever solidified the image of a MASH unit in the minds of people around the world through both a movie and long-running television sitcom. *M*A*S*H* was set in South Korea, near Seoul, during the Korean War.

The series focused on the group of doctors and nurses whose job was to heal the wounded who arrived at this Mobile Army Surgical Hospital by helicopter, ambulance, or bus.

The hospital compound was isolated from the rest of the world. One road ran through the camp; a mountain blocked one perimeter, and a minefield the other. Here the wounded were patched up and sent home—or back to the front.

On Jukeboxes Everywhere…

- "Hoop-Dee-Doo"—Mellomen
- "All My Love"—Bolero
- "The Bigger the Figure"—Louis Prima and His Orchestra
- "Yakety Yak Polka"—Liberace
- "Castle Rock"—Frank Sinatra
- "Half as Much"—Rosemary Clooney
- "It's So Nice to Have a Man Around the House"—Dinah Shore

Playing in Theaters

- *The Manchurian Candidate*
- *MacArthur*
- *The Bridges at Toko-Ri*
- *Men in War*
- *Pork Chop Hill*
- *The Last Picture Show*
- *M*A*S*H*
- *Battle Hymn*
- *War Hunt*

Crash Course

Highlights of History

- Acupuncture was first used as a medical treatment in 3700 BC by Chinese ruler Shen-Nung.
- The Taj Mahal was commissioned in 1632 by Shah Jahan to honor his wife Mumtaz, who died in childbirth.
- The Republic of Israel was established May 14, 1948.
- Armored knights raised their visors to identify themselves when they rode past their king. This custom has become the modern military salute.
- In the Holocaust between 5.1 million and 6 million of Europe's 8 to 10 million Jews were killed. An additional 6 million "unwanted" people were also executed.
- On June 26th, 1945, the charter of the United Nations was signed in San Francisco by fifty countries. (The text of the charter was in five languages: Chinese, English, French, Russian, and Spanish.)
- The first country to abolish capital punishment was Austria in 1787.
- Although construction of the Notre Dame Cathedral in Strasbourg started in 1015, the spire was not completed until 1439.
- Napoleon took 14,000 French decrees and simplified them into a unified set of seven laws. This was the first time in modern history that a nation's laws applied equally to all citizens. Napoleon's seven laws are so impressive that by 1960 more than seventy governments had patterned their own laws after them or used them verbatim.
- The longest-reigning monarch in history was Pepi II, who ruled Egypt for ninety years, 2566 to 2476 BC, although some sources add another four years and others another six to that reign. The second longest rule in history was France's Louis XIV, who ruled for seventy-two years, 1643 to 1715.
- The Eiffel Tower is 984 feet high.

- Julius Caesar and Napoleon Bonaparte both suffered from epilepsy.
- The USSR set off the largest nuclear explosion in history, detonating a fifty-megaton bomb (twenty-six hundred times the power of the Hiroshima bomb) in an atmospheric test over the Novaya Zemla Islands on October 30, 1961.
- The very first bomb dropped by the Allies on Berlin during World War II killed the only elephant in the Berlin Zoo.
- The worldwide "Spanish Flu" epidemic which broke out in 1918 killed more than thirty million people in less than one year.
- The world's largest art gallery is the Hermitage in St. Petersburg, Russia. Visitors would have to walk fifteen miles to see the 322 galleries, which house nearly three million works of art.
- Work on St. Peter's Basilica, Rome, began in 1506. Construction took over a century, reaching completion in 1615.
- Measuring 1,483 feet, the Petronas Tower in Kuala Lumpur, Malaysia, is the world's tallest building.
- The term "devil's advocate" comes from the Roman Catholic Church. When deciding if someone should be sainted, a devil's advocate is always appointed to give an alternative view.

Vietnam Conflict (1959–April 30, 1975)

Commonly referred to as the Vietnam War, or sometimes the Vietnam Conflict, this prolonged engagement in Southeast Asia is also known in other corners of the world as the Second Indochina War. The Vietnamese call it simply the American War

The Players

Supporters of the Communists (North Vietnam)

- Democratic Republic of Vietnam (North Vietnam)
- National Front for the Liberation of South Vietnam (NLF); also known as the Viet Cong
- Vietnam People's Army (VPA); also known as the North Vietnamese Army (NVA) or the People's Army of Vietnam (PAVN)

Supporters of the Republic of Vietnam (South Vietnam)

- Army of the Republic of Vietnam (ARVN); South Vietnam
- The United States of America
- Australia
- Canada
- New Zealand
- Philippines
- Korea
- Thailand
- Montagnards (aboriginal hill tribes of southeast Indochina)

The Issues

The nearly sixteen-year war was partially a remnant of French colonial rule that ended in 1954 after the acceptance of the Geneva Conference agreements. When scheduled elections for reunification of the nation in South Vietnam were canceled by President Ngo Dinh Diem, his actions were immediately denounced by Ho Chi Minh and other Communists expecting to benefit from the expected outcome, and Diem's government faced great opposition from the Viet Cong as a result.

The Viet Cong were masters of guerrilla tactics and employed them at will during their assaults. Diem's army accepted aid and recommendations from the United States but failed to suppress the guerrillas' establishment of the NLF.

U.S. naval vessels reported being attacked by North Vietnam in 1964, although there is speculation the events did not happen and were used as a ruse to pass the Gulf of Tonkin Resolution in Congress for authorization to bomb North Vietnam after a second attack. The first combat troops arrived from the United States in 1965 and would number more than half a million within three years.

Nearly all land battles were waged within the area of South Vietnam amongst not only the thousands of North Vietnamese Army troops that managed to infiltrate the west and north regions but also the thousands of civilian Vietnamese in South Vietnam that supported the North and fought for them. The Americans came to refer to these groups as the Viet Cong.

Due to this saturation dynamic, it became difficult and dangerous for South Vietnamese troops and their allies to determine who was friend and who was foe. Where many tragic examples can be sited by veterans, the My Lai Massacre in March 1968 was a result of mistrust in which U.S. troops killed hundreds of civilians in a South Vietnamese village believing it to be a Viet Cong stronghold. Americans were frequently attacked by the large numbers of NLF forces embedded in South Vietnam.

Part of the successful penetration garnered by the VPA and NLF fighters rose out of a vast network of hidden trails, now referred to as the Ho Chi Minh Trail. The North Vietnamese used their mobility from these trails to enter Cambodia and Laos, where American forces were not authorized to follow.

In a "Secret War," battles were waged covertly by the Americans on these trails, and they used planes flying deep into North Vietnam to damage the trail as well as destroy factories and bases supporting the North.

The escalation of the war officially began on January 31, 1965, after orders were issued to mobilize the Eighteenth TAC Fighter Squadron from Okinawa. A red alert sounded for the pilots and support personnel to deploy and participate in Operation Flaming Dart—an attempt to cross the seventeenth parallel into North Vietnam. This mission was part of strikes on Pleiku airbase on February 6 and other targets in North Vietnam on February 7.

It's interesting to note it took more than an hour for the forty-nine Thunderchief aircraft to deploy, creating a continual sound of rolling thunder. From this point forward the war was no longer confined to land battles in the South.

CRASH COURSE

AND IT WAS ON

The departure of the aircraft from the Danang Air Force Base left it unprotected.

The opportunity for attack was not lost on the enemy, and the South Vietnamese military was unable to provide much defense. After several such attacks at various bases, the U.S. Air Force bases were provided additional protection by the thirty-five hundred marines deployed to South Vietnam on March 8, 1965.

Public opinion supported this maneuver because the popular belief at that time indicated Vietnam was part of a worldwide struggle against Communism.

The primary goal of the war was to reunify Vietnam, securing its independence, but the policy of the North Vietnam was not to dismantle other non-Communist governments in Southeast Asia.

The marine assignment was merely a defensive action, but with the deployment numbers increased to two hundred thousand within seven months, it was obvious the U.S. military had moved into an offensive strategy, playing on the strengths of their training.

South Vietnamese forces suffered heavy losses in battles over the next few months and began to see increasing desertions and low morale.

Given the shifting tide, U.S. commanders categorized their situations as critical but felt success would be attained. The commanders recommended an aggressive change in their defensive posturing and the sidelining of the South Vietnamese.

With the South Vietnamese Army units out of the way, the U.S. involvement became an open-ended commitment.

GRENADES

A grenade by definition is a small bomb of combustible material designed for short-range use and ignited to produce an explosion via outward pressure of gas expansion on the containment matter. The required elements are the combustible matter and a means of ignition.

Different combustion materials can be used for different types of explosions depending upon the desired result, such as spreading fire or smoke. The ignition mechanism can be either a time delay or impact variety. The function of both is to set off the explosion after the grenade is a good distance from the soldier.

A simple time-delay type of grenade is the Molotov cocktail—a bottle of flammable liquid containing a rag sticking out acting as the fuse. The liquid is spread out on impact and lit by the rag. This type of grenade can easily explode in the user's hand, so most grenades employ more sophisticated ignition systems. The time-delay grenade is used to kill or hurt nearby enemy soldiers and is designed to be easy to use and deploy while remaining durable.

Conventionally, the design consists of an outer iron shell holding a chemical fuse and a surrounding reservoir of explosive matter pouring in via a filling hole. The firing mechanism is triggerd by a striker inside the grenade held in place by a lever on top. The soldier grips the device so the striker is pushed up against the device, pulls out the pin so nothing holds the lever in place, and tosses the grenade at the target.

The spring throws the striker against the percussion cap igniting a slow burning fuse. The end of the element is attached to the detonator, usually a capsule of combustible material, which ignites the explosive material, setting of an explosion around the sides of the grenade and creating a much larger explosion that blows it apart. Pieces of metal are thrown outward, injuring anyone and anything nearby.

While these time-delay grenades are effective, they are unpredictable in effectiveness and provide the enemy the chance to counterattack. If tossed inaccurately, the enemy can scoop it up and return the volley!

Impact grenades work similarly to bombs deployed from airplanes that explode upon hitting the target. Soldiers typically deploy these via a grenade launcher to provide the speed needed for the impact.

Austrians had grenade launchers attached to their assault rifles.

These must remain unarmed until actually fired as any accidental contact can set it off. They have an automatic arming system triggered by the propellant exploding it out of the launcher.

The fuse mechanism is like that of a time-delay grenade, but with a detonator instead of a chemical delay element igniting the explosive material. The spinning motion of the grenade exerts a strong force that pushes the weighted pins out as the grenade flies, releasing the pins and allowing the pins to strike the percussion cap upon impact, creating the main explosion. There are dozens of variants of this type of device, many with far more elaborate arming and ignition systems but utilizing the basic principle in most of cases.

Weapons of Vietnam

- Smith & Wesson Mark 22 Mod. 0 Pistol
- F-1 Submachine gun (Australian)
- M3/A1 grease gun (U.S., ARVN)
- M16 assault rifle (U.S.)
- Remington 870 pump action shotgun (U.S.)
- M-40 sniper rifle (U.S. Marine snipers)
- Browning M2HB .50-caliber heavy machine gun
- M61 fragmentation hand grenade
- M79 grenade launcher

River Warfare

River warfare was one of the more successful of Vietnam warfare tactics. Controlling the rivers meant controlling communication routes and preventing resupply and movement of enemy forces. The PBR (Patrol Boat, River) was the go-to vessel in these applications because it could easily be beached for troops to load or unload, and its hydro jets could be easily reversed. It was also helpful that damaged units could be transported via landing craft and modified to serve as dry docks.

Large choppers could lift the PBRs to place them wherever needed, especially on isolated waterways that the enemy would presume no one would patrol.

The vessels were heavily armed and commanded by a four-man crew operating the gun mounts. Their speed and armor made them hard to hit, fast, and versatile.

These were used for patrols and to transport smaller infantry units and were supplemented by PCF swift boats—larger, inshore vessels.

Beach landing craft were utilized for strongholds in larger scaled operations. These were slow and clumsy and more easily damaged by short range weapons and grenades.

Vietnam-Inspired Entertainment

Music

- "Blowin' in the Wind"—Bob Dylan
- "Paint It Black"—The Rolling Stones
- "California Dreamin'"—The Mamas and the Papas
- "Turn Turn Turn"—The Byrds
- "Time of the Seasons"—The Zombies
- "Bridge Over Troubled Waters"—Simon & Garfunkel
- "You Really Got Me"—The Kinks
- "Give Peace a Chance"—John Lennon
- "Nowhere to Run"—Martha and the Vandellas
- "All Along the Watchtower"—Jimi Hendrix
- "American Woman"—The Guess Who
- "War"—Edwin Starr

Hollywood Depictions

The following films of varying critical acclaim depict the soldier's life during the Vietnam War.

- *We Were Soldiers*
- *Born on the Fourth of July*
- *Full Metal Jacket*
- *Apocalypse Now*
- *Platoon*
- *Good Morning, Vietnam*
- *Hamburger Hill*
- *Forrest Gump*

MRI Machine

July 3, 1977, marked a monumental day in medical history. The first human being was placed inside an MRI machine and photographed. Five hours later, one fuzzy image was produced. The machine, labeled Indomitable, is now inside the Smithsonian Institute. Today, an MRI machine can produce detailed pictures of the body in just seconds. The technology involved is complicated but is a giant breakthrough in the field of medicine.

How It Works

MRI stands for magnetic resonance imaging. The heart of the MRI system is a large magnet. A horizontal tube, called a bore, runs through the magnet and allows a patient to slide inside. The magnet is so large it is rated with a unit called a tesla. The magnet works by imposing a tremendous magnetic force while a patient is inside the bore. The magnet causes the nuclei of hydrogen atoms within the cells of the body to react in certain ways specific to their atomic properties. For example, the protons of hydrogen atoms have a spin of 1⁄2, and will align in a certain way to the magnetic field. Images are then captured of the cell activity, and the MRI is able to detect many things, including tumors, infections, torn ligaments, tendonitis, cysts, and strokes.

A Giant Magnet

Any metal objects in the room during the MRI can potentially be sucked inside the machine with great force, a great danger to the patient inside. The force of the magnet increases exponentially as objects move closer to the machine. Patients with metal inside their bodies cannot undergo an MRI, one of the downfalls of the technology, as many people are ineligible for testing.

The Functional MRI

An fMRI, or functional magnetic resonance imaging, involves using an MRI to measure haemodynamic (blood flow) response in the brain and spinal cord. The blood flow directly corresponds to neural activity and can give doctors and scientists a plethora of information about the way a brain is functioning.

Advantages

- The fMRI can noninvasively measure the neural activity of the brain without any risk of radiation damage.
- Measuring the blood flow inside the brain can potentially tell scientists more about cognitive activity.

Disadvantages

- The fMRI only measures neural activity but does not account for the influence of outside nonneural activity on the brain.
- Some theoretical models suggest that the signals given by the fMRI are too vague and unspecified to be considered scientific.

The New Lie Detector

The fMRI could possibly be used as lie-detecting technology that would be far more advanced than the long controversial polygraph. Since the fMRI can measure blood flow and neural activity in the brain, the testing can aid in the detection of lying, as researchers have pinpointed the areas of the brain that are used for recognition and creation. When patients are placed in the fMRI machine and asked certain questions, the imaging can detail which areas of the brain are called upon during the answering of questions, allowing researchers to determine whether the answers are being recalled or created.

Ireland's Turn
The Troubles, 1963–85

Northern Ireland was embroiled in a period known as "The Troubles" between 1963 and 1985.

The strife began when the nation's prime minister, Viscount Brookeborough, stepped down after two decades in office, threatening the Ulster Unionist powerhouse that had dominated Northern Ireland politics since 1921.

The damage, however, had already been done.

The two-thirds Protestant majority wielded exceptional power, especially when it came to getting their Unionist party representatives appointed to high offices.

To add insult to injury, only property owners—translation Protestants—were allowed to vote, and those who held property in more than one district could vote as many as six times.

But political appointees were only the beginning.

Catholics were marginalized on all fronts. Enduring police harassment was as commonplace as breathing, and they were excluded from public service.

It's no wonder then that Catholic representatives in Parliament turned a blind eye to the partitions established when the Unionists took control more than forty years earlier.

And yet, social reform had managed to filter down to the benefit of Catholic neighborhoods.

Britain's postwar Labor party had introduced welfare to the North with widespread success. It was a culturally blind program, meaning services were rendered regardless of religion.

The most immediate benefit of this program was the Catholics' access in the 1950s to higher education that, in turn, created a more enlightened populace less content to tolerate the injustices of the status quo.

But let's not jump ahead too quickly.

Much like the world-altering Civil Rights Movement taking shape in the United States, Northern Ireland's "troubles" were just getting started in 1963.

Troubled times

Economically, Northern Ireland profited in the postwar boom.

By the 1960s, however, the industrial surge was tapped, and plenty of fingers pointed in Brookeborough's direction. Of course, he found little solace—or protection—within his own party, forcing his unceremonious exit in 1963.

Terence O'Neill stepped in to take his place and brought with him a strong slate of economic-recovery measures.

Brookeborough's ineffectiveness had contributed directly to Northern Ireland's festering political and social climate, and O'Neill knew sweeping change would be an impossibility if he allowed the pot to boil over.

That's when the trouble—er, Troubles—began.

O'Neill's first bold step was to meet with Sean Lemass, the Republic of Ireland's prime minister, in a historic gathering forty years in the making. He also tested the waters with nationalists in the north, raising hackles among the Unionists because—on paper—the Republic's constitution still claimed the entire island of Ireland.

Hope swelled among Catholics, and plunged among Unionists, who felt their power structure teetering on the brink of collapse. As emotions raged and violence finally erupted, the Reverand Ian Paisley emerged as a central Unionist figure in the struggle.

In 1966, the showdown escalated with the simultaneous anniversaries of the Battle of the Somme and the Easter Rising, considered a historically significant uprising for the Protestant and Catholic communities respectively.

In May and June of that year, the violence culminated when a loyalist terror group known as the Ulster Volunteer Force murdered two Catholics and one Protestant, making them the first casualties of The Troubles.

Tempers Flare

As tensions mounted, Irish Catholics proved a harder sell for O'Neill than he ever anticipated.

Not surprisingly, the minority remained unconvinced their new leader's priorities were actually in their best interests, and they took exceptional issue with the sluggish pace of his reform initiatives.

But as is the case with most revolutionary movements, organization and strength in numbers go a long way toward making a group feel protected and prepared to fight the good fight.

And thus, the Northern Ireland Civil Rights Association (Nicra) was formed in 1967.

The association called immediately—and vehemently—for an end to seven pervasive "injustices" that contributed to the fragmentation of the state. The request fell on deaf ears, and the people took to the streets.

Much like the parallel movement in the United States, the civil rights demonstrations that followed began as peaceful marches, but by 1968, the political and social climates had turned violent and confrontational. In October of that year, marchers in Derry met with the swift and brutal Royal Ulster Constabulary in what can only be described as an old-school melee.

O'Neill found himself swept in front of the British government with a lot of explaining to do and not a whole lot of answers to provide.

The result was a sweeping reform package, and Northern Ireland finally won the more equitable allocation of council houses, and community advocates for the airing of grievances.

But the initiative represented only a partial victory in that it failed to establish a one-man-one-vote system.

Within months, the cycle began all over again.

Civil rights protesters flooded the streets; the Royal Ulster Constabulary answered with force; everybody hated everybody else.

O'Neill's ill-conceived general election in February 1969 turned into a fiasco when nobody showed up to vote. He resigned in exasperation two months later.

Crash Course

Army of the People

Flanked by aggression, O'Neill's successor, James Chichester-Clark, sallied forth with relentless reform measures. The results were mixed, at best:

- Militia groups organized on both sides of the coin.
- Civil rights confrontations became more intense and violent.
- The annual Apprentice Boys march in August 1969 was followed almost immediately by three days of rioting in Belfast.
- Chichester-Clark was forced to call in reinforcements, and a small contingent of British troops squelched the Battle of Bogside, as it became known.
- Although necessary, Chichester-Clark's SOS sent a clear signal that Northern Ireland was in real trouble.
- Politically, he responded by drafting the joint Downing Street Declaration with British Prime Minister Harold Wilson.
- The sweeping document proved more an act of appeasement than action: It promised equality and freedom for all, while reaffirming Northern Ireland's station as a part of the larger United Kingdom as long as that remained the will of the majority.
- Reform finally appeared within reach. Attempts were made to regulate council housing as well as a full-scale investigation being launched into abuses of power by law enforcement.
- In fact, the investigation resulted in a recommendation to disband the B Specials auxiliaries, disarm the police and establish in its place an Ulster Defense Regiment under the thumb of the British Army. The plan backfired.
- Loyalists rebelled, and Catholic communities became the targets of their rage.
- A reinvented Irish Republican Army emerged as the perceived savior of the Catholic minority.

- The rebels had been largely inactive since 1962, primarily because their largest operatives had been locked away. As tensions mounted in 1969, the Provisional IRA broke officially from the IRA.
- While it shared the ideas of civil rights, defending the Catholic community, and the unification of Ireland, the PIRA fancied itself a little harder edged. Specifically, the militant group didn't just want to crush the British government, it wanted to make its perceived oppressors wish they'd never been born.
- In the other corner was the Ulster Volunteer Force, a loyalist paramilitary group, that joined forced with the Ulster Defense Association in 1971.

Bloody Sunday

In March 1971, Chichester-Clark resigned and was replaced by Brian Faulkner.

Wash. Rinse. Repeat.

Civil strife under the new regime reached such unprecedented levels that Faulkner decided he had no choice but to revisit an old standby: internment. For those a little slow on the uptake, that was a policy by which suspects in any suspected terrorist activity could be held—indefinitely—without trial, and it took effect on August 7, 1971.

Not surprisingly, the measure failed to actually detain any significant players in the Provisional IRA movement.

Violence escalated, and the body count topped 150 in the final months of 1971 alone.

Frustrated by the mounting unrest, the British Army lashed out and adopted increasingly brutal policing tactics.

On January 30, 1972, the Parachute Regiment was deployed by the army to suppress yet another riot during a civil rights march in Derry. The troops shot and killed thirteen demonstrators and mortally wounded a fourteenth.

The bloodbath, which became known as Bloody Sunday, fueled the fire and swelled the rolls of the IRA. The army responded by dispatching more troops to the province.

And yet, life was far from hunky-dory on the other side.

Despite the movement's ability to attract tens of thousands of supporters to rallies across the island, the recently formed Ulster Vanguard, an umbrella organization for loyalist groups, met with mounting disapproval from the Protestant community.

British Prime Minister Heath responded by removing security responsibilities from the Northern Ireland government's chore list and appointed a secretary of state for the province.

On cue, the Northern Ireland government resigned in outrage, and Heath instituted direct rule from Westminster.

Share and Share Alike

The fallout from the dissolution of Northern Ireland's government on March 28, 1972, was graphic and severe. In fact, it ignited the single bloodiest year of the Troubles era, with the body count reaching 496 before the close of the year.

The brutal year culminated on Bloody Friday, when the PIRA detonated simultaneously more than twenty bombs killing nine people in Belfast.

But a new plan was afoot in Britain.

On the table, was a plan to create a new Northern Ireland Assembly.

The new government would be elected by proportional representatives, creating a power-sharing system for both Protestants and Catholics.

A pie-in-the-sky Council of Ireland was also a tenet of the plan, designed to give the Irish Republic a role in Northern Ireland's affairs.

The slate of candidates in June 1973, actually produced a majority of pro-power-sharing representatives, but the anti-power-sharing minority made it clear bipartisan pleasantries would never fly.

Work began in January 1974.

The Sunningdale Agreement—named for the Berkshire town where the negotiations took place—did, in fact, establish a fourteen-member Council of Ireland, but one could drive a truck through the holes in its bylaws. On the upside, the agreement did allow for the future possibility that the Irish Republic might one day wield decision-making powers in Northern Ireland.

The anti-power-sharing Unionists—who felt they'd lost their voice in the Sunningdale negotiations—bided their time, and instead used the British general election of February 1974 to foil the agreement's progress.

Anit-Sunningdale candidates swept the referendum, taking eleven of Northern Ireland's twelve parliamentary seats. The assembly had not only been morally decimated but had lost its very real standing as the voice of the people.

Chaos ensued.

The British government refused to hold new assembly elections.

On May 14, 1974, the assembly restated publicly its support for the agreement reached at Sunningdale.

Later that same day, a recently formed coalition of unionized Protestants known as the Ulster Workers' Council went on strike.

Three days later, thirty-two people were killed in Dublin and Monaghan when loyalists detonated a series of bombs.

It took less than two weeks for the province to experience total breakdown, complete with roadblocks, power outages and the screeching halt of most industries.

On May 28, 1974, the pro-Sunningdale unionist members of the power-sharing executive resigned, restoring direct rule immediately.

It lasted another twenty-five years.

Hunger Strikes

Despite some very concerted efforts, repeated attempts to broker peace in Northern Ireland over the ensuing decade failed.

In 1976, the British government also removed the status of "special category" paramilitary prisoners. Since 1972, paramilitary prisoners had held some of the rights of prisoners of war. With their special status removed, these everyday, normal criminals were now confined—with all the usual suspects—in the new Maze Prison near Belfast.

Fancying themselves as freedom fighters, PIRA let the clever protests fly.

They refused to wear prison-issue duds during the "blanket" protest and smeared feces on the wall during the "dirty" protest of 1978. We'll say.

By 1980, the civil disobedience escalated to a hunger strike and was followed by another in 1981.

The second hunger strike was led by Bobby Sands, who was nominated while incarcerated for the vacant Westminster seat of Fermanagh and South Tyrone—and won.

There was no question left that the strikers had won heartfelt and effective community support, but British Prime Minister Margaret Thatcher refused to make any concessions.

Sands died on May 5, 1981, and another nine prisoners expired before the strike was halted in October.

Sinn Fein, the political arm of the IRA, took up the cause in 1981. It miraculously found a way to contest elections without abandoning its violent policies in the process. The practice seemed to work for them.

In 1983, Sinn Fein leader Gerry Adams defeated Gerry Fitt to win the Westminster seat for West Belfast. Sands's death had not been in vain.

Peace at Last?

The hunger strikes of the early 1980s represented a particularly testy period between Northern Ireland and the British government. It certainly didn't help that Prime Minister Thatcher barely avoided being blown to bits by an IRA bomb attack at the Conservative party conference in October 1984.

Let's just say she wasn't really in good spirits when Irish Republic-supported proposals for Northern Ireland's future slid across the table. Forever the diplomat, however, Thatcher recognized the political force Sinn Fein had become, and she had grown weary of the endless cycle of violence the inaction had created. She and Garrett FitzGerald came to terms on what would become known as the Anglo-Irish Agreement, signed in November 1985.

Per the agreement, Northern Ireland would remain independent of the Republic as long as that was the will of the people—the majority, at least—in the north. *But,* the Republic was given a legal say in the province's operation for the first time in history, and the agreement created the Intergovernmental Conference for the express purpose of discussing security and political issues.

The only way Northern Ireland could reclaim its forfeited power would be to agree to the power-sharing model, and we all know how well that worked the first time. The agreement was panned—OK, detested—by both Sinn Fein and the Republic's opposition party, Fianna Fail, for having the audacity to acknowledge that Britain was entitled to have a say in Northern Ireland's affairs.

Center-ground nationalists embraced the progressive—and potentially constructive—development. Unionist believed unequivocally that the agreement placed the final nail in the coffin. They might as well get out before a united Ireland became a reality.

And with the usual fanfare, the unionists responded with mass demonstrations, strikes and marches as well as the resignation of all fifteen unionist Westminster seats.

Even though the violence continued for at least another decade, the unionists buried the hatchet somewhat and began cooperating with the government in 1987. In 1998, the Good Friday Agreement was brokered ending the cycle of violence.

Vietnam Continues

In 1967, the political situation in South Vietnam stabilized slightly when President Nguyen Van Thieu and Vice President Nguyen Cao Ky assumed power. The calmer period allowed the South Vietnamese Army to collaborate more efficiently and effectively with the growing allied forces.

Tet Offensive

After luring forces into the Quang Tri Province in January 1968, the North Vietnamese broke truce agreements that had traditionally been observed as part of the Tet holiday. Instead, a surprise offensive was launched in more than a hundred cities—in Saigon, the U.S. Embassy was attacked—with the intention of provoking a national uprising.

The response of the American and South Vietnamese forces was swift and decimating despite the offensive maneuver.

The North Vietnamese recognized—after the fact—that the Tet Offensive had been successful in reducing Viet Cong forces but it brought a far greater consequence: It became the turning point of the American involvement in the war and profoundly affected domestic support. Not since the bombing of Pearl Harbor during World War II had such an intelligence failure been revealed.

In the United States, an anti-war movement was gaining momentum and then President Richard Nixon called for Americans to support the war effort. With revelations of the My Lai Massacre and similar events, outrage was sparked not only nationally but internationally.

The civilian cost of the war was believed to be too high, which was again questioned when the body count of Operation Speedy Express exceeded ten thousand Viet Cong guerillas, with only forty U.S. losses.

It certainly didn't help that at least half of the Vietnamese dead were civilians.

Crash Course

Marching Onward

Sweden had proclaimed neutrality for Cambodia in 1955, but found the North Vietnamese Army and the Viet Cong used their lands as a base of operations. While Cambodian Prince Norodom Sihanouk tolerated these occurrences and sought to avoid further involvement in the conflict, he changed his opinion under pressure from Washington in 1969, informing the groups they were no longer welcome.

Sihanouk's move allowed U.S. President Nixon to launch Operation Menu, a secret massive bombing mission on the Viet Cong and North Vietnamese Army operations along the border of Cambodia that essentially violated Cambodia's long-held pronouncement of neutrality.

Although Nixon respected Cambodia's sovereignty, the measure was necessary.

In a fourteen-month period, more than 2.75 million bombs were dropped—hidden from the American public—a number exceeding the total bombs dropped in World War II by all of the Allied forces combined.

Sihanouk was deposed in 1970, and the country's borders closed. The United States and South Vietnamese continued to launch missions into Cambodia to attack enemy bases in an effort to buy time for the South.

The South Vietnamese Army launched Operation Lam Son 719 in an attempt to cut the Ho Chi Minh Trail in Laos, but the offensive was a violation, again, of neutrality.

This formality had long been overlooked, with battles having been fought there in part of the Secret War.

South Vietnamese forces retreated after meeting strong resistance.

Literally running out of gas, soldiers abandoned vehicles and forced their way onto American helicopters evacuating the wounded. Many were forced to hang onto the skids of the aircraft.

One task of U.S. aircraft was to destroy any abandoned equipment, be it tank, truck, or helicopter, to prevent enemy forces from gaining any benefit of the items.

It is estimated that more than half of the invading South Vietnamese troops were captured or killed outright.

The entire operation was a failure.

By 1971, both New Zealand and Australia had removed their forces from the war theater and the U.S. count was decreased to 196,000, with more to withdraw in 1972 amid peace protests across the United States. By this time, various world leaders tried to help South Vietnam and North Vietnam reach a peace agreement at the Paris Peace Accords, but the countries disagreed, and North Vietnam quit the talks.

The United States launched a heavy bombing campaign on Hanoi in December 1972 in an effort to force North Vietnam to continue the talks. The tactic worked and led to an agreement in 1973.

Of course, both sides quickly broke the agreement and started fighting again.

On April 30, 1975, the South Vietnamese capital of Saigon fell to the Communist forces of North Vietnam.

The war was over.

More than 1.4 million military personnel were killed in the conflict, while estimates of civilian fatalities range up to two million. The war ended with the dissolution of South Vietnam and the failure of U.S. foreign policy.

Aircrafts of Vietnam

- Boeing B-52 Stratofortress—heavy bomber
- Bell AH-1 Cobra- attack helicopter
- Boeing CH-47 Chinook—mass transport/cargo helicopter
- Bell UH-1 Huey—gunship helicopter
- Republic F-105 Thunderchief—fighter plane
- McDonnell Douglas F-101 Voodoo—fighter/reconnaissance plane
- Lockheed C-130 Hercules—cargo plane
- Sikorsky CH-54 Skycrane - helicopter

New Breed of Warfare

Helicopters were introduced to the military battlefield during World War II, but they were relegated to performing minor service roles as supply craft and rescue missions in the Indochina theater under the operation of the First Air Commando Unit.

While the helicopter proved its usefulness, the airborne machines—small and puny by today's standards—were limited in capability.

By the advent of the Korean War, helicopters were more abundant but still served mainly support roles of search and rescue or medical intervention. The helicopter was still not serving the military in a combat role.

Although plans had been made to use helicopters for ferrying troops during the Korean War, the army was prohibited from operating large aircraft as a direct result of a law put in place at the creation of the U.S. Air Force in 1947.

To circumvent this issue, an agreement was signed between the army and air force that continued limitations upon the army's fixed-wing aircraft under the existing law, but restricted the conceptual functionality of the helicopter in the combat arena. With the new agreement in place, a new path emerged for the use of large helicopters.

The effort was too little too late for the Korean War but became the new concept of warfare for the Vietnam conflict: air mobility. Vietnam became known as a helicopter war.

What the horse had been to the First Cavalry of World War I, the Huey became to the U.S. troops in Vietnam. As the war raged, the army would continually redefine its use of the helicopter.

Lethal Weapons

When American H-21 helicopters were first used to ferry South Vietnamese troops into battle against Viet Cong guerillas, the guerrillas fled when the choppers landed. But at the important battle of Ap Bac, they soon learned they could bring down the helicopters with relative ease and began to stand their ground.

Communist training manuals would describe how to shoot at the H-21 and Huey helicopters, recommending shooting ahead of the target rather than directly at it. This provided a greater chance of hitting the target. It also instructed where to shoot the vehicle to create the most damage.

Meanwhile, the U.S. Army fully embraced the concept of "air mobility" as American involvement in Vietnam dramatically increased. In turn, it began moving massive amounts of troops by air.

Some combat operations involved more than one hundred helicopters simultaneously, as well as fixed-wing aircraft support to drop bombs and rockets on the enemy.

Now instead of armies engaging across vast fronts, advancing slowly, and holding ground, the army would quickly carry troops into hostile territory, deploy them, and remove them the instant the fighting ended.

While the overall strategy was questionable as no territory was ever really held, the tactic was very successful.

Helicopters provided quick, effective mobility for troops while maintaining a tremendous element of surprise.

An enemy sitting unchallenged for weeks could suddenly find itself under assault from troops brought in by helicopter.

In fact, large transport helicopters like the CH-47 Chinook were developed for this purpose.

But the workhorse UH-1 Huey became the most popular helicopter for moving troops into and out of battle.

The army also used armed helicopters to support ground troops, eventually dedicating helicopter gunships like the AH-1 Cobra for such purposes.

A helicopter could be equipped with guns, grenade launchers, rockets, or even guided missiles and provide rapid and wide-ranging fire against an adversary on the ground.

By the middle of the war, the helicopter had become as important to the army as the tank, the armored personnel carrier and the jeep. And the Huey was the most symbolic weapon of the Vietnam War.

Air mobility came at a heavy price, though.

Between 1962 and 1973, the United States lost 4,869 helicopters, 53 percent due to enemy fire. The high rate of operational accidents occurred largely due to mechanical breakdowns as a result of lax maintenance. Vietnam's heavy jungle canopy also made helicopter operations difficult, with few places to land a wounded helicopter.

The United States was a pioneer, however, in the use of choppers in combat, leading the way for other countries to employ similar tactics.

None would ever succeed in creating such large "airborne cavalry" units as the United States, but some did mimic the concept of helicopters used to ferry troops in and out of combat areas quickly and while under fire.

EARTH-SHAKING MOVEMENTS

Earthquakes are some of the most destructive natural disasters that can occur. They can cause thousands of deaths, and spur other natural disasters such as tsunamis, fires, famines, and landslides. Earthquakes occur when the earth's tectonic plates shift, and the fault slips.

The Richter Scale is a base-10 logorithmic scale used to measure an earthquake's strength. Its infinite measurements can be negative or positive. A 5.0 tremor is roughly the same as a 32-kilaton blast, which has about two-thirds of the explosive force of the atomic bomb that the United States dropped in 1945 over the Japanese city of Nagasaki.

An increase in a whole number, such as going from 5.0 to 6.0, indicates a tenfold increase in the amplitude of the seismic waves of an earthquake. Here are some of the most powerful earthquakes in history:

New Madrid Fault, Dec. 16, 1811

The quake that shook the point where four U.S. states meet—Missouri, Kentucky, Arkansas, and Tennessee—measured at nearly 8.0 on the Richter scale. Some who experienced the jolt claimed the shock waves spread so far across the country that church bells rang in Boston. The topography of the land was so affected that the Mississippi River flowed backward, as the land was lifted high enough to change the currents.

Great San Francisco Earthquake, April 18, 1906

A 7.8 magnitude quake, this natural disaster caused approximately three thousand deaths and more than $500 million in property damage. Buildings in the San Francisco Bay area crumbled to the ground, waterlines broke, and streetcar tracks were twisted into metal disasters. Most of the deaths of the tragedy were a result of a large fire caused by the tremor. The fire spread rapidly, but with the water mains busted, the blaze was impossible to control. People as far away as Oregon and Nevada claimed they felt tremors from the earthquake for nearly one full minute.

Turkmenistan, Oct. 5, 1948

This 7.3-magnitude quake is believed responsible for the death of more than two-thirds of the population of Ashgabat, Turkmenistan, or about 110,000 people. It was the most devastating quake to ever hit Central Asia up to that time, and the city was reduced to rubble and ruin. In 2002, the government issued coins to commemorate the lost lives of the tragedy of 1948.

Southern Chile, May 22, 1960

At 9.5 on the Richter scale, this disaster was the strongest earthquake ever recorded in history. It actually consisted of several quakes that struck together over several hours, causing a large tsunami to follow. Landslides, volcanic eruptions, and flooding pounded the area for days, effectively decimating the Chilean coast. The ensuing tsunami then moved across the Pacific Ocean and ravaged Hawaii. Overall, the disaster was responsible for more than 5,700 deaths in Chile, Hawaii, Alaska, Japan, and the Philippines.

Alaska, March 28, 1964

The most powerful earthquake to ever strike the United States, the quake that struck Prince William Sound registered 9.2 on the Richter scale. The quake itself took only fifteen lives, but the tsunami that followed towered nearly two hundred feet over Alaska, killing more than one hundred people and causing over $300 million in damage.

China, July 27, 1976

Measuring 7.5 on the Richter scale, this quake occurred along the Pacific Ocean's Ring of Fire, a belt that has endured a large amount of seismic activity and weather disasters over the years. This particular quake hit Tangshan, a city near the northeast coast of China. Of a population nearing one million, the quake caused somewhere between 250,000 and 780,000 casualties.

Indonesia, Dec. 26, 2004

Off the west coast of Sumatra, a 9.1- magnitude quake and its subsequent tsunami killed around 230,000 people in several countries. The quake caused enormous, devastating waves in the Indian Ocean; full extent of its damage is unknown. Scientists report that the tremor was so large that it shifted the earth's rotation on its axis by nearly one full inch, a truly awe inspiring phenomenon.

The F-Scale

Theodore Fujita introduced the Fujita Scale in 1971 to categorize tornados by intensity and area. The scale, also known as the F-scale, was divided into six categories:

- F0 (Gale)
- F1 (Weak)
- F2 (Strong)
- F3 (Severe)
- F4 (Devastating)
- F5 (Incredible)

In 2007, the National Weather Service revised the Fujita Scale, relating the damage caused by a tornado to the fastest 1/4-mile wind at the height of a damaged structure. The 2007 Fujita Scale evaluates wind speed in this way:

F Number	Fastest 1/4-mile (mph)	3 Second Gust (mph)
0	40-72	45-77
1	73-112	78-118
2	113-157	119-163
3	158-206	164-210
4	207-260	211-262
5	261 and up	263 and up

POP QUIZ #9

1) How many Americans died during the Korean War?
 a) 20,000
 b) 35,000
 c) 54,000
 d) 66,000

2) When was acupuncture first used?
 a) 3700 BC
 b) 1400
 c) 1750
 d) 1980

3) When was the spire of Notre Dame Cathedral completed?
 a) 1015
 b) 1253
 c) 1398
 d) 1439

4) When was the first MRI used?
 a) 1881
 b) 1935
 c) 1977
 d) 1983

5) What size earthquake shook San Francisco in April 1906?
 a) 8.0
 b) 7.8
 c) 7.5
 d) 9.1

6) Who developed the F-Scale?
   a) Theodore Fujita
   b) Thomas Edison
   c) Isaac Newton
   d) Albert Einstein

Answers:

1) c 3) d 5) b
2) a 4) c 6) a

Theater 101

- Aeschylus is considered the Father of Greek Drama.
- French dramatist Pierre Beaumarchais financed the shipping of ammunition and supplies to colonists during the American Revolution and even offered the services of his own boat, *Le Fier Roderique.*
- Robert Cummings real name is Bruce Hutchens.
- Greek playwright Sophocles wrote more than one hundred plays, introduced the revolutionary third actor and broke away from the trilogy format.
- The musical *Bye Bye Birdie* was based loosely on the life and times of country and western legend Conway Twitty.
- Playwright Israel Horovitz is related to a member of the rap group Beastie Boys.
- Seems a little bland, but the tyrannical father in Neil Simon's first play, *Come Blow Your Horn*, is in the wax-fruit business.

The Space Race

The competitive regard with which the United States and the Soviet Union held one another was evident in many aspects of the Cold War. Superiority in every field was key to each country, and anything less deemed failure.

Each nation invested billions of dollars and man hours in research and development of various forms of technology to be applied in agriculture, communications, and transportation, all with applications that furthered their nations both economically and militarily.

The most prominent of competitions that emerged from the Cold War was the quest to be the first to explore space. Each country created its programs and plans to achieve the goal with one common and questionable factor: time.

The space race was on.

First Successful Orbiter – Winner: Soviet Union

The Soviets laid claim to the first milestone in the race with the launch of Sputnik I on October 4, 1957, and the technology was used to determine the accurate density of the upper atmosphere.

With the realization of the economic and military implications of the Soviet success, fear set into political debate in the United States. The Eisenhower administration formed NASA with the sole aim of besting the Soviets in the race.

The success of Sputnik served to bolster public opinion in the Soviet Union regarding their technical prowess as they continued to recover from war.

Until this time, the United States held the belief of its superiority in all realms of technology and advancement. Their countereffort to regain technological supremacy included an overhaul of many aspects of the government and education systems, down to the curriculum taught in schools nationwide.

Greater emphasis was placed upon science and mathematics programs in schools.

The National Defense Education Act was passed by Congress.

The NDEA was intended to fund reform and construction of schools; provide student fellowships and loans for higher education;

and support several new approaches in vocational education to offset the defense industry's workforce shortage.

Four months after Sputnik I, the United States countered with successful launch of Explorer I at Cape Canaveral. Data captured by Explorer I led to the discovery by James Van Allen of a radiation belt eventually named after him.

Many failed launch attempts followed the initial success with Explorer I, but at least things were finally getting interesting.

Communications in Space – Winner: United States

The United States did attain superiority in launching the first communications satellite in December 1958, which relayed a Christmas message from President Eisenhower. By July 1963, a satellite that could retain an established and stationary orbit was successfully launched. The feat allowed citizens to view television broadcasts via satellite communication transmissions.

Animals in Space – Winner: United States

Officially, Americans could claim the first successful launch of animals into space for scientific study. Fruit flies were sent up on a rocket captured from the Germans in 1946. The Soviets sent a dog named Laika into orbit inside Sputnik II in 1957. The dog was not to return to Earth and died as a result of stress, dehydration, and heat exhaustion several days after successfully achieving orbit. Within three years the Soviets were successfully launching *and* returning dogs from space orbit. The American space program countered with the launch of Ham the Chimpanzee, prior to their first human orbiter.

Man in Space – Winner: Soviet Union

The first man successfully launched into space was Yuri Gagarin of the Soviet Union in Vostok I, which achieved a 108-minute planetary orbit. Alan Shepard of the United States completed a suborbit mission three weeks later. John Glenn became the first American to orbit the Earth on February 20, 1962.

Other Firsts – Winner: Soviet Union

With the vitality of the American program, the Soviet thirst for "firsts" in the space race never relented as they achieved other triumphant firsts: first dual manned flight, first woman in space (Valentina Tereshkova), first flight with more than two crew members, and the first space walk.

The Moon – Ultimate Winner: United States

The competitive air between the two nations continued with the pursuit of placing man on the moon. Initially, this required the successful launch and exploration of the moon via photography by means of unmanned craft. The Americans accomplished the feat with the Luna probes of the Pioneer program.

Program for the People

U.S. President John F. Kennedy and his vice president, Lyndon B. Johnson, sought to create a program that captured the American public's interest in space and found it within the Apollo program. The program appealed not only to citizens but politicians seeking to throw their support behind an initiative that benefited both society and the military.

The focus of the Apollo program was simple: Put a man on the moon.

The Soviet Union was ambivalent at the time about human visits to the moon, wanting neither defeat by another power nor the incurred expense of such a monumental project. It would be 1964 before the Soviets committed to a lunar landing program in opposition to that of the Americans.

Kennedy proposed a joint program utilizing a moon landing with American and Soviet astronauts and simultaneously improving weather-monitoring satellites of the day. Nikita Khrushchev wanted no part of such a joint venture, regarding it a ruse for stealing Soviet space technology rather than a collaborative effort for the betterment of both nations. The Soviet program began to crumble following multiple launch failures and the death of several top engineers within their program.

In December 1968, an Apollo orbiter successfully orbited the moon, carrying the first humans to celebrate Christmas in space: a successful splashdown followed days later.

The Soviets did trump the American program by attaining the successful unmanned probes reaching the moon.

But the crown jewel of space exploration was claimed by the Americans when they sent the first person to actually set foot on the lunar surface on July 21, 1969. Neil Armstrong served as commander of the Apollo 11 mission and climbed down the ladder of the lunar lander module.

His steps—and momentous words—broadcast via satellite to millions of televisions worldwide rang out: "That's one small step for man, one giant leap for mankind."

The accomplishment did not result in a territorial gain for the United States as any ownership rights of the moon were declined.

To the Moon and Beyond

Space programs continued to evolve in pursuit of exploration of other planets.

Venus was the first, passed by the U.S. Mariner II in December 1962, following the 1960 Soviet probes of both Venus and Mars.

The data gathered on the planets reflected temperature and atmospheric pressures, but as there were no cameras to capture images there was not much public attention to the success.

The Soviet Venera 7 project captured the first photos of Venus's surface.

U.S. Mariner 4 passed Mars and transmitted images in 1965.

The Soviets landed their Mars 3 craft on the surface in 1971—again, unable to transmit pictures.

The 1976 U.S. Viking lander captured and transmitted the first photos of the Martian surface.

The U.S. Mariner 10 passed Venus en route to Mercury in 1974, a feat unchallenged for nearly three decades.

That's What He Said: Neil Armstrong

- I guess we all like to be recognized not for one piece of fireworks, but for the ledger of our daily work.
- I think we're going to the moon because it's in the nature of the human being to face challenges. It's by the nature of his deep inner soul... we're required to do these things just as salmon swim upstream.
- In much of society, research means to investigate something you do not know or understand.
- It suddenly struck me that that tiny pea, pretty and blue, was the Earth. I put up my thumb and shut one eye, and my thumb blotted out the planet Earth. I didn't feel like a giant. I felt very, very small.
- It's a brilliant surface in that sunlight. The horizon seems quite close to you because the curvature is so much more pronounced than here on earth. It's an interesting place to be. I recommend it.

The Checkered Flag

While the starting line of the space race is clearly visible, the end of the race is subject to debate.

Five lunar landings beyond the 1969 Apollo landing, Americans turned from moon exploration to new ventures.

Skylab focused on gathering further data, and the Space Shuttle was designed to return intact from space exploration and be used repeatedly.

The Soviets enjoyed less success.

They created a design similar to the Space Shuttle, but the project never really got off the ground because of the nation's declining economic position. The cost of the arms race had taken its toll on the Soviets, and the economy eventually collapsed.

Of course, the Soviets won't let a little financial disaster stand in the way of bragging rights.

The Soviets claims to have won the race by successfully launching the first man in space, yet the Americans argue walking on the moon means they deserve mad props.

Either way, as the Cold War began to ebb, and other nations began to pursue their own space exploration programs, the race between the two world powers became less evident.

Star Gazing for the Ages

The next time your kids don't want to pay attention when NASA's doing its thing, tell them they might want to consider a few modern conveniences they'd be living without if it weren't for the space race:

- Ready-to-eat and freeze-dried foods
- Powdered beverages
- Water-resistant clothing
- Auto-tinting
- No-fog eyewear
- Package-sealing techniques

These are just a smattering of the everyday items we only enjoy because of space program technology.

Likewise, satellites are orbiting the Earth relaying information on everything from weather and ecologic data to human activity, communications, and music.

Again, all of this is possible thanks to micro-tech applications that evolved from space race research programs.

Toward the end of the twentieth century an apparent resurgence of the space race was at hand in the form of a European space agency with a plan to send a manned mission to Mars by the year 2030.

The agency is teaming with Russia on the project.

U.S. President George W. Bush announced a similar plan, Crew Exploration, in 2004 that would involve a manned return to the moon as well as a mission to Mars on a similar timeline.

Several other nations now capable of space exploration include Japan, China, and India. While China's funding capabilities are no match for those of the United States or European endeavors, the successful manned space flights and space station plans that have been developed clearly show the potential of their programs.

We See You: Spy Satellites

The touted space race was also a parallel effort in the development of space for military purposes by both the U.S. and Soviet governments originating in each country's development of reconnaissance satellites.

Like other programs of the space race, the Soviet Zenit program developed in opposition to the U.S. Air Force's Discoverer, which ultimately produced successful payload recoveries in the summer of 1960—one day apart.

The Americans squeaked their accomplishment ahead of the Soviets once more.

Both powers continued to develop extensive space programs; the difference being that the Americans typically designed models and prototypes only to abandon projects while the Soviets completed building and launches of their prototypes.

Space Race Entertainment

The following movies and television series were all inspired by actual events or perceived possibilities of space exploration.

- *The Right Stuff*
- *Apollo 13*
- *Mission to Mars*
- *Armageddon*
- *Space Camp*
- *Star Trek* (Television and Movie Series including four spin offs)
- *Space Balls*
- James Bond film series
- *Battlestar Galactica*
- *Star Wars*

What Is the Internet?

For starters, when most people think of the Internet, they think of the World Wide Web. It is important to note that while this is the newest and most popular part, it is not the extent of the Internet. The Internet is based on many protocols, standards that control the way communication is held between two endpoints. Protocols allow computers all over the world to access common files and one another. The TCP/IP protocol allows computers to describe data to one another through a network.

- TCP stands for transmission control protocol. TCP takes information and breaks it down into tiny pieces to be sent in packets to another point or computer.
- IP stands for Internet protocol. The IP takes the packets sent by the TCP and directs them through computers to get to their appropriate destinations.
- In a sense, the TCP is the packager, and the IP the shipper.

Other Common Terms

- SMTP: simple mail transfer protocol – works with e-mail
- FTP: file transfer protocol – guides the uploading and downloading of file between computers
- ISP: an Internet service provider – allows the computer to connect with a server

The Internet Race

In the 1950s, the US was in the midst of a space race with the Soviet Union. With the Russian launch of Sputnik in 1957, the US immediately created the Advance Research Projects Agency (ARPA) in order to regain the nation's technological superiority.

Armed with the challenge, ARPA set out to develop a computer network. They created four interface message processors (IMPs) as gateways to let computers enter other systems using telephone lines. By 1971, 23 host computers provided access to other computers, forming a network. Within ten years, there were more than 200 host computers, including several in other countries. The agency's work, first called ARPAnet, is now known as the Internet.

British research scientist Tim Berners-Lee took the network idea a step further. He developed a way to link a set of documents and make them available to other computers around the world. His World Wide Web of information was launched in 1990. He created Uniform Resource Locators (URLs), the Hypertext Transfer Protocol (HTTP), and Hypertext Markup Language (HTML) so that people could use computers to access information in the linked documents.

World's First Website

- The world's first website was http://info.cern.ch. Launched on August 6, 1991, it is still accessible. It first explained the World Wide Web concept and gave users an introduction to getting started with their own websites.
- Today there are more than 150 million websites.

Slobodan Milosevic

From 1989 to 1997 Slobodan Milosevic served as president of Serbia, and from 1997 until 2000, was president of the Federal Republic of Yugoslavia. He led the Serbian Socialist Party from its foundation on.

During the Yugoslav wars of the 1990s and the war in Kosovo in 1999, Milosevic was a key political figure and a highly controversial wartime leader. In 1999, he was indicted for crimes against humanity in Kosovo, for breaching the Geneva Conventions in Bosnia and Croatia, and for genocide in Bosnia.

In 2000, he conceded to the charges. Milosevic was arrested in Yugoslavia on corruption charges and was sent to trial in The Hague. He died before his trial concluded, after spending five years in prison during the deliberations.

- Milosevic began his political career after befriending Ivan Stambolic, whose uncle was the president of the Serbian Executive Council.
- By 1978, Milosevic had become the head of one of Yugoslavia's largest banks, thanks to Stambolic's support.
- In 1986, he was elected chairman of the Belgrade City Committee of the League of Communists, replacing Stambolic, who left to lead the Serbian Communist Party.
- In April 1987, Milosevic became the largest force in the Serbian political scene.
- In Spring 2007, self-titled "vampire hunters" broke into his tomb and put a stake through his heart, in hopes of preventing Milosevic from coming back from the dead as a vampire. It is unknown whether the group actually believed in his propensity to come back and harm others, or if the act was simply a political protest.

Diana Frances Spencer: Modern Day Cinderella

Born into the British aristocracy, Diana was the youngest daughter of Edward John Spencer, Viscount Althorp, later John Spencer, eighth Earl Spencer, and his first wife, Frances Spencer, Viscountess Althorp.

She was born at Park House in Norfolk, England, on July 1, 1961. When her parents divorced in 1969, Diana's mother took her and her younger brother to live in an apartment in London's Knightsbridge section, where Diana attended a local day school. That Christmas the Spencer children went to celebrate with their father, and he subsequently refused to allow them to return to London and their mother.

In 1976, Lord Spencer remarried, and during this time Diana traveled up and down the country, living between her parents' homes—with her father at the Spencer seat and with her mother off the west coast of Scotland. Diana did not get along with her stepmother.

The Spencers had been close to the British royal family for centuries, rising in royal favor during the 1600s. Diana's maternal grandmother, Ruth, Lady Fermoy, was a longtime friend and lady-in-waiting to Queen Elizabeth, the queen mother.

In 1977, at the age of sixteen, Diana briefly attended Institut Alpin Videmanette in Rougemont, Switzerland. At about that time, she first met her future husband, who was dating her sister, Lady Sarah.

Diana reportedly excelled in swimming and diving and longed to be a ballerina. She studied ballet for a time, but at 5 -feet, 10 inches she was deemed too tall. Diana moved to London before she turned seventeen and lived with three roommates until 1981.

Meanwhile, Prince Charles's love life had always been the subject of press reports, and he was linked to numerous glamorous, aristocratic women. In his early thirties, he was under increasing pressure to marry. In order to gain the approval of his family and advisers, any potential bride was expected to have a royal or aristocratic background, be a virgin and a Protestant.

Their engagement came on February 24, 1981, as the heir to the throne presented the future princess with a ring consisting of fourteen diamonds surrounding an oval sapphire. The couple married on July 29, 1981, at St. Paul's Cathedral, as Westminister Abby could not accommodate the seating required for the ceremony.

The ceremony was considered a fairytale wedding and was watched worldwide. Diana's wedding gown was made of the finest lace and had a twenty-five-foot train. The only slip of the day occurred when Diana reversed the order of Charles's middle names when reciting her vows. The couple had two sons, Prince William of Wales, born June 21, 1982 and Prince Henry of Wales, born September 15, 1984.

Starting in the mid- to late 1980s, the princess became very well known for her support of several charity projects. This stemmed from her role as Princess of Wales as she was expected to visit hospitals where she comforted the sick and assumed the patronage of many charity organizations. In April 1987, Diana was one of the first high-profile celebrities to be photographed touching a person infected with HIV/AIDS.

In the late 1980s, the marriage of Diana and Charles fell apart, a fact that was at first suppressed, then sensationalized. Both the Prince and Princess of Wales allegedly spoke to the press via friends, each regarding the marriage's demise. Charles and Diana were officially separated on December 9, 1992. In December 1995, the queen asked Charles and Diana to obtain a divorce, which was finalized August 28, 1996.

In accordance with the rules of British royalty, as Diana was no longer married to the Prince of Wales, and therefore ceased to be royalty-by-marriage, Diana lost the style, Her Royal Highness, and instead was titled, Diana, Princess of Wales. However, Diana was still officially a member of the royal family, since she was the mother of the second and third in line to the throne.

The Fairy-Tale Ends

After the divorce, Diana retained her apartment in Kensington Palace and it remained her home until her death. Her work became more humanitarian than political in nature. Diana worked particularly in conjunction with the Red Cross and campaigned to rid the world of land mines. She was extremely aware of her status as mother of a future king and prepared to do anything to prevent harm to her sons.

The People's Princess died on August 31, 1997, after a high-speed car crash in Paris. The vehicle was attempting to allude paparazzi obsessed with Diana's relationship with Dodi al-Fayed. She, Fayed, and driver Henri Paul were killed in the wreck.

Diana's funeral took place in Westminster Abbey on September 6, 1997, and was greeted by as much international attention as her wedding. Services were attended by all members of the royal family. Her sons, William and Harry, walked behind her casket along with her brother, Earl Spencer; her ex-husband, Prince Charles; and Charles's father, Prince Philip.

During the service, Elton John sang "Candle in the Wind," which was originally written for Marilyn Monroe. He changed the lyrics to start with "Goodbye, England's Rose" and brought many people, including Harry, to tears.The princess's grave is on an island within the grounds of Althorp Park, the Spencer family home.

Memorial Awards and Tributes

- Diana Memorial Award: Given to youths demonstrating unselfish devotion and commitment to causes advocated by the princess.
- Diana, Princess of Wales Memorial Playground, in Kensington Gardens.
  Diana, Princess of Wales Memorial Walk, between Kensington Gardens, Green Park, Hyde Park, and St. James's Park.
- Diana, Princess of Wales Memorial Fountain, opened July 6, 2004, on the southwest corner of Hyde Park.

Project Phoenix

In February 1995, the Search for Extraterrestrial Intelligence Institute (SETI) used the world's largest radio telescope in the Southern Hemisphere to search for extraterrestrial civilizations. The Parkes 210-foot radio telescope in New South Wales, Australia, listened for radio signals from another planet. In September 1996, the project moved from Australia to the US, setting up at the National Radio Astronomy Observatory in Green Bank, West Virginia. Observations then moved on to Puerto Rico.

The Phoenix Project computers simultaneously monitored millions of radio channels, examining nearby, sunlike stars. Researchers had picked out specific stars—about 800 of them—that they believed to be most likely to host long-lived planets capable of supporting life. They then assigned 2 billion very narrow channels, 1 Hz wide, to examine for each star.

Because of the ability to detect slowly-drifting signals and the application of near real-time data processing, Project Phoenix was the most comprehensive and sensitive SETI program ever conducted. More than 11,000 hours were spent observing 800 stars with telescopes in Australia, West Virginia, and Puerto Rico; however, no ET signals were detected.

> The signal-processing techniques developed for use in Project Phoenix have proven useful in the detection of breast cancer.

Crash Course

More Famous Firsts

- In 1903, Maurice Garin was the first official winner of the Tour de France.
- Charles Curtis was the first American Indian to become a United States senator in 1907. He represented Kansas until resigning in 1929 to serve as Herbert Hoover's vice president.
- Colin Pitchfork of Narborough, Leicestershire, England, became the first person to be convicted because of evidence provided by DNA fingerprinting
- Marie Sklodowska Curie became the only person to ever win two Nobel Prizes when she received a prize for chemistry in 1911. She won her first prize in 1903 for physics.
- The first black hole thought to be discovered was reported in 1970. Cygnus X-1, is about seven thousand light-years from earth.
- The first female Pulitzer prize winners came in the twentieth century:
  - 1921—Edith Wharton, fiction, *The Age of Innocence*
  - 1923—Edna St. Vincent Millay, poetry, *The Ballad of the Harp-Weaver*
  - 1983—Ellen Taaffe Zwilich, music
- In 1951, Florence Chadwick became the first woman to swim across the English Channel in each direction.
- In 1952, George Jorgenson was the first person in the world to receive a sex-change operation.
- In 1953, Elizabeth II was the first monarch to have her coronation televised.
- In 1957, a dog named Laika aboard the Soviet satellite Sputnik 2 became the first living creature to ever orbit the Earth.
- In 1998, Carlos Santana became the first Latino inducted into the Rock and Roll Hall of Fame.
- Eileen Collins went to space in 1999, becoming the first woman to command a space shuttle mission.

- On October 20, 1999, Abdurrahman Wahid became the first elected president of Indonesia.
- When she was elected to the Senate in 2000, Hillary Rodham Clinton became the first first fady to be elected to a U.S. national office.
- Steve Fossett became the first balloonist to make a solo flight around the world, landing in Australia on July 4, 2002.

Terrible Acts

The terrorist organization known as al-Qaeda has claimed responsibility for several of the most heinous acts of international terrorism over the past fifteen years. In simplest terms, al-Qaeda is a radical fundamentalist Islamic organization led—at least at one time—by Osama bin Laden and committed to the destruction of Israel and to the eradication of all American influence in the Middle East.

The following is only a sampling of the terror incidents in recent history for which al-Qaeda or a related cell is suspected or has accepted responsibility:

October 12, 2000: The USS Cole, an American naval destroyer, was targeted by suicide bombers while refueling in the Aden harbor in Yemen. The blast killed seventeen and wounded another thirty-nine aboard the Cole.

September 11, 2001: Terrorists claiming allegiance to bin Laden hijacked four U.S. commercial passenger planes, transforming them into weapons. The hijackers flew two planes into the World Trade Center in New York City, while a third crashed into the Pentagon in Washington, D.C. The fourth plane crashed into a field in Pennsylvania, and it was believed the terrorists had intended to fly it into the White House. More than three thousand people—including the passengers and pilots of all four planes—were killed in the attacks.

April 11, 2002: A truck filled with natural gas crashed into a synagogue in Djerba, Tunisia, killing seventeen. Most of the dead were German tourists. This event is considered historically significant because it is believed to be al-Qaida's first organized attack outside of Afghanistan since the September 11, 2001, attacks on the United States.

October 6, 2002: Suicide bombers attacked the Limburg, a French oil tanker, leading to the spill of more than ninety thousand barrels of oil.

October 12, 2002: A Bali, Indonesia, nightclub frequented by tourists was bombed, killing two hundred.

November 28, 2002: Three men drove a sports utility vehicle into an Israeli-owned hotel in Kenya. The death toll was thirteen—ten Kenyans and three Israelis—and the Mombassa hotel was destroyed. Almost simultaneously, two surface-to-air missiles were launched at a passenger plane departing for Israel. One missile missed the target and the other failed to explode as it brushed past.

January 5, 2003: Twenty-three people are killed and 100 wounded when a a suicide bomber attack's Tel Aviv's old Central Bus Station.

March 13, 2003: Serbian prime minister Zoran Djindjic is assassinated by snipers.

December 5, 2003: Forty-six people are killed in a suicide attack on a train in southern Russia. Four days later, six more people are killed when a bomb explodes in Red Square in Moscow.

July 7, 2005: The first suicide bombings in Western Europe killed fifty-six people and injured more than 700. The targets were a double-decker bus and three Underground trains. Three weeks after these bombings, there was an another attempted attack on London. Only minor injuries were sustained because the explosives failed to detonate properly.

Terror Timeline: September 11, 2001 (all times are EST)

8:45 a.m.: American Airlines Flight 11 crashes into the north tower of the World Trade Center in New York. It had set off from Boston en route to Los Angeles with ninety-two people on board.

9:03 a.m.: United Airlines Flight 175 crashes into the south tower of the World Trade Center. It had departed Boston for Los Angeles carrying sixty-five passengers and crew.

9:10 a.m.: In Florida, U.S. President George W. Bush is reading to children in a classroom when his chief of staff, Andrew Card, whispers news of the attacks into his ear.

9:20 a.m.: The FBLI begins delving into reports of passenger planes being hijacked.

9:29 a.m.: The first casualties are reported.

9:30 a.m.: Bush declares: "We have had a national tragedy. Two airplanes have crashed into the World Trade Center in an apparent terrorist attack on our country."

9:40 a.m.: American Airlines Flight 77, carrying sixty-four people from Washington to Los Angeles, crashes into the Pentagon in Washington. One side of the five-sided structure collapses.

9:43 a.m.: Abu Dhabi television reports it received a call from the Democratic Front for the Liberation of Palestine, claiming responsibility for crashing two planes into the World Trade Center. The claim is later refuted.

9:45 a.m.: The White House and the Capitol are evacuated.

9:50 a.m.: All airports in the United States are shut down. The south tower of the World Trade Center collapses.

9:58 a.m.: An emergency dispatcher in Pennsylvania receives a call from a passenger on United Flight 93 who says "We are being hijacked! We are being hijacked!"

10:00 a.m.: Flight 93—bound for Los Angeles from New Jersey—crashes eighty miles southeast of Pittsburgh.

10:12 a.m.: British Prime Minister Tony Blair describes the attacks in the United States as "the most terrible shocking event."

10:25 a.m.: An exploded car bomb is reported outside the State Department in Washington.

10:29 a.m.: North Tower of World Trade Center collapses.

12:39 p.m.: Bush addresses the American people for the second time and pledges to hunt down and punish those responsible.

1:20 p.m.: Bush leaves Barksdale Air Force Base in Louisiana and is flown to Offutt Air Force Base in Nebraska.

1:27 p.m.: A state of emergency is declared by the city of Washington.

1:44 p.m.: The Pentagon reports five battleships and two aircraft carriers will be deployed along the East Coast to provide upgraded air defense for the New York and Washington areas.

2:00 p.m.: The U.S. Securities and Exchange Commission closes the stock market.

2:48 p.m.: New York Mayor Rudy Giuliani says the eventual death toll from the attack may be "more than any of us can bear."

4:25 p.m.: The American Stock Exchange, the NASDAQ, and the New York Stock Exchange announce they will remain closed the following day.

4:30 p.m.: Bush leaves Offutt Air Force Base aboard Air Force One to return to Washington and deliver a nationally televised address.

5:20 p.m.: The forty-seven-story building adjacent to the ruins of the World Trade Center collapses.

8:30 p.m.: Bush addresses the nation on television and hints that at a strong U.S. response against the "terrorists who committed these acts and those who harbor them."

Child Prodigies

A child prodigy masters a skill or art at an unusually young age. Typically a prodigy is defined as someone who masters the fundamentals and skills of a certain field by the age of twelve.

- The word Wunderkind is sometimes used as a synonym for prodigy. It can also be used when referring to adults, such as Steven Spielberg, who achieved great success very early in their careers.
- American psychologist Michael O'Boyle recently discovered through the use of an fMRI, which measures brain activity, that the mental operations of prodigies are strikingly different than those of typical humans. His research documented that the blood flow to certain parts of the brain of a prodigy calculator was nearly seven times the amount of typical blood flow in a human doing math.
- The fMRI measures activity in certain locations of the brain to gain a better understanding of how a particular brain is functioning. They are currently being tested as possible lie detectors!

A Few Famed Child Prodigies

- Kim Ung-Yong – Earned a Ph.D. in physics before turning fifteen.
- Zerah Colburn – Able to multiply six-digit numbers in his head at age nine.
- Blaise Pascal – At age eleven, worked out the first twenty-three propositions of Euclid.
- Ruth Lawrence – Youngest student to enter the University of Oxford, at age twelve.

Notable Young Achievers

Temba Tsheri

At the age of sixteen, Temba Tsheri, a boy from Nepal, reached the top of Mt. Everest with a hiking group from France. He was the youngest person to ever climb Mt. Everest, which stands at 29,035 feet and claims several climbers' lives per year.

Ruth Elke Lawrence

At the age of eleven, Ruth Lawrence passed an entrance exam and was admitted to Oxford to study mathematics. She was the youngest person ever to attend the prestigious college and had to be accompanied to class by her father. Then, she graduated the program in just two years, while most students take three. Lawrence currently teaches at Hebrew University in Jerusalem.

Tatum O'Neal

In 1974, ten-year-old actor Tatum O'Neal won an Academy Award for her roll in the film Paper Moon, making her the youngest actor to ever win an Oscar. After such early success, her career turned to focus mainly on television.

Balamurali Ambati

Born in 1977, Balamurali Ambati graduated from NYU at the age of thirteen. He then went on to Mount Sinai's School of Medicine, from which he graduated four years later, becoming the youngest doctor in the world in the year 1995. Currently teaching and researching in the field of ophthalmology, Ambati has won countless awards and received many honors for his medical achievements.

THE DIAMOND TRADE

The global diamond trade is one of the bloodiest businesses in the world, continuing to fund civil wars all over the globe. Human rights campaigners have warned that international standards and regulations of the diamond trade tend to disappear as major diamond-selling holidays such as Valentine's Day and Christmas approach.

- An eight-year civil war in Liberia has been continuously funded by the illegal diamond trade. Diamonds are smuggled and sold in the international market, providing wealth and resources to rebel factions and regimes.
- Globally, marketers of diamonds are required to provide a store policy about the sale of conflict diamonds, alerting customers of the legality of the diamond. But in a street survey in 2006, it was found that only 18 percent of stores surveyed could provide proof of a conflict diamond policy; 22 percent admittedly did not have any such policy in their store.
- A report by Global Witness revealed that diamonds were being smuggled out of the Ivory Coast of Liberia and sold in international markets. Laborers were forced to work in diamond pits in the northern part of the country, extracting enough diamonds to produce nearly 300,000 carats per year—worth over $25 million.

Buying Clean Diamonds

Shoppers should always be wary when buying diamonds and ask appropriate questions before completing a sale. A customer can ask the vendor to produce a policy on conflict diamonds, to provide the location from which the diamonds were purchased, and to offer a written guarantee from the store's diamond supplier verifying that the diamonds are conflict-free.

The ABCs of Cloning

Cloning can seem fairly complicated, but when broken down into simple terms, it is quite understandable.

DNA Cloning

In order to clone a gene, a DNA fragment of the gene must be extracted from the chromosomal DNA. This is done using enzymes that basically pull apart the DNA strand. They are then connected with a plasmid that has been cut apart with similar enzymes. This fragment of DNA connected with the plasmid is called a recombinant DNA molecule. When introduced with the appropriate host cells, the DNA will then reproduce with the host cell DNA. Ta da! Cloning.

Plasmids can hold up to 20,000 base pairs of foreign DNA.

Reproductive Cloning

Reproductive cloning is the process of creating an animal that contains the same nuclear DNA as another. Using the somatic cell nuclear transfer (SCNT) process, genetic material from the nucleus of the donor cell is transferred to an egg whose nucleus has been removed. The egg containing the DNA from the donor must then be treated with electrical currents to stimulate the cell division process. Once the egg reaches a suitable stage of development, it must be implanted into a host animal, where it continues to develop until the birth stage. Boom! A cloned sheep.

Fast Facts About Cloning

- The first animal ever cloned was a tadpole in 1952.
- Since the first cloned mammal, Dolly the sheep, many large and small animals have been cloned, including, goats, mice, pigs, rabbits, cats, and cows.
- Attempts to clone certain animals, such as dogs, chickens, and monkeys, have been unsuccessful. It is believed that certain species may be more resistant to somatic cell transfer than others.
- Reproductive cloning is actually highly inefficient. Nearly 90 percent of attempts at cloning fail to produce desired results in offspring, and a successful procedure might take nearly 100 nuclear transfers. Furthermore, cloned animals tend to have low immune system function and high rates of disorders, tumor growths, and infection.
- Because of the many risks and the inefficiency of animal cloning, most scientists believe that cloning humans would be ethically irresponsible.

Therapeutic cloning, or embryo cloning, involves the production of stem cells, via embryos, that can be studied and used to develop treatments for Alzheimer's, cancer, and other diseases.

NATO

NATO, which stands for the North Atlantic Treaty Organization, is the most powerful defense alliance in the world. Formed in 1949, NATO aimed to protect the freedom and civilization of its membering countries by promoting stability worldwide. An agreement was formed to state that an attack on one NATO country was to be treated as an attack on all NATO countries, each forming an alliance to respond and come to one another's aid.

Timeline

NATO currently has 26 members and several applicants for future memberships. Over time, countries have been added to the alliance.

- The Treaty of Brussels, which was signed in 1948 between Belgium, the Netherlands, France, Luxembourg, and the United Kingdom, is often considered to be the precursor of NATO's development.
- The treaty resulted in the Western European Union, but soon it was realized that the United States' involvement was needed in order to combat the military power of the Soviet Union. Talks were initiated, which led to the signing of the North Atlantic Treaty in 1949.
- The North Atlantic Treaty was signed by the five Treaty of Brussels nations, as well as Canada, the United States, Italy, Norway, Portugal, Denmark, and Iceland.
- In 1952, Greece and Turkey joined the treaty.
- In 1954, the Soviet Union proposed to join NATO in order to help preserve peace in Europe. Every single country inside NATO rejected the proposal.
- In 1955, the Soviet Union created the Warsaw Pact, a counteralliance to NATO. It quickly dissolved in 1991, when the USSR broke apart.

- In 1999, the Czech Republic, Hungary, and Poland gained NATO membership.
- Estonia, Latvia, Lithuania, Slovenia, Slovakia, Bulgaria, and Romania became NATO members in 2004, inducted at a ceremony in Washington, D.C.
- In 2008, Croatia, Bosnia, Serbia, and Montenegro are expected to join the NATO alliance. They are already members of NATO's Partnership for Peace alliance.

NATO has one civil and two military budgets. Each member nation allocates money into the budget using a cost-sharing formula. Each nation also provides resources for the organization's daily expenditures and needs.

The G8

The Group of Eight, set up during the oil crisis and recession of the 1970s, was created to ensure the stability of global economic issues and challenges. In 1973, the Library Group was formed between senior financial officials of the United States, Europe, and Japan. Two years later, the French joined in, and the group decided to meet annually. The countries, France, Germany, Italy, Japan, the UK, and the US, became known as the G6, and later the G7 and G8 when Canada and Russia joined.

- Though G8 members decide on policies related to economics and finances, compliance with the decisions is completely voluntary, as there is no real international law enforcement body.
- A different country holds the presidency of the G8 each year and is responsible for hosting the annual meeting, the G8 Summit. In 2006, Russia hosted the summit, and in 2007, Germany held the meeting in Heiligendamm.
- The G8 has been criticized as an organization that lacks representation by major economies such as China and India, and it is regarded by some as a body that only represents the elite industrialized nations of the world, ignoring the well-being of many other states.
- There have been disagreements within the G8 over the US war in Iraq, the Kyoto treaty, and international concerns such as global warming.

Hezbollah

The most powerful military force in Lebanon, Hezbollah formed in 1982 with financial support from Iran. Also called the Party of God, the organization is Shi'a Muslim and also serves as a large political force in the Lebanon parliament.

Hezbollah's military wing is called the Islamic Resistance and is believed to have well-trained fighters and missile capabilities that pose threats to Israel, its main target.

The main initiative of Hezbollah is to dissolve the nation of Israel, which members believe occupies Muslim holy land unrightfully. Hezbollah was created in the early 1980s in response to the Israeli invasion of Lebanon. The group currently draws heavy support from the Lebanese because of its involvement in Israel's withdrawal from South Lebanon in the year 2000.

Hezbollah has also gained support for providing health care and social services throughout Lebanon. They have a television station, al-Manar, which is widely received by the Lebanese, with support from Iran and Syria.

Hezbollah has been subject to many attacks, bombings, and kidnappings. Organizations such as the CIA, the UN, and Israeli military groups have targeted Hezbollah leaders in the recent past. In a car bombing in 1985, the CIA allegedly attempted to assassinate Hezbollah leader Mohammad Hussein Fadlallah. The attempt failed, however, and Fadlallah survived.

The United Kingdom considers the military part of Hezbollah to be a terrorist organization but views its political party as a legitimate force.

The Darfur Conflict

The Country

Darfur is a province in the west of Sudan, which is the largest country of Africa. Darfur is roughly the size of France. The majority of the population of Darfur is black African, and the country is under Arab control.

The Conflict

The Darfur Conflict began in 2003. For a long time, tensions between black African farmers and Arab herders have created opposition groups and boiling conflict around Darfur. In 2003, rebel groups began attacking the government in a violent revolt. Over two million citizens of Darfur had to flee their homes to escape the violence.

The government's retaliation of the revolt wreaked havoc on the country. Military aircraft bombed entire villages, and militias would then ride though the desecrated villages and rob, rape, and steal. Survivors and refugees believe that the violence was part of a deliberate attempt to rid Darfur of the black Africans. These refugees live in camps across Darfur, hiding from the violence, and many have crossed the border into Chad to escape. Foreign aid agencies have entered Darfur from all over the world to help the refugees, but many report that the spreading of violence has made it difficult to remain inside the country.

- A peace deal was signed in 2006 by the African Union in order to end the conflict. Part of the agreement was that the government would disarm the Janjaweed militia, but the disarmament was slow in taking off. The government of Sudan signed the peace agreement to help rid Darfur of violence, but little has been done on their part as well.
- The African Union has sent nearly 7,000 soldiers into Darfur to monitor the ceasefire outlined in the peace deal.

- Britain and the United States have pushed the United Nations to become involved in the peace mission for Darfur, but the Sudanese government has forbidden the UN from its territory, making things rather difficult.

There are many estimates of the number of casualties that have occurred as a result of the Darfur conflict, but all are well into the hundreds of thousands. The UN reports that at least 450,000 have died as a result of violence, disease, and starvation caused by the wars in Darfur.

> Scientists report that the scale of climate change that has occurred in Darfur because of manmade global warming is unprecedented around the world. Some believe that this drastic climate change is a partial cause, or contributor at least, of the Darfur conflict. The rapid desertification of the land and fast reduction of rainfall because of drying, heating climates has caused migration and turmoil between farmers, herders, and landowners.

The Arab League

The Arab League is a voluntary association of Arab-speaking countries that seeks to strengthen relationships between member nations and serves to protect the common good of Arab nations. The league was founded in Egypt in 1945, at the end of World War II, when many Arab nations were still under colonial rule.

- The Arab League has twenty-two member states, including Palestine.
- The population of the league reaches nearly 300 million, across an area totaling nearly 5.25 million square miles.
- A council rests at the top of the Arab League, comprised of representatives from each state. Every nation has one vote, no matter the nation's size, and meetings are held twice per year.

Amr Moussa, a popular charismatic diplomat in the Arab world, currently holds the title of secretary-general of the Arab League. As the leading member, the secretary-general is elected by nomination from at least two member states and is then selected by a council to serve for a five-year term. Moussa has served as an ambassador in India and to the United Nations. He served as Egypt's foreign minister before becoming head of the Arab League.

THE EUROPEAN UNION

The European Union is a compilation of European democratic nations that seeks to transform Europe into a sort of single body, with common currency, open trade, and a common foreign security policy.

- The Treaty on European Union was signed in 1991, officially beginning the European Union.
- The Union is governed by a council of ministers, with each individual member country represented by several members. A commission and a parliament are also governing sections of the EU, regulating the currency and holding regular elections.
- In recent years, many formerly communist countries have joined the EU. There are currently twenty-seven members:

Austria	Cyprus
Belgium	Czech Republic
Bulgaria	Denmark
Estonia	Malta
Finland	Netherlands
France	Poland
Germany	Portugal
Greece	Romania
Hungary	Slovakia
Ireland	Slovenia
Italy	Spain
Latvia	Sweden
Lithuania	United Kingdom
Luxembourg	

EXTRA CREDIT: Any individual country, once part of the EU, must ratify the constitution in order for it to take effect.

THE NOBEL PRIZE

The Nobel Prize is an international award administered by the Nobel Foundation in Stockholm, Sweden. The Peace Prize was first awarded in 1901 to International Committee of Red Cross (ICRC) founder Henry Dunant. Since then, the Nobel Prize has been awarded for achievements in physics, chemistry, physiology or medicine, literature, and peace. Each prize consists of a medal, personal diploma, and a cash award. In 1968, Sveriges Riksbank established The Sveriges Riksbank Prize in Economic Sciences, in memory of Alfred Nobel, founder of the Nobel Prize.

The First World War was contradictory of what the peace activists honored by the Nobel Peace Prize had worked so hard to establish. So, the Nobel Committee, located in neutral Norway, decided to award only one prize in 1917 to the ICRC. During the war, the ICRC worked to protect the rights of prisoners of war on all sides, including their rights to contact their families.

Again, little more than twenty years later, the world was embroiled in another war. This time, Germany attacked Norway, and within two months the entire country was occupied. No Peace Prize was awarded until 1944. And it was only appropriate to award the prize again to the ICRC. In the midst of chaos, the ICRC had promoted the "fraternity between nations" that Alfred Nobel had referred to in his will when making provisions for the Noble Peace Prize.

- Since its beginning, 797 people and twenty organizations have been awarded the Nobel Prize. Some have been awarded more than once, but only thirty-four women have been awarded a Nobel Prize. Marie Curie received two Nobel Prizes, her husband, Pierre, daughter, Irène Joliot-Curie, and son-in-law, Frederic Joliot, also received Nobel Prizes.
- Two Nobel laureates have declined the Nobel Prize: Jean-Paul Sartre in 1964 and Le Duc Tho in 1973. On the other hand, four laureates were forced to decline the Prize. Adolf Hitler forced Richard Kuhn, Adolf Butenandt, and Gerhard Domagk to decline the prize; however they later received the Nobel Prize diploma and medal, but not the prize money. And, in 1958, Boris Pasternak was

forced to decline the Nobel Prize in Literature by the Soviet Union.

- The youngest Nobel laureate is Lawrence Bragg, who was twenty-five years old when he received the Nobel Prize in Physics with his father in 1915.
- The oldest Nobel laureate is Leonid Hurwics, who was ninety years old when he was awarded the Nobel Prize in Economics in 2007.

Nobel Prize Trivia

- Theodor Mommsen, age eighty-five, was the oldest person to win the Nobel Prize in Literature.
- Rudyard Kipling became the youngest when he won the price for literature at age forty-two.
- Mommsen was born over 134 years before the most recently born laureate, Orhan Pamuk.
- Bertrand Russell, who died at ninety-seven, lived longer than any other prizewinner.
- The oldest living laureate is Aleksandr Solzhenitsyn, who was born in 1918.
- The laureate who lived the shortest time afterward was Albert Camus, who died three years after receiving the award at age forty-six.
- TV and radio personality Gert Fylking began the tradition of shouting "Äntligen!" (Swedish for "At last!") when the award winner was announced.
- The first Asian laureate was Rabindranath Tagore.

U.S. Presidential Tidbits

Presidential Bachelors

- James Buchanan, president from 1857 to 1861, was a lifelong bachelor. He asked his orphaned niece, Harriet Lane, to be the White House hostess during his term.
- Grover Cleveland was a bachelor when he entered the White House in 1885; however, he married Frances Folsom in 1886.

Hail to the Chief

John Quincy Adams was the first president to be honored by "Hail to the Chief." The song was composed by James Sanderson and first played in the United States in 1812. The wife of John Tyler (the tenth U.S. president) was the first person to think of having the U.S. Navy band play "Hail to the Chief" to announce the arrival of the president. It became the official musical tribute to the president in 1954.

1600 Pennsylvania Avenue

The White House was not always called the White House. Built for the U.S. president to live in, it has been called the "President's Palace," the "President's House," and the "Executive Mansion." President Theodore Roosevelt officially gave the White House its current name in 1901.

Designed by James Hoban, who was awarded a gold medal for his work, the White House took eight years to construct. It has 132 rooms, thirty-five bathrooms, and six levels. There are also 412 doors, 147 windows, twenty-eight fireplaces, eight staircases, and three elevators.

- The White House requires 570 gallons of paint to cover its outside surface.
- John and Abigail Adams were the first to live in the White House.
- The White House keeps five full-time chefs on staff, who can serve as many as 140 guests for dinner and hors d'oeuvres for more than 1000.

- The White House also provides a tennis court, movie theater, jogging track, and a bowling alley for its residents to use.

While in office...

- James Polk was the first president to have his photograph taken.
- Theodore Roosevelt was the first president to travel outside the country when he visited Panama.
- Franklin Roosevelt was the first president to ride in an airplane.
- William McKinley was the first president to ride in an automobile.

President Harry S Truman was not given a middle name. He once explained, "I was named for Harrison Young. I was given the diminutive Harry and, so that I could have two initials in my given name, the letter S was added. My grandfather Truman's name was Anderson Shippe Truman and my grandfather Young's name was Solomon Young, so I received the S for both of them."

Notorious Art Thefts

- The most notorious art theft in the world has to be the robbery of 1911 in Paris, France, at the Louvre. Employee Vincenzo Peruggia stole the famed Leonardo da Vinci painting Mona Lisa. Peruggia hid in the museum until it closed and then concealed the painting under a smock while he escaped. The incident transformed the Mona Lisa into perhaps the most well-known painting in the world. Two years later, Peruggia tried to sell the painting in Florence and was arrested. The Mona Lisa was returned to the Louvre with a whole new level of fame and notoriety.
- Edvard Munch's painting The Scream was lifted in 1994, when thieves, who stole in through the window, took it from the Oslo National Art Museum. The men tried to ransom the painting to the government of Norway but were caught within several months. Having left a piece of the frame at a bus stop, they left a trail behind them and were soon convicted.
- In late 2002, robbers stole two Van Gogh paintings from the Van Gogh Museum in Amsterdam after breaking into the building through the roof. The men worked so quickly that they had vanished before the police arrived, even after setting after the alarm system upon entry. Fortunately, the men left hair inside two hats in the museum and were convicted on DNA evidence. However, the paintings, the missing link to proving the two men's guilt, have never been recovered. View of the Sea at Scheveningen and Congregation Leaving the Reformed Church in Nuenen together are worth more than $30 million.
- In August 2003, two men joined a guided tour through Drumlanrig Castle in Scotland. They subdued a guard and stole Leonardo da Vinci's Madonna with the Yarnwinder. The men convinced bystanders that they were police practicing a protocol; and escaped in a white Volkswagen. The painting is still missing, and the two men were never caught.

- In August 2004, two armed thieves entered the Munch Museum of Oslo, Norway, in broad daylight. Masked, they stole two Edvard Munch paintings, The Scream, and The Madonna, after threatening workers with their weapons. The two paintings combined were worth an estimated 100 million euros. In May 2006, three men were convicted to prison sentences, and the paintings were recovered. The painting that they stole was actually a different version of The Scream than was lifted before, as Munch had created four different versions of the painting.
- In February 2008, the art world was ransacked again—this time in two thefts in Switzerland within one week. On Wednesday, February 6, thieves broke into the Seedamm-Kulturzentrum cultural center in the town of Pfäffikon, stealing two Picassos, Horse Head and Glass and Pitcher, estimated to be worth $4.4 million combined. The following Sunday, three armed men stole Cézanne's Boy in a Red Vest, Monet's Poppies Near Vétheuil, van Gogh's Blossoming Chestnut Branches, and Degas' Count Lepic and His Daughters, worth an estimated total of $163 million, from the E. G. Bührle Collection in Zurich.

Oldest Person to Ever Live

Jeanne Louise Calment was born in 1875, and died 122 years later, making her the oldest person to ever live thus far. Born in Arles, France, a year before the invention of the telephone, Calment is believed to have met Vincent van Gogh at the tender age of thirteen.

ALTERNATIVE FUELS

Ethanol

Ethanol, which comes from plants, is a renewable fuel that is rapidly moving to the front burner of fuel research. Most ethanol is made from corn and other sugary plants, created through the process of fermenting the plant sugars into alcohol.

E85

Pure ethanol cannot be used for transportation fuel, but it can be blended with gasoline and other substances to create an efficient and earth-friendly alternative to traditional fuel. E85 is a blend of 85 percent denatured ethanol and 15 percent gasoline. E85 can be used in special engines designed to burn the particular properties of ethanol gas, called flex fuel vehicles. Flex fuel is only offered in special markets but is becoming more common around the world.

A higher percentage of gasoline is added to flex fuel sometimes during colder winter months to ensure that an engine can still start in harsh climates.

FFVs

Flex fuel vehicles were introduced as early as the 1880s. Henry Ford designed a car that ran on ethanol, and later built a Model T in 1908 that could run on either ethanol or gasoline.

Modern FFVs can only run on a blend of ethanol and gasoline, with the maximum percentage of ethanol topping out at 85. Cars, trucks, and SUVs are now made as FFVs and require the same maintenance and have the same efficient qualities of regular gas-powered vehicles.

One drawback to driving an FFV is that the ethanol-gasoline blends, such as E85, contain less energy than gasoline, reducing fuel efficiency by around 20 percent. The cost of E85, however, is usually lower than pure gasoline and is more easily replenished and earth-friendly to produce.

One of the biggest benefits of E85 and FFVs is the fact that replacing gasoline with ethanol will reduce the demand for foreign oil, at least for the Western countries in Europe and North America. The

United States is currently the world's largest ethanol producer, as most ethanol is extracted from corn, a major agricultural product of both the United States and Mexico.

> E85 also reduced greenhouse gas (GHG) emissions by nearly 15 to 20 percent when compared to the production and use of gasoline. E85 is less volatile than gasoline and therefore emits far les gases such as carbon monoxide and other carcinogens upon evaporation.
>
> There are nearly 6 million FFVs on the road today in the United States alone.

Biodiesel

Biodiesel is a fuel that is extracted from agricultural products like vegetable oils. Most biodiesel in the United States is produced from soybean oil, but a large number of recycled cooking oils, plant oils, and animal fats can be used to make the product.

A process called "esterification" is used to make biodiesel. Industrial alcohol, such as methanol or ethanol, is used to convert the oils into a fuel that can be used to power a motorized vehicle. Additionally, most diesel engines can be run on biodiesel without any special modifications to the hardware.

B5

While B100 is pure biodiesel, B5 is the most common biodiesel blend, consisting of 5percent biodiesel and 95 percent regular diesel fuel. Registered with the EPA, biodiesel is legal to use on and off road.

Approximately 600 fleets of trucks in the United States use biodiesel blends to fuel their engines. Biodiesel can be more expensive than petrodiesel, but no extra maintenance is involved in the transition between the two fuels.

Like ethyl-based fuels, biodiesel can help reduce the Western dependence on foreign oil as well as reduce greenhouse gas emissions and environmental contamination.

Crash Course

Little-Known Facts About the Arms Trade

The global arms trade involves the proliferation, sale, and technological advancement of weaponry and war resources.

- The United States spends over $400 billion every year on the procurement of weapons. This total is almost as much as the rest of the world's expenditures combined.
- In recent conflicts, more than 80 percent of casualties have been civilian, and close to 90 percent of these deaths are caused by small arms.
- The United Nations, a global organization set up after World War II to preserve peace and international cooperation, has a budget that is only two percent of the world's military expenditure.
- The most recent data about the arms expenditures of the United States is from 2005. It showed that the US military budget was close to 29 times as large as the combined expenditures of six rogue nations, including Cuba, Iran, Libya, North Korea, Sudan, and Syria.
- Arms and military expenditures are the largest business in the world, with a global expenditure of around $1 trillion every year.
- The United States, France, Russia, and Britain spend the most money on arms trade of any nations in the world.

Historic Bad Boys

Darius and Xerxes might have set the standard in the Ancient world, but these guys took no prisoners—at least, not without making them wish they were dead:

Mao Zedong (40 million + slaughtered)

A founder of the Chinese Communist party, Mao Zedong founded the People's Republic of China in 1949. In 1915, he wrote the longest graphite ever recorded, criticizing the Chinese school system and Chinese society. His protest contained over four thousand Chinese characters. As a political leader, he was responsible for more than thirty million deaths, most of which resulted from hunger and starvation in China during the Great Leap Forward. He also killed tens of thousands during China's Cultural Revolution.

Peter the Great

Born in 1672, Peter the Great was a czar and emperor of Russia during the eighteenth century. Standing around six feet, seven inches, he was a commanding figure who got his start as a foot soldier in battle against the Turks. It is believed he actually tortured and executed one of his own sons for treason in 1718.

Idi Amin (100,000-500,000 killed)

A former dictator of Uganda and a heavyweight boxing champion, Idi Amin was one of the most notorious and bloody rulers in African history. He was a proponent of Hitler and often defended the Holocaust and the Nazis. Amin, who threw his name in the race to be king of Scotland, is rumored to have eaten his opponents.

Pol Pot (70,000-1.7 million killed)

Pol Pot is the common name used to refer to Saloth Sar, leader of the Communist movement Khmer Rouge in Cambodia. He was the prime minister of Cambodia for three years beginning in 1976. During his rule, he imposed "agrarian collectivism" by which he moved city dwellers to the country to work in forced-labor projects and collective farms. Between slave labor, starvation, executions, and neglect, Pol Pot is estimated to be responsible for anywhere between 700,000 and 1.7 million deaths in Cambodia. In 1979, when Vietnam raided Cambodia, Pol Pot fled to the jungle. He was arrested and imprisoned by other Communist leaders. He died under house arrest in 1998.

Saddam Hussein (2 million + killed)

Saddam Hussein was president of Iraq from 1979 until 2003. He was largely involved in the coup that brought the Ba'ath Party to power. In power during the Persian Gulf War, Hussein remained popular among Arabs who disliked the West and its intervention in the Middle East. Although the exact number of casualties during his watch remains disputed, Hussein was convicted of crimes against Iraqis, Kuwaitis, Kurds, and Shia Muslims. as well as dissidents, many of whom were discovered in grisly mass graves. He was sentenced to death by hanging and executed in December 2006.

The Deadliest Wars of the 20th Century

World War II (1939-45) - 20 million died
World War I (1914-17) - 8.5 million died
Korean War (1950-53) - 1.7 million died
Chinese Civil War (1945-49) - 1.2 million died
Vietnam War (1965-73) - 1.2 million died

Older Than Dirt

Face it, no matter how bad you might feel about yourself at this very moment—bathroom lights do tend to be the most unforgiving—remember you have youth on your side. The most beautiful thing about studying history is that it reminds you how old everything around you really is. Consider the following:

Oldest City in the World

Archaeologists on a dig in 2001 discovered what they believe to be the remnants of an ancient city in western India off the coast of the Gulf of Cambay. Submerged beneath the water, the city stretched 5.6 miles and is believed—based on carbon dating—to trace its roots to 7500 BC. Of course, dating remains a tricky practice, and most historians still believe the earliest cities, located in Mesopotamia, predate this site by as many as 4,500 years.

Oldest Tavern in America

The Bell in Hand Tavern, located in Boston, is the oldest and longest running tavern in the United States. Established in 1795, the haunt has reportedly never closed and counts Paul Revere and President William McKinley among its storied clientele.

Oldest Company in the World

Based in Osaka, Japan, the Kongo Gumi Company, a construction business, is the longest operating company in the world. The business started in AD 578 when it built the Shitennoji Temple, and it continues to build as a subsidiary of the Takamatsu Corporation. It has had a hand in building many famous temples and buildings around Japan, including the Osaka Castle in the sixteenth century.

Oldest Person to View the Earth from Space

U.S. astronaut John Glenn became a national hero when he rode the shuttle Friendship 7, orbiting the Earth three times. He was the third American to enter space, and the first American to orbit Earth. Glenn returned to space at the age of seventy-seven to test the effects of space travel on an elderly body.

Record Holders: Planet Earth

- **Highest mountain: Mt. Everest**
  Mt. Everest grows nearly four millimeters per year, as two tectonic plates continue to push against each other.
- **Highest waterfall: Angel Falls**
  Located in Venezuela, the waterfall drops 3,212 feet.
- **Hottest place on Earth: Azizia**
  Located in Libya, Azizia reaches 136° Fahrenheit, or 57.8° Celsius.
- **Coldest place on Earth: Vostok, Antarctica**
  Vostok reached -129° Fahrenheit, or -89° Celsius, breaking the world record.
- **Largest ocean: Pacific**
  The Pacific takes up 32.6 percent of the earth's surface.
- **Longest river: The Nile**
  The Nile stretches 4,160 miles, or 6,695 kilometers.
- At 630 feet high, the tallest constructed monument in the world is the Gateway Arch in St. Louis, Missouri. The stainless steel arch designed by Eero Saarinen was constructed to commemorate the Louisiana Purchase. It was completed on October 28, 1965.
- Built to demonstrate the strength of iron, the Eiffel Tower in Paris, France, was the tallest building in the world in 1889. It is twice as tall as the Washington Monument. The tower is painted every seven years and takes 50 tons of paint to complete the job.
- Ka Lae (South Cape) Island in Hawaii is the southernmost point in the United States.
- The southernmost city is Hilo, Hawaii.
- The lowest point in the US is Badwater Basin in Death Valley, California. It is 282 feet below sea level.

Pop Quiz #10

1) Which country had the first man in space?
   a) Soviet Union
   b) United States
   c) France
   d) Germany

2) What year was the world's first website launched?
   a) 1969
   b) 1975
   c) 1983
   d) 1991

3) What city was Princess Diana born in?
   a) London
   b) Paris
   c) Norfolk
   d) York

4) Who won the first Tour de France?
   a) Maurice Garin
   b) Colin Pitchfork
   c) Florence Chadwick
   d) George Jorgenson

5) How many people were killed in the July 2005 bombings in London?
   a) 43
   b) 56
   c) 212
   d) 700

6) Tatum O'Neal won an Acadamy Award for her role in what movie?
   a) *Gone With the Wind*
   b) *Annie*
   c) *The Little Match Girl*
   d) *Paper Moon*

ANSWERS:

1) a
2) d
3) c
4) a
5) b
6) d

Last Call

Increased global terrorist activity in the early twenty-first century reignited public health awareness—and quite frankly, hysteria—related to bioterrorism and chemical warfare. Nothing like the threat of global annihilation to keep you on your toes, right? Given the renewed interest in some of the nasty little bugs modern health care has nipped in the bud, it's always interesting to find those unfortunate souls, like Janet Parker, who were in the wrong place at the wrong time. Parker is the last reported person to die from smallpox. Ironically, this medical photographer was exposed to the disease during a 1978 laboratory accident, and she died shortly thereafter. Two years later, the World Health Organization declared the virus eradicated, but it didn't stop people from clamoring for new vaccines when the threat of bioterrorism erupted almost three decades later.

And what about those executions? Capital punishment wasn't always such a touchy subject, but some of the more gruesome—yet totally socially acceptable methods of their day—eventually took their final bows. The French halted public executions via guillotine on June 18, 1939. Too bad for Eugene Weidman whose execution was slated for the day before. Of course, just because they stopped publicizing the events didn't mean the French *really* stopped letting heads roll. You could ask Hamida Djandoubi, except his was France's last *real* execution by guillotine—even if it was behind prison walls on September 10, 1977.

For once, the United States was actually more progressive than its European counterparts when it came to putting prisoners to death. The last public execution in the United States took place in Owensboro, Kentucky, in 1936, three full years before the French nixed the use of the guillotine. And the drama surrounding the case was so strong it almost overshadowed the historic final act. Rainey Bethea, a twenty-two-year-old black man, was convicted of killing a seventy-year-old white woman. More than two thousand people witnessed his death.

Jonathan Walker could have taught Nathaniel Hawthorne a thing or two about branded criminals. In 1844, Walker had "SS" branded into the palm of his right hand. His crime? Walker had been charged with helping secure passage to the Bahamas for American slaves, so "slave stealing" became his scarlet letter. It was, however, the last time that particular form of punishment was practiced—at least formally—in the United States.

When Frank Wathernam walked out of Alcatraz Prison on March 21, 1963, one can only imagine how he felt to be the last federal prisoner to leave The Rock. The structure which remains one of San Francisco's major tourist attractions is more likely to host gawkers than hardened criminals these days, and we're sure no one is more pleased about that than Wathernam.

Americans take their cars pretty seriously, so any serious automotive buff knows that the last of Henry Ford's Model T's cruised off the assembly line on May 26, 1927, but the last Packard—produced by the Studebaker-Packard Company—didn't put on its parking brakes until late 1958. A true American automotive era ended in April 2007, when Oldsmobile produced its last vehicle after more than 105 years of production.

While personal transportation has its merits, the British ushered in a new era for public transit on July 6, 1952, when the last streetcar made its final tour of London before being replaced by more economical buses. But economy isn't for everyone. Just ask the millions of people who had the opportunity to take a transcontinental flight on the luxury Concorde before the historic aircraft was officially retired on October 24, 2003.

Edward VIII became the last British monarch to abdicate his throne, but at least he had a good reason. He bolted from his regal duties on December 11, 1937, and married Wallis Warfield Simspon some six months later.

Adrian II was the last married Catholic pope. Because he was already married when he ascended the papal throne in 867, the shrewd pontif simply refused to give up his wife—or sex—during his five-year appointment.

Uncas, son of Chingachgook, was the *Last of the Mohicans* in James Fenimore Cooper's 1826 novel by the same name.

After three-quarters of a century, Communism officially crashed and burned in the Soviet Union on August 29, 1991.

TOP SEVEN MOST RIDICULOUS QUOTES IN HISTORY

7) "There is no reason for any individual to have a computer in their home."
Kenneth Olsen, president and founder of Digital Equipment Corporation,1977

6) "Airplanes are interesting toys but of no military value."
Marshal Ferdinand Foch, French military strategist and future World War I commander

5) "[Man will never reach the moon] regardless of all future scientific advances."
Dr. Lee Forest, Father of Radio, 1967

4) "[Televison] won't be able to hold on to any market it captures after the first six months. People will soon get tired of staring at a plywood box every night."
Darryl F. Zanuck, head of 20th Century Fox, 1946

3) "We don't like their sound. Groups of guitars are on the way out."
Decca Records, rejecting the Beatles, 1962

2) "For the majority of people, the use of tobacco has a beneficial effect."
Dr. Ian G. Macdonald, Los Angeles surgeon, quoted in *Newsweek*, 1969

1) "The 'telephone' has too many shortcomings to be seriously considered as a means of communication. The device is inherently of no value to us."
Western Union Internal Memo, 1876

Final Exam

1) Which religious leader is credited with launching the Protestant Reformation?
   a) John Locke
   b) Thomas Hobbes
   c) John Calvin
   d) Martin Luther

2) Who in 1687 published *Mathematical Principles of Natural Philosophy*?
   a) Charles Darwin
   b) Sir Isaac Newton
   c) Thomas Paine
   d) René Descartes

3) Who was Louis XIII's chief minister who strengthened the king's power and simultaneously weakened the power of the Hapsburgs throughout Europe?
   a) René Descartes
   b) Charles de Gaulle
   c) Napoleon Bonaparte
   d) Cardinal Richelieu

4) French Protestants are known as what?
   a) Huguenots
   b) Hapsburgs
   c) Pralines
   d) None of the above

5) Which of the following statements about Laika is not true?
   a) He was the first dog sent into orbit.
   b) He died of stress, dehydration and heat exhaustion.
   c) He was launched into space on Sputnik I.
   d) It took three years for the Soviets to figure out how to successfully launch and return dogs to Earth.

6) Which of the following was not a battle waged during World War I?
   a) Ypres
   b) Somme
   c) Stalingrad
   d) None of the above

7) Which parties fought on the side of the North Vietnamese during the Vietnam War?
   a) The Viet Cong
   b) The Vietnam People's Army
   c) The People's Army of Vietnam
   d) All of the above

8) The elite class of Celtic intellectuals were known as what?
   a) Druids
   b) Runes
   c) Wiccans
   d) None of the above

9) The particularly bloody period in Northern Ireland's political and social history between 1963 and 1985 is referred to as what?
   a) The Terrors
   b) The Troubles
   c) The Tyranny
   d) The Tempest

10) Russia's Czar Nicholas II married Princess Alexandra of Hesse-Darmstadt, granddaughter of which monarch?
   a) Catherine the Great
   b) Queen Victoria
   c) Queen Elizabeth II
   d) Mary Queen of Scots

11) What was the first animal to be cloned?
   a) Sheep
   b) Tadpole
   c) rat
   d) cat

12) NATO has how many members?
   a) 3
   b) 15
   c) 21
   d) 26

13) Darfur is a province of what country?
   a) Algeria
   b) Sudan
   c) South Africa
   d) Kenya

14) Who was the White House hostess during James Buchanan's term?
   a) His daughter
   b) His wife
   c) His mother
   d) His niece

15) What was the deadliest war of the twentieth century?
   a) World War II
   b) World War I
   c) Korean War
   d) Chinese Civil War

ANSWERS:

1) d	6) c	11) b
2) b	7) d	12) d
3) d	8) a	13) b
4) a	9) b	14) d
5) c	10) b	15) a